W9-ASB-760

ANCIENT MEN OF THE ARCTIC

E 99
99
.E7
G358

ANCIENT MEN OF THE ARCTIC

by J. LOUIS GIDDINGS

Alfred · A · Knopf NEW YORK

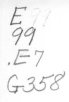 1967

150709

© *Copyright 1967 by Ruth W. Giddings,*
Executrix of the Estate of J. Louis Giddings

Library of Congress Catalog Card Number: 65–11122

THIS IS A BORZOI BOOK
PUBLISHED BY ALFRED A. KNOPF, INC.

© Copyright 1967 by J. Louis Giddings

All rights reserved under International and Pan-American
Copyright Conventions. Distributed by Random House,
Inc. Published simultaneously in Toronto, Canada, by
Random House of Canada Limited.

Manufactured in the United States of America

FIRST EDITION

ACKNOWLEDGMENTS

Since the time span of this book extends to the author's student days, I am sure he would have inserted in its acknowledgment section some wry remark about the improbable task of properly expressing thanks to each one of a lifetime full of friends, teachers, colleagues, students, advisers, and employees! I could not begin to list them all here. Yet they form a real part of the background of my husband's book and I know he would have wished to thank as many as possible for their individual contributions. On his behalf I wish to thank in particular those friends who gave such expert field assistance in Alaska on Louis's various expeditions, contributing so much by their presence, namely: Helge and Gerda Larsen, Froelich Rainey, David Hopkins, Henry Staehle, Hans-Georg Bandi, and Emil Haury. My sincere thanks go, too, to Louis's many other scientific associates over a period of some thirty years—those with whom he exchanged ideas and from whom he learned so much in the course of long evenings in our cabin in Alaska, or before other fireplaces in Pennsylvania, in Denmark, and in Rhode Island.

In the same vein, a debt is owed to the many fine student assistants who worked in the field and laboratory with Louis, particularly, recently, William S. Simmons III and Douglas D. Anderson.

For the generous financial aid to his research endeavors Louis was always most grateful. Those institutions and men of imagination who sponsored his scientific reports enabled him to test the new ideas explored throughout the pages of this book. Specifically, they are: the National Science Foundation; the Arctic Institute of North America; the Wenner-Gren Foundation for Anthropological Research; the Office of Naval Research, Department of the Navy; the American Museum of Natural History; Brown University; and the Universities of Pennsylvania and Alaska.

I should mention the close camaraderie enjoyed so much by Louis and his many friends in the United States Geological Survey. Without their help and without the similar enthusiastic cooperation of the Radiocarbon Laboratory at the University of Pennsylvania, the story of ancient Alaska's history might not have developed here as it does.

I know Louis would have wanted to make special mention of the native helpers and their families who worked for him on various expeditions: Almond Downey, Tommy Lee, Shield Downey, Murphy Downey, Robert Lee, Truman Cleveland, Nelson Greist, Robert N. Cleveland, Julian Towkshjea, Lewis Nakarak, Saul Sokpilak, Tommy Kalinek, Peter Bussidor, and Thomas Jawbone.

Most important, without the steady encouragement and skillful advice of Louis's friend and editor, Angus Cameron, this book might never have been written, and to him I am most grateful.

Although some of the drawings for the volume were done by Louis before his death, many other illustrations were needed and I thank the various students and other friends at Brown University and Haffenreffer Museum who contributed much effort in this regard. In particular, Mrs. Judith Huntsman was competently helpful in various ways and made many of the drawings that were needed, and Miss Dorothy Day generously gave her time to make drawings of flintwork. The all-important coordination and final composition and editing, a task that was much more difficult because of the circumstances, was done by the museum's administrative assistant, Mrs. Marjorie Tomas. Without her careful eye for detail with map work, and long, untiring effort at editing and other work, the completion of this volume might never have been accomplished. To her my husband's book owes its greatest debt, and for that I extend my sincere thanks.

Many other friends and institutions who generously provided illustrative material are gratefully noted below:

Douglas Anderson for Figs. 10, 28, 43, 54, 66, and 67
Carroll Bisson for Fig. 55
Henry B. Collins for Fig. 59
The Danish National Museum for Figs. 12, 13, and 30
Dorothy Day for Figs. 78, 80, 86, 131–2, 139, and 142

Almond Downey for Fig. 117
David M. Hopkins for Fig. 94
Judith Huntsman for Figs. 8, 11, 14–17, 19, 24–7, 29, 35, 37–41, 47, 51–2, 61, 65, 68–9, 77, 83, 98, 101, 105, and 133–4
Eigil Knuth for Figs. 106–7
Helge Larsen for Figs. 33b, 36, 42, and 79
Froelich G. Rainey for Fig. 87
The Smithsonian Institution, Bureau of American Ethnology for Figs. 56–8
Henry Staehle for Figs. 9, 20–1, 31, 49, and for the jacket photograph
Marjorie Tomas for Figs. 23, 32, 127, all maps, bibliography, index, and (with Judith Huntsman) for the glossary
The United States Geological Survey for Fig. 2.

The quotation from John Muir's *The Cruise of the Corwin* (1917) is reprinted by permission of the Houghton Mifflin Company.

RUTH W. GIDDINGS

Haffenreffer Museum
Bristol, Rhode Island

CONTENTS

ILLUSTRATIONS

CHAPTER XIV

CHAPTER XV

CHAPTER XVI

MAPS

INTRODUCTION

BY *Henry B. Collins*

T HIS BOOK is the best possible measure of the loss that American
archeology has suffered in the untimely death of Louis Giddings. Although Giddings has described the results of his Arctic
work in more than fifty scientific papers and monographs, it is this
single retrospective volume that shows most clearly the magnitude
of his accomplishments.

Giddings's interests were wide and he has written on such
diverse topics as dendrochronology, archeology, ethnology, Eskimo
kinship, and mythology. He was, however, primarily an archeologist
and it was here that he made his most important contributions—
discoveries that are basic to our understanding of the origin and development of Eskimo culture. First, in 1948, came the discovery of
the 4,500- to 5,000-year-old Denbigh Flint complex at Norton Sound
on the Bering Sea coast of Alaska. This microlithic assemblage, containing stone implements comparable to those of the Old World
Mesolithic and Paleolithic, was unlike anything previously known
from America. While pre-Eskimo in the sense that it predated any
known form of Eskimo culture, the Denbigh Flint complex is now
generally recognized as the primary local source from which Eskimo
culture developed. Giddings's excavations at Cape Krusenstern on
the Arctic coast of Alaska between 1958 and 1961 revealed a remarkable record of human occupation extending from the present back to
at least 3000 B.C. Here, on a series of 114 old beach ridges that
stretched in curving parallel rows as much as two miles back from
the present shore, were found the campsites and artifacts of the
Denbigh Flint people and of eleven other prehistoric cultures. Nine

of these, on the beaches extending seaward, represented successive stages of culture that were later than Denbigh, while two others, on a terrace beyond the beaches, were older. The Cape Krusenstern sequence thus afforded clear evidence of the chronological position of the Denbigh Flint complex in relation to other stages of prehistoric culture in the western Arctic. Finally, as a capstone to his Cape Krusenstern discoveries, Giddings located and began the excavation of what is undoubtedly the most important archeological site ever found in the Arctic—a huge stratified site at Onion Portage on the Kobuk River in the interior of northern Alaska. The site, which covers some two acres, is eighteen feet deep, with more than thirty distinct, undisturbed culture layers containing in vertical succession the hearths and artifacts of the culture stages previously found on the Krusenstern beaches as well as more Indian-like manifestations.

In the present volume we have a vivid account of these and other discoveries and of the events—sometimes humorous and often exciting—that led up to them. There is something in the nature of serendipity in Giddings's discoveries, for if ever a Prince of Serendip went questing through the Arctic, it was Louis. He never found less than he set out to find and he often found more, much more, than he sought. But it was never by sheer luck or chance; it was by careful planning and expert knowledge of what was known and what was needed. With an intimate awareness of the environment and its relation to man's activities, and with a keenly developed sense of problem, Giddings was often able to answer the question inevitably put to the archeologist: "How do you know where to dig?" His approach was always imaginative; he was ever alert and ready to seize upon a clue that might add a new dimension to the problem he was working on, or that would add greater time depth to the culture sequence he was constructing.

Giddings had a remarkable gift of expression, and from the opening pages of this volume the reader feels as if he were on the scene himself, sharing the excavator's excitement and suspense as one discovery leads to another. Giddings's own work and findings are described not in isolation but in relation to the discoveries of other archeologists and in the context of Arctic archeology as a whole. Essentially, however, this is a personal narrative, in which the vicissitudes of Arctic travel, episodes of camp life, and associations with the Eskimos are so skillfully interwoven as to seem a fitting part of the serious task at hand—the continuing and persistent effort to trace the origin and early history of man in this Arctic environment.

Giddings was led to the field of Arctic archeology through his interest in dendrochronology, in which he had been trained by Dr. A. E. Douglass, director of the Laboratory of Tree-Ring Research of the University of Arizona. While at the University of Alaska as a member of the staff of the department of anthropology, Giddings inaugurated a program of tree-ring research that resulted in the first actual dating of archeological sites in the Arctic. In 1939, with Froelich Rainey, then professor of anthropology at the University of Alaska, and Helge Larsen of the Danish National Museum, he went to Point Hope on the Arctic coast and participated in the discovery of the spectacular Ipiutak culture, a strange and wholly unexpected form of prehistoric Eskimo culture that was characterized by a highly developed style of ivory carving and engraving resembling both Old Bering Sea art and the Scytho-Siberian art of northern Asia. Other features of the Ipiutak culture seemed to point to the interior, which suggested the possibility that the huge Ipiutak village of over six hundred houses had been a seasonal settlement occupied by people who came to the coast to hunt seals and walrus in summer and who spent the winter in the interior hunting caribou. To test this possibility and to collect samples for tree-ring dating, Giddings spent the summers of 1940, 1941, and 1947 investigating old Eskimo sites on the Kobuk River in the interior of northern Alaska.

The travel experiences of 1940, which Giddings describes here for the first time, were truly impressive. Arriving at Allakaket on the Koyukuk River by airplane, he set out alone on foot for the headwaters of the Kobuk. The maps then available showed a large blank space between the two rivers. With a compass as his only guide he traversed some ninety miles of this unmapped territory in which there were no trails or markers for foot travel, stopping at regular intervals to collect cores from living conifers for tree-ring dating. Living on birds and fish, for he took no other food, and plagued by mosquitos and gnats, he reached the Kobuk River six days later. Here he built a light raft (without ax or hatchet) and floated sixty miles downstream for three days until he met the first people, two families of Shungnak Eskimos at their summer encampment at the mouth of Mauneluk River. After three weeks of excavating sites on the upper Kobuk he bought a small canvas-covered kayak in which he traveled alone to the next inhabited village, Kiana, one hundred fifty miles downstream, investigating old sites along the way.

In the spring of 1942, before joining the Navy for wartime service in the South Pacific, Giddings traversed almost all of the Kobuk River on snowshoes and by dog team on a special mission for the

U. S. Army Engineers. This second difficult set of journeys is not even mentioned in the present volume, presumably because it had nothing to do with archeology.

At the end of the third season's work on the Kobuk, Giddings had recorded an extensive body of ethnographic information, had excavated seventy-three houses at twelve different sites and had established a tree-ring chronology for the last thousand years of Eskimo culture in this part of Alaska. The results of these investigations have been described in some twenty papers and monographs. Two of them, *Forest Eskimos*, in the *Museum Bulletin*, University of Pennsylvania, and *Kobuk River People*, published by the University of Alaska, provide valuable information on the ethnography and mythology of the Kobuk Eskimos. *The Arctic Woodland Culture of the Kobuk River*, a monograph published by the University Museum and containing a detailed description of the Kobuk excavations, is one of the major works of Eskimo archeology and the finest example in Arctic literature of linkage between the archeological past and the ethnographic present.

In 1948, under the sponsorship of the Arctic Institute of North America, Giddings began a four-year program of excavations at Cape Denbigh—situated at the entrance to Norton Bay at the upper end of Norton Sound—excavations that were to mark a turning point in Eskimo archeology. His primary purpose had been to collect materials that would extend his tree-ring chronology and to learn more of the archeology of Eskimos who had lived in an area where the forests approached the sea. These objectives were accomplished but were overshadowed by a far more important find—the discovery of the Denbigh Flint complex that was to provide an insight into the beginnings of Eskimo culture.

Excavations were begun at Nukleet, a large site on the southeast side of Cape Denbigh. It was a rich site that produced over 2,000 fragments of pottery lamps and cooking pots and 4,000 artifacts of stone, bone, antler, ivory, and wood. The site had probably been occupied as late as the eighteenth century A.D., and the materials from the lower parts of the seven-foot deposit appeared to be slightly older than the oldest of the Kobuk sites (A.D. 1250) and contemporaneous with the intermediate or Punuk stage of culture on St. Lawrence Island. The stone implements at Nukleet were all of rubbed slate; there was hardly a trace of stone chipping. However, at another site, Iyatayet, on the northwest side of the Cape, a few tests beneath the grass roots had revealed chips of flint. The fact that no such chips had been found at Nukleet suggested that the Iyatayet site was culturally different and probably older. Consequently, in mid-July Giddings and his crew established camp and began excavating at the new site.

The upper few feet of the Iyatayet deposits contained materials comparable in every way to those at Nukleet. Beneath them, however, and separated in some places by a buried sod line, were materials of a very different kind, including thin, hard, check-stamped pottery, small stone lamps, and large numbers of chipped stone implements. Giddings recognized that this underlying culture layer, which he named Norton, was closely related to the earliest form of culture, called Near Ipiutak, found at the Ipiutak site at Point Hope. The Norton culture has been radiocarbon dated at around 400 B.C. The later Nukleet people had dug into this older layer when building their houses, and this was the explanation for the flint chips that had been found earlier near the surface of the site.

The Norton people, in turn, had established their village on a still older site, but in this case one that had been abandoned for more than 2,000 years. This lowermost occupation level, separated from the Norton culture by a sterile layer of sandy silt, was named the Denbigh Flint complex. It was the earliest evidence of man known from the Arctic coast, and its most distinctive artifacts were unlike anything ever before found in America.

The Denbigh artifacts, made mostly of obsidian, chert, chalcedony, and jasper, included hundreds of microblades and the cores from which they had been struck; delicately chipped bifaced end and side blades made from microblades; various types of burins—a highly specialized form of stone tool which Paleolithic and Mesolithic hunters of the Old World used for cutting and grooving bone and ivory, but which had not been found before anywhere in America; tiny artifacts, evidently engraving tools, made from burin spalls, a wholly new type of implement; a wide variety of flakeknives, end scrapers, side scrapers, and keeled scrapers; harpoon blades; "Folsom"-type gravers and a single, rather crude, fluted point; and several points comparable in form and chipping technique to Angostura and Plainview, types known from Paleo-Indian sites in the western United States.

The Denbigh Flint complex opened new and exciting vistas in Arctic archeology. Here was an early American culture whose two most important features—burins and microblades—were also the most characteristic features of the Old World Mesolithic and Paleolithic. Although burins were previously unknown in America, a few microblades had been reported from Arctic sites, including those of

the Dorset culture in the Canadian Arctic. Other Denbigh implements—"Folsom" gravers, a fluted point, and several Angostura
and Plainview points—resembled those from Early Man sites on the
Western Plains, while others such as flakeknives, slender finely
chipped end blades, side blades, and harpoon blades appeared to be
the prototypes for forms that were characteristic of Ipiutak and Near
Ipiutak, the early Eskimo cultures that had recently been discovered
at Point Hope, Alaska. In short, the Denbigh Flint complex was an
early American culture that had close affinities with the Old World
Mesolithic and Paleolithic, may have been related in some way to
early Paleo-Indian cultures of western North America, and shared
certain features in common with early Eskimo cultures in the Arctic.

The significance of the Denbigh Flint complex may be best understood if viewed in the light of previous theories and later discoveries.
Some twenty years ago I suggested that the deepest roots of Eskimo
culture were to be found in the Mesolithic cultures of northern
Eurasia, with the early Siberian Neolithic of the Lake Baikal area as
an intermediary stage. The small, slender, chipped stone arrowpoints of the Ipiutak culture were closely similar to those occurring
at early Neolithic sites in Siberia. The bone and ivory arrowheads
and lances of the Ipiutak Eskimos with stone blades inserted in the
sides were directly comparable to the side-bladed implements of the
European Mesolithic and Siberian Neolithic. Other parallels between
Mesolithic and early Eskimo included art motifs, pottery lamps,
steep-sided conical-based cooking pots, and barbed bone fish and
bird spears. The oldest known Eskimo cultures were, of course, far
removed in time and space from the European Mesolithic. Later discoveries, however, have greatly lessened the gaps and strengthened
the postulated cultural relationship. With the discovery in the late
1940's of the pre-Eskimo Denbigh Flint complex in Alaska and of
early Neolithic sites on the Lena River in Siberia, two highly important traits—burins and microblades—were added to the list of features shared in common by the Mesolithic and early Eskimo and
pre-Eskimo cultures of America. Similarly the postulated relationship between early Eskimo and Upper Paleolithic-Mesolithic art has
been strengthened by Helge Larsen's excavations in the Trail Creek
caves on Seward Peninsula, northern Alaska, in 1949–50. Materials
from the lower levels of one of the caves, radiocarbon dated at
4000 B.C., included Denbigh-like flint implements and a Mesolithic-
like bone point with a groove for side blades and an incised decoration closely resembling that of the Maglemose (Mesolithic) culture
of northern Europe.

From all indications, Ipiutak and Near Ipiutak were not the only western Eskimo cultures that had been influenced by the Denbigh Flint complex. In 1960 Giddings excavated a site called Battle Rock on the Arctic coast near Cape Krusenstern that was somewhat older than either Near Ipiutak or Okvik, the oldest stage of the Old Bering Sea culture. The chipped stone implements at Battle Rock were intermediate in form and flaking technique between Denbigh and Near Ipiutak. They were accompanied by a highly specialized type of bone arrowhead characteristic of both Near Ipiutak and Okvik, and antler objects decorated with deeply incised straight and curving lines to which long sharp spurs were attached—a form of decoration typical of the oldest style of Okvik art, previously known only from Okvik sites on St. Lawrence Island and the northeast coast of Siberia. These and a number of other specific trait resemblances between Okvik and Near Ipiutak show that the two cultures were more closely related than has sometimes been assumed. Future work will no doubt continue to break down the rather sharp distinction once made between Okvik and Near Ipiutak and bring further evidence that both these early Eskimo cultures, and indeed Eskimo culture as a whole north of the Aleutians, were derived from the pre-Eskimo Denbigh Flint complex.

Obviously enough it is in the eastern Arctic, rather than Alaska, that we have the most unequivocal evidence of the ancestral role of the Denbigh Flint complex in the formation of Eskimo culture. Soon after Giddings's discovery of the Denbigh Flint complex at Norton Sound, sites containing materials of a closely similar nature were found by Solecki, Irving, Hackman, Skarland, and Campbell at a number of localities in the Brooks Range in the interior of northern Alaska. Still later discoveries by MacNeish, Harp, Giddings, Meldgaard, Knuth, Taylor, Lowther, Larsen, Mathiassen, and Maxwell have extended the range of Denbigh-like microlithic cultures far to the eastward—from the Arctic coast of Yukon Territory, Victoria Island, Hudson Bay, and the Ungava Peninsula in northern Canada all the way to northeast Greenland and Disko Bay on the Greenland west coast. The original Cape Denbigh site and the related sites to the eastward are representative of what Irving has called the Arctic Small Tool tradition.

The Canadian and Greenland manifestations of the Arctic Small Tool tradition are also referred to as "pre-Dorset," because they represent a stage of culture that was ancestral to a later microlithic culture, the Dorset, which was the basic, original form of Eskimo culture in the central and eastern Arctic. The clearest evidence of this relationship is provided by the T 1 site on Southampton Island in Hudson Bay, excavated by the Smithsonian Institution and the National Museum of Canada in 1954 and 1955. This site, with four radiocarbon dates ranging from 675 B.C. to 60 B.C, yielded a large body of material—several thousand artifacts of stone, walrus ivory, and bone—which represented an older form of Dorset culture than any known from previous excavations in Canada or Greenland. T 1 implements that are typologically comparable to those of the Arctic Small Tool tradition are microblades, burins, and tiny implements made from burin spalls. Other T 1 implements were closely similar to types found at early Neolithic sites in Mongolia and Siberia. These were—in addition to microblades and burins—long rectangular side blades chipped on one or both surfaces, microblades with notched tangs, small delicately chipped triangular end blades, and thick, rectangular-sectioned implements similar to European backed blades but struck from the outer edges of prepared cores or chipped blades. The fact that the most characteristic implement types of early Dorset culture have their counterparts in the pre-Dorset microlithic assemblages of the American Arctic and the early Siberian and Mongolian Neolithic shows that the Arctic Small Tool tradition was the primary source from which the eastern form of Eskimo culture was derived. The pieces of the puzzle thus fall neatly in place and in so doing give us in large part the answer to the much-discussed question of the origin of Eskimo culture, a development stemming directly from Louis Giddings's breakthrough discovery of the Denbigh Flint complex on the Bering Sea coast of Alaska. Giddings's final report on the Cape Denbigh excavations, *The Archeology of Cape Denbigh,* will stand as a major landmark in Arctic archeology, and was published by Brown University in 1964, only a few months before his death.

In 1956 Giddings began the series of investigations of "beach ridge archeology" that were to yield such brilliant and unexpected results in the years immediately following. The camps and villages of modern Alaskan Eskimos, who are dependent on the sea for their livelihood, are always located near the water's edge. However, on St. Lawrence Island and at Point Hope on the Arctic coast, ancient Eskimo village sites had been found on older beach ridges far back from the present shore. As sea-mammal-hunting Eskimos must live within easy access to the sea, it was obvious that the beach ridges on which the old villages were situated must earlier have lain beside the water at the time the villages were occupied. Realizing that the location of old Eskimo sites in relation to old beach lines was a dependable guide to chronology, Giddings set out to search for favorable localities where a long succession of old beaches might reveal successive stages of prehistoric Eskimo culture.

The first locality to meet these requirements was Choris Peninsula in Kotzebue Sound, where there were nine beach ridges, the oldest a mile back from the present shoreline. The most recent beaches contained house pits and caches of modern and late prehistoric Eskimo cultures of the post-Thule period that ended about A.D. 1400. On the intermediate beaches lay hearths and artifacts of the 2,150-year-old Norton culture that Giddings had earlier identified at Cape Denbigh. The three oldest beaches contained the oval house pits and distinctive artifacts of a culture new to the Arctic, which Giddings named Choris, a culture in some respects related to but older than Norton. Finally, on the terraced hillside beyond the oldest beach ridges were found microblades presumed to be those of the Denbigh Flint complex.

The beach ridge sequences at Cape Prince of Wales at Bering Strait and at Cape Espenberg at the southern entrance to Kotzebue Sound yielded essentially the same results, but here with a well-defined Denbigh occupation discernible on the oldest beaches. At Cape Espenberg the Choris beach was more than a mile and a half back from the shore, and the Denbigh culture flints were restricted to a still older beach crest two miles inland from the sea.

Important as these discoveries were, they were eclipsed by those at Cape Krusenstern at the northern entrance to Kotzebue Sound where, with research grants first from the Arctic Institute of North America and the American Philosophical Society, and in later years from the National Science Foundation, Giddings began to work in 1958. The rows of Krusenstern beaches, 114 in number, extend from one and a half to three miles inland from the sea. The beaches are not only more numerous than those previously investigated but also reveal a longer and more continuous record of human occupation. Eskimos of every culture period known in northern Alaska have left their traces here. Moreover, the Krusenstern beaches and the higher ground beyond them added two and possibly three new stages of culture to the Alaskan sequence.

The first eight ridges, those nearest the shore, contained materials ranging from modern to late prehistoric Eskimos back to about A.D. 1400. Beaches 9 through 44 contained in orderly sequence the campsites, house ruins, and artifacts of Western Thule, Birnirk, Ipiutak, Near Ipiutak, and Norton, covering a time span of from about A.D. 900 to 400 B.C. Next came a series of beach ridges with campsites of Choris and the somewhat older Trail Creek–Choris culture (500–1500 B.C.). On these beaches were found a number of projectile points which in shape, size, and fine diagonal flaking were closely similar to the Paleo-Indian types from the Western Plains known as Angostura and Scottsbluff. These are of particular importance as indicating the relatively late persistence in the Arctic of implement types like those used by ancient hunters thousands of years earlier in regions to the south. Beach 53 contained one of the greatest surprises: the ruins of five winter houses and five summer lodges of a whale-hunting people whose large stone tools and weapons, including side-notched points, were unlike any previously known from the area. This new culture, which Giddings named Old Whaling, has been radiocarbon dated at around 1800 B.C. Included among the Old Whaling implements were several that resembled the Paleo-Indian Brown's Valley points from Minnesota. The side-notched points of Old Whaling were closely similar to those of the later Archaic culture known as Old Copper, from the Great Lakes region, dated at around 3200 B.C.

The oldest Krusenstern beaches, like those that had been tested elsewhere, contained flints of the Denbigh culture: a late phase on Ridges 78 to 80, and an earlier phase on Ridges 83 to 104. Denbigh flints were also found on the lower slope of a terrace behind the oldest beaches.

Higher up the same slope, on the top of a 500-foot-high terrace locally known as the Palisades, Giddings found materials of still another kind. These he had described as Palisades I and II, two new cultural assemblages that were not found on the beaches below and that therefore were probably much older. The Palisades II implements included a point resembling another Paleo-Indian type, the Milnesand, and short, stubby side-notched points unlike those of the Old Whaling culture. The Palisades II implements were all lime-encrusted and somewhat patinated. On the basis of the physical appearance of the artifacts, their position behind the old beaches, and the known antiquity of similar side-notched points at other localities, Giddings postulated an age of around 6,000 years for the Palisades II assemblage. Accompanying the Palisades II flints were a number of others that differed in their state of preservation, form, and chipping technique. They included large coarse flakes made in a manner suggestive of the Levalloisian of the Old World Paleolithic forms, five crude chopping tools that also recalled early Paleolithic forms, and a single large percussion-flaked bifaced implement. None of these flakes and implements would be described as patinated. Instead, they had undergone a complete chemical change from presumably an original chert to a coarse gritty material. This small collection of chemically altered flakes and artifacts was called Palisades I. Giddings points out that the high bench on which the Palisades implements were found had not been subjected to glaciation at any time during the Wisconsin period and that the Palisades I material could therefore be of great antiquity.

While Giddings's beach ridge chronology was accepted for the brilliant accomplishment that it was, several of his colleagues, including myself, expressed doubt concerning the age attributed to Palisades II. The two new cultures at Cape Krusenstern—Old Whaling and Palisades II—were both characterized by side-notched points. Those of the Old Whaling culture resembled the side-notched points of the Great Lakes Old Copper culture known as Raddats, and from their position on the beach ridges and the C-14 date for Old Whaling, were 1,000 years later than the Denbigh Flint complex. The side-notched points of Palisades II, on the other hand, were closely similar to another Old Copper manifestation called the Burst Stemmed, and these, Giddings thought, were more than a thousand years older than Denbigh. The question that arose was whether there really had been two separate and distinct populations at Cape Krusenstern, one of them 2,000 years older than the other, both of which had made use of side-notched points. Might not the undated Palisades II material represents a phase of culture related to Old Whaling, despite the difference in shape of its side-notched points?

Giddings realized that the "horizontal stratigraphy" of Cape Krusenstern could not provide a conclusive answer to this particular question. What was needed was a stratified site and, hopefully, one deep enough and old enough to provide a vertical testing of the relative ages of the Krusenstern beach and Palisades assemblages. And here we have the final and most dramatic example of Giddings's uncanny knack of "knowing where to dig." In 1941 he had excavated four late prehistoric Eskimo house ruins at Onion Portage, about 175 miles up the Kobuk River, and in one of them—House 1—he had found three microcores and a single microblade. These seemed puzzling at the time and even more so in later years after discovery of the Denbigh Flint complex with its microblade industry at sites on the Bering Sea coast and in the interior of Alaska. Giddings had often speculated on the significance of these ancient Denbigh-type artifacts in a house at Onion Portage that had been occupied as late as A.D. 1400. The most likely explanation was that the inhabitants of the house had found the microcores and microblade at some nearby site of Denbigh or Denbigh-like culture. No such site had been found at Onion Portage. There was, however, the intriguing possibility that the later Eskimos here, just as at Cape Denbigh, had sunk their house pits into the surface of a much older site. If so, then Onion Portage held promise of providing the vertical stratigraphy needed to sustain or modify the Krusenstern sequence. In 1961, while the work at Cape Krusenstern was under way, Giddings made a trip to Onion Portage to see what might lie beneath the floor of the house he had excavated twenty years earlier.

What he found surpassed his most sanguine expectations. House 1 had indeed been built on an earlier site, but a site of such magnitude, complexity, and richness as one could hardly imagine. Giddings's excavations of 1961, 1963, and 1964 showed that the Onion Portage site was some two acres in extent and as much as eighteen feet deep. The deposits consisted of alternating layers of sterile sand and over thirty thin, dark-colored strata one above the other containing the hearths and artifacts left by people who had camped there at different times in the past. This buried site with its vertical succession of habitation levels is the deepest site known from the interior of Alaska and the finest example of sharply defined stratigraphy ever found in America. As Giddings points out, the explanation for this remarkable site is that Onion Portage is a caribou crossing, a place where every year for thousands of years the caribou moved back and forth between the interior and the coast, and where man waited to intercept them.

The thirty and more culture layers were grouped into seven bands, representing seven different cultures. Most of the cultures found at Cape Krusenstern were present, and in the same sequence. But some of the Onion Portage assemblages, particularly those in Bands 2 and 5, had no counterparts on the coast and seemed to represent periods when the site had been occupied by Indians instead of Eskimos.

The characteristic implements of the Denbigh Flint complex—microblades, cores, burins, and burin spalls, and small delicately chipped end and side blades—were found in abundance in the five layers of Band 4 at a depth of five feet. Band 6, with twelve or more layers reaching a depth of ten feet, gave final proof that Giddings had been correct in his assessment of the antiquity and relative chronological position of the Palisades II assemblage at Cape Krusenstern. Band 6 proved to be the cultural equivalent of Palisades II; five feet deeper and therefore much older than the

Denbigh layer, it contained considerable numbers of side-notched points, some of which were almost identical with those of Palisades II.

Artifacts that have thus far been found in the deepest levels of the site, called Band 7, are few in number but of unusual significance. They consist of a core and several small thick microblades entirely unlike those of the Denbigh Flint complex but similar to some found by William S. Laughlin at an 8,000-year-old site in the Aleutians, which in turn were similar to cores and microblades found at the 11,000-year-old Shirataki site on the island of Hokkaido, in Japan. The bottom layers of Band 7, where the artifacts were found, had been folded over as a result of solifluction, a phenomenon associated with alternating cold and warmer periods that may have occurred at the end of the Wisconsin glaciation. As the work at Onion Portage continues, there is a reasonable expectation that this single site will reveal a record of continuous human occupation since postglacial times.

The hope expressed in the closing words of this book was not to be realized, for Louis Giddings did not return to Onion Portage in 1965. It is good to know, however, that the work there is continuing and that others—his colleagues, friends, and wife—will carry to completion the important task he had set for himself.

H. B. C.

Bureau of American Ethnology,
Smithsonian Institution

ANCIENT MEN OF THE ARCTIC

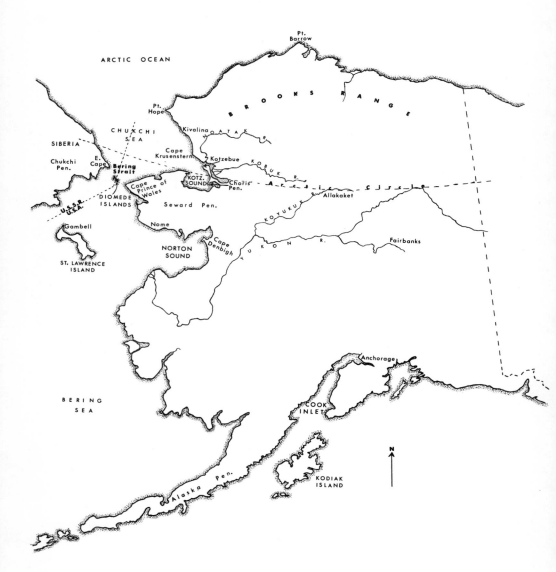

Map 1. Alaska

(1)

WHY DO WE DIG?

A SHADOW more substantial than a hawk's fell across the floor of my pit, and I looked up with a start. Nakarak and Sokpilak, each encased in a swarm of mosquitos, had come to the edge of the excavation and were bent over examining the small flints I had recently placed on a folded cloth bag.

"We have been thinking about these little things," said Nakarak, relaxing his face into what he intended as a smile.

I tapped sand off my trowel, laid it aside, and climbed to my feet out of the excavation. It was time for a rest, anyway, and my friends seemed to have something weighty on their minds. The day was warm. We sat in shirt-sleeves on the dry tussocks of bunchgrass, looking downslope from the terrace to the beach where the surf washed lazily over the rocks and sand.

"We have been thinking about that little chief," said Nakarak, spreading his hand at the height of his knee. I remembered the story of the dwarf chief to which he referred, for he had told it to us the year before, and his enthusiasm for this abandoned village called Iyatayet, which was the scene of the story, may have had something to do with our deciding to test it. The remarkable facts about this ancient mound on Cape Denbigh, an Alaskan peninsula jutting into the North Bering Sea (Map 1) were not so much the house pits and half-frozen accumulations left by fairly recent Eskimos as the deeper layers—unexpected—that contained the stone tools of two distinct peoples who were only possibly the ancestors of Eskimos. The older of these people had lived at the site five thousand years ago and had left the extraordinarily small and delicately flaked flints that we now regarded.

"We were thinking," continued Nakarak, "how hard it would be for us to make these small things, and it seems to us that maybe the chief was small all right, but everybody else was small, too." Sokpilak, who seldom spoke English though he understood it, nodded in agreement.

Nakarak's story was about a thriving village of full-sized people ruled over by a benevolent but autocratic chief no more than two feet tall. He had first told us the tale as an amusing one at odds with the teachings of the Swedish Covenant Church to which he and most of his Eskimo neighbors of Shaktoolik, Alaska, belonged. Like his friends, however, Nakarak had been a Christian too short a time to have discounted all the rich, pagan lore of his forebears. One might still remember the old stories and wish they had substance. One might even, now and then, draw upon them to explain objects or happenings for which missionaries and the schoolteacher had no ready explanation.

We sat for a while, visualizing a whole village of miniature people who made weapon points and knives to suit their size and who, accordingly, left none but these minuscule flints.

My companions were reasonable and intelligent men, both in their middle sixties, the fathers of families, and successful members of a modern Eskimo community. We worked and joked together, and we held in common a deep appreciation of the cliffs and seas and tundras of Cape Denbigh. Earlier that summer we had stood on a lookout point high above the sea watching white whales in their raids upon schools of silvery herring. We had searched the frozen banks to the east for mammoth teeth and ivory, had climbed the cliffs for murre eggs, and had discussed the many uses of other living things—plants and animals—found near our camp. In none of this had I been called upon to explain the mysteries of nature; yet now I was clearly expected to pass judgment on their profound new theory. How could I say that I believed in a village of dwarfs —however pleasant the prospect? Yet merely to shrug them off would be inadequate indeed. It seemed better just to talk, hoping for words to explain this intriguing dilemma. My listeners were silently attentive, and I tried to choose simple English words that they would not fail to understand.

I began by reminding them of objects they had helped to dig out of recent houses: arrow shafts, harpoon heads, ivory needle-cases—and now these small flints. Then I explained about archeologists—that they are not ordinary collectors like tourists who come ashore each summer from the supply ships, for they do not keep any of the collections for themselves. Instead, the real aim of archeologists is to learn the history of forgotten people, and any artifacts they dig up are put in museums for all to see. Furthermore, they must be trained in colleges and then get experience with older archeologists before they can find sites to dig on their own. They had watched, I said to Nakarak and Sokpilak, how excavations proceed. After a site is tested, if it is shown to contain buried objects, the excavators begin very careful digging. Gradually the walls of an old house are brought into view and then after scraping and brushing even more carefully, the floor is exposed. The things lying on that floor tell something about the people who left one day and never came back. A knife handle with a slate blade still wedged in its slot, a feather setter of bone, a broken arrow-point, and wood shavings show that here a man sat preparing his arrows and spears for a hunt—and over there by the hearth a pile of boiling stones and a broken clay pot show where his wife prepared dinner. The artifacts and all other information are studied and compared, and soon another part of prehistory is known.

I went on, explaining that if I seemed to know more than they about the small flints of our site, it was because I had seen similar ones from sites of Siberia, Europe, and other parts of the world. As an Arctic specialist part of my job was to learn about Indians of the Canadian woods, Eskimos of the coast and tundra, the Chukchi of Siberia, and even the Lapps of Europe, who came to Alaska a few years back to help introduce tame reindeer. By reading and talking with other specialists, and especially by studying collections in museums, I had learned more about Eskimos than they themselves knew. Nakarak and Sokpilak took this in good stead, faces impassive, and waited for me to go on. I realized that this did not yet explain why the small blades were not necessarily made by small people.

Shifting to a new line, I pointed out that they and their friends and neighbors speak the Malemiut dialect, while Eskimos only a few miles farther south speak Unalik. Another noteworthy fact is that all the Eskimos living farther north on the continent, for two thousand miles between Point Barrow and Greenland, speak a dialect so nearly identical that they can understand each other better than Malemiut speakers can understand Unalik. When explorers and scholars began to comprehend that Eskimos were much alike across the whole of Arctic North America, they wanted to know how long this had been so. And they wanted to know where these people, who harpooned seals and whales from skin boats and boiled their stews over oil lamps, had come from in the first place. Were they once American Indians, like those farther south, who had gradually learned to make a living in the coldest parts of the world? Or had their ancestors been Asians, living somewhere in or north of the great Siberian forest? Archeologists and ethnographers have puzzled over these questions for a long time, and to find the answers they have traveled north to try, in the short thawing season, to dig history out of the ground.

From many years of study, we know now that Eskimos have lived across all of Arctic America since the Thule period at least a thousand years ago, using nearly identical weapons and tools in their hunts for whales, walruses, seals, fish, and birds. Some things are different, of course. The Bering Sea kayaks, for instance, are broad and heavy for pushing between ice floes in a seal hunt, while the Greenland kayak is long and slender, low to the water, a speedy boat for outrunning seals in the open, and shallow enough to be righted easily by a hunter if he tips over in the water. Yet, whatever their differences in culture, their likenesses are greater.

Here I paused, wondering how close I had come to proving there were no miniature people. My listeners scarcely moved, but waited patiently for me to go on. Enjoying such unaccustomed attention, I continued, explaining next that archeologists have now learned that before the Thule period there were very different ways of life between the east and the west. Two thousand years ago on St. Lawrence Island, only two hundred miles from Cape Denbigh where we sat and talked, Eskimo hunters of whales and walruses engraved ivory and antler implements with lines, scrolls, circles, weird animals, and grotesque human faces. This showed that their ceremonies were more elaborate than the later ones of Thule culture. We call the people who dwelled there "Old Bering Sea" people, and while they have been traced, through their special kinds of tools and weapons, as far north as East Cape in Siberia and the Diomede Islands, they do not seem to have regularly visited North American shores.

The oldest remains in Arctic Alaska that we knew about, until we came to Cape Denbigh, were in the great Ipiutak village of

Point Hope (Map 1), where certain hunters of walrus and caribou built more than seven hundred houses, over who knows how long a time, but dating back to the beginning of the Christian era, and buried their dead with such strange things as carved face masks and ivory chains. But neither the Old Bering Sea nor the Ipiutak people ever went as far east as Canada, so far as we know. The earliest people there, preceding the Thule, appear to have been the Dorsets, who kept no dogs and used no drills, and who are thought by some anthropologists to have been as much Indian as Eskimo.

This brought me back to the strange things we were finding at the bottom of our mound at Cape Denbigh that summer of 1949. Here, I explained, was where my studies and training came in. Since nothing quite like this combination of Denbigh flints had been seen before, we were trying to learn where their makers came from. The smooth and razor-like small flints—not made into anything in particular—we call microblades.[1] They were formerly made also in several other parts of the world. Only a few years ago, in fact, some, along with spearpoints and scrapers, were found on the edge of a hill overlooking an old river channel on the campus of the University of Alaska near Fairbanks. Specialists who examined these Campus-site artifacts said they were identical to flints collected from the Gobi Desert of Mongolia and also from sites in the forests of central Siberia, where they might be 5,000 or even 8,000 years old. Whoever our oldest Denbigh people were, they flaked flint-like rock in a special way exactly as other early, full-sized men did in other parts of the world.

Nakarak and Sokpilak had listened intently, and now they made no move to go. I slowly realized they were still waiting for a more specific answer to their proposal.

"Now among these small flints," I said, "are some kinds that I have never seen before." Taking up a small piece just excavated, I pointed out that twenty ribbon-like flakes had been struck from both faces of the original microblade, shaping it into a point as small as the blade of a penknife (Fig. 1). Such delicate flaking might more understandably have been done by a jeweler than by a man with primitive tools. Explaining that in other parts of the world blades less refined, but altogether as small, were once set into grooves in the sides and ends of arrow and spearheads of bone and antler, acting as knives to widen the wound of a stricken beast,

[1] For full definitions of technical terms see the glossary, pp. 385–91.

1. A small point from Cape Denbigh. This was made from a microblade and shows the careful flaking work that was typical of Denbigh craftsmanship. Length, 1¼ in. (3.3 cm.).

I suggested that these small tools were probably once used in similar ways here by full-sized men, not by a race of dwarfs. Besides, I said, from measuring lengths of bones, anthropologists know that there have been and still are races of varying heights, but none are known from the Arctic who were greatly taller or shorter than men today. The first men in America, whenever they came and whoever they were, and all of those who descended from them, were most likely full-sized people—no larger, no smaller, than the tall and short people we know today.

My last words had a summary tone, and my two listeners made preliminary motions toward getting to their feet. After a moment of silence, Nakarak spoke with deliberation, saying: "We thank you for explaining all these things to us. We do read a little, and we go to Bible School in the winter, but no one has ever explained these things to us before."

They got up to go. As they did, Nakarak added, as though to emphasize his appreciation: "We understand those things better now. The world has had big people and small people—and we think it must be true that the little chief was one of the smallest, all right, and we think all the other people in this village were pretty small, too!"

(II)

A SEARCH FOR
OLD BEACHES

T HE FLAT, grass-covered shoreline at Cape Krusenstern, the
northern limit of Kotzebue Sound (Fig. 2; Map 1), is deceptively bland to those who sail past in boats. "A most dreary expanse
of low moorland," remarked Henry W. Elliott, a tourist of the
1870's.

Now that hunters seldom camp there, the only landmark for
many miles is a forty-foot tower of weathered spruce poles. The
Eskimos whom I asked about the origin of this structure gave a
choice of answers, each stated with authority. One group said it had
been built of driftwood by native whale hunters for use as a lookout
place in the annual spring hunt. Others said government engineers
had unloaded the poles from a ship and built the tower high
enough for them to see it with their instruments from the neighboring hills. A more interested observer might note, however, the brass
marker of the United States Coast and Geodetic Survey that is
driven into the ground between its four legs. Whatever its intended
function, the tower affords an excellent, if slightly wobbly, vantage
point for scanning the countryside.

One climbs into the full force of the wind, avoiding loose
rungs on the built-in ladder. Grasping the rail about the narrow platform at the top, and slowly adjusting to swaying with the gusts, he
looks out landward across a remarkable terrain. The broad,
brownish-green beach crest upon which the tower stands is but one

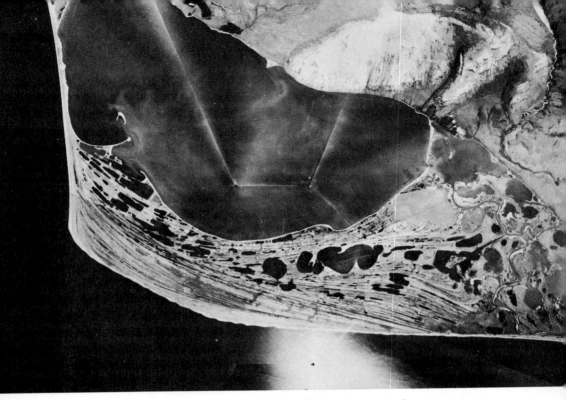

2. Aerial view of Cape Krusenstern, Alaska.

of dozens of similar crests stretching away like the furrows of a gigantic garden.

No longer monotonous, the landscape becomes rich in detail. Immediately below, one sees half-buried logs of driftwood, probably tossed by storms to the height of the beach, and arrangements of weathered wood and whalebone, quite certainly the work of man. Belying its appearance from the sea, the first crest has been walked upon by many men, and signs of their tenting, digging, and storing soon become evident in patterns of rectangles and circles formed by the ground-hugging leaves of various plants. Similar areas on the surfaces of other crests, beyond, testify to their also having been the sites of human activity. Lines running along the crests were made by men and animals for whom the old, parallel beaches were natural highways. Between the crests, sheltered from the wind, the vegetation grows taller and in a variety of hues, and moist spots encourage sedges and thick-leaved plants. Far back from the ocean, some of the swales hold water, making canals. Still farther back, swales join to become ponds, and, finally, in the distance, the con-

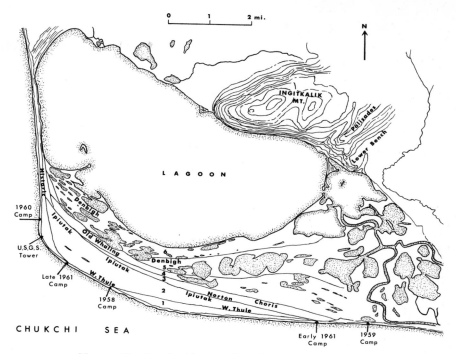

Map 2. The beach ridges at Cape Krusenstern, Alaska:

Segment	Beaches	Sites and Age
1	1–8	Recent
2	9–19	Western Thule, about A.D. 1000
	29–35	Ipiutak, about beginning of Christian era
3	36–44	Norton, about 500 B.C.
	44–51	Choris, about 1000 B.C.
4	53	Old Whaling, about 1800 B.C.
5	78–80	Late Denbigh, about 2500 B.C.
6	83–104	Early Denbigh, about 3000 B.C.
		Lower Bench, about 3500 B.C.
Ingitkalik Mt.		Palisades II, about 6000 B.C. (?)
		Palisades I, much older

tinuous water of a wide lagoon stretches three miles to the slopes of Ingitkalik Mountain (Map 2). Dark-green channels spread like a net across the more remote beach ridges—they are the sealed-over frost cracks that dissect only the older and more settled ground

(Fig. 72, p. 201). Ducks and dowitchers fly up from the ponds now and then, and a glitter in the distance is the sunlight reflected from the wings of wheeling terns.

One looks again at the evenly undulating ground and wonders if the old beach crests, now left remote from the sea as new beaches formed, might not carry, in series, the leavings of many generations of hunters and travelers. If they do, have we not at Cape Krusenstern an unequaled archeological sequence—an orderly succession of people who resettled at the ocean edge whenever a new beach formed? This was my hope upon first climbing the tower at Cape Krusenstern in August 1958, when it looked as if our search for beach ridge sequences of archeology had reached a climax in this apparently endless series of fossil shorelines.

The successions of beaches here and elsewhere were built by the changing habits of wind and sea. In earliest times there was but one beach—if, indeed, any—rather than cliffs, along the shore of a body of water. Then, in certain areas, an unaccountable change in the prevailing winds and a slight shift in offshore currents deposited heavier concentrations of sediment along the shore in certain places, making a new beach rise in front of the old. The height of this new beach was great enough not to be overrun by high tides, which might have washed it away. After a period of stability, another change in the elements caused a third beach to rise in the same way, until here at Cape Krusenstern there are more than 114 such old ridges. It seemed likely that the successions of people at the coastal edge might have matched the beach formations— that is, we know that present-day people camp at the water's edge; as ancient people would have done the same, their leavings should be found on the most ancient beaches now far back from the sea. This book will tell a little of what has been learned of the successive peoples who inhabited those beaches—not only the Denbigh people, already introduced, but people whose cultures have been given such names as Western Thule, Ipiutak, Norton, Choris, and Old Whaling.

THE SUMMER of 1958 began at a leisurely pace. With my son Jim and two undergraduate assistants from Brown University, William Simmons and Terrell Robinson, I had driven across the continent from Rhode Island to central Alaska. While this was a familiar route to me, and Jim, then eleven, had been born in Fairbanks, neither of the others had previously crossed the Canadian border. We stopped often during the first few days, pondering such phenomena of the north woods as a porcupine crossing the road, bear tracks in the sand, and groups of colorfully dressed Ojibway Indians strolling through the streets of a Manitoba town.

For me, the trip from New England to Alaska is a proper prelude to the challenge and mystery of a summer of search and excavation in the Arctic. As we drive across the hundreds of miles of prairie where herds of antelope feed in the early morning and the bleached bones of steers suggest those of vanished bison, I am impressed again by the immense space through which Early Man spread across the Americas. On this occasion we talked about the misleading drawings one still sees in books about Indians showing brutish, long-haired Asians trekking determinedly in pursuit of American animals now extinct. We felt how unlikely it was that men would move always southward through these vast forests and prairies, as though led by bellwether mammoths and Pleistocene ponies, all seeking together a utopian home. Had we been pioneers in these places, we would most likely have wanted to pound in our stakes and settle at one or another good camping place, as Indians had done since long ago.

In the Rockies we climbed a small mountain near Toad River Lodge, and at Teslin Lake we bargained with a group of inland Tlingit Indians for a beaded moosehide jacket. Later we took in the sights of Whitehorse, a town still vaguely reminiscent of the days of '98 (Map 4). Driving on past the steely slopes and blue waters of Lake Kluane, we questioned again the motives of those fictional migrants who, some theorists maintain, hurried through the great game belt of the sub-Arctic forest; and we concluded that such early men could only have lacked appreciation of good country.

Our group, on the other hand, did rush along the "migration" route, even though in the opposite direction, for it took us only ten days from Providence, Rhode Island, to Fairbanks, a distance of some five thousand miles. After a visit with anthropologists at the University of Alaska and a study of its archeological collections, we stored the car and traveled by air the remaining five hundred miles to Kotzebue. We were keen with anticipation of the sites we should find on the coast, whatever they might be: those of migrants or simply of permanent dwellers on hospitable shores. Our plan that year was to excavate the remainder of an old site at Choris Peninsula, study the succession of beach ridges upon the inner of which the old sites stood, and then traverse the coasts of Kotzebue Sound in search of other and—hopefully—broader expanses of parallel stranded beaches (Map 3).

ARRIVING in Kotzebue, one man sees the town differently from another. Young Captain Otto von Kotzebue, the Russian explorer whose name it bears, sailed past in 1816 without even noticing the wide inlet on the south shore of which the settlement now lies. To the younger members of my group, the town was, at first sight, a collection of unpainted walls and false fronts like those of a Hollywood western, all facing a littered beach, fish racks, and rows of howling dogs. But to me, Kotzebue will always have a different stripe. I first saw it in the winter of 1934 when, as a student and would-be writer, I squandered my last savings to spend the winter in an Eskimo village. After a long and sometimes hazardous flight by bush plane and a landing on what appeared to be an endless snowfield, I watched scores of energetic people in fur clothing emerge, apparently, from rows of snowdrifts. Each drift, I soon learned, encased at its windward end a house or a store, the interior of which was warm and friendly and smelled of coffee, seal oil, and fresh-baked bread. Even today newcomers are quick to sense in Kotzebue the spiritual well-being of its people which triumphs over the more visible litter on paths and beaches and the occasional rowdiness of a few celebrants. As a town in the modern sense, Kotzebue began with the establishment of a Friends' Mission in 1896. This was followed by a little gold rush in 1898, and the subsequent gathering of traders and Eskimos who settled on the first beach ridge nearest the water. Earlier men had preceded them, though, both on that beach and on the inner, more ancient beaches.

In 1940 I had excavated the remains of old pit houses on Beaches 2 and 3 at the west end of the town, and now Bill Simmons and I studied large aerial photographs of the locality and walked back to the oldest beach ridges, hoping that some of the spots on the crests detected in the photographs might prove to be the marks of ancient settlement. Soon disillusioned in this, we returned to the village hungry to invest some of our funds in dollar hamburgers and half-dollar ice-cream cones at the counter in Rotman's store.

Later, all of us strolled the mile-long waterfront path that serves also as a precarious street for the town's few wheeled vehicles, in hope of finding Almond Downey, our native boatman and assist- ant of a previous year. From his friends we learned that he was camped with his family ten miles away across Hotham Inlet at the whaling station of Shesualek. This is a temporary tent village that each summer briefly accommodates nearly the whole inland com- munity of Noatak. Families gather here as they have done for at least a century, and probably a great deal longer, to hunt the big seal (*oogruk*) before the ice leaves, and the white whale for some weeks longer. While we might have hired a man with a boat and motor to take us across the inlet, I knew that the cost of a bush plane for the short hop would be little more, and the prestige to be gained for the Downeys would make it well worth while. There is nothing like having an airplane land back of your tent with the word that a season of adventure is about to begin. This decided, we soon hired a plane, buzzed the settlement, and landed dramatically abreast of the Downeys' tent.

Almond Downey (Fig. 3), a rugged, genial Eskimo, then twenty-nine, was eager to be traveling again. Ruth, his wife, smiled and nodded assent as she laid out crackers and cups for tea, and the two older children, Lydia and Percy, created a small storm by

3. Almond Downey, my Eskimo assistant for several seasons.

instantly rolling up their reindeer-skin sleeping bags, ready to go. A baby, Mary, peering out of the back of her mother's parka, would offer no impediment to this family whose ancestors had spent a good part of every summer camping in the lee of their upturned skin boats.

When the time came for us to leave, Almond tested the wind, scanned the sky, and said he would fold up his tent and meet us with his boat in Kotzebue as soon as the weather calmed, perhaps that night. Looking down a few minutes later as our Piper Cub leaped into the air from the rough beach crest that served as a landing strip, we saw that the whole community had assembled to see us off. As we wheeled to gain altitude before crossing the inlet, I carefully studied the pattern of old beaches spread out below. Here, again, was evidence that one shoreline had succeeded another, by some process we did not fully understand, until crests lay paralleling one another like the ripples on a pond. Depressions on some of the earlier beaches were clearly those of house or cache pits overgrown for centuries with moss and willows. Beach ridges like these were to be our summer hunting ground.

The Downeys met us in Kotzebue as planned, and next day our travels began. Almond's boat was a large skiff that his father had built of planks whipsawed from crooked-grained Noatak River spruce. Designed for use on the river, it was commodious rather than sleek in appearance, but when burdened by Almond's family of five together with our foursome and all our tents, gasoline, food, and other supplies, it lay as low in the water as an outbound tanker. Almond's pride was high, nevertheless, because he had pre-invested a good part of his summer's salary in a new 35-horsepower motor that pushed us along with reassuring strength. After a long day's journey, we pitched camp, under a cold midnight sun, at Choris Peninsula.

THE IDEA of a special kind of "beach ridge archeology" had become, for me, a unique challenge. The summer of 1958 was not to be an ordinary season of digging sites to extend our knowledge of Eskimo beginnings. Rather, I intended to use our information about cultural successions to learn whether or not series of beaches had formed with predictable regularity. Archeologists in Scandinavia had found that the earliest settlements lay on former sea beaches now high on mountainsides. This was explained by the fact that the beaches during the Pleistocene (the Ice Age) were covered by heavy glaciers; then, eight or ten thousand years ago, when our present, warmer period began and the ice melted, the land, released of its burden, slowly rose upward—not unlike a cork that will bob up when freed of whatever has pressed it down. Thus, very old beaches in Scandinavia may now be as high as seventy feet above the present waterline. The beaches we were examining in Alaska, though, seemed neither to have been lifted nor depressed, but were left unmolested by the elements, free to build forward as often as new surges of sediment came along.

Beach ridge archeology thus seemed logical enough. Its main premise is that any people in this part of the world who live near a shoreline will prefer to camp on a sand or gravel beach from which they can most conveniently scan both land and sea. Food—fish, seals, and whales—is available just off the shore, increasing in abundance at certain seasons. The shore itself is a convenient place for storing boats and supplies as long as their owners remain close enough to protect them from damage by wind and tide. The stable shore is always more attractive than any beach ridges behind it, and thus it will accumulate most of the leavings of the people of its period, receiving progressively less only when it is left too far from the sea by the build-up of a new shoreline.

Assuming that this is so and that each beach crest bears the cultural leavings of the people of its time, why had we not put the principle to work earlier? Observant archeologists had, for some time, noted the location of older sites on back beaches. Henry B. Collins of the Smithsonian Institution recorded in 1932 that the order of age of the six settlements at Northwest Cape on St. Lawrence Island (Map 6, p. 152) corresponded to their distance from the present shoreline: the town of Gambell, where people now live in plank houses on the surface, had been preceded by an older town of pit houses, straddling earlier beach ridges; and that, by a still older one, from which the waterfront cannot now be seen. A half-mile farther back, the large mound of a sizable village abandoned some 1,000 years ago lies on a beach ridge from which people today, were they to camp there, could not even see a seal, much less give effective chase. Still farther back, a large village ruin of 1,500 or 2,000 years ago lies on the earliest beach ridge to have formed at the foot of a steep hillside. Finally, a still earlier settlement on the

slope of the hill itself was presumably occupied before any permanent gravel beach existed. Collins pointed out the significance of
the distance from the sea and realized that the edge of beach ridge
formation at that particular point might be estimated once the
villages were dated, though he relied for his dating on the changing
styles of art and implements.

Those of us who excavated at Point Hope, halfway between
Kotzebue Sound and the northern tip of Alaska, both in 1939 and
later, again noted the relation of beach ridges to old settlements.
We saw that many parallel old beaches form the peninsula on which
Point Hope lies (Fig. 42, p. 126), but we could not recognize on
them a uniform succession of house pits and villages. Nor did we
have encouragement from other sources. Not even geologists had
seen reason to believe that the beach ridges in various parts of
western Alaska were the result of fairly regular deposition.

I FIRST acquired faith in beach ridges as time markers in 1956
when, observing the regularity of cultural succession on nine old
beaches at Choris Peninsula (Map 3) and remembering other such
series, I envisioned in them a kind of horizontal stratigraphy that
might carry with it a built-in calendar. But this was still a hypothesis
that had to be rigorously tested. I had also learned that year that the
beach ridges at Choris had grown more slowly than had those at
either Point Hope or St. Lawrence Island, where twenty or thirty
beaches had formed, presumably in not much more than 2,000
years. The radiocarbon dates of charcoal from house floors of ancient residents on the next to oldest Choris beach indicated an age
greater than 700 B.C. If the old village had stood on the edge of the
sea some 2,700 years ago, as we believed it had, the seven beaches
that formed subsequently would have had 400 years each in which
to form. Beach ridges thus gave evidence of forming at different
rates in different localities. But had they formed in response to the
same surges of climate? As we surveyed the ridges and swales at
Choris and examined the archeological leavings on the later crests,
we reached the conclusion that these beaches had not formed haphazardly but with some degree of regularity through time from some
unknown effects of wind and tide. Though their rates of formation
might differ because of the direction of currents and prevailing
winds, their major crests would be substantially the same.

.   .   .

BY JULY 10, 1958, we had completed the excavation of the old Choris site begun two years earlier. Intriguing though this work had been, with its outlining of a previously unknown form of culture presenting great oval houses and the earliest pottery yet encountered on these coasts, I was as eager as a tiger hunter to get on and track down other beach ridge series in Kotzebue Sound. Consequently, we packed the boat again and, heavily loaded with people and gear and depending upon relative calm for plying the shallow waters of the Sound, moved on. We stopped as often as sheltering banks or small inlets appeared, in order to walk the small beaches and look for series of earlier crests. On the south side of Chamisso Island (Map 3) we halted briefly to examine the narrow, sandy shelf left by two or three beach deposits in succession, but house pits here gave no signs of being more than a few hundred years old. Farther south, on the shore of Seward Peninsula where the Kiwalik River mouth is bordered to the west by long ribs of former beaches, we made an overnight camp and searched, as I had done in the area once before, for flint chips or house depressions. The succession of ridges there, though promising for short-range studies, again failed to produce anything earlier than the Thule culture of a thousand years ago, the presence of which we had previously ascertained.

Next, traveling at night when the winds ordinarily die down, we reached the village of Deering at the mouth of the Imachuk River. No sooner had we nosed into a sandy beach just inside the river mouth than the village children and loose dogs were on hand to meet us, followed by nearly all the rest of the fifty or so residents. It came as a surprise to the Downeys—but not to me—that they at once discovered relatives in this community where they had never been before. In our travels together along these coasts, I cannot remember a place where Almond failed to find an uncle, a great aunt, or at least a cousin or two, all of whom extended to his family and the rest of us the full range of their hospitality. While the Downeys disappeared into a weathered frame house, the rest of us, trailed by small admirers, walked down the beach path in front of the boarded-up windows and storefronts of this waning town to search out an excavation made by Helge Larsen of Denmark in 1950. There, on the crest of the second gravel beach, was the rectangular floor of a large house of the Ipiutak culture, built in an early century of the Christian era, from which Larsen's party had removed quantities of well-preserved artifacts. We saw at a glance that the position of this site could not help us much with beach ridge reconstruction, however, for the shoreline had eroded in recent decades or centuries, removing all other beaches that might have served as dating criteria.

The following day we walked some six miles to the mouth of the Kugruk River and sketched and photographed a more promising series of beach ridges. Here the deposition had been rapid, and the earliest house pits we could find were clearly more recent than those of Thule culture. In an eroded muck bank just inside the back of the beach ridges where the river turned toward its outlet, we examined the bones of extinct mammals washing from Pleistocene deposits. The tusk of a mammoth—coated with blue vivianite formed from phosphorus in the ground—proved too heavy for us to carry back to Deering, though that night a group of men from the village retrieved it with their boat and set about sawing it into segments to carve into images and spoons for the souvenir trade.

Returning tired from a day of walking and testing the beaches with shovels, we paused to rest on high ground at the top of a bluff overlooking the mouths of two neighboring rivers. On this clear day one could see bare, blue mountains around the northern and eastern rims of Kotzebue Sound and, away to the west, a low-lying gray streak that we knew to be Cape Espenberg. Regarding it, I remembered that other archeologists had considered it to be an unpromising region of blowing sand. The water, shallow and dangerous in that direction, would not permit one to get close to the shore until he had reached the point, and for a short while I weighed the hazards of travel in that direction against the time that might more profitably be spent in excavating known sites in previously discovered beach ridge sequences. We all wanted to see and test for ourselves new terrain, however—even an uninhabited place like Cape Espenberg—so, after returning to Deering and waiting again for a dead calm, we set out in Almond's boat, hugging the shore until we reached a point where the shallow, muddy bottom forced us farther and farther seaward and out of sight of land.

Although he never spoke of it, I knew Almond's apprehension for his boatload of valuable cargo and his new motor in shoals of this kind. As long as the water remained calm and we had a foot or more of clearance for the propeller we were in no immediate danger, but as soon as the wind blew up—which it did long before we were within sight of the Cape—there was double danger from the short, choppy waves. The propeller dug regularly into the muddy bottom, and spray blew with force into the boat. One of us had to bail continuously, while the rest kept busy trying to guard the gear from getting completely drenched. Tents and tarps were weighted or lashed down. The small children, enjoying themselves, made a play camp under a dome of canvas while we huddled miserably in our raincoats and poled into the wind as often as the motor succumbed to its propeller's fight with the mud. Seek as we might for a change of expression on Almond's face that would tell us what we already knew—that the situation was dangerous—we found none. Tilting the motor to clear bottom in the trough of a wave, and simultaneously scanning the horizon for signs of an inlet, he displayed no outward hint of the tenseness that we felt. Now and then he sounded with a paddle, noting minute changes in depth. Just when I was calculating our chances of jettisoning part of the cargo and turning around to go with the wind across the raging center of the Sound, I noticed that his paddle showed a progressive deepening of the water: one inch, two inches, then another were gained, until at length he restored the paddle to the inner edge of the boat and chose a course that angled, at first dangerously, into the wind. He had found a channel, and he knew that if he could read the signs, it would lead him toward the flat and shadowy shoreline. Now we bailed constantly as water sluiced into the boat, but we were traveling with greater speed and great hopes of reaching the shore safely.

A little later the children emerged, beaming with good nature, to see why the boat had spoiled their game by no longer rocking with the waves. We had entered a small inlet just south of the Cape proper, where slanting sunlight turned a marshy shore into green and gold as flocks of terns, ducks, and shore birds rose in shrill and clattering alarm. Within minutes after landing, a tepee of driftwood, half-covered by a tarpaulin, became an outdoor living room in which Ruth Downey brewed tea and laid out the lunch, while the rest of us admired the landscape and speculated about the height of the whitecaps on the brown, churning sea (Fig. 4). Cape Espenberg was going to be worth the effort after all.

After a long rest, we decided to explore the small Espenberg River at the mouth of which two Eskimo families lived in plank and driftlog houses. On both sides of the river entrance were sand dunes. I knew from aerial photographs and the reports of archeologists that this shoreline consisted of shifting sand, stabilized only

4. Setting up the tepee for a lunch stop at Cape Espenberg. In background is Kotzebue Sound.

in parts by vegetation. Unlike the coasts from Deering around the other side of Kotzebue Sound, these had neither gravel nor small pebbles—only sand. Yet I knew from the photographs that even these sand dunes were denuded beach ridges, though each ridge was much broader than those of gravel elsewhere. From the boat, sheltered in the calm stream by the high dunes on either bank of the river, we sought a camping place where wind would not fill our tents and food with drifting sand. Though we had seen two houses high on a grass-covered dune, they were not suitable for summer living, being primarily winter quarters. We felt obliged to start the motor and move on upstream in search of a better camping place. At length, perhaps a mile from the river mouth, we came to a grassy bank littered with driftwood where we pulled ashore and raised our tents.

On walking to the highest dune in the vicinity, I could see the northern shore of Cape Espenberg, along the Arctic Ocean, and found that there were, indeed, old beach lines to be discerned both in the rows of dunes near the sea and in the broad, flat, sod-covered stretches of solid ground between long marshes. The bare dunes of the first beach were still in the process of forming and shifting, but the crests behind that active front were increasingly flat. Those nearest our camp had been completely covered with turf at one time or another, but even the most stable of them had been cut into by currents of wind, and once these cuts had been opened, the wind widened its channel, undermining the surface, until it produced depressions and cross channels (blowouts) at frequent intervals. The very broad and shallow swales here, on the other hand, were continuous marshes and lakes—difficult to cross and covered with a profusion of low vegetation. Scrutinizing the surface of the ridge behind our camp as I walked back, it took only a short time to find gray and black chips of chert and a piece of a broken clay pot impressed in its outer surface with thin, parallel markings. This was an exciting disclosure, for this type of decoration was neither recent nor that done 1,000 years ago by the Thule or Birnirk people; and the Ipiutak people of 2,000 years ago were not known to have made pottery. The sherd, in fact, was similar to others found on the oldest beach at Choris Peninsula, where pottery—the oldest known in the region—was made about 700 B.C.

By the time I got back to camp, the Downeys had their large, white tent up and the camp stove roaring with a fire of dry sticks. The scent of boiling salmon issued forth, and Ruth explained that she had already received a visit from our neighbors at the mouth of the river, who had brought us one of the first salmon of the season. After dinner, fired by the small discoveries on our beach ridge, we turned to a still older, parallel beach immediately in front of a stable bank which presumably had once been a Pleistocene shore. In Alaska archeologists seldom find things of value on the surface, for vegetation obscures small objects. They must look, instead, for signs of ancient digging that show through a cover of thick moss and sod. Here, exceptionally, we could walk slowly across naked blowouts on this presumed oldest postglacial beach and, bending now and then for a better look, find the chips, bone fragments, and stone tools of those who had once known this crest as their oceanfront camp (Fig. 5).

Presently one of the men shouted, and we converged like sea gulls on his discovery. Lying one beside the other in a blowout were the fragments of a large pot, its pieces still together after decades of slow dispersion of the supporting sand. Within the radius of this ancient camp lay also fragments of knives and scrapers of silicified slate, whitened bones of seals, and hard, blackened lumps of cemented sand from a fireplace. All this testified to the conclusion of a successful hunt and a feast before a windbreak or in a tent

5. Beach ridge blowouts, Cape Espenberg. Russ Giddings is at lower right examining artifacts. The beach ridge extends back to top of picture, its sides sloping gently in either direction.

at a time when the beach crest was sod-covered and habitable.

Farther along came an even greater prize: a microblade—one of those thin, parallel-edged flakes of flinty material made by the old Denbigh people of five thousand years ago whose remains we knew until then only from Cape Denbigh on the North Bering Sea coast and sites of mountain passes in the Brooks Range to the north and east (Fig. 102, p. 263). Still farther along we found a burin (a small but highly specialized flint implement with faceted edges, used as a groover or chisel) and a fragment of a side blade showing meticulous workmanship, both of which were also characteristic tools of the Denbigh people (Figs. 6, 7, and 109). We guessed then and know now from later experience that the beach had been occupied by two peoples at different times: those of the Denbigh Flint complex and, later, those of a Choris-related culture. This wide,

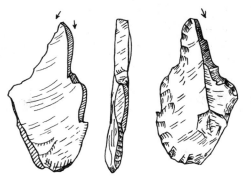

6. Front, side, and back views of a burin, Denbigh Flint complex. Arrows show where flakes were removed. Length, 1½ in. (3.8 cm.).

7. Three views of a side blade, Denbigh Flint complex. Length, 1⅝ in. (4.0 cm.).

inner beach crest had evidently been stable for hundreds of years. Excitement ran high that evening as we discussed the indications at Cape Espenberg. My hope of using beach ridge sequences both for dating archeology and for discovering new sites appeared about to be fulfilled, since even these disturbed, sandy crests were yielding the information we wanted.

As the days passed, however, and we slowly walked the fifteen-mile-long crests of the old beaches, we learned that large-scale archeological work was going to be difficult. Search though we might, we could not find the remains of early house pits on the older beaches. If houses had been built—and no doubt they had—they must have become deeply buried by the ever-moving dunes while the beaches were still young. On the other hand, there were other rewards from our minute scrutiny of the beaches, especially the earlier ones. Artifacts found both singly and in conjunction with burnt areas gave us a good picture of the earliest people to occupy the mile-and-a-half-wide series of ridges. We slowly learned that the very earliest beach to form at Cape Espenberg was not the one at the edge of the old, permanent ground, but was in a series that had been mostly covered over by the later beach ridges we had been examining, protruding at an angle at a lower elevation farther toward the eastern tip of the peninsula. Here we found artifacts of the Denbigh Flint complex, but none from a later period.

As we sat in the tent each evening sorting out chips and labeling the artifacts of the day's collection, we were elated anew by the importance of our discovery. The Denbigh people of the coast, it would seem, had not only camped at seal-hunting points where the forest met the sea, but had traveled, undoubtedly by boat, along the beaches of treeless parts of Seward Peninsula, camping here and there as Eskimos have done in more recent times. Also, we now knew that in searching for further Denbigh sites, we could ignore the later beaches of a series and walk directly to the very earliest— if, indeed, another series long enough to reach back to those remote times could be found. Since we had a number of radiocarbon dates relating to the Denbigh Flint complex, we could also be sure that the earliest beaches, which yielded the Denbigh artifacts, must have formed before 2500 B.C.

The final part of our project that summer was to investigate the area north of Kotzebue—in particular, Shesualek and Cape Krusenstern. Before departing from Cape Espenberg, however, we left Mrs. Downey and the small children in camp and made a quick trip as far as the village of Shismaref, some seventy miles southwest along the coast (Map 3). Everywhere the beach was the same: sand backed by sand dunes. Sometimes a short series of beach ridges paralleled one another, but none appeared to be wide enough to add anything further to the information we had secured at Cape Espenberg.

Landing on the shore of the wide inlet behind Shismaref, we were met by an old couple—the wife with vertical tattoo lines from lip to chin—who invited us into their small tent for coffee. Seeing the size of the tent, we hesitated about all crowding into it—especially when we saw that it was already reasonably full of bedding and supplies—but our hosts insisted, and we packed ourselves in, one by one, until Jim, the last, squeezed in far enough to tie the tent flaps together. Just then heads began to poke through the spaces between ties—the faces of boys Jim's own age, all studying him with quiet interest. When our hostess poured coffee, Jim, still holding his cup and saucer, declined. The woman then lifted a kettle from the stove, asking if he would like hot water. Anticipating cocoa, Jim nodded and held his cup out for her to fill. But, while his audience watched and we drank our coffee, nothing further came his way. At length, feeling obliged to save face, he lifted his cup and downed the hot water, evoking murmurs of admiration from his peers who, no doubt, judged this to be a custom of boys from wherever in the world he had come.

After a few minutes of animated conversation between the Eskimos, Almond turned to explain that this was another of his "uncles"—one he had never met or even heard of before. From there on, the hospitality of Shismaref continued to be open and enthusiastic. No sooner would we examine a burial or house mound in the not very old village site behind the present community than we would be asked again to drop in to someone's tent or house for another cup of coffee.

In examining the old village, I soon realized that the sand-filled house pits that were being dug into by natives for ivory and oil-soaked timbers must be the same ones that Otto von Kotzebue had investigated in 1816 while they were still occupied by the presumed ancestors of these present residents of Shismaref. Von Kotzebue described the houses as lying in a straight line at the shore, supposedly on the first beach ridge. He and his companions were explorers from Russia, and he wrote in his journal that although dogs had dashed out to meet them, the owners of the houses had all vanished or hidden, abandoning their possessions for the moment. Von Kotzebue had walked to the roofs of the underground houses, then entered one by crawling through an entrance tunnel only three feet high that brought him to a room described as ten feet long, seven feet wide, and seven feet high. This was a storeroom full of black blubber in squares a foot across, and it contained "sieves with long handles," presumably ice strainers used in winter fishing. He then crawled through a second tunnel only two and a half feet high and seven feet long, emerging through a circular doorhole into the house proper. This had a plank floor, a raised sleeping bench, ladder-like drying racks, and a window of transparent membrane. The outlines our group saw here and in neighboring sites indicated that von Kotzebue had faithfully described the Shismaref of his day.

Our welcome was in sharp contrast to that of von Kotzebue, however. Back on their ship, the *Rurik,* von Kotzebue and his crew saw two skin boats, each containing ten men, rowing rapidly toward them. Pulling alongside the *Rurik,* these men, wearing short shirts or none, with heads bare and hair cut short, and with ivory labrets protruding from holes below the edges of their mouths, threatened the invaders with their lances while producing "the most piercing cries and hideous grimaces." The muskets the Russians pointed at them failed to frighten the Eskimos—presumably they had not yet learned about firearms—but the display of bright Russian sabres glistening in the sun soon silenced their cries and they drew away soberly in their boats, even though they followed the ship for a distance, perhaps more out of curiosity than malice. We, by way of contrast, finally pulled away from Shismaref so kindly treated and full of coffee that we spoke for a while of giving up that beverage for the rest of our journey.

THE BEACH RIDGES at Shesualek were our next hunting ground. After no more than the usual small crises of coastal travel in a river boat, we reached Kotzebue again, then continued north across the bay. Here again, at Shesualek, I felt confident that we would find a beach ridge sequence of pit houses to dig. We camped temporarily in the Eskimo tent village that was rapidly decreasing in size as the various families completed drying their meat and returned to their winter homes on the Noatak River. It was still populous enough, nevertheless, to be a mecca for the well-traveled Downeys. Neighbors gathered to hear with unflagging interest all the details of our progress and the people we had met since we had lured the Downeys away, and I became aware of Almond's strong determination to find things of enough importance to hold us in this camp, among relatives and friends, for the remainder of the summer. The five-mile-long peninsula of Shesualek proved to be composed entirely of beach ridges, but the earliest ones were truncated and short, lacking any signs of cultural material. Toward the tip of the peninsula, on the other hand, some fifteen beach ridges all contained pits that were clearly defined even through the thick sod and frequent patches of willow thicket.

The obvious pits of houses—recent ones that still displayed protruding posts—were easily found along the first two beach crests, but the earlier pits we found seemed nearly all to have been storage chambers of one kind or another. These cache pits, continuous from the present to the earliest tent village, indicated use by spring and summer campers as storehouses for the meat and skin of seals and whales, and it rather seemed that Shesualek had seldom been

the site of winter dwelling. The one exceptional area we discovered
lay at the west end of the oldest part of this beach series, where it is
cut off by the existing high sea beach. Here were the remains of
four deep house pits with the long tunnels characteristic of other
Kotzebue Sound house pits dating to A.D. 1200 or 1300.

Three of the pits, unfortunately, had been dug into by an elderly Eskimo whose English name is Frank. Frank showed us with
pride the ragged holes, like enlarged fox burrows, that he had made
over the years. The members of my party found it hard to share his
enthusiasm, particularly when we saw that the artifacts he had
most recently recovered were of an older style than we had expected, more nearly like those of Western Thule sites at Point
Hope and Thule culture sites of eastern Canada and Greenland.
Frank, who had never heard of the government's regulations for
preserving antiquities, was accustomed to working just enough
each season to secure a few souvenirs to sell the tourists at Kotzebue.
While the holes he had dug showed that he seldom penetrated beyond the walls and floors of the house pits, he had thrown out debris
in a welter of splintered timbers, hearthstones, ash, animal bones,
and other floor leavings. Only one of these pit houses had been left
with its outer edges intact. A single hole, just large enough to admit
our friend with his short-handled shovel, seemed to have done little
damage. I asked Frank if he would let us excavate this site, and in
a most agreeable manner he waved permission, pointing out that
he had as much as he could do, for some seasons, to find all the
ivory in the other pits. Besides, he explained, this one was not worth
his trouble, as the house had clearly burned down, leaving nothing
of value. Thanking him, and politely turning down his offer to dig
another hole in our house pit to help us get started, we set up our
instruments, mapped the surface, and began a methodical excavation.

Day after day as we removed the sod and then trowelled carefully as far as the receding frostline permitted, Frank and his friends
would squat at the rim of the excavation and offer suggestions in
both Eskimo and broken English. Soon, however, the playful comments turned to murmurs of respect. I began to feel that Frank,
given a different opportunity, might have become a creditable archeologist himself, for he was obviously a clever artisan and one whose
interest in his predecessors at Shesualek was as genuine as that of
a historian.

Frank had been right in one respect. Our pit was that of a dwelling that had burned, and part of its contents had been destroyed in the process. Near the walls and at the floor we came to masses of wet charcoal and red ash. Slowly this sodden matter left its mark on our clothes and faces. Perhaps fortunately, it rained a great deal while we excavated the house, and this helped to wash away the blackness from both the house floor and our bodies. Rain did not discourage our visitors, however. They were always at the edge of the pit ready to comment on each new find and each emerging view of that last day at home of the ancient residents of the house. They made jokes, too, about our appearance, their broad faces trembling with mirth as rain dripped down their parka hoods and hat brims.

I considered it lucky that Frank could gloat over his correct assumption that the house had burned, for, without this, he would have lost face immeasurably regarding its contents. In spite of the burning, or perhaps because of it, preservation of ivory, bone, and even wood artifacts was good at both the floor of the house and its tunnel. The ash and the frost retained by insulating charcoal had worked in our favor, and now as Frank saw each new object turn up he could not refrain from evaluating it in terms of what it would bring in the Kotzebue trade. An ivory fish lure in the form of a pickerel (Fig. 8), even the scales of which were indicated by minute etching, gave him particular concern. I knew his discomfiture, and while I might have fallen back upon my official permission to excavate archeological sites at Shesualek, this would hardly have made immediate sense to Frank, who had a "squatter's right." At length I came up with a way to keep good will and at the same time reduce the number of self-appointed admirers and critics at the pit edge. I hired Frank by the day for the remainder of our stay. He and one of the experienced members of my party moved to the least damaged of the neighboring pits, taking most of the spectators with them. From it they salvaged what information they could from the

8. Pickerel fish lure of antler from Shesualek, Western Thule culture, about A.D. 1100. Length, 4 in. (10 cm.).

parts of the house that were still intact and gained a collection of artifacts that could at least be ascribed to another single household. Frank soon began to show pride in his trowelling skill, and I suspect that he has by now become a staunch upholder of the Antiquities Act.

Each day at lunchtime we walked a few yards to Frank's box-like winter house on the ocean beach crest. The inner house, made of driftwood logs, was hardly larger than a small tent, but a storm shed of vertical poles through which we entered the house proper was somewhat larger. Upon approaching the house, one saw sod walls that continued up and over the roof in a breadloaf form, the sod on top nourishing this late in the season low stalks of magenta fireweed. On the roof was an assortment of whale vertebrae and ribs saved for the fashioning of tools and furniture. At the brow of the first beach overlooking the sea, Frank had a cabin-like cache raised on four corner posts well out of the reach of dogs. The dogs themselves were tied to separate stakes above high-tide line on the beach. Each animal had dug his sleeping nest in the sand among clumps of the luxuriant dark-green grass that abounds in such favored places. The frame of a kayak lay rotting by a trail to the beach and the remains of plank boats together with a skiff still used, added up to a course of cultural change—possibly progress.

As one entered the outer door of Frank's house, he was at first overwhelmed by the strong odors of half-dried fish, seal meat, and rancid seal oil. Hanging from every rafter and hook were rawhide lines, snowshoes, dog harnesses, clothing, sealskin bags, and the comfortable clutter with which Arctic coast dwellers surround themselves. The house proper, still warm from the heat of the stove, contained a commodious bunk softened with a thin mattress, down sleeping bags, and scraped caribou hides. On the table were a short-wave radio, a Bible, a stack of comic books, and, usually, some of the dishes from a hasty breakfast. Soon the small space became dense with tobacco smoke and other new odors as we opened our containers of salmon, sardines, and cheese.

One day as we talked, I asked our friends about the last locality in which I planned to spend the final weeks of the season. This was listed on my map as Cape Krusenstern. It was known to the natives as Sealing Point. Both Almond and Frank assured me that there were beaches in series at Sealing Point, yet they could not remember seeing signs of people earlier than those who had camped at the

Point during the last generation or two. As my questions about Sealing Point continued, however, Almond began to recall more about the place, for he had spent some seasons with his parents in that vicinity. Once, he and his father had dug a deep cold-cellar for storing meat at the edge of a frozen muck bank. Again, he had helped to take care of the Noatak reindeer herd during a season when it foraged near Cape Krusenstern. Then came a conjecture to which I listened with interest. The reindeer had liked to make trails a long way back from the salt water, near the edge of a large lake, and he thought their trails were along ridges like these at Shesualek. This and the fact that it was now August, when midnight became quite dark and we would have only a short time left in the field that summer persuaded me that it was time to take advantage of the next suitable weather to travel up the coast.

Rather than move the entire camp, I decided on a quick trip of reconnaissance. Almond, Bill Simmons, and I took advantage of a light load and began the trip while the water was still uncomfortably rough for a river boat. With more speed than usual, and drenched with spray, we bounded over the choppy waves just offshore from the unchanging gravel beach that leads from Shesualek's peninsula to the mainland. Soon a low, tundra-covered plateau with willows on its slope capped the beach. Occasionally silhouetted at the rim of this high ground were the decaying tepees of driftwood that mark old, pre-Christian, Eskimo graves (Fig. 9). At length we beached the boat and hauled it up at a point where high ground turns inland and a brackish stream sometimes opens to the sea. At this time of year the beach was sealed off, and, in order to get into the channel behind, we used driftwood rails and rollers to slide the boat over to the calm water. Here, protected from the wind, we threaded through a network of shallow channels for several miles until we reached a wide lagoon (Map 2). This, I could see from my topographical map, was the body of water separating Cape Krusenstern from the mountain slopes behind. Almond knew of a good camping place, and we headed for it without appreciable delay. After a somewhat windy trip across the length of the lagoon, we made camp on the lagoon shore where it is separated from the sea by only a thin strip of beach.

As the wind had now blown up much too strong for further travel by boat, we put up tents and set out to walk southward in search of possible beach ridges. Mounting the oceanfront beach on

9. Fallen tepee burial of perhaps 100 years ago on the beach nearest the sea, Cape Krusenstern.

the west side of the Cape, we saw that beach ridges did indeed stem from it, at an angle, one after the other, as though cut off by some early intrusion of the sea. We were too low to the ground to make sure, but there seemed to be many more than at Shesualek. They were not similar at all, however, to the broad, sandy crests at Cape Espenberg. More like those at Choris Peninsula, they were firm with gravel underneath and displayed no marks of wind attrition. Their crests appeared formidable to archeology, for few breaks seemed to occur in the long-established sod of the older ridges. But then I observed that trails, usually one to a crest, moved along each old beach, just as Almond had remembered. We angled off on one of these crests, watching for signs of man, and soon found flint chips in places in the trail where hooves of reindeer had destroyed the sod. It became apparent that the patches of greener grass and, perhaps, also the small mounds and depressions about us were signs of dwellers who had once camped on these now stranded beaches. Flint chips like these were not made by recent people. We had found none on the Thule beaches at Shesualek. I was tempted to walk away from the sea right then to learn how much promise this new beach crest might hold, but rather suddenly a gray blotch on the horizon that had been wavering in the distance in a sort of mirage effect peculiar to the Arctic came into focus as a tower. Almond promised us a good view from its top, and we turned toward it with anticipation. This was our first of many contacts with that venerable landmark, the United States Coast and Geodetic Survey tower.

Seen from its top, the beach ridges suggested a great garden that has for some seasons lain fallow. The gardener of the ridges, or furrows, might have been Gulliver and we, on our tower, Lilliputians, for the shortest distance from the tower to the lagoon was one and a half miles, across (we now know) more than a hundred old beach ridges. The longest continuous ridges extend eight miles or more from east to west, bending slightly northward. As we left the tower and walked through the wet swales and up onto the dry crests of beaches, sometimes as broad as highways and again as narrow as country lanes, we began to realize that any people who lived in northwestern Alaska might sooner or later have camped on the beach of their time at Cape Krusenstern. Some beaches were a foot or two higher than others, but in the main the unaltered crest of each reached six to nine feet above the mean-tide level of today. As we continued to walk away from the tower and the sea, wading across shallow ponds and examining the bare ground at the top of each beach, we collected enough chips and stone artifacts to indicate that there was indeed a range of cultures back through time. From recent, Eskimo-like Thule to the exotic Ipiutak culture of two thousand years ago, there were abundant flakes and occasional artifacts.

Farther back, our luck dwindled and the signs of people became scarcer, but then, a mile from the sea, more of the chips discarded by flintworkers again began to appear. Finally, only a few beaches from the lagoon edge, we began to find a variety of small objects: flakes of blue, gray, and black chert and red jasper, and, now and then, obsidian. Then Bill handed me a small, gray flint. "This looks like a burin," he suggested. It was! More than that, it was a special kind of burin, unmistakably a cutting and engraving tool of the old Denbigh people (Fig. 6). Nakarak and Sokpilak, my Eskimo friends from Cape Denbigh, would have recognized it and known that their dwarf people had hunted here! Small though it was, this object told us that the season had become successful beyond all expectations. Here in the rows of this giant's garden we had a progression of cultures laid out horizontally through the centuries, one succeeding another, with the unmistakable promise that we had only to search and dig on each beach to learn something of what two hundred or more generations of Arctic people had been like in this part of the world.

THE OUTER BEACH
AND THE
CHANGING
ESKIMOS

THE MEASUREMENT of time formerly meant little to Eskimos. In the minds of the oldest people at Kotzebue Sound the past, so far as their recollections and hearsay are concerned, can be limited simply by the term "a long time ago." The ethnographer must ask specific questions if he wants to learn when. "Did you yourself see this happen?" he may ask. If the answer is "No," he presses on: "Did your father or his brothers see it?" Like as not, the answer is "Maybe," which is simply, "I don't know and care little." Narratives that the questioner assumes to be historical thus often turn up with disquieting elements of the supernatural. A detailed story that I recall about an apparently flesh-and-blood local hero describes him at one point turning incredibly athletic and jumping across a wide river without wetting his feet. It is no good to argue such inconsistencies. "People used to do things they can't do now," said my informant. Consequently, we found no particular enlightenment from native sources as to how long it might take for a new beach ridge to form. Kotzebue Sound legends give assurance that remarkable things have happened some time in the past, but they afford no

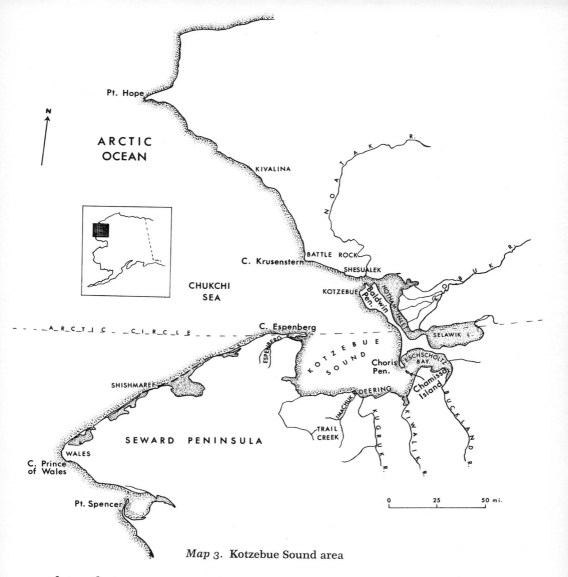

Map 3. Kotzebue Sound area

dates that we cannot arrive at more securely by walking the old beach ridges and judging for ourselves.

Returning for a second season to Cape Krusenstern on an early July morning in 1959, I was particularly concerned with the outer beach—the one now at the water's edge. Had it been there long? Was it young or already near the enigmatical time when a beach must retire from the ocean as a new ridge is formed? I had been excavating earlier in the summer near Cape Prince of Wales (Map 3) with William Simmons and Samuel Friedman, both Brown

University students. The Swiss archeologist, Hans-Georg Bandi, had just joined us at Kotzebue, where we arranged passage on the *Pauline*, a small "schooner" that carried supplies and passengers up the rivers and along the coasts. Lester Gallahorn, the Eskimo skipper, now in his seventies and wise to the vagaries of weather, had agreed to take us and our gear as far as Cape Krusenstern on his profitable, longer trip up the coast. At Cape Krusenstern we would meet the Downey family and other Eskimo assistants and spend as much time there as possible to learn what we could from the beach ridges.

We waited in Kotzebue many hours for the wind and rain to let up, and, as often happens there in summer, the propitious hour turned out to be bedtime. The clouds had broken, truly enough, but the wind had hardly ceased, and the old, unpainted boat its cargo and passengers stowed in an oily single chamber that served as hold and cabin, wallowed precariously through the swells as the seasoned skipper encouraged his equally seasoned motor with wrench and hammer, and a young assistant steered. Those of us who preferred the chill on deck to the motion and fumes below scanned the shore for the place we planned to set up camp, somewhere near the tower. We did not reach our destination, however, for the waves increased as we approached the Cape, and it seemed best to land at the closer end of the beach ridge area. Our vessel towed behind her a whaleboat laden with goods for a coastal village farther north and, behind that, an empty skin boat. When the skipper dropped anchor as near to the shore as he dared, we drew the bobbing umiak alongside the schooner and, after several precarious relays with the small boat, safely transferred our gear and food to the surf-washed shore. It was well into the morning hours when we waved a relieved farewell to the other passengers and crew of the *Pauline*. Tired, and still feeling the nausea of the three-hour voyage, we put up only our individual sleeping tents, covered the more perishable supplies against moisture, and said good night as the red sun gave promise of a clear, warm morning.

After a year of waiting, however, curiosity about the beaches was, for me, more overwhelming than need of sleep, and I could not turn in without a fond look at these ridges that I now expected to tell us far more than anyone had guessed about the ancestry of the Eskimos and the peopling of the American Arctic. I stepped from the clean gravel on which we had pitched our tents and walked to the ten-foot-high crest of the first broad, sod-covered beach ridge. We had landed where a river-like channel periodically breaks through the shore to drain the lagoon directly into the sea. Here there was essentially only one ridge—the one at the present ocean-front that continued westward two or more miles to become part of the parallel series. The distance to the tower was about nine miles (Map 2).

A few steps away on the beach crest I saw an old house and approached it. This and another nearby proved to be half-under-ground houses of an old style. Unlike the house of Frank, our digging companion at Shesualek, that was built on the surface and then banked by blocks of sod, each of these was excavated to a depth of three feet, walled within the excavation, and provided with a peaked roof complete with skylight. In place of a tunnel or a storm shed, each house had a short entrance passage sloping gradually from the ground surface to the floor. Earth had been heaped over the whole, excepting the window, transforming the house into a mound. I peered into the nearest hut and saw that it had been occupied recently, for it contained a camp stove, cooking utensils, and scraps of bedding. The other still had its stovepipe, but little usable furniture, and the skylight had been broken in.

Walking farther, I came to an entire series of houses now col-lapsed into pits, each with a true tunnel stretching from the rectan-gular house proper toward the sea. The ends of driftlogs and whale bones still extended above the grass and sod, showing that these houses had been abandoned for some decades. It occurred to me that they might be the precise "many habitations" seen by von Kotzebue on August 14, 1816, on the low tongue of land extending forward from the high ground at Cape Krusenstern. People had been "running to and fro on the shore," and two large skin boats had at-tempted in vain to catch up with them "as the wind, which blew briskly, had given the 'Rurik' wings." Von Kotzebue was speaking of winter houses rather than summer camps, when he described "habitations on this tongue of land," for they lay "under ground" and "appeared like little round hills, with fences of whalebone." I stood for a moment looking out to sea, where small whitecaps broke and the *Pauline*'s mast was just disappearing in the west, and I imagined myself an Eskimo in 1816 standing in awe at sight of my first great ship and then setting out on the run to help friends launch a skin boat, yet failing, when all was done, to board this fabulous craft of which there had previously been only vague and legendary rumors.

Fifty-eight years later, Henry Elliott, an American official, was also speaking of houses represented by some of these pits when he said of Cape Krusenstern that "its inhabitants greet your vessel as it passes out and up the coast with the usual dress parade—climbing upon the summits of their winter houses, and . . . running in light-hearted mirth along the beach."

Behind these long-abandoned houses, a hundred yards or more, I saw the remains of whalebone structures. Some appeared to have been the posts of caches on stilts, but one was a fence of whale jawbones enclosing a space somewhat smaller than a room in one of the buried houses. This I presumed to be a burial place, although the fence may once have supported a storage platform.

By now the sun had become warm and friendly, counteracting the harshness of the wind. Fully awake, I walked to the limit of the tall grass that outlined the former village site, and then beyond, to where the grass became short and sparse, giving way to sedges and the soft, close-cropped turf of long-established surfaces. Earlier in the summer, this first beach would have been lavishly colored by low, flowering plants, but now, at mid-season, blossoms were left only on patches of blue forget-me-nots, pincushions of green out of which moss pinks grew, and on solitary yellow Arctic poppies. On the moister ground of the swales behind the beach ridge, blue irises stood singly and in small clusters.

I walked slowly, scanning the ridge for further signs of human workmanship, and soon saw a white object a short distance away. This proved to be a human skull, bleached and weathered by long exposure on the surface, sphagnum moss growing in its orbits. A mandible lay nearby. I picked up the long, typically ridge-topped skullcap of a male Eskimo in one hand and the wide mandible in the other and found that the condyles fitted where they should and that the teeth came together in an edge-to-edge bite, showing that these were parts of a single skeleton. Not far away a pattern of tall green grass and the bases of driftwood posts standing a few inches above the ground showed where a tepee burial had once been made (see Fig. 9). This explained the skull, which had undoubtedly lain on the platform along with its other bones, properly caparisoned and furnished with tools, weapons, and food for a future life. We had puzzled the previous year over why, often, skulls lay on the ground away from the graves, while the remaining bones of the skeleton had vanished. We decided that in most cases colonies of ground squirrels had made their homes in these burial places, and, after many generations, the burrowings had created a kind of slow sand-trap into which bones gradually sank from sight, excepting the skulls that were too globular to fall into the burrows. Another possibility was that larger animals had frequently dragged away the skulls after the burial structure had fallen apart.

This reminded me of a rather amusing incident that had occurred at the end of the previous season. We had accumulated skulls from exposed places along the first and second beaches here at Cape Krusenstern. They could be used, even without the rest of the skeleton, as study specimens in the laboratories of the university. Almond Downey and his brother Murphy, who had been with us during the last weeks of the previous year's field trip, had expressed, at first, a slight aversion to handling skulls. Since, however, we were not interested in excavating the burials of recent Eskimos—not even those of the few standing old tepee burials—they soon, along with the rest of us, felt no compunction about collecting the old, detached specimens. Such skulls required little of the attention that goes with methodical archeological work; we simply picked them up where we found them and, on reaching camp, deposited them in a large cardboard box that stood at one end of the cook tent. Now and then someone made an uneasy joke about the growing hoard, and Almond and Murphy once indicated with wry laughs that it was just as well their mother did not visit our camp and look into the box, for she, in particular, believed dead men's bones brought bad luck.

The cardboard box of skulls was still with us on the final trip that previous season to Kotzebue from our field site. We anchored our skiff as close to shore as possible and all waded back and forth unloading the wooden crates of small artifacts and the gasoline drums of larger bone implements, stone tools, and collections of animal bones. At last we came to the skulls. Almond, wearing rubber boots, waded to the edge of the boat, picked up the box, and turned with it toward the high shelf of dry beach before the waterfront houses. As usual when a boat comes to town, people had gathered to watch, comment, and perhaps joke, but were also ready to help if the need arose. Now Almond began to feel wet, oozing cardboard where the bottom of the box had lain in the boat. Anticipating disaster, he glanced ahead just far enough to see, for the first time, that his mother stood, tall and stern as befits a parent, watching his progress. To keep his load from tumbling into the water, he had no choice but to plod on to dry ground. Having barely done so, he felt the wet paper begin to give way in his hands. Before he could set it down, the box burst open in an avalanche of bleached and staring skulls. Neither we nor the spectators uttered a word or a laugh, nor did Almond's mother change her expression as her two sons stiffly set about retrieving these unwelcome belongings and stuffing them as best they could into the remnants of their former container. As far as I know, none of us ever mentioned the subject again.

EVEN MORE COMMON than skulls on this first beach at Cape Krusenstern were circular or rectangular concavities. Most of these, I noted as I continued my walk, were old enough to have become rounded over with the same velvety sod as the rest of the beach, but some, more recent, supported tufts of tall grass. All marked former cold-storage places for meat and fish. The round ones were the remnants of deep caverns, probably square below ground when in use, in which Eskimos once stored whale, walrus, and seal meat, as they still do today (Fig. 10). Occasionally the proprietor of such a cache has invited us in to look over his wealth. A trap door lying

10. Entrance to a recently used meat cellar, first beach, Cape Krusenstern.

flat on top of the mound is removed and we climb down a short ladder into the cold locker. The air inside is at or below the freezing point, even in early summer, for the ground around the concavity is frozen throughout the year. Hanging like pelts in a furrier's establishment are slabs of gray meat and white blubber, each with a long blue fleece of mildew. Last year's whaleskin may have a stronger flavor than this year's, but it is not spoiled and will keep even for another season. The owner quickly chooses a slab of meat and we climb out before too much warm air has penetrated the artificial cave.

The shallow and narrow rectangular pits were more puzzling, for they are not commonly encountered on the coast today, but these of the first beach at Cape Krusenstern reminded me of fish caches used by riverbank Eskimos and Indians of the interior. They seem to have been more popular on the coast in early times, giving way to the deep cold cellars with the late post-Thule surge of intensive whale hunting.

Farther along the shore I saw outlines in the distance which, when I drew closer, I recognized as driftwood frames for modern canvas tents and the racks for drying meat and fish. Two families had evidently camped together here in recent seasons. Lying about on the ground were tin cans, bottles, parts of rusted traps, a broken dog sledge, snowshoe frames from which most of the babiche netting had rotted away, and the ubiquitous oil drums that were scattered along these coasts during World War II. A few heavy logs of driftwood had been pulled up beside the tent frames for use as firewood and building material. This was a camp used by hunters in spring or fall and, possibly, during the whole summer. Those who had appropriated this part of the ridge had spent more than one season here and would probably come again when hungry for seal meat or nostalgic for the sights and scents of the Cape.

THE DRIFTWOOD that some liberality of sea current now deposits along the shores of Cape Krusenstern does not all originate in neighboring streams. I learned this after some thirty years of collecting samples of living trees and driftwood logs in Alaska and Canada and measuring and cross-comparing their annual rings. But more later of tree-ring dating, or dendrochronology. Just now it suffices to say that most driftwood on these shores is expelled from the mouth of the Yukon River (Map 1) and is carried by currents of Bering Sea north toward Bering Strait where some of it enters the Chukchi Sea in the open season. The driftwood that does enter is diverted to the east by a great eddy of the sea and moved northward along the coast of Alaska as far as Point Barrow. Although coal and oil are the fuels now most widely used by Eskimos in towns and larger villages, many industrious families nonetheless still scour the beaches for driftwood, hacking their marks of ownership into the logs, and dragging them to the slope of the beach to be retrieved later by sledge or boat. In times past, the Eskimos along the Chukchi Sea coast depended almost wholly upon drifting logs for their winter houses, cooking fires, and a wide range of manufactures, from boat frames to bent-plank barrels and buckets. Less wealthy in wood than people living near the mouth of the Yukon River in the North Bering Sea, they have tended to be conservative in its use, employing whalebone and antler as building materials and, around the north coast of Alaska, depending upon sod blocks for some support of structures as well as for insulation.

East of Point Barrow one no longer finds driftwood logs from the Yukon drainage, but presumably only those from the Mackenzie River of Canada. Vast quantities of wood are disgorged from the Mackenzie each summer and liberally distributed westward along the shores of Arctic Alaska. Driftwood paths suggest that whatever wood from the two currents converging on Point Barrow is not deposited before it reaches the point enters the great circumpolar drift of Arctic sea ice north and west of Point Barrow and either reaches the shores of Siberia or travels all the way to the North Atlantic. Old maps frequently showed the arrows of drift currents moving southward through Bering Strait, but native residents have long known, and recent studies have proved, that the current, slow though it may be, persistently flows from the Pacific Ocean north to the Arctic Sea through Bering Strait. Such items as palm wood, coconuts, and especially floats from the nets of Japanese fishermen wash up on beaches from Cape Prince of Wales northward. We can imagine the puzzlement and perhaps challenge that ancient residents of this region must have felt on finding strange objects and even wrecked boats and bits of writing that may have drifted north now and then from the islands of the Pacific and the shores of China.

.   .   .

AT THIS POINT in my walk, I could see the Coast and Geodetic Survey tower at the westernmost point of Cape Krusenstern and knew, from the previous season, what I should find if I continued walking along the shore. There would be other abandoned tent camps, a dozen or so remains of surface burials under tepees on the first or second beach crest, another small, half-buried village of a century or so ago beyond the tower, then a reindeer herder's abandoned tent camp littered with gear, and, beyond it, a fenced-in Christian Eskimo cemetery containing half a dozen graves, each with its homemade cross and footboard of carved driftwood.

The sun was now quite warm and I climbed up on one of the tent frames nearby to gain a wider perspective of the beach ridges and the ocean. Many questions floated through my mind. Had this solid beach upon which structures were built for decades changed at all since Europeans first saw these shores a century and a half ago? Presumably not—unless we have been misled by historical records. The region has been known to westerners for all too short a time; but could there have been a period even within the Christian era when the affairs of these shores were completely cut off from those of neighboring Asia? I reviewed the historical evidence in my mind.

THE FIRST Europeans to reach Bering Strait were the Cossacks —if we may call them Europeans at all. Seventy years after Yermak's Russian Cossacks, escaping the Czar's troops, established themselves in western Siberia in 1557, their amazing descendants had pressed across the whole vast expanse of Asia, subjugating tribes and imposing tribute as far east as the Pacific Ocean and Bering Strait. Simeon Deshnev, one of these later Cossacks, was hardly an explorer in the European sense. A ruthless trader, his allegiance to the Czar was so tenuous as to make it all the more remarkable that he left even a short historical note. Building three small, decked boats on the Kolyma River, he set out in 1647 to travel eastward along the Arctic coast of Siberia. Failing to accomplish his mission before ice made further passage impossible, he tried again the following season with seven boats, and succeeded in taking three of them around Bering Strait. While Deshnev appears to have remained at the Strait only long enough to force upon the natives his rights to trade, he became the first to describe American Eskimos. These were most likely residents of the Diomede Islands in the center of the Strait, who wore labrets—artificial teeth thrust through their under lips—as no Siberian Eskimos have apparently ever done. Deshnev did more, though, than describe these people—he captured some of them as they were rowing by in their boats, for what purpose we are not told.

Bits of information such as this indicate that contacts between the natives of America and Asia were long a going concern, as they clearly have been in all subsequent accounts of Bering Strait. According to historical records, these native peoples of the islands and opposite sides of the Strait were no strangers to one another even though their relationships may often have been hostile or restricted more or less to formal patterns of trade. Later Cossacks also knew about Alaskans. In 1711 Sin Popow gave a detailed account of what the Chukchi had observed of the land to the east, including the testimony that in summer the Americans sailed over to Siberia in their skin boats in a single day; yet these facts were ignored in the western world until James Cook discovered, and named, Bering Strait. Earlier, in 1728, Vitus Bering had sailed north and back through the Strait, but had strangely enough failed to see either the Alaskan mainland or the islands of the Strait.

As far as the mainland is concerned, the first Europeans to see the Eskimos of Alaska north of the Aleutian chain were Captains Cook on the *Resolution* and Clerke on the *Discovery*—and of course their crews—in 1778. The natives of Cape Denbigh and Norton Bay are described by Cook as living the same kind of life that we know for their successors a century and more later. They already used iron knives, coveted tobacco, and wore glass beads. European goods had clearly preceded Europeans in all this part of the world.

In 1790, a summer gathering of Eskimos at Cape Rodney, near the present site of Nome, was described by Martin Sauer, a spokesman for the Russian Billings expedition. The Eskimo men of the group, tall, handsome, and healthy, had boldly approached the ship, hoisting an inflated bladder to signify that they wished to come aboard. They wore clean and new skin clothing, including half-boots embroidered with hair of different colors and trousers dyed yellow or red, worn with the hair turned in. Their parkas were cut with a flap behind and before, reaching to the knees and open at the sides up to the hips, as are the parkas of some Hudson Bay Eskimos today. The hair of these men was "cut almost as short as if shaven." The intensity with which they offered objects in trade— jade adz blades, weapons, and articles of clothing in exchange for beads and knives—gives the impression that they were accustomed to dealing with strangers.

Sauer put together clues as to the identity of their sources of trade and came up with the right answer, but probably the wrong reason. The ship's interpreters, one from the North Pacific island of Kodiak and the other from an island of the Aleutians, could not understand these residents of Cape Rodney. On the other hand, a Cossack crew member from the Anadyr River of the Chukchi Peninsula, whose mother was a Chukchi, made himself understood perfectly well in the Chukchi language. Sauer concluded from this that the people of Cape Rodney were not Americans but Chukchis. More probably, from Sauer's description, they were true residents of Alaska who frequently met Chukchis at the trading fairs and knew enough of the Asian language to carry on bilingual conversations. Though Eskimos, they could scarcely have understood the divergent dialects of southern Alaska any better then than do Bering Strait Eskimos today. The trading continued for two days, becoming more intensive as the natives invited the seamen ashore and displayed choice skins of marten, river otter, and varieties of fox, which the sailors avidly purchased for iron, metal buttons, and more of the prized blue glass beads. July is no time, of course, for trapping fur-bearing animals—particularly not those that live far from Cape Rodney in a forested environment. The skins had no doubt been hoarded, after their receipt from inland tribes, for trading later in the summer with Siberians at one of the traditional rendezvous.

This nearness to Asia and the ease with which people in skin boats have been able to navigate the fifty-six miles between continents, with a convenient stopping place halfway between, shed light on why the Eskimos of Kotzebue Sound and the Bering Strait region differ in appearance and in many customs from their Eskimo relatives in Canada and Greenland.

Voyagers coming after the Cook and Billings expeditions found more time on their hands for penning descriptions of the natives in their journals. Von Kotzebue, failing in his hunt for the fabulous passage through the heart of the continent to the North Atlantic, spent many hours communicating with Eskimos and recording their ways. His failure was thus anthropology's gain. Captain F. W. Beechey spent even longer in Kotzebue Sound. His ship, the *Blossom,* lay at anchor for some time in 1826 and 1827, leaving his men free to explore their surroundings from small boats. They had been sent by the British government to meet the eminent explorer John Franklin who, after his second land expedition through Canada, had prearranged to meet the ship and be returned home by sea from Kotzebue Sound. While Beechey's men did not always deal amicably with the natives, they did vividly illustrate and write of their experiences.

Some years later Franklin again became unwittingly responsible for records of the western Eskimo. Sailing from England in 1845 in command of the well-equipped ships *Erebus* and *Terror,* he intended to end the long search for a northwest passage through Arctic ice from the Atlantic Ocean to the Pacific. When the ill-fated expedition was not heard from within a reasonable time, ships of rescue were dispatched from England to all likely points where rescue or aid might be given. The *Herald* and the *Plover* thus sailed halfway around the earth to make their base in Kotzebue Sound, and we are indebted to their officers, especially Seemann, Pim, and Captain Maguire of the *Plover,* for sensitive observations of the Eskimos at a time just before the western Arctic was invaded by whaling ships and disinterested seamen from all parts of the world. Although the Russians never established themselves as far north as Seward Peninsula, one named Zagoskin faithfully described the Eskimos of the lower Kuskokwim and Yukon rivers.

Following 1848, when Captain Roys pushed his whaling ship *Superior* into the Chukchi Sea and discovered the undreamed-of resources of those waters, the Eskimos underwent an intensive change of culture surpassed only by that brought by missions and schools in the 1880's and 1890's. Then, with the purchase of Alaska from Russia in 1867, all manner of American adventurers, journalists, and scientists, curious to know what this frozen "folly" might mean to the nation, began to produce an unending, though often sketchy, record of the Eskimos.

STILL PONDERING the first beach at Cape Krusenstern, I felt sure it had been settled more persistently before the days of whaling ships than after. Those who had lived in the houses with long entrance tunnels had done so when iron and tobacco came from Siberia rather than from the whalemen of New Bedford and the traders of Honolulu. I tried now to reconstruct the life on this beach before 1850, when the western Eskimos were still little changed from times gone by. I sat in the old tent frame and leisurely pictured for myself an Ahngun and Noolaak (man and wife); drawing upon the background provided by those explorers of the early nineteenth century who had sojourned in the area, I tried to visualize this couple and their neighbors as they went about their lives throughout a year.

I T IS AUTUMN, and Ahngun, returning from a hunt, bends into a chilling wind. He, like some of his neighbors, is six feet tall and has a long, prominent nose that distinguishes him from most of those who live in the villages farther north. His hair is black, straight, and coarse, yet tonsured like that of a friar—close-cut on the top with a band two inches wide covering the forehead in front and circling about to where it becomes long and hangs down the back of the neck. His cheekbones are prominent and his chin and jaw are square and strong. A slight mustache darkens the upper lip but he habitually pulls out the few hairs that grow from his chin. Now Ahngun raises his parka hood as protection against the wind until its wolfskin ruff frames his face. The parka, reaching mid-thigh, is fringed with coarse fur; at its back, as though the man were half beast, hangs the tail of a fox.

Beneath the parka Ahngun wears trousers of dog skin, and these fit into boots of caribou leg fur, soled, at this season, with the heavy, waterproof hide of a big seal. Over his right shoulder protrude the feathered ends of arrows and a quiver of de-haired, oiled, caribou skin. The bow in his left hand has a double bend. He has achieved this shape by wrapping the bow a few inches from either end in wet wood shavings, holding it over a fire until the wood is steamed, and then staking it down to the earth in the form of a cupid's bow. Made of spruce driftwood, it is backed with a cable of heavy strands of braided sinew that may be adjusted to the moistness of the weather by twisting near the center with a small ivory tool he carries at his belt. Still attached to his wrist is the *munera,* a hollowed-out buckle of ivory worn to absorb the lash of the bowstring. In his quiver Ahngun carries an assortment of arrows, some equipped with multi-barbed points of antler for shooting waterfowl or caribou and others with blunt or lobate tips for stunning, rather than piercing, birds, rabbits, and other small game. In his right hand he carries by the neck a snow goose that he has been fortunate enough to strike with a sharp arrow as it flew up from one of the rapidly icing ponds.

As he nears his tent, he sees Noolaak bent forward over some thin-sided wooden containers. She has collected *mashu* (polygonum roots) to be roasted in the ashes, and a quantity of berries: blueberries, crowberries, lingenberries, and a few of the last yellow cloudberries of the season. When the larger boxes are full, the berries will be allowed to freeze and will be stored in the ice cellar where they will remain until the time comes to chop them out with an adz for mixing, still half frozen, with frothy fat, as a winter treat.

The tent is conical and broad at the base. Unlike a tepee, however, it has no smoke hole, for the skins that cover it are sewn tight against the wind. It has a built-in floor of wood. In it one may light a lamp for illumination at this season of the year, providing warmth as well, though ordinarily the tent is unheated. Ahngun's family has already moved to the winter house, and the tent is no more than a storage place that will soon be taken down for the season.

Noolaak, resting from her exertion, stands, throws back her hood, and reaches for the goose. Her parka is long, in an apron-like extension before and behind, and the hood is large enough to admit the head and shoulders of an infant that she carries, straddling her back and upheld by a belt, inside her coat. Her long hair, parted down the middle, is collected at the sides into two long braids ornamented with strings of beads. The couple walk together a few yards to the winter house. This appears as a mound of earth in the top of which is a square frame covered by a transparent section of whale intestine drawn taut to form a translucent window. Standing near the mound is a tall platform upon which are stored the kayak, lashed upside down for protection against wind and dogs, a harness for the dogs, and other belongings of animal skin that might be chewed apart by beasts. A smaller structure, a little house on tall poles, can be reached only by a notched log ladder. Here are stored the skins, furs, and garments not presently in use.

The doorway to their home, like a ship's hatch, is covered by a tightly fitting curtain of deerskin. Ahngun pulls this aside and steps down a ladder to the floor below ground level where, still standing upright, he removes his quiver and holds it in one hand with his bow. Then he bends forward and crawls through a dark tunnel toward a dim glow and the sound of children playing. At the end of the tunnel he stands again and pushes aside a second deerskin curtain, then crouches to step through a round doorway into the plank-lined room. Noolaak follows, securing the curtains as she goes. Anuga (grandmother) is sewing by the combination of waning daylight and light from her lamp. She sits on fur bedding at the edge of a low bench to one side of the room. Across from her, a similar sleeping place is marked off by a log and filled with young willows over which rolled-up bedding may be spread out. Between the two sleeping places is a fireplace at center, now covered with boards to furnish a table and to prevent the ash and charcoal from being displaced. The remainder of the house is evenly floored with planks and split logs. These are split once or several times by driving series of antler wedges into them and then planing the faces with adzes.

The interior of the dwelling is clean and tidy. The newcomers remove their outer clothing and then, wearing only skin trunks and the short, soft boots that are customary indoor attire winter and summer, sit about in the warmth of the lamp. A ladder-like frame hangs from the rafters over the lamp. This is a drying rack that will be necessary, when snow comes, for removing moisture from mittens and boots. The lamp itself is a shallow oval of stone about eighteen inches long. A thick wick of sphagnum moss rests against an edge, allowing the flame to be increased by simply spreading hot oil, with a stick, from the wick around the rim of the lamp. No fire will be built in the hearth this day because Anuga has only to hang the clay pot of meat and soup for a while over the flame of her lamp to provide the family with an evening meal.

While it is still daylight, Ahngun, donning a parka minus the ruff and with the hair turned inside, pulls on a second thin, transparent rain parka, sewn from strips of seal intestine, and sets out in his kayak to hunt near the shore. Pulling swiftly with his double paddle alternately on one side and the other, he moves through the spray toward a flock of eider ducks. Then, securing his double paddle behind ivory guards lashed to the deck of his kayak, he slips his single-bladed paddle from beneath a rawhide strip bound to the deck and stealthily glides closer to the flock. His bird spear lies on the deck ahead. When the birds take alarm and begin to fly, he slides the paddle blade under a lashing, reaches into the cockpit for a foot-long, grooved throwing stick, fits the concave end of the bird spear into a pin at the tip of the throwing stick, and, just as they pass him close to the water, heaves the spear with the full force of his arm plus the added length of the stick. The spear has a light shaft, but its tip is a heavy, sharpened piece of antler with barbs along the edges, and halfway down the shaft are three prongs that project forward ready to grasp a duck's foot, leg, neck, or wing with their inward-formed barbs. The flock is dense, and he aims for the group rather than for an individual. The tip strikes one bird, and simultaneously the wing of another is caught between a side barb and the shaft. Swiftly paddling to the scene, Ahngun retrieves both birds, strikes their heads against the deck, and slips them toward his feet inside the kayak. Then he places his spear on deck in position for another shot. Later, if he sees a seal, he follows nearly the same tactics as before, paddling quietly toward the point where he expects the beast to surface again, but using a heavy sealing dart with a detachable head.

At dusk he returns to shore, drags his craft onto the beach, and removes from it the birds and the seal that will provide his family with nourishment and lamp fuel for a day or so.

The winter season comes round. Ahngun and his wife wear double layers of clothing—undergarments of fawn skin, with the hair turned in, outer ones of heavy caribou skin, with the fur out, trousers of dog skin, and stockings of heavy fur inside fur boots. A hunter so dressed may stand hours at a time in a frigid wind, patiently waiting for game. Ahngun now hunts seals in open water that forms near the middle of Kotzebue Sound. Harnessing his five heavily haired, sharp-eared dogs to a sledge provided with stern posts and runners extending far enough back to provide standing space for the driver, he transports his kayak, before daylight, out across the smooth ice of the Sound to the steaming edge of the open water. Here he and other hunters paddle through the broken ice waiting for seals, which they spear with heavy, toggle-headed harpoons and play, like fish, at the ends of rawhide lines. If the seal is a heavy one, the harpoon line is allowed to drag an inflated seal bladder from the stern deck of the kayak. This serves as a float and deterrent until Ahngun can mount solid ice, dig in the ice pick at the butt of his harpoon, and by leverage tire out the animal until it can be dragged to the ice edge and slaughtered. When he returns successful from a hunt, Ahngun finds his dogs straining with excitement at their harness. They have been in their places all this time, the sledge and the center trace anchored by lines tied to small bridges made by picking holes through the ice.

While Ahngun is thus occupied, Noolaak has walked back to the slope of the nearest hill where she rebuilds her ptarmigan fences, removes the snared birds, and looks to her rabbit snares set among the denser alders and willows.

In midwinter the couple provide Anuga with sufficient food and leave her in charge of the children while they spend a few days in the nearest village. Here, while Noolaak moves into her sister's house, Ahngun takes his place in the *kazigi,* or ceremonial house, to which all men belong. This is a large room, square, with a long, deep entrance tunnel, the inner end of which opens upward in a circular hole through the floor. In place of the wide sleeping benches of dwelling houses, where people lie with their heads to the fire and feet to the wall, one may here make his bed anywhere at all on the planked floor or on the narrow bench that lines all the walls of the room. The *kazigi* is essentially a men's workshop and dormitory, and is the scene of secular entertainment and religious ceremony for the village. During the day, while the women in the ordinary household dwellings prepare food, sew tents, bedding, and clothing, and mind the children, the men sit about in the *kazigi* with their wolverine-hide tool bags open, whittling sledge runners, repairing snowshoes, making buckets and boxes, and discussing the adventures of the past fall and the prospects of hunting in the coming spring.

At night the men roll out their skin robes and sleep. Upon waking in the morning, they smoke their long-stemmed, stone-bowled pipes, drink a quantity of water, and go to work again. Lunching on a light meal of dried fish, they wait until later for the big meal of the day. The women at home, meanwhile, build up fires and boil meat in the late afternoon. At mealtime, they issue forth from their separate tunnels and converge upon the *kazigi.* Once there, they either lift the smoke-hole cover and pass down dishes of food or crawl in through the tunnel to sit in the shadows while the men dine together in the light of a central lamp. If several men customarily eat together, their women prepare a communal dish.

Today Ahngun and his friends kneel before a six-foot-long, narrow wooden dish along the center of which is heaped the steaming meat brought together from the cooking pots of several households. It is served in its own dense broth, and the men waste no time in attacking their meal.

Ahngun, leaning forward, picks out a large piece of meat with his fingers, grasps an edge of it in his teeth, and with a flash of his sharp, iron-bladed knife cuts it loose just beyond the tip of his nose. They all eat with great speed, half chewing the meat before swallowing it, and uttering no word until the dish is empty or their stomachs full. Now, leaning back with a loud belch of appreciation, Ahngun talks with his neighbor. A second course, a dish of broth, is passed, and each man drinks what he wants before passing the bowl along and joking with his fellow diner. When the men are satisfied and in good spirits, the women remove the dishes and silently leave the *kazigi*, returning to the houses where they and their children ladle deep into the clay cooking pots for whatever soup and morsels remain. While the men frequently visit their wives and families during the time of their residence in *kazigi*, they may not do so upon those ceremonial occasions when the animals that are propitiated before hunting would resent the association of the hunters with women. While in the *kazigi*, the men prepare ceremonial buckets, dance masks, and figurines for their boat crew that will go out in late spring to intercept any big whales that may pass Cape Krusenstern.

The *kazigi* is also frequently the scene of dancing and sorcery. The preparation for almost any undertaking requires certain ceremonies and magical performances. The failure of game to appear at the proper season must also be alleviated by shamanistic séances in which the magicians call upon deities beyond the horizon and under the sea to aid them in enticing game animals back to the realm.

Walruses and seals, for example, are controlled by a hideous hag who lives in the deep water between Choris Peninsula and Chamisso Island. The shaman, who is the chief performer at a drum dance, must visit her and arbitrate in person if the luck is to be improved. For this, men, women, and children gather in the *kazigi* and sit upon the floor until space remains only near the doorway where the shaman will begin his ordeal. Near center, drummers sit stiff-backed in a row, their legs straight ahead, each holding in his left hand, by its wooden or ivory handle, a tambourine-like which simple music is evoked from a taut membrane across the drum. In the right hand each drummer grasps a thin wand with drum. The faces of the drummers, without expression, glisten in the lamplight. At first the wand lightly strikes only the rim of the open side of the drum, but as the music follows its patterned course, there comes a time when heavy blows bend the wand to a point where it touches and resounds sonorously against the center of the membrane. Tones are thus varied, and the beat, unfamiliar to Western ears, becomes to the accustomed listeners now intense, now ominous, now light and humorous, setting the stage by its intricacy for the enticement of spirits.

Soon a man rises to his feet, puts on a special coat of white skin and a pair of white mittens, places over his head a band of loon skin, with the beak forward, and wedges a wing feather over each ear. He begins to stamp violently with his right foot in time to the drumming, then throws out his arms in wild gesticulations as he expresses with unaccustomed workings of his facial muscles the elements of the pageantry of which he is a part. Through stylized motions, the listeners see in him a man who is also a loon and who may become, by his gestures, a seal, a bear, or an ogre. He typifies a legend, becoming first the hero and then the adversary.

Four men next stand, chanting, stamping, and gesticulating in unison. An old woman rises to join them, but her dance differs from theirs: her feet remain close together. She does not stamp or rage, but follows the drumbeat with sinuous motions of her upper body while gracefully pushing against air with her gloved hands. The men sometimes shout, throwing their voices as a yodeller does to add an effect of violence or intensity. Now the shaman rises and, to the music of the drums, improvises, stating in a musical form what it is he is called upon to do—through what obstacles he must force his body to meet with the awesome creatures of another world. Time is unimportant. Hour after hour the preparations go on—drumming and dancing—until the group begins to identify with the shaman and to see in him a creature different from the very ordinary neighbor that he is most of the week. They sway in unison with his swaying; they chant to the beat, men, women, and children, whether or not they know the words of the songs. The shaman begins to perspire. His face is dark red in the lamplight.

Now comes the moment of dramatic intensity when the shaman, ecstatic and buoyant with the support of the group, asks to be tied hand and foot. As the rawhide lines are drawn tight and knotted and he lies helpless on the floor, ostensibly so weak as scarcely to be able to make himself heard above the low beat of the drums, he demands that the lamp be removed. Soon after the light is gone, people hear the shaman stirring, clearly freeing himself from the lashing, rising above his earthly body, and flying about the inside of the room. The listeners feel the wind from his body sweep through the *kazigi*, and then the cold air as the skylight lifts. They hear the scream of the shaman as he leaves the building and his diminishing cries as he soars away to enter a particular spirit world.

Now they wait, tense and frightened, while the shaman is somewhere bargaining for their souls and their well-being. The drums continue their soft, precise rhythm. People begin to hear a noise in the distance—a screaming that becomes louder—louder and nearer—until, with a roar, a body enters the room and the skylight slams shut. They hear the spent voice of their shaman begging for the light to be brought, and when it is, they see him, still tied as before but his face distorted and his body steaming with sweat. Helpers free him and he begins to tell, in a voice still shaking with emotion, of the battle he has given to fly through the air and then down through the water to a place where he has met the walrus-headed dogs who guard the cave in which lives the Old Woman of the Sea and how he has threatened, begged, and promised until she has acquiesced and he has become free to return home. She will release the seals at once and the hunting will soon improve.

Ahngun and Noolaak sit through the séance with apprehension and awe; yet they leave it with a rare feeling of exhilaration and well-being. Later, back in their own house, away from the village, they talk about it often and remark how fortunate they are in having a shaman who can be depended upon to know the songs and cast the spells that will enable the group to make contact with the spirits and grow rich in food and health while others perish.

In late spring, when the sun comes back and the ice begins to break in the Sound, Ahngun at first hunts seal alone in his kayak but soon goes to join his whaling crew at the Cape. Here the men spiritually isolate themselves and camp at the edge of the water beside their readied boat. Farther along they see whaling crews from other camps and villages, and they wait, fasting, until a momentous spout is seen far down the channel and the black hulk of a whale stirs the sheen of the water. As the whale approaches, all hastily slide their boats into the water. Ahngun paddles in unison with his fellows until, with good fortune, the skin boat and its crew of eight slide onto the back of an emerging whale just long enough for the harpooner in the bow to thrust his heavy weapon down into the beast's head. Backing away and releasing floats as the rawhide line falls from the gunwales with a hiss and the whale attempts to escape by sounding to the bottom, they just miss being tipped over by the line itself and now find their work half done. It remains only to follow the beast and to strike again as often as he surfaces, weakening him in vital places until he drowns for fear of surfacing or dies of wounds. He is then towed to the edge of the ice for the ceremonial drink of fresh water that will ensure the return of the whale in future years.

In summer, Ahngun and his family set up a tent camp at a place propitious for the white whale hunt. Working with partners who have their own kayaks, Ahngun helps to drive these small whales into shallow water where they cannot sound and joins in stabbing them with fixed harpoons. Big seals are killed at the edge of the ice, and an occasional herd of walrus is attacked by a group of men in a skin boat.

With summer, too, comes traveling and trading. Late in the season, all families who have good boats sail down to Kotzebue to meet the people who come from the neighboring coasts, the interior, and even Siberia. Here Ahngun guards his hoard of dry meat and seal skins until he can convert them into the few exotic things he needs: from the interior, birch-bark containers and wolverine hides for trimming winter parkas, and from Asia, iron, tobacco, beads, and a small brass bell. After the trading is over, the families move into the hills for communal hunts of caribou, or hunters go singly in hopes of securing a few more skins with which to make the many items that give protection from the elements throughout the year.

At length the season grows cool and Ahngun, smoking his long pipe one early morning, turns to his wife and says that the time has come to clean out the winter house and move back indoors again where they will be warm and content when the ice returns.

STILL PERCHED on my tent frame and pondering for a while the full life of these old dwellers in Kotzebue Sound, I recalled that they, like Eskimos everywhere, gave explorers the impression that they were content with their surroundings and its resources and, furthermore, could conceive of no life elsewhere in the world for which they would willingly give up the advantages they knew. Travelers often spoke of the "miserable" Indians of the interior who, like as not, "eked out" an existence, but they admired and tended to emulate the Eskimos.

What is this continuity called Eskimo? One may follow its geographical distribution for six thousand miles or more around devious coasts. It reaches from the Pacific Ocean around the Bering Sea, past Bering Strait, and across the whole northern coast of Alaska and Canada down to Labrador and across to Greenland (see Map 4). "Eskimo" is first of all a language. Excepting only the Aleuts of the southwestern peninsula of Alaska and the islands beyond, the speakers of one dialect easily master that of another. While the Aleut language is also Eskimo, it appears to have been cut off from the mainstream of Eskimo speech long enough to have become differentiated, as, for instance, one Germanic language differs from another. Around the truly Arctic shores of the realm of Eskimo speech from Bering Strait to Greenland, people all understand each other with but little difficulty. Their pronunciations may differ, but their words and constructions are the same.

With respect to physiognomy and body-build, Eskimo means less. Throughout the whole range, we find a physical type that is not easily identified with other races of Americans or Asians. Men of this cast are long-trunked and short-legged, have small hands and feet and a long head keeled over the top like an upturned whaleboat, and possess minor traits in common that appear to be genetically passed along from one generation to the next. But in some areas this Eskimo physique becomes rare, as though submerged by an ancient or bordering physical type. Men of Kotzebue Sound, for instance, tend to have a short trunk, long legs, a prominent and even hooked nose, and a medium to short, rather than extremely long, head. Siberian Eskimos along the eastern shore of the Chukchi Peninsula and on St. Lawrence Island blend with their Chukchi-speaking neighbors and may, in most cases, be distinguished physically from Eskimos of mainland Alaska.

With respect to ways of life, there are too many local stamps of culture to allow the isolation of many tools or manners that are universally Eskimo, and Eskimo alone. Perhaps I first realized this the day before Christmas 1934, in Kotzebue. A group of schoolchildren had blocked my way on the path, urging me to go that night to the school building and see their Christmas pageant. Their parents would be there and I must come too. I would be especially pleased, they said, because their play was going to be about *real* Eskimos. It had not occurred to me until then that the people of Kotzebue did not call themselves by the English word "Eskimo" but by their word "Inuit," or men. They had learned about "Eskimos" from the schoolbooks. I attended the play and joined with the hundred or more parents and villagers who followed every movement of the actors with murmurs and sighs of keen appreciation. Then I saw why the children, working a Christian theme into an Arctic setting, felt that they were playing out as exotic a part as do children elsewhere who play the parts of wise men on camels. The setting was one of snow houses, which these children had never seen, ladder-like sledges with paper dogs harnessed in fan shape, and "Eskimos" wearing strange garments with peaks and tails.

The differences between groups of Eskimos are indeed manifest to those who search for them. These Kotzebue Sound people, I recalled, shared their cycle of raven myth, their masked dances, and perhaps the squareness of their wooden underground houses and central fireplaces with Indians of the northwest Pacific coast. They employed fish seines and trapping methods like those of their neighbors along the wooded rivers. They made composite pipes with bowls like those from ancient China, and they smoked Asian tobacco, holding their breath with the smoke in their lungs. They built conical tepees like those of the central Siberian tribes and the Indians of more temperate North America. Yet, on the whole, the continuities between them and the Eskimo speakers to both north and south were prominent and numerous, tending to outweigh the differences.

Who, then, are the Eskimos and where did they come from in the first place? Once I posed this question to a rheumy-eyed old man who removed his pipe from his mouth and said:

> A long time ago, they tell us, there was nothing here but water—no land at all. Raven, he fell to worrying about this and then he saw some stumps of bunchgrass floating by and he got

in his kayak and chased them. He paddled close to one and he hit it with his spear and he put the line around it and pulled it back to shore where he packed it down tight. Then he got in his kayak and went hunting again and he kept spearing grass roots and packing them down next to the first one and then there was land —and then there was land all around. And when he had made enough land, Raven called the people together and said: "Now you have land to live on." And that was how we came to be here in the first place.

When I attempted cautiously to learn where Raven had stood when he first stepped into his kayak, and how he could paddle to shore before land existed, and where the people were when he called them and said land was ready, the old man simply returned his pipe to his mouth and said between his teeth: "We don't know about that. We only know what they tell us."

I STEPPED DOWN from the tent frame now and, feeling both hungry and sleepy, turned back toward camp. To my left lay the crests of many beach ridges, brown-green in the dry sunshine. The answer does not lie in this first beach ridge, I thought, nor in the historical records, nor in the memories of the oldest Eskimos; but perhaps if we ask the same question with shovels and notebooks of one ridge after another, through the whole series here at the Cape, we shall come nearer to answering the question of Eskimo origins than anyone has done before.

(IV)

THULE: ARCTIC
ARCHEOLOGY
BEGINS

T
HE OUTER BEACH at Cape Krusenstern does not everywhere
mark an even progression. A mile or so east of the tower it bends
perceptibly inward where, at some time in the not too distant past,
a persistent eddy from the sea seems to have cut back into the older
beach ridges, removing the parts of some before the outer beach
could mend itself with a crest high enough to resist the water
(Map 2). In this area one day during our first season at the Cape,
1958, as our crew walked along a substantial crest that had once
lain well inland, we found ourselves close to the coarse, blue grass
that marks the outer beach and also in the midst of a small village
of house and cache pits. I recognized the pits as too large and deep
to be recent. One or two seemed to have more than one room, joined
by tunnels. Houses of this type had not previously turned up in sites
later than the thirteenth century A.D. or in phases later than Western Thule, with whose culture we tentatively identified them.

Turning over a square of sod in the basin of one of the large
pits, we soon found in the black, bone-filled earth an arrowhead of
antler with the unmistakable shaft stem of a Thule type (Fig. 11).
At first puzzled by the occurrence of these older houses so close to
the sea, we then realized that this locality once lay several beach

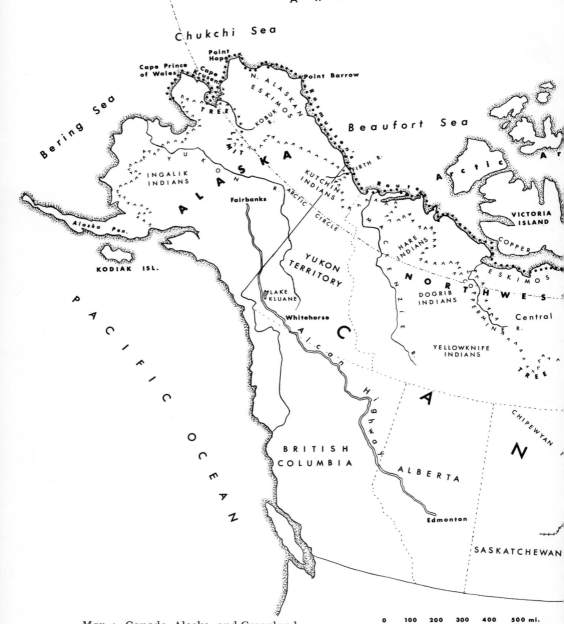

ARCTIC OCEAN

Chukchi Sea

Point Hope

Cape Prince of Wales
Cape Krusenstern

Point Barrow

Bering Sea

N. ALASKAN ESKIMOS

Rasmussen's

Beaufort Sea

TREE

KOBUK R.

MIT

ALASKA

YUKON

FIRTH R.

Arctic

INGALIK INDIANS

KUTCHIN INDIANS

Route

VICTORIA ISLAND

Fairbanks

ARCTIC CIRCLE

MACKENZIE R.

HARE INDIANS

COPPER

Alaska Pen.

ESKIMOS

KODIAK ISL.

YUKON TERRITORY

NORTHWES

Central

PACIFIC OCEAN

LAKE KLUANE

DOGRIB INDIANS

Whitehorse

COPPERMINE R.

Alcan

C

YELLOWKNIFE INDIANS

TREE

CHIPEWYAN

Highway

N

BRITISH COLUMBIA

ALBERTA

A

Edmonton

SASKATCHEWAN

0   100   200   300   400   500 mi.

Map 4. Canada, Alaska, and Greenland

GREENLAND

POLAR ESKIMOS

Thule

:h i p e l a g o

BAFFIN ISLAND

ARCTIC CIRCLE

Godthaab

IGLULIK ESKIMOS

MELVILLE PEN.

ETSILIK ESKIMOS

T E R R I T O R I E S

Naujan

DANISH ISL.

FROZEN STR.

DARKNESS LAKE

Region

CARIBOU ESKIMOS

MAGUSE R.

Padlei

SOUTHAMPTON ISLAND

NEW FOUNDLAND

IMIT

Eskimo Point

HUDSON BAY

TREE LIMIT

NASKAPI INDIANS

LABRADOR

Thyazzi

N. KNIFE R.

Churchill

MONTAGNAIS INDIANS

ANS

A

D

A

he as

M A N I T O B A

ONTARIO

QUEBEC

11. Antler arrowhead, Thule culture. Length, 9 in. (22.2 cm.). (*From Mathiassen, Vol. I, 1927*)

ridges farther inland before the capriciousness of the sea cut away the front beaches it had so carefully built.

That night in camp, while trying to decide whether to dig this new site then or later, I sketched for the students of our group the history of Thule culture. "Thule" meant to the ancients the farthest north habitable region. Later, it came to mean the specific part of Greenland where the world's most northerly people still lived and, to two young Danes, Knud Rasmussen and Peter Freuchen, the spot where they established their trading post among the Polar Eskimos. Anthropologists now perhaps acknowledge all three meanings when they see in Thule a whole culture or way of life. This differs from others particularly in the daring way its people hunted whales and moved freely over ice floes and polar lands—lands that long ago became the base across the whole American Arctic coast for the Eskimos as we know them today.

KNUD RASMUSSEN and Peter Freuchen met in Denmark in 1909 only after each had already explored in Greenland. Pooling their resources, they went on a prolonged lecture tour and so stirred themselves with recollections of Greenland that they decided to form an expedition of their own. Rasmussen was a dark-haired man of medium height, born in Greenland to a mother who was part Eskimo and to a father who had been a missionary in the Arctic for a quarter of a century. Young Rasmussen's intimate knowledge of the Eskimo language and of Eskimo ways were to stand him in good stead all his life. Even though his features were sharp and aquiline, Eskimos in Canada and Alaska as well as in Greenland sometimes refused to believe that he was not one of themselves. His fertile mind and mastery of the two languages gave him the rare ability among ethnographers to rise above the role of mere translator and say in eloquent Danish precisely what it was his Eskimo informant had intended to express, whether in poetry or prose. It was he who was the organizer—the orderly member of the team—who planned far ahead and pressed toward his goal even while appearing outwardly to have no care in the world.

In contrast, Peter Freuchen, a blond giant who appeared at first a stolid type, possessed a free imagination and a spontaneous nature that often led him into unnecessary adventures. With his open heart and keen sense of the ludicrous, it is no wonder that he became famous as a raconteur and, toward the end of his life, caught the fancy of television viewers.

While the partners were still unloading their supplies and building houses at Thule, Rasmussen began planning scientific excursions. Thule was to be more than a trading post: it was to serve as the base for various explorations (Fig. 12). Out of this determination grew the five "Thule Expeditions." The first four, financed variously from Denmark, brought forth Greenlandic studies of the ice cap, of the physiography of the north coast, and of the mythology of a remote people on the east coast. Then came the ambitious Fifth Thule Expedition to North Canada. Its members remained in the field between 1921 and 1924. Planned on the basis of his and Freuchen's experiences, Rasmussen counted on it to solve the problem of Eskimo origins. A group photograph taken in Godthaab, the capital of Greenland, at the beginning of the expedition in 1921 shows the seated leaders fit and youthful after fifteen years of rigorous Arctic travel and exploration (Fig. 13). Rasmussen was forty-two, and Freuchen, wearing a heavy beard

12. Headquarters building for early Danish explorations in Greenland. Thule Mountain is in background.

13. Members of the Fifth Thule Expedition, 1921. Seated, left to right: Peter M. Pederson (ship's captain), Knud Rasmussen, Peter Freuchen, Jacob Olsen (interpreter). Standing, left to right: Kaj Birket-Smith, Therkel Mathiassen, Helge Bangsted (secretary).

and looking stern, was thirty-five. Standing behind them in the photo and wearing hooded anoraks specially fitted with pockets for notebooks were the two young university-trained scientists of the expedition: Kaj Birket-Smith, twenty-eight, and Therkel Mathiassen, twenty-nine. Fully aware of the volume of work expected of them in the next few years, these two anthropologists had studied at the University of Copenhagen, where they had been steeped in Eskimo lore and had learned to understand some of the language.

Looking back, we see that these and the other expedition members more than fulfilled their promise. The bound volumes of natural history and, principally, archeology and ethnology resulting from this Fifth Thule Expedition fill a foot and a half of a bookshelf; and yet they are not excessive. The styles of writing vary. That of Mathiassen, the archeologist, is impersonal and evenly descriptive, giving the reader all the statistics he needs along with vivid word pictures of places and objects. Birket-Smith, the ethnographer, describes living people and the things they use, as might a candid photographer who records many views of his subject while himself remaining out of sight. Rasmussen is warm and personal in his portrayals of everyone he meets; yet he spares no detail. Only Freuchen has contributed little to these scientific works—nevertheless, in his private writings he paints both himself and others in lively colors with a broad, romantic brush. His is a continuous Arctic adventure, and he tells us of his fears, his loves, and his hardships as though he were a character in some picaresque tale. In all the accounts, however, whether statistical or narrative, we sense that the members of the expedition had placed themselves exactly where they wanted and were doing the work they most enjoyed, remaining all the while deeply sympathetic toward the people whose past and present they were there to record.

Headquarters for the expedition was made on an islet that they called "Danish Island," north of the large Southampton Island in Hudson Bay (Map 4). From here they were usually free to move in all directions. The most remarkable journey of the many made by expedition members was undoubtedly the final excursion by Knud Rasmussen with two Polar Eskimos—a man and a woman— from Danish Island all the way across Canada and Arctic Alaska to Bering Strait. For Eskimo theory and history, however, we are even more concerned with the work of the two young scientists.

Birket-Smith moved westward to study the inland tribes— those of the Caribou Eskimos west of Hudson Bay and north of the forest out across the barren grounds of Canada. These single-minded people, he learned, depended for food on migrating herds of caribou and held a fatalistic view of nature and the spirit world. Their independence of both the sea and the forests and their simple ways obliged him to interpret all Eskimos in a new guise.

Mathiassen's task was, in some ways, the most difficult of all. Often working alone during two short summer seasons when the ground was thawed enough for him to dig, he managed to excavate old house ruins both north and south of Danish Island—from Southampton Island northward to Melville Peninsula and back around the west coast of Hudson Bay.

The "Central Regions," which Rasmussen had chosen as a center of operations, are central because they fall halfway between the better-known parts of the Eskimo habitat in Greenland and Labrador on the one side and Alaska and the Mackenzie River region of Canada on the other. It was toward this treeless region of islands, inlets, lakes, and rocky barrens—all inhabited by Eskimos —that questions of origin had long been directed. The earlier theorists, from the time of the Danish missionary Cranz in 1770 until the last part of the nineteenth century, had largely agreed on a single explanation: that the Eskimos were originally north Asian tribes, who, pushed ever farther into northeastern Asia by more advanced or hostile tribes, took the easy way out and migrated into Alaska and ultimately to Greenland. The peopling of the American Arctic thus required no particular strain on the imagination and no essential change in the migrants themselves. The question of origin was relegated to another part of the world and had little further interest for historians.

With the acceptance of Darwinian evolution, however, anthropologists began to apply the principles of progressive change to their own fields, and it was perhaps inevitable that Eskimo culture should be seen by some as a current stage in the progress from simple beginnings to complicated devices and ideas. Henry Rink, in 1871, arranged what he took to be the key elements of Eskimo culture in an order of complexity. When his analysis was done, it seemed to Rink that the primitive beginnings would have occurred in the interior of Alaska. Simple tribesmen, slowly perfecting their devices and inventing new ones, would have learned to support themselves beyond the timber and on the sea ice, becoming the first Eskimos. Once free of the protective trees, Eskimo culture would have spread in several directions, improving as it went. All might have gone well with Rink's hypothesis had it not been for a tenet of evolution. In the biological view of what happens to animals and plants through time, the geographical lines of progress must be kept clear even though primitive forms may persist, especially at the outer edges. Observers now began to point to the Central region, west of Hudson Bay, and to suggest that the Eskimos here were less progressive—less advanced—than those of either Alaska or Greenland. Franz Boas's work on Baffin Island in 1883 and 1884 proved these suggestions to be true.

Boas, trained in Germany as a physicist and geographer, was destined to lead American anthropology proudly into the twentieth century. From his educational background and instincts, he set a pattern for ethnographic thoroughness in his study of the tribes of the Central region. Soon any theorist, safe in his university study with Boas's reports in his hands, could examine for himself the ways of the Central Eskimos. He could see that they, unlike their neighbors on either side, lacked deep and permanent winter houses, for they lived a migratory life, whisking about in winter with dogs and sledges and erecting, for the moment, snow houses wherever on ice or land they chose to hunt; in summer they switched to tents and boats. Not only did these Central Eskimos qualify as prototypes by refusing to settle in fixed villages; they also, as Boas's study of folklore showed, occupied an Arctic Eden. The Eskimos living on either side of them, knowing nothing of each other, each pointed to the Central region as their traditional place of origin.

Later, Boas spearheaded studies of Asia and America that seemed to show a closer early relationship between the old Siberians of northeast Asia and the Indians of the Pacific shores of America than between either of these and the Eskimos. By the beginning of the present century, the new information and the massive attack led by Boas made it increasingly difficult for students to see the Eskimos as having spread out of Asia like icing over a cake, progressively coating the north of America. The Eskimo people and their culture seemed more and more to have originated in America, having somehow issued from ancient Indians. No longer orphans of the Old World, the Eskimos had become, in theory, an expanding wedge only recently pushing out from a place of origin in the Central Regions toward Bering Strait, where they were now still in the process of cutting off the Indian cultures from their Asian parentage.

The larger fragments of the circumpolar picture-puzzle once again seemed to fall into place; yet it remained for another Danish investigator to test the new assumptions and formulate the evolution of Eskimo culture. H. P. Steensby blew dust from many an old source and focused on each distinct part of the Eskimo area. Dividing his realm geographically, he first listed the separate resources of each. He then added animals, plants, rocks, and ice, and heaped the Eskimos and their customs on top, with special emphasis on their means of exploiting raw materials. The result was his *Anthropologeographical Study of the Origin of the Eskimo Culture*, published in 1917, where group after group could be compared: those of Baffin Island, Labrador, the Thule district, south and east Greenland, the Arctic archipelago, the Mackenzie River, Asia, and elsewhere as far away as Kodiak Island and the Aleutians of the North Pacific Ocean.

By listing for each area the things made, done, or thought by its people and then comparing these elemental life-ways, or "types," Steensby found, first, that the regions overlap in ease and actuality of communication. That is, most of the types extend from one region into those touching it, changing only slightly. From this he concluded that the whole Eskimo territory is a cultural unity.

Next, he found a great dichotomy of culture. An Eskimo summer culture could be distinguished from an Eskimo winter culture. This distinction, greatest among the Arctic Eskimos, faded to the south at both ends of the Eskimo range. In brief, the most northerly winter culture is that of people who move out on the actual sea ice to hunt seals in a variety of specialized ways. Their swift means of locomotion is the dog sledge and their principal weapon, the harpoon. At the beginning of winter, their habitation may be an earth house; later, on the sea ice, it is inevitably a snow house. The complementary summer culture exists largely inland, where the land provides caribou and the rivers, fish. The Arctic Eskimos then live in tents, use a kayak for transportation, and lances, bows and arrows, and salmon spears as their principal weapons.

The sub-Arctic Eskimos, who live in most places south of the Arctic Circle, correspond closely to the Arctic ones in their summer culture, but in their winter culture they live in earth houses and center their lives on coastal hunting in which they use harpoons while moving across the water in kayaks and umiaks.

Steensby now asks which of these forms—the Arctic or the sub-Arctic—is the older. In answer, he points to three significant groupings of the types. In the first are methods and implements distributed among both the Arctic and the sub-Arctic Eskimos. These include ways of hunting caribou and the uses of salmon spears, bows and arrows, and tents. In the second group are the methods and implements used by sub-Arctic Eskimos both in the western and the eastern areas but not recently in the central area. These include the continuous use of kayaks and their appurtenances for hunting on the sea. In the third group are those types found in the Central region that tend to disappear toward the west and the east. Among these are ice-hunting methods, the ladder-like dog sledge, and the snow house.

Now, says Steensby, it becomes clear that the elements of the second and the third groups, particularly such things as snow houses, could hardly have been devised first in the warmer regions where their use would be slight. Thus, while the specialties of the Central Eskimos might reasonably have spread into neighboring areas where they could be useful, if not essential, it is unlikely that they originated there. Steensby concluded from this testimony of types that the Arctic form of Eskimo culture was the older.

He next looked for the origin of Eskimo culture in the area where its older form was still found—by elimination, the Arctic archipelago—those large islands of most remote Arctic Canada north of the Hudson Bay region. Here were the essential ice for winter dwelling, the aquatic mammals, the caribou herds, and, formerly in greater numbers, the musk oxen. We must finally assume, says Steensby, that if one form of Eskimo culture preceded another, it, in turn, was preceded by an even older culture that we cannot designate as Eskimo. This gives us a "Preeskimo" culture. Next, the "Palaeeskimo" is "an original North Indian form of culture, the winter side of which has become specially and strongly developed by adaptation to the winter ice of the Arctic Ocean." This has been overrun in large part by the "Neoeskimo" culture and population that originated around Bering Strait and was influenced by the neighboring peoples of Asia, including, most likely, seafarers and fishermen like the modern Japanese. The American Indian influence will thus have been expended primarily on the Palae-eskimo before the Neoeskimo "immigration."

Steensby discovered, by peeling away series of types like the layers of an onion, what he believed to be stages in the development of Eskimo culture. Here was a blueprint for further investigation. In particular, it was a blueprint for archeological excavation, and one could hardly discover archeology in the Central region that did not show Steensby to be either right or wrong! Steensby, in effect, did archeological work without scratching the surface of the ground and without committing himself as to the dating of his several groups of types.

The archeological challenge was more real to Therkel Mathiassen on the Fifth Thule Expedition. He wished to find the actual dwelling sites of ancient Eskimos in this area where recent Eskimos had seldom settled down in one place long enough to leave surface traces of their dwellings. A few clues existed. Down through the years, sea captains and other travelers had collected artifacts in the Central Regions that appeared to Mathiassen quite unlike those of the Eskimos living there today. And in the Thule district of north Greenland, from a deep, frozen deposit—a "kitchen midden" resulting from some early people who had lived on the spot a long time ago—came tools made differently from those of the present Eskimos. Since earlier Greenlanders would logically have come from the Canadian Arctic archipelago, it stood to reason that one might find there the same types of early deposits.

Also, the Central Eskimo tribes fear and respect a class of legendary beings known as the "Tunit." Elsewhere, as far away as Alaska, the Tunit may be only troublesome spirits, but within the Central region they take a more worldly cast. Mathiassen learned with interest that the local Tunit had been "big, strong people who lived in permanent winter houses and hunted the whale and the

14. Simple and composite house forms, Naujan, central Canada. Width of house at left, 20 ft. (6 m.). (*From Mathiassen, Vol. I, 1927*)

walrus; their men wore bearskin trousers and their women, long boots." These and other details of Tunit life had less the ring of myth than of history. It did not take the archeologist long to recognize certain stone-filled depressions covered with moss as the remains of old houses. These, affirmed the Eskimos, were where the Tunit had lived, and Tunit ruins, it soon became clear, existed in many parts of the Central region.

Mathiassen settled down in the summer of 1922 to excavate the houses of Naujan, the "sea gull place" (Map 4). Here, between a long, narrow lake and the sea, on gravel terraces from forty to seventy feet above sea level, occurred groups of house pits, stone-lined graves, and tent rings. The house outlines were round and their tunnels short. Two houses joined their tunnels in what appeared to be a single outlet, and another house took the shape of a clover leaf, its stem being the tunnel (Fig. 14). Since Eskimos are now accustomed to building their houses as near the sea as possible, Mathiassen wondered about the elevation of the Naujan village. Why should people have carried their building materials and supplies so far up the slopes and away from the water—especially the heavy bones and skulls of whales? Could the village once have lain nearer to the sea and the land have risen enough since abandonment to leave it both distant from and high above the water?

By stripping the houses and adjacent areas of their sod to allow the warmth of the sun to thaw a few centimeters of ground a day, it became possible in the course of two months to excavate ten houses, two of them the composite kind. The simpler house forms of Naujan later proved to be like those in many other old settlements in the Central region. As a special type, it is known as the "whalebone" house. Circular in outline and excavated a foot or so beneath the surface of the ground, its walls were built of the bones of whales, particularly the skulls. Over these was erected a roof of whale jaw-bones and ribs covered with animal hides, stones, and turf. The short doorway or entrance passage, hardly a tunnel, opened into the house at or below the level of the house floor. Inside, the dwelling had a low ceiling, the back half even lower because of its slightly elevated sleeping area lined with slabs of stone.

The excavations at Naujan soon revealed other differences between the ancient house builders and the Iglulik Eskimos who presently inhabit the region. The old site was one of resident hunters who secured most of their food from the local sea and tundra. The present Iglulik prefer to go far away on the sea ice during most of the winter. The immense deposits of bones and other refuse showed that the houses were occupied year after year. Whale bones and baleen—the black, springy substance that grows in the mouths of whales—could easily have been removed from animals beached near the village, but a large quantity of walrus, seal, and caribou bones showed that these animals had been transported to the village by sledge or boat from many distant points of interception. Other bones in the floors and middens were those of birds, bears, fish, and musk oxen. It was clear from the beginning that these bones represented animals actually hunted and killed.

Weapons for taking seals and walruses were easily recognized from the close resemblance of their parts to those from other Eskimo regions. Three types of small harpoon heads for sealing were distinguished (Fig. 15), some with inset slate blades. Along with these heads, which were detachable from the shaft to act as toggles under an animal's skin, were found other parts of the harpoon: bone, ivory, and antler foreshafts; socket pieces for the foreshafts cut to fit the ends of wooden shafts; the wooden shafts themselves; finger rests to aid in propelling the harpoon; and, for attaching to the base of the shaft, ice picks with which the hunter might open his seal holes through the ice and make ice anchors to brace himself against the pull of a wounded beast at the end of his line. Other harpoon heads and blades, much too large for seals, were nearly identical to those used in distant parts of the Arctic where Eskimos recently still harpooned the great whales (Figs. 16 and 24b). Clearly, whaling for the early villagers had been an important aspect of procuring food. Yet now this region is not frequented by whales. The waters, too shallow to allow them to pass through, must once have been deeper when so many were caught.

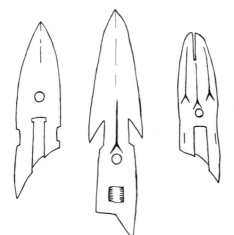

15. Three types of harpoon heads used at Naujan in taking seals. Length of antler head at right is 3 in. (7.6 cm.). (*From Mathiassen, Vol. I, 1927*)

16. Whaling harpoon head of ivory, Naujan. Length, 7 in. (17.7 cm.). (*From Mathiassen, Vol. I, 1927*)

Other kinds of hunting equipment at Naujan are known to recent Eskimos in Alaska and elsewhere, though they are absent among the present natives of the Central region. These include the bladder dart, a seal-hunting weapon used by hunters traveling individually in their kayaks; light bird spears, propelled by throwing boards from the kayak, with three side prongs set halfway down the shaft; wolf killers of baleen (these are bent and inserted into a bait and left for the wolf to swallow—to his later keen regret);

and the weights of bolas, the peculiar bird slings that open in the air like the spokes of a wheel and wrap themselves about the wings and necks of flying birds. Other Thule-like tools and objects of Naujan that are foreign to the Iglulik are sledge shoes of baleen; splitting wedges; mattocks for cutting turf; hand drills; meat hooks; winged buttons; hair ornaments and chains of walrus ivory; bird figures with human foreparts, probably used in a game similar to jacks played by some modern Eskimos; and dolls with a cross over the back and breast (Fig. 17).

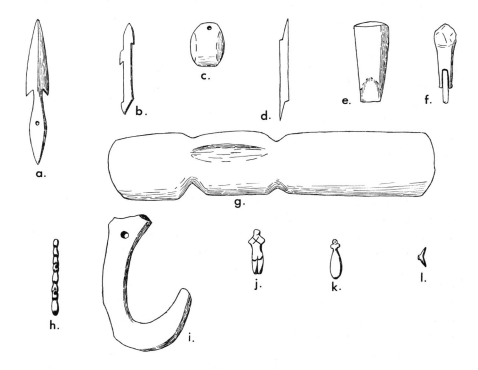

17. Objects found at Naujan that are typical of pieces from the widespread Thule culture:

a) bladder dart, antler
b) prong, antler
c) bola weight, bone
d) wolf killer, baleen
e) wedge, ivory
f) drill, wood; point, slate

g) mattock, whale rib; length 15 in. (38 cm.)
h) chain, walrus ivory
i) meat hook, antler
j) doll, ivory
k) bird, ivory
l) button, ivory

(From Mathiassen, Vol. I, 1927)

In most other respects, however, the Naujan people seem to have passed along their techniques and inventions to their Iglulik successors. Their sinew-backed bows; a variety of arrowpoints; long, ladder-like dog sledges and harness parts; snow knives, snow probes, and snow shovels (showing that the settled people of Naujan also knew how to build themselves snow houses when away on journeys); blubber lamps for cooking and illumination; and cooking pots of soapstone, along with cups and bowls of wood and baleen, show continuity over a long period.

The old Naujan people were respectful of their dead. Rectangular graves of heavy stone often lay still undisturbed in the vicinity of the village. In these small tombs, the body was laid on its back but drawn up at the knees to fit the short enclosure. Grave goods were placed beside the body either in the grave or in a small chamber created of stones just outside. Strangely, however, only the men's graves seemed to contain the goods to accompany them into another world. The skeletons at Naujan and other Thule sites all proved to have the body-build, head form, and bony structure of modern Eskimos, rather than of Indians.

AN ARCHEOLOGIST'S LIFE in the Arctic is seldom without incident, but if there had been a question about whether or not the Tunit were still active and resentful of having their houses torn apart, Mathiassen might have felt that he was a special target of their anger in that winter of 1922 following the excavation of Naujan. He and Jacob Olsen, the interpreter and secretary of the expedition, set out early in the fall to cross Frozen Strait in order to return to the base at Danish Island. Their whaleboat proved too small to break through the early ice, however, and the two Danes reluctantly turned back to spend the winter, with short supplies, on Southampton Island. Making the best of a bad situation, they teamed up with the Eskimos who lived there, fishing through holes in the ice and hunting with them. Their few remaining rifle shells were quickly used, and tea and tobacco also ran out, for they did not hide their luxuries from the people whose houses and food they shared.

But later, farther inland at Darkness Lake, where they had gone with some of the Eskimos in search of caribou, things became even worse. Those Eskimos with whom they now hunted began to grumble about the scarcity of food. They also remembered, after one or two people became sick, that their Danish guests had broken some of the local taboos—excavating ruins, smashing the skulls of caribou with a hammer to get at the brains, and doing other equally unacceptable things. One night Olsen overheard their hostess, an unhappy woman who now blamed her headache on her guests, asking her husband to kill the strangers. Needless to say, the Danes next day thanked their hosts for their hospitality and moved on. Later, in another household, a man's rifle accidentally discharged, and the bullet made six holes in the folds of Mathiassen's inner skin garment, fortunately with no other damage. Though they gradually became accustomed to their enforced intimacy with Eskimos, in February, when word came that the Strait was solidly frozen, neither man turned down the opportunity to hurry back to the warm expedition building on Danish Island with its wealth of food, tobacco, and books.

During the following summer Mathiassen, calling upon the others of his party to help him take advantage of the short thawing season, excavated house pits and whole villages at several other points as far away as the north shore of Baffin Island and as far south as Eskimo Point on the west shore of Hudson Bay. The Naujan story was repeated in one archeological site after another. While differences in the styles of artifacts occurred regionally, a larger pattern emerged of an early culture long preceding that of local Eskimos. This pattern, now known to be both widespread and old, was appropriately christened by Mathiassen the "Thule culture." With its principal "types," so clearly defined by him in his two-volume work, *Archaeology of the Central Eskimos*, the Thule culture immediately took its place as a standard against which to measure other Eskimo, or Eskimo-like, cultures of the Arctic.

As to the age of this Thule culture, the unusual elevation above sea level of Naujan and other sites suggested to Mathiassen a means of dating. The land here might be expected to have risen at a more or less regular rate since the release of pressure by continental glaciers. On the basis of the rate of rise of land along the coast of Norway, he estimated one thousand years to have passed since the beginning of Thule culture in the Central Regions.

While he failed to find signs of a "Palaeeskimo" culture stratum, Mathiassen called attention to the close correspondence of his Thule culture to Steensby's "Neoeskimo." One might now envision a surge of Neoeskimos spreading eastward from the Bering Strait region, reaching the Central region of Canada about one thousand years ago, and, allowing a short time more for further migration, becoming the first Eskimos to reach Greenland.

Even as Mathiassen finished his masterful delineation of Thule culture, however, his partner in fieldwork, Birket-Smith, was evolving a new hypothesis, modifying that of Steensby, that would reaffirm a Canadian rather than an Asian or an Alaskan origin for Eskimos. In brief, the present-day Caribou Eskimos, living inland the year around and depending almost wholly on migrating caribou, still maintain the oldest patterns of Eskimo culture that he called "Proto-Eskimo." Some of the caribou hunters moved to the coast and learned to hunt on and under the ice of the sea, changing their culture to Steensby's "Palaeeskimo." As the Thule culture moved eastward, however, the Palaeeskimo patterns became more and more altered by ideas from the Bering Strait region. The resulting "Neoeskimo" pattern prevails in much of the Eskimo realm today, although a fresh advance from the interior obliterated the old Thule culture in the Central Regions and became, instead, the phase of culture now evident among the Iglulik Eskimos.

In either view, the Tunit and the Thule people may have been one and the same—but whether the legends have grown out of recent guesses about old houses and graves or have persisted from the time of the Naujan village to the present may never be known.

THE FINDING of a Thule settlement at Cape Krusenstern, two thousand miles west of Naujan, would give us, we hoped that summer of 1958, an opportunity to test whether Thule culture represented people on the move or simply a slow change of styles and hunting methods for all of those who happened to live in the different parts of the region. If the greater number of types, in Steensby's sense of the word, proved to be identical, or nearly so, with those of the Central Regions, and if these were proven to be more or less contemporary in both parts of the Arctic, we could hardly question a rapid migration, in one direction or the other, of the Thule people themselves. On the other hand, if only half the types were shared, and our western sites had in common many things as distinct as the rectangular winter house of poles, we would have to think more strongly in terms of a free passage of *ideas* across tribal lines, while the people moved but little. The spread of tobacco smoking from Asia to the Eskimos in the last two centuries, for example, required no change in dialect groupings, or even in hunting territories. Rather, the platform pipe and Circassian tobacco passed from hand to hand heedless of language and traversed the continent long before European explorers had joined hands across the Northwest Passage.

We now wished to excavate and date enough house pits on our beaches to learn what elements of culture had preceded tobacco smoking in a drift across the Arctic, as well as those, such as the ladder-like sledge and legends about Raven, that had failed to do so.

(V)

WESTERN THULE

PERHAPS IT WAS Percy Downey who finally determined when we should dig our first deep Thule house. The season was now late —mid-August 1958. We had completed our trip of sampling beach ridges around Kotzebue Sound—Chamisso Island, Deering, the mouth of the Kugruk River, Cape Espenberg, Shismaref, and Shesualek—and, finally, here at Cape Krusenstern we were uncovering a tantalizing variety of flints on the many old beaches (Map 2). Our crew after a brief separation was together again and now included Almond's burly, taciturn brother, Murphy. Upon finding the large, Thule-like house pits and artifacts, I had briefed the students on the history of Thule, and now we were trying to decide whether to halt other, more exploratory work in order to dig these Thule pits—a comparatively heavy type of excavating. This was where Percy came in.

Percy was four years old; his sister Lydia, six. Percy had long regarded himself as the leader of our expedition, and once or twice when his influence became far greater than his stature, we were inclined to agree. In his miniature hip boots and blue denim jacket, with or without breeches, Percy always took his place at the bow of his father's cumbersome boat to heave and strain with the rest of us at getting it launched. Another self-appointed task was to retrieve the anchor or change its position when the boat required deeper water as the tide dropped. Fending off his sister if she came to help, he would hoist the heavy anchor to his shoulder, stagger manfully under its weight, and, carefully calculating its next position, lower it. Never punished or scolded, Percy seemed to be taught, if taught at all, by the gentle persuasion of his parents.

Our supply of shovels, toward the end of that season, was still plentiful, but trowels of the best quality had dwindled, through wear, to one apiece. An archeologist's well-polished trowel is as personal and essential to him as was a knight's sword, and each evening upon returning to our camp on the oceanfront beach two miles east of the lookout tower, we habitually stabbed our trowels into a particular patch of sod beside the cook tent. One morning, though, the trowels were missing. A frantic search revealed nothing. Ruth Downey, hearing our sounds of distress, emerged from her family's tent, baby Mary's quizzical head looking out from her perch under her mother's parka. When told of our loss, Ruth had no answer, and Lydia shook the braids at the side of her head to show that she, too, knew nothing of the trowels. Then, as though directed by a single mind, all eyes turned toward Percy. Having already reset his anchor experimentally a half-dozen times, he stood in the boat, poling back and forth in a wide arc a few inches above the shallow, muddy bottom offshore.

Almond walked slowly to the edge of the water. This was a man's sensitive business. First searching the sky as for a change of weather, he turned at length to the boy, and said: "Sonny, where did you put the trowels?" Percy looked up from his work, puzzled. His small brow wrinkling under a fringe of coarse, black hair, he replied: "Over there," pointing to the beach. The group of onlookers, poorly concealing their concern, marched to the indicated spot. There were no trowels. Almond tried again. "Sonny," he asked, "did you throw them?" Agreeably, Percy nodded. "Where?" "In the water," said Percy, waving his arm about the perimeter of the boat. Now we all plunged in shoepacs and boots into the mud and shallow water. Percy climbed out of the boat and explored the water with even greater assiduity than the taller people around him. After some lapse of time we had searched all the mud within a long stone's throw of the boat. Nothing like trowels turned up.

There was no recourse but to consider the trowels lost. Turning our backs on Percy, whose day, though young, had already been a complete success, we trudged off to work with some old, poorly made spare trowels. Thus handicapped, it seemed wise to spend the remaining few days of the summer shovelling more and trowelling less. We would dig the deep Thule house one way or another.

The five presumed house pits of the Thule group were given numbers from 4 through 8. In general, our system was to assign numbers to all houses we had found by the end of a season, whether dug or not. Mostly for our own future convenience, the number and location of each house were spotted on a large-scale map of the area. At Cape Krusenstern, we began the numbering on the most recent beaches, assigning higher numbers to houses on older beaches, and often skipping numbers that could be assigned in subsequent years if other houses turned up close by.

We excavated the largest of these Thule houses first, the one designated 7 on the tenth beach back from the sea, because it seemed to promise a complexity of rooms and passageways. Before commencing, we set up our theodolite over a stake at a high point on the edge of the rim of the larger pit, took elevations for contour mapping, and laid out reference points on the ground at convenient intervals where they would be least subject to covering by "back dirt," the earth and debris thrown from the excavation before the artifacts can be recovered. Once the surface was mapped, we began cutting the thick mossy sod in straight lines that followed roughly the probable shape of the underground floors, then cleared the enclosed space of its sod. We either cut squares of a size that one man could easily tip over and carry to the edge of the excavation or, working together, rolled up a long, heavy strip of this thick carpet, continuing to roll it off the mound and over to a convenient spot where it could be unrolled and examined for stray cultural items. When the last of the sod carpeting was removed, we turned to the rich black earth thereby exposed and scraped its top for whatever cultural items there might be. Anything found there was likely to represent later campers on the site rather than the original dwellers and had to be so labeled for future studies.

Below the six inches or more of sod and inch or two of black dirt, the earth was coarse with sand and gravel and gray from the absence of organic matter. This was a largely sterile zone, two to four feet deep, composed of the earth that had been dug out of the original excavation together with that which had been heaped over the house—the latter having crept downward in the process of attrition that reduces a rectangular house to a rounded shallow pit. Objects in such an unproductive layer are nevertheless mainly those of the culture to which the house itself belonged, for people long ago, like their descendants of recent years, sat upon the mounds of their roofs scanning the sea and mending equipment while children climbed up and perhaps dropped playthings. Roofs

also served then, as now, for the preservation of raw materials:
a bit of whale rib, the tine of an antler, or last winter's cooking
stones that might again be useful.

The digging of House 7 required many hours of cautious
shovelling for all of us. Pivoting our shovel handles across our
thighs in such a way as to scrape up a small pile of earth, as we
could with trowels, we searched each bladeful for a bone fragment
or man-made object, which, when found, was carefully set aside.
As our little piles of earth grew to shovelfuls, they were then heaved
out of the excavation as far as they could comfortably be thrown.
If we had correctly estimated the size of the structure below, there
was no need to move this back dirt again; we knew, through tests,
that little of value was being covered by the rim of dirt growing
from our hundreds of separate shovel throws. At a depth of about
two feet near the center, and somewhat less at the edges, we came
to the rotted remains of fallen wall and roof timbers. These had to
be carefully cleaned and, if they still clung together (showing the
position of a beam), mapped in their various positions before
removal from the pit. Still, House 7 was telling us little about the
people to whom it had been home. Attempting to bring order to our
excavation, we concentrated on taking the walls down to the level
of the center. Here, nearly three feet deep, the bases of once
vertical poles that remained long frozen each year were better preserved and they could be cleaned and exposed in nearly the same
position they had occupied in the original walls of the house.

The walls of the main room, we found, had been of driftwood
poles laid horizontally and dovetailed, as in a modern log cabin.
Outside the walls we found only clear sterile gravel. The large room
now seemed nearly ready for the removal of the treasure that we
anticipated: the accumulation of litter that usually covers the floor
of an unswept, long-occupied house. But as the front wall emerged,
something seemed amiss. Those of us now working with trowels
and brushes faced those who were exposing the walls and deeper
floor of the narrow entrance tunnel. As expected, a step led down
from the house floor into the floor of the tunnel (Fig. 18). The signs
were clearing, as they should, under the slow manipulations of our
smaller instruments. Only to the right of the tunnel did the front
wall, as one looked toward the entrance, offer an unexpected disturbance.

Concentrating on this area, we soon discovered that another

doorway had opened here from the main room into an ash-filled room (Fig. 19). Our earlier calculations had not, unfortunately, allowed for this complication and there was no recourse but to shovel away the thick rim of accumulated back dirt and, beginning with the layer of sod, repeat the entire process. At length the walls of the new room were exposed, revealing a small, rectangular kitchen. A third room, recognized from the beginning by shallow surface indentations, lay ahead of the main room and to the left of the tunnel.

Suspense mounts as the outlines of an entire house come clearly into view. Our trowels are at last within reach of the main goal, but we must use self-control and continuous good judgment to keep from cutting too quickly into the rich, dark substance that should yield all manner of familiar objects and, with luck, a few forms never seen before. That stage had now been reached; we had worked around the walls of the main room, the kitchen, and the large lateral bedroom; the general shape of the main tunnel and the short one leading from it to the bedroom had become clear; and we had carefully refrained from removing the last bit of rich soil that would expose the floor, although in some of the looser material on the floor of the main room I had recovered two ivory salmon-spear barbs, a nearly complete woman's knife or ulu blade, an ivory sealing dart, and some arrowhead fragments. We could see too that bones were numerous, as was usual in a house where a hunter's family had eaten many a satisfying meal. Recent Eskimos are known to be tidy, and it is hard to understand why their ancestors lived amidst the rubbish they did, but their tossed-aside bones of fish and game as

18. Bill Simmons clearing the floor and tunnel of Western Thule House 7 at Cape Krusenstern, 1958.

well as their litter of broken or misplaced tools and weapons afford
a valuable record for archeology. All bones are eventually identified
and counted, and the tabulation tells much about the eating habits
of the residents.

It was evening when we stacked our shovels at the edge of the

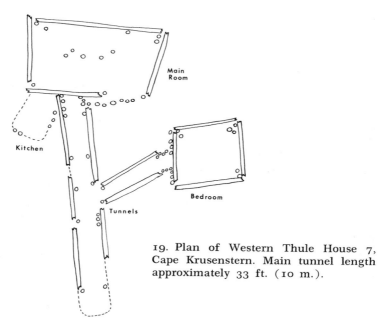

19. Plan of Western Thule House 7,
Cape Krusenstern. Main tunnel length
approximately 33 ft. (10 m.).

excavation and gazed with pride and anticipation at the now clear-
cut walls of the composite house and at the dark ground between,
looking forward to the next day or so when we would recover the
belongings of the people who had built and lived in the house. With
the satisfaction a farmer must feel for his wheat the night before
he reaps, we turned back toward camp, a pleasant place consisting
of the Downeys' tent, where they, their children, and the other
native workers all ate and slept; a second white tent where Ruth
Downey spread the meals for those of us who preferred such
things as beans, bread, and canned meats to the seal oil and
stronger meat favored by the Eskimos; and, beyond this, the small
tents in which we each found room for our air mattress and sleeping
gear, duffel bag, notebooks, writing equipment, personal library, and
other accoutrements of a season. Tired after a hard day's shovelling,

we cleaned, catalogued, and stored that day's take of artifacts and then turned in for a good night's sleep on a beach still lit by a glow from the northern sky.

During the night I was gradually awakened by a weird sound quite unlike that of the usual wind and surf. As I listened, it reminded me of a sound I had heard but once before, during World War II in New Guinea: the clatter caused by myriads of small hermit crabs in their borrowed shells migrating in the moonlight on a tropical beach. I hurriedly pulled aside the mosquito netting and peered through the short tunnel of my tent. As much of the beach as I could see from this snail's-eye position seemed to have become suddenly forested. Then I recognized the truth, and our peculiar predicament. I was looking at the legs of reindeer. We were completely surrounded by a herd! Most of the animals simply stood and rested, but some milled quietly about like the winding current in a quiescent stream. Lying prone, with only tent walls as protection, one has an indescribably vulnerable feeling. Reindeer, when frightened, stampede like cattle, but perhaps with even less leadership and discretion. What would happen if these animals suddenly took fright? Would they not trip on our tent ropes and, veering away, trample us in our low tents? Slowly, so as not to spread alarm, I stuck my head out of the tent tunnel until I could see that all my companions were equally surrounded. Jim's tent was nearest mine. At first calling hoarsely, and then more loudly as I drew no more than puzzled looks from the animals nearest me, I caught Jim's attention and explained that he must lie quietly until we could come up with a better plan of action.

In time, knowledge of our predicament spread through the individual tents and on to the big Eskimo tent. These reindeer comprised the whole Noatak herd of 900 to 1,000 animals. Ordinarily hard to approach in the daytime, they were nevertheless accustomed to the tents and odors of their native herders and, thus far undisturbed, were spending the night in what they must have mistaken for the camp of their owners. Herding during the summer in this part of Alaska is extremely lax. The Eskimos to whom this herd had recently been transferred from the Federal government were probably ten miles away, beyond our beach ridge sequence, and unlikely to round up their beasts for some time This was the period when the animals customarily ate young leaves of willows for a while, before they were encouraged by their owners to go over the hills to the river to begin a winter of lichen-eating—the

20. A small part of a reindeer herd silhouetted against the sea, Cape Krusenstern.

principal means of sustenance for both domesticated reindeer and wild caribou.

We in the small tents now stuck our heads out of our separate tunnels and began to plan a concerted move. But by this time murmurs had started to issue from the big tent. Then Murphy Downey, who had worked as part-time herder the year before, slowly emerged from his doorway and sauntered cautiously out among the deer. Taking no alarm, the animals nevertheless made way for Murphy until, edging toward our tents little by little he induced movement enough from the nearby reindeer to set the whole herd into a slow walk away from camp. Soon we were all able to come out from our tents, ready for an early breakfast, and grateful that the great brown mass of future steaks and stews had surged westward along the beach ridges (Fig. 20). Reindeer from Asia were first introduced to Alaska by our government in the 1880's as a source of meat and hides to replace the native herds of caribou that were becoming scarce from overhunting. Though reindeer herding has never been developed to the extent it was hoped, both the government and some of the natives still own small herds.

The beach, which had been carpeted by a thin sod, now looked as if an army had passed through—or, more precisely, a herd of reindeer. Halfway through breakfast, someone agitatedly remembered that the herd was last seen moving in the direction of our Thule settlement. Forsaking our meal, we rushed off to work—some of us at a trot. Sure enough, the herd, looking like a low cloud on the horizon, appeared to have come to rest on the site. The closer we came, the more certain it seemed that our carefully exposed floors, ready for their final dissection, would certainly be trampled by these brainless creatures. Throwing the herd into a short sprint of retreat with our precipitous arrival, we advanced apprehensively to House 7. The back dirt had indeed been trampled and piles of animal bones were scattered, but beyond this, unbelievably, no damage had been done to the house itself, probably because of its depth and sheer walls. Later in the day two of the reindeer herders, accompanied by a blue-eyed Irish shepherd dog they had trained to round up the deer, dropped in for a visit (Fig. 21). They understood our concern for the excavation and promised to collect the entire herd and drive it back to their camp. Apparently they did so, for we had no more such nocturnal visitors.

AS WE CONTINUED work on House 7, the rich floor layer in the main room and kitchen yielded, that day and the next, a wide variety of artifacts and bones along with evidence as to where people had slept and how they had prepared their food. The kitchen floor was half a foot thick in red to yellow ash, and black in spots with charcoal from half-covered fires. Throughout this moist paste

21. John Stalker, reindeer herder, and his dog.

22. Sherd of a Western Thule pot with curvilinear markings, Cape Krusenstern.

23. Probable shape of the pot from which the sherd came.

occurred the sherds of broken pottery vessels. Enough fragments of one such vessel were recovered to allow its partial reconstruction (Figs. 22 and 23). It represented a slightly conical cooking pot with a flat-topped rim and holes for suspension and was capacious enough to hold three or four gallons of liquid. The outer surface was covered with concentric circles impressed in the wet clay by striking repeatedly with a rounded paddle on which had been carved series of raised circles. This was a method of designing that lasted, we now know, from about A.D. 700 to 1400, encompassing the Western Thule period of culture which was first identified at Point Hope in 1939.

The elongate kitchen had slightly irregular walls, presumably because its roof had been a light, removable cover. The doorway from the kitchen into the house had been narrow enough to close with a hanging skin. Looking through this aperture from the main room, we could imagine the housewife controlling her open fire, having to breathe in some of the smoke as she boiled and roasted food for her family. The rest of the house, with no other fireplace, had been heated and lighted by round, dishlike pottery lamps, the fragments of which were found in several parts of the excavation. From the many animal bones, deep ash, and quantity of broken pots, we knew the house had been occupied for a long time.

The large, rectangular main room, its greater dimension opposite the length of the tunnel, had been floored with planks and small split logs. This flooring, although now largely decayed, ran parallel to the length of the tunnel at the left side of the room, apparently marking off a sleeping area, while the remainder ran at right angles.

Having observed this much, we now set to work briskly with our trowels, lifting up layers of old matted floor debris, shaking them apart cautiously so as not to break their more delicate contents. In this way we began to find some of the good things lost or intentionally left behind by members of the family. Among these were sealing dart and toggle harpoon heads of the same type found by Mathiassen in the Central Regions, arrowheads, the working end of a mattock of whalebone, a pair of snow goggles, an ivory bodkin, and a whaling harpoon head (Figs. 15, 16, and 24). The large harpoon head, carved of whalebone, is nearly identical to those used in recent times in the pursuit of baleen whales. Along with a number of other whalebone objects it assured us that these people practiced whaling of the kind recently done by trained crews in large skin boats. The snow goggles were carved of a single piece of antler and had a nose groove and two flanges designed to fit closely over the eyes. A long narrow slit in each flange allowed a wide sweep of horizontal vision without letting in a blinding glare from the low-lying sun on spring and fall sea ice.

The bodkin was a special revelation. We gathered round and studied it closely. A four-sided object, blunt at the end that held a narrow slit and drawn to a point at the opposite end, this piece was decorated on all four long faces. Three of the faces had panels of engraved lines containing the combinations of straight or slightly curved lines that we recognized as typically Western Thule. These elements in similar combinations occurred again and again throughout this house and, as we later learned, throughout the site.

The fourth face of the bodkin, in sharp contrast, contained only a small area of formal engraving and, beyond that, a lifelike scene showing two men standing on land, a man sitting in a boat, and a caribou. These figures were outlined with a minimum of marks yet with a skill that portrayed a scene from life far more

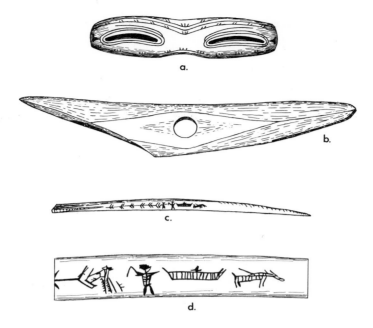

24. Western Thule culture objects from House 7, Cape Krusenstern:
  a) snow goggles, antler; length, 5¼ in. (13.3 cm.)
  b) whaling harpoon head, whalebone; length, 9¾ in. (24.7 cm.)
  c) bodkin, ivory; length, 7¼ in. (18.4 cm.)
  d) enlargement of the engraving on the bodkin

realistically than could have been done using simple stick figures. With only rare exceptions—in sites of Eastern Thule culture and in a site at Wales, Alaska—such drawings were not known to occur before the first historic contacts in the western Arctic. The style of engraving on this piece is nearly identical with carvings done by recent Eskimos on drill bows to record their hunts and travels. The differences in detail, however, are remarkable, and perhaps reveal game pursuits and processes not known among recent Eskimos of this region.

Both men in the engraving appear to be casting weapons with throwing sticks, or spear throwers. The caribou clearly has a spear from one of these thrusts piercing its shoulder. While it has long been assumed that prehistoric Indians in more temperate regions used throwing sticks, or *atlatls*, of special types to kill deer and other land animals, no one, so far as I knew, had suggested that Eskimos might have used theirs except for hunting from their kayaks on the water. Here, nevertheless, both the two men and the caribou are shown standing. The boat appears to be another subject,

unrelated, for it is out of line with the men and the animal. While
at first the crosshatched boat appears to be an umiak like those in
recent engravings, we see that the bow and stern pieces, which are
always in line with the gunwale in umiaks, here continue upward
at the same angles as the bow and the stern. The man sits in the
center, as he might do in a kayak or canoe, but not in a large skin
boat that would be awkward to paddle from this position. The boat
is clearly neither umiak nor kayak as we know them; rather, it

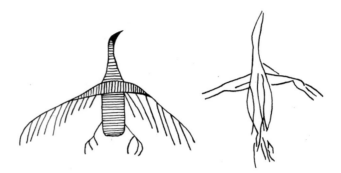

25. Thunderbird (left) carved on an Eskimo spear rest.
(*From Nelson, Part I, 1899*). Bird carving (right) from
House 7, Western Thule culture.

resembles the birch-bark canoes described by the first western
explorers on the Kobuk River. We are thus obliged to see in this
single small engraving both the un-Eskimo practice of hunting
caribou on foot with spears propelled by throwing sticks and boats
shaped like birch-bark canoes.

Another realistic carving on a discarded basal piece of reindeer antler depicts a bird with both wings partially outstretched.
This is nearly identical with recent Eskimo drawings of a mythical
creature, the Thunderbird—a bird so large it can carry away a
white whale in its talons (Fig. 25).

From other parts of the house, the floors of the tunnels, and
the small, square, floored room that probably served as an extra
bedroom for the family, came many items in a good state of preservation—arrowheads of several Thule types, wound plugs for stopping the flow of blood and thus retaining the valued fluid inside
wounded seals, harpoon heads, a handsomely decorated needlecase
of ivory (Fig. 26), and a wide variety, both whole and fragmentary,
of other tools, weapons, and containers.

26. Ivory needlecase, Western Thule culture, Cape Krusenstern. Length, 3⅝ in. (9.2 cm.).

The main tunnel, thirty-five feet long and a foot or more deeper than the floors of the rooms, contained at its outer end a large stone and a whale vertebra, evidently used as steps for entering and leaving the house.

As usual upon cleaning the floors of structures like this, we finally took up the rotten floorboards to retrieve anything that might have become more deeply buried as well as to check for any possible lower floor. Lifting one such board near the center of the floor of the main room, between the bases of two supporting posts, I was pleased to find a rectangular cavity in the earth. This small well, cribbed with miniature logs, had apparently been a storage place for valuables. It was packed with caribou and seal hair along with the bones of seal flippers and a few sharp fishbones, probably intended for some special use. Placed within the hair, as though intentionally for protection, was a double-headed seal-drag handle of ivory with the head of a seal carved on one end and the head of a bear on the other (Fig. 27). Also included within the hair were a broken, decorated brow band, the tip of a blunt arrow, and a knife blade of green slate hafted in a two-piece wooden handle with its sinew lashing still preserved. The seal hair and "finger" bones may have represented whole seal flippers stored there for future use, perhaps as patching material to be used with other sewing equipment. Strips of sinew and a simple tubular needleholder with sinew protruding were also included. This cavity, then, was a cache for sewing equipment as well as for some of the owner's most valued carvings.

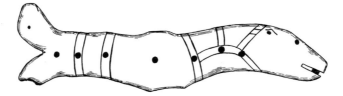

27. Seal-drag handle of ivory. Length, 3¼ in. (8.3 cm.).

The charred edges of fallen wall and roof logs of the main room and the tunnel suggested that a blaze from the kitchen had set fire to the house and that, even though the burning was only partly destructive, the owners had left precipitately. A puzzle that we never solved was the presence of a human mandible—that of a large man—on the house floor, and a thigh bone, possibly of the same individual, on the floor of the tunnel. These did not appear to have intruded from some later burial, and, as they would have been gruesome souvenirs, we can only guess that they must have been carried into the abandoned house by burrowing foxes.

From the more than six thousand bones complete enough for identification, we learned that the people of House 7 subsisted largely on small seals and caribou during the winters they lived there: while the bones of small seals made up half the total, those of caribou came to a surprising thirty-six per cent, showing either that these hunters were exceptionally persistent as compared with later Eskimo dwellers on the coast, or that caribou were plentiful during this period of occupation. Next in order of prevalence were the bones of big, or bearded, seals; those of dogs, several skulls of which appeared in the house floor suggesting that the animals may have been eaten; and those of walruses and birds. Rare bones were those of moose, white whales, big baleen whales, sheep, ground squirrels, and muskrats. The skull of a mountain sheep had probably been brought to camp by hunters returning from the high mountains of the neighboring Brooks Range. Moose, on the other hand, are creatures of the forest. They were extremely scarce in this region from the time of historic contact to the last decade or so, although they are now increasing phenomenally and pushing out to the coast. These facts suggest either that the climate at the time our Thule village flourished was similar to that of the present or that moose, ordinarily shelter-loving, expand their range to the open tundras and coasts whenever the forests become over-populated. Whatever the climate, however, the people of House 7 had lived well for some winters in their commodious house.

AFTER HOUSE 7, with its revelation of a Western Thule phase of culture at Cape Krusenstern that was closely related in many ways to Thule culture farther east, we turned during nearly two whole seasons to more exploratory findings on earlier beaches; yet work

28. Excavated floor of House 6, Cape Krusenstern. Entrance tunnel is at top of photo; kitchen angles to the right.

on the relatively recent Thule beaches did not entirely stop, and by the end of the 1961 season we had managed to excavate each of the other four Thule house mounds. Quite possibly the group formed a contemporary settlement even though three of the houses lay three beaches farther inland than the other two. There were, nevertheless, minor stylistic differences between the two groups, and we cannot rule out the possibility that two beach ridges formed between the times of occupation of the two sets. Each of the houses had been built on the same plan. The lower walls of the main room and tunnel—and a second living room, where present—were made of horizontally laid poles; the kitchen walls had been at least partially constructed of upright driftwood timbers. Each kitchen angled from the right front wall in the same manner as had that of House 7 (Figs. 19 and 28). They varied in size, but all had thick deposits of ash and charcoal. House 5 had a secondary living room joined to the tunnel in the same fashion as did the one in House 7. In the vicinity of each house were two or three shallow cache pits, but neither here nor in the houses were there signs that whale ribs or jawbones had been used in house construction.

Whale bones had been used, however, in a small village or cluster of houses two miles farther east. There, the outward signs had led us to believe the houses would date much later than Western

Thule. Whale bones still protruded from the edges of the pit and the bleached stumps of jawbones testified to some kind of above-ground structure, perhaps a cache. Furthermore, the tufts of tall grass growing out of the pits indicated a more recent date than had the old turf in the first settlement. Excavating House 25 of this eastern group in 1959, which first appeared as a large, roundish,

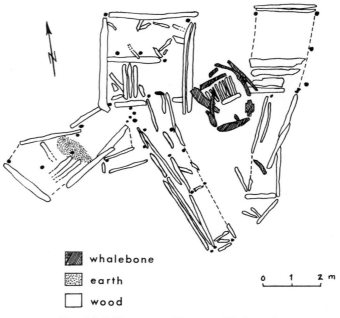

    ▨ whalebone

    ▨ earth

    ☐ wood

    0   1   2 m

29. "Double" House 25, Western Thule culture.

pitted mound of an uncertain number of rooms, we were surprised to find that we had actually uncovered a small rectangular house floor and tunnel with a cache pit lined with whale ribs to the left of the entrance, and, beyond that, a larger house floor with a tunnel and a kitchen (Fig. 29). This larger house had a form identical to most other houses of the Thule group, and we suspected that the close proximity of the two tunnel entrances indicated a double house, the smaller one perhaps serving as the home of grand-parents.

    The second house of the eastern group, House 27, which we excavated in 1961, was again a truly composite house. The kitchen of this one opened to the left, rather than to the expected right, of a rectangular main room. Two side tunnels had opened at intervals from the right side of the long entrance tunnel, each into a four-sided bedroom. In both these large house complexes there were quantities of bones from whales: jawbones, ribs, and vertebrae, as well as others less suited to building. This could be evidence either of more successful whaling or of a new style in house construction—perhaps a western equivalent of the Eastern Thule "whalebone house."

The range of artifacts recovered (Figs. 30 and 31) closely paralleled that of the Western Thule group of house pits, but some new elements and stylistic changes showed that Houses 25 and 27 were closer in time to house pits of the so-called "Old Kotzebue" phase of culture. This "whalebone" settlement was, in any event, the most

30. Front and back view of a doll carved of ivory, late Western Thule culture (about A.D. 1300), Cape Krusenstern. Height, 3¾ in. (9.5 cm.).

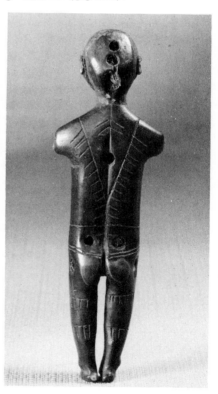

31. Antler fishhook, late Western Thule culture. Length, 4⅛ in. (10.5 cm.).

recent one excavated at Cape Krusenstern to which we could apply the phase-name Western Thule. It now appears to date at about A.D. 1300, while the older settlement is estimated at A.D. 1000.

THE EXCAVATIONS at Cape Krusenstern along with those of related cultures excavated by Henry Collins at Wales, Helge Larsen at Point Hope, and James Ford at Point Barrow now make possible a comparison of Thule culture both eastern and western. Many of the smaller artifacts of Thule culture are duplicated in Alaskan sites and these assemblages are called "Western Thule." The similarities suggest that their makers in different parts of the world shared a common cultural background that they drew upon, wherever they were, for their everyday manufactures. Thus, judging from certain well-preserved artifacts in our sites and in Thule sites of eastern Canada, we see that people who almost certainly spoke Eskimo carried on some nearly identical pursuits using nearly identical tools and weapons.

They used large uncovered skin boats for the pursuit of baleen whales in the open sea; they cut up the whales in front of their villages and employed some of the bones in constructing houses and caches; they harpooned seals with thin toggle harpoon heads of similar types and fitted the whole harpoon assemblage with bulbous, heavy socket pieces, finger rests, and ivory ice picks; they hunted from kayaks with harpoons that had inflated seal bladders attached as floats, and from their craft they propelled side-barbed bird spears with throwing boards; they hunted caribou with sinew-backed bows and antler-tipped arrows; and they slung wheel-like bolas with multiple ivory weights into flocks of seabirds. Their two-piece knife handles held slate and, occasionally, a bartered metal blade. Their mattocks for digging, their wedges for splitting drift-wood, and their drills for working ivory, antler, and wood were of the same form. Women cut fish and meat with stemless slate *ulus,* tended their seal-oil lamps—used for illumination and some cooking—and used ivory combs with narrow, ornamented handles in putting up their hair. Thule artists even engraved bits of ivory with realistic figures showing boats, tents, and human figures. It is on the strength of dozens and even hundreds of close resemblances between artifacts that we draw conclusions of close ties of cultural continuity between the Thule peoples of the east and the west.

If identities of these kinds were found in every aspect of the life of these two ancient groups, we would be justified in saying that people moved but recently from one area to the other. Minor and regional differences might even be explained by the time re-quired for a long and slow migration. When Western Thule arche-ology was still hidden in the ground and nothing earlier than Thule was clearly seen for the east, it was entirely reasonable for Mathias-sen and others to speak of a Thule migration along the Arctic coasts of America, where the Thule people were believed to have been the first human settlers. Nor was there doubt of the direction of such a migration. Greenland, commonly supposed to have been only recently freed from ice at its margins and hence only recently populated, would have been the end point in a migration, not the beginning. Since the Thule people were quite certainly Eskimos in physique and culture, as compared to the Indians either nearby or those farther to the south in any direction, the point of origin of such a migration obviously lay to the west. For a while it seemed likely that archeologists working in Alaska might even turn up actual sites of a Thule people on the march.

The sites that were excavated on the coasts of Alaska and on St. Lawrence Island over many years, however, failed to produce such a site or series. The differences in the sites that seemed early enough were overwhelming when one looked at them for Thule origins. But now, at last, we have sites at Cape Krusenstern, Shesualek, and at least two other points in Alaska that show such close relationships to Eastern Thule sites as to indicate continuity and direct or rapid descent. Unfortunately, only a few radiocarbon dates thus far relate to the Thule problem. To know whether the Thule culture was earlier in the west or in the east we must await more dates and interpretations of dates. Tree-ring dating indicates that its last stages in Alaska were as late as A.D. 1300. Certainly Thule culture had a wide time range at both ends of its geographical range.

In Alaska, the Thule culture seems to have been a mixture half of pure Thule and half of something derived from local inheritance and exploitation of the local enviroment. Furthermore, the Western Thule phase lacks some of the specializations of the east. The Eastern Thule people traveled by sledge; they harnessed their dogs, fan-wise, to long, ladder-like sledges lacking built-up stanchions or sides; though they spent parts of the winter, probably in snow houses, waiting at the breathing holes of seals, at the same time they maintained substantial stone houses on land where they cooked with soapstone pots suspended over half-moon-shaped soapstone lamps; they also built stone caches and buried their dead in chambers of heavy stone slabs.

The Western Thule people, on the other hand, dug their large composite houses deep into the earth and depended upon an attached kitchen and clay pottery for much of their cookery. They made twined baskets of grass, going so far as to impress basketry into the inside of a fresh-made pot. They constructed log caches both above and below ground and buried their dead in log tombs. Some of their working tools—heavy, pecked stone adz heads and thin, circular scrapers of coarse stone—were like those more recently used by Indians of the Northwest Pacific coast and the Alaskan interior. While they probably kept dogs, they left none of the sure signs we see in Eastern Thule of having regularly used their dogs to pull sledges.

For all these differences, we nevertheless see in the Thule culture, both east and west, a continuity as strong as, and similar to, that between the modern Eskimos of Alaska and those of Canada and Greenland. This makes the question about migration less urgent. We now know that recent Eskimos of Bering Strait, of Point Barrow, of Melville Peninsula, and of eastern Canada were preceded by Thule Eskimos who, in turn, were preceded by still earlier Eskimo-like peoples. Might not those early populations also have been stable, changing their culture but slowly to fit the styles of the times? For the moment, then, we may shelve the question of migration at this earlier period and speak instead of the spread of a culture remarkably similar on all the Arctic coasts between Labrador and Bering Strait. Here at Cape Krusenstern we had the unique opportunity of walking with our digging equipment back beyond the Western Thule houses and onto the old beach ridges to learn what people had preceded those of Thule and what they had been like.

BY NOW we had studied the beaches and were familiar enough with their contents to know roughly which concentrations of pits or other surface signs would indicate which periods of culture. We also knew that groups of beaches ran at slightly different angles. That is, successive sets of beaches had formed in slightly different directions—undoubtedly the result of major changes in wind direction that affected the offshore currents and coarser sediments as they moved slowly southward. The six such changes since the present series of ridges began to form at Cape Krusenstern are shown in Map 2. Segment 1, the beaches currently forming, is in two parts, either because part of the shoreline has washed away just east of the tower or because an eddy in the south-flowing current has prevented gravel and sand from accumulating there. It thus far boasts eight substantial ridges. Just behind them, on Beaches 9–19 of Segment 2, are all the Western Thule sites so far known at the Cape. Segment 2 ends at Beach 35, and the earliest segments continue back to Beach 114, which curves about the lagoon shore.

It is on the middle beaches, 20–28 of Segment 2, however, that the immediate predecessors of the Thule villagers must have walked and camped; yet, search as we might, no house pits turned up on those ridges. Later, we found two house pits related to the Birnirk culture (an early form of Thule), but they were noncommittal as to their beach because they had been dug into the northwest corner of Segment 2 where several ridges merge. Some deep caches that had been walled with vertical poles came to light, but these contained few artifacts. We can only say of the middle beaches of Segment 2 that, compared to others, they were thinly populated, perhaps reflecting a sparsity of food animals when the beaches fronted the sea. Whatever the reason, they do not reflect conditions on the older beaches, for just as the Segment 2 ridges ended in a burst of Thule culture, they also began with a relatively dense population carrying one of the most specialized and bizarre cultures of the Arctic: that of Ipiutak.

(VI)

THE ARTISTS
AND MAGICIANS
OF IPIUTAK

THE DISCOVERY of the original Ipiutak site at Point Hope, one hundred miles northwest of the Cape Krusenstern beaches (Map 1), will always seem more dramatic to me than the opening of Tut-ankh-amen's tomb. It was, in fact, my introduction to Arctic archeology. The year was 1939 and I had been doing research in tree-ring dating at Alaska College (now the University of Alaska) when Professor Froelich Rainey returned to the campus from a congress of anthropologists in Copenhagen. There, he explained to the three or four of us who shared laboratory and curatorial space in the college's museum, he had talked with Danish archeologists about a joint field trip to the north coast of Alaska. In particular, he had worked out a scheme with Helge Larsen, a curator in the National Museum of Denmark and the best prepared of the younger Arctic men, to go to Point Hope to explore the huge midden mound called Tigara (which is also the official name of the present village —Map 5) that Knud Rasmussen had so interestingly described after his epoch-making sledge journey across Arctic America in 1924.

Rasmussen had thought Tigara might hold the key to the western origin of Thule culture. It lay halfway between Point Barrow, where the Birnirk phase of culture had been recognized as an early form of Thule, and the Bering Strait region, where on St. Lawrence

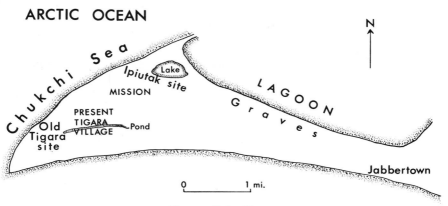

ARCTIC OCEAN

N

Chukchi Sea

Ipiutak site

Lake

MISSION

PRESENT TIGARA VILLAGE

Old Tigara site

Pond

LAGOON

Graves

Jabbertown

0   1 mi.

Map 5. Point Hope

Island and the Diomedes the most ancient cultures clearly had formed a base for the emergence of Thule culture (this will be discussed further in Chapter 8). Rainey explained to us that the mound at Point Hope was big enough to encompass many house pits and that it probably contained layers of debris comparable to those of the big mounds on St. Lawrence Island and at Point Barrow, where people were known to have resided for two thousand years at points that had long been and still were excellent sealing and whaling locations.

Tigara was then a village of about two hundred and fifty Eskimos, and even now each spring its men form crews to go out in skin boats and harpoon or shoot the great baleen whales that provide them with sufficient food and oil to last throughout the year to come. Rainey, who had excavated on St. Lawrence Island, and Larsen, who had worked in a number of sites in Greenland, agreed that it was the most promising unexplored spot in the Eskimo region. The expedition, Rainey explained to us, was now practically assured. It was to be sponsored jointly by the American Museum of Natural History in New York, the Danish National Museum, and Alaska College. The Danes would pay Larsen's way to Alaska and back, and the Americans would furnish travel and subsistence for the two scientists while they were in the field as well as the means for hiring a crew of Eskimos to assist in the digging.

Excitement around the museum became intense as summer approached. I had no thought of being asked to join the undertaking, for my research dealt with Arctic trees and buried wood and their dating by the tree-ring method. This method, also called dendrochronology, is based upon the tendency of trees of certain species,

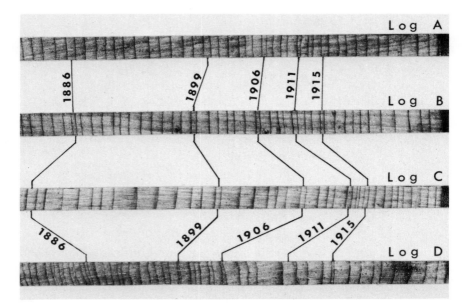

32. Four log sections showing ring patterns. The thin rings, representing years of meager growth, are dated to each other.

mainly conifers, to reflect in the growth of their rings the annual changes in climate. From matching patterns of thick and thin rings, it can be ascertained that certain logs or wood grew in adjacent areas at the same time. At a forest edge in the dry Southwest, for instance, the trees show patterns of thick and thin rings corresponding to the degree of rainfall during the winter preceding growth. By these patterns, one tree or fallen log may be cross-dated to another that has grown in the same environment; and when a tree is freshly cut, its rings can be dated to the Christian calendar (Fig. 32). If the logs have been long dead, as in a cliff dwelling, they can still be cross-dated in a relative chronology, revealing such information as when a room was built and then when it was remodeled. In the Arctic the growth of rings at timberline, or northern treeline (see Map 4), depends mainly on the temperature during the growing season. Thin rings form during a cool, rainy summer, and thick ones when the ground thaws early and the skies remain clear.

I was the first to apply this system successfully in the western Arctic, and after three years of such work, including a year with the late A. E. Douglass, the originator of the method, at the University of Arizona, I had begun to find new applications for it.

In a test case, I had recently obtained permission from Rainey to make narrow razor cuts along the edges of certain artifacts of coniferous wood from an archeological site on St. Lawrence Island. Comparing the plots of these pieces, I soon found that the artifacts from related levels sometimes cross-dated. That is, their patterns of ring structure showed that they had been fashioned from driftwood that came originally from trees growing contemporaneously somewhere on northern river banks, most likely the Yukon.

On one occasion I discovered cross dating between two plots from pieces of wood that had been excavated in different years from the Kukulik Mound on St. Lawrence Island (Map 6). When I happened to need these pieces another time and was looking for them in the dozens of shelves and drawers in which the St. Lawrence Island artifacts were temporarily placed for cataloguing and description, Rainey became interested. He took one of the plots and from its catalogue number tracked down its corresponding piece of wood. When he retrieved his specimen, I already had mine—a piece of a deep food dish carved of spruce wood—and had reviewed the ring widths. A quick check showed that I had measured and identified the rings correctly from the center to the edge of the vessel and that they appeared to have been from near the outside of the original tree. This piece had been excavated for the museum by Otto Geist in 1934. The other piece, according to its catalogued information, had been excavated by Rainey, in 1937, from a layer comparable to that of the first but some feet away in the same large mound. Now Rainey, with his sample, walked to my desk as all other work in the laboratory came to a temporary halt. Even as we put the second fragment to a test, all could see at a glance that the pieces, though differently weathered, fitted together to form a complete bowl.

In the next few weeks, similar tests showed that tree-ring dating could be used not only to find the parts of wooden objects that belonged together, but also to date at least the later occupation of the Kukulik Mound. Then one day Rainey asked me if I thought buried wood from a mound as far north as Point Hope could be cross-dated. I felt sure that it could. He next asked if I wanted to postpone my summer plans for a collecting trip at timberline and join the expedition to Point Hope. I did indeed!

The days went slowly for me during the next few weeks, but finally July 4 arrived—the date set for our departure. Helge Larsen, a tall, dark-haired Dane with the jutting brows and prominent nose of a Plains Indian chief, yet the attentive eyes and expressive face of one who expects others to be both interesting and amusing, had arrived from Denmark and marveled with us at the unusual summer heat on College Hill. The temperature late that morning reached 90° F. in the shade. This seemed hardly the way to begin an Eskimo summer, particularly since we were already within a hundred miles of the Arctic Circle.

Our flight in a five-place Bellanca had to be postponed from mid-afternoon until evening because no breath of air stirred the river from which we were to take off on floats. Nor did a few degrees of evening coolness end our troubles. The load of our sleeping equipment, clothing, and food, which filled every spare nook, was so heavy it seemed doubtful that the plane could rise even if the stream were ruffled by a gale. At length, after several attempts at flight, the pilot regretfully informed us that supplies and baggage must be lightened by half. Rainey and Larsen, after a discussion, came to a reasonable conclusion. They knew that Point Hope boasted a cooperative store of the Alaska Native Service. Why could we not leave the heavy cases of food behind and take with us only the vital sleeping gear, clothing, and technical equipment? Now once more, while Mrs. Rainey stood beside a pile of our discarded provisions waving good-bye, the plane roared out to the center of the stream—and again it plowed the water like a tugboat. As we returned despondent to the shore, the pilot encouraged us with word that we must try again in the cool of midnight. After more restless hours, at midnight—just when the traditional Independence Day baseball game was starting in Fairbanks—we climbed aboard and found that by rocking the floats our pilot could lift his craft off the water and manage, barely, to clear the tops of the trees at the far bend of the river.

The flight of some six hundred miles took us across country which was then, twenty-five years ago, not too commonly used as a passenger route. We landed to take on more fuel at the Koyukuk River, where Athapaskan Indians stood about watching in their shirt-sleeves. Airborne again, we soon left the forest and experienced a dramatic change of scene. In place of the steaming greenery of the interior, we saw, first, brown tundra and then a sea full of broken ice. At Point Hope the ice covered the Chukchi Sea, leaving only narrow leads between the floes. Taking advantage of one of these, our pilot set us down on the water and taxied to the gravel beach on the south side of the village (Fig. 33a). Here we were met by scores of running Eskimo men and boys in the soiled, medium-weight parkas they use in the transition period between winter and summer. Then came our first shock of the season. Upon alighting from the plane, a continuous blast of icy wind whipped our summer coats about us and we learned with dismay that the temperature was 34° F. Almost at once native seamstresses who had arrived on the scene noted our measurements and contracted to make us warm fur parkas and skin boots.

Other surprises came fast on the heels of the first. Two school-teachers who invited us in to their house and gave us a bowl of *chili con carne* made of reindeer meat told us that their plane was due momentarily to take them away to a new assignment, and they also mentioned, with satisfaction, how successful they had been in using practically all their winter food supplies so that they had no surplus to transport. The only other non-Eskimo in the village, they told us, was the resident missionary—the ancient archdeacon of the Episcopalian Mission—who, they said, would under no circumstances sell us food from his dwindling stores. A little later, opening the door to the cooperative village shop, we saw at a glance that life in the Arctic can be trying even for latter-day explorers. The shelves contained some hardware and heaps of pelts, but the only food, as the native storekeeper agreeably pointed out, was a few packages of old and very dry figs. What should we do? we asked as we watched our plane fly away south. The schoolteachers answered without hesitation: we could do what everybody else in the village did—we could eat meat from the spring catch. The cold cellars of the Eskimos were still supplied with whale and walrus meat and we might even be fortunate enough to obtain a fresh-caught seal from a successful hunter.

We allowed ourselves a fleeting thought of the cases of tasty sausages and cheeses we had left behind, and then turned a little apprehensively to arranging our lives at Point Hope. We had no trouble in renting the small, one-room winter house of a native family who were to spend the season in another village. After half a day of scrubbing floors and walls and removing some odorous dog troughs and containers of rapidly thawing meat stuffs from the storm shed, we moved in our bedding, duffel bags, and supplies. A quick search through these for the food of civilization netted

33a. Point Hope Eskimos watch the arrival of a plane, 1939.

us little. A few chocolate bars, two pounds of blue cheese, a bottle of cognac, and two cartons of cigarettes (for three heavy smokers) were all that we could muster. It became clear at once that since we must subsist on quantities of meat and whaleskin, we ought to have a cook who would understand these exotic staples and be able to serve them in the most enticing local fashion. We thus hired Violet, a young and businesslike Eskimo woman who appeared each morning to start the fire and brew tea and bring the pot of whalemeat to a new boil. She left us, then, to our morning ablutions, but returned later, when we had gone to work, to wash our dishes and tidy up the house. When at noon we came in hungry, Violet would again warm the whalemeat; on more fortunate days we might have a change of menu for the evening meal, enjoying the boiled ribs of a walrus or the liver of a seal.

THE GREAT MOUND of Tigara appeared from a distance to be all that Rasmussen had claimed. As we walked upon its crest, however, no degree of optimism could hide the disheartening facts. Each house pit, including those recently occupied, had been dug into by the people of Point Hope. The mound looked as if it had been bombed repeatedly from the air. Questioning some of the interested onlookers who accompanied us everywhere during the first few days, we learned that the old site had long since become a

33b. Two Point Hope women: Emma and Naksuguruk. Surrounding them in the excavation are the whale ribs that once supported a house.

source of ivory and other items to sell to the crews of government ships that came late in the summer. Of even more use to the villagers was the buried driftwood that had been used in construction, some of it oil-soaked and therefore highly flammable—now an excellent fuel. We paused to talk with two old women who stood in a pit deeper than they were tall and tried to hide our feelings when they pointed with pride to the objects they had unearthed with their makeshift picks and wooden shovels (Fig. 33b). Obviously none of these structures, not even those with parts of their floors still intact, would offer us the kind of controlled excavation for which we had come so expectantly to Point Hope.

One opportunity did remain, however, to learn something about the succession of peoples there. This was to lay out squares and dig between the craters in hope of finding at least a few layers of archeology below the surface debris created by present-day villagers. This plan worked very well and for me, being new to the game, it was difficult to understand why my companions continued to be something less than elated. Having studied archeology at the University of Arizona and having visited sites of the dry Southwest, I could now see the techniques I had learned applied to a region where conditions were in sharp contrast to those in Arizona. Here, laying out a series of squares with our plane table

34. Froelich Rainey (left) and Helge Larsen (right) cataloguing artifacts at Point Hope, 1939. Garments purchased from Eskimos are being aired on the roof of the shed.

and mapping them at the same time, we proceeded to remove earth in six-inch levels, recording artifacts as we went along. Kneeling in our newly purchased parkas and high skin boots, we peeled away with trowels the thin segments of midden that thawed each day. As soon as we had removed the thawed ground and its artifacts and bones, we moved on to other squares, and so on during the day, rising at intervals to stamp circulation back into our feet while the wind blew with uninterrupted force off the persistent floe ice. As I acquired skill with the trowel in those first days of digging, striving for that careful touch that leaves no mark on wet and half-frozen artifacts, I developed a fascination for the unique feel of the culture-bearing earth underneath—a feeling, perhaps, such as a sculptor acquires for his clay.

In the evenings we cleaned and numbered the materials of each day's labor, wrapping them for protection and storing them in containers that we marked with the numbers of the appropriate squares and levels (Fig. 34). Larsen had brought with him from Denmark a bag of numbered copper discs, and one of these went into each container with the appropriate number entered into a notebook so that if other means failed we could still identify groups of objects when they were ready for unpacking and study in one or another of the distant museums. By day, as we scraped at the frozen midden, and in the evening, as we sat about the table in the warm cabin, Rainey and Larsen talked archeology. While they could identify nearly every object we recovered, there were times when all of us consulted the voluminous photographic plates in Nelson's *The Eskimo About Bering Strait* or Murdoch's *Ethnological Results of the Point Barrow Expedition.* These heavy books and a few smaller ones were part of the reason we could enjoy no store-bought food. Yet there never came a time, I am sure, when we would have traded a single volume for ten times its weight in provisions, and I was soon reading these sober books as avidly as if they were novels. Each day brought with it also discussions of other archeological sites and excavations. We compared our findings with those of Collins, Mathiassen, and Jenness, and went over in great detail all the problems that confronted archeologists of 1939 in their attempts to piece together the prehistory of the Arctic.

Despite this enthusiasm, after two weeks of excavating our Tigara squares not even I could pretend that our enterprise was any kind of success. Although I had not yet recovered enough samples of wood to date levels exactly, we did not require such precise dating to know that most of Tigara had been built no more than three or four hundred years ago. Whatever this site had to say about the development of Eskimo cultures, much more had already been said at Point Barrow and at Bering Strait.

By now, however, we were comfortably entrenched at Point Hope, enjoying our all-meat diet, reconciled to not smoking, and accumulating all manner of ethnographic information from the friendly Eskimos who offered us the open hospitality of their village. Through their generosity we even enjoyed an occasional break in the monotony of our diet. Now and then there was boiled fresh fish in place of the bits of sea-going mammals that usually graced our table. And one day we were given a marvelous gift: two sea-gull eggs apiece, gathered by an enterprising Eskimo from the bird cliffs north at Cape Lisburne. We walked to our house that evening tired but keen with anticipation. Violet, sure enough, plunged the large, blue, brown-spotted eggs into boiling water as we walked through the inner door of our hut. Soon, faces washed and hair combed for the occasion, we sat at our accustomed places at the table, rubbing our hands in anticipation. Violet placed the steaming eggs in the center of the table and we passed them around. Each cracked an egg simultaneously. Instead of the firm, white substance we expected, there streamed from Rainey's and my shells a watery mass of red and yellow, filling the bottoms of our tin plates. Larsen's sniff of surprise was greater than ours, however. Staring up at him out of an equally colorful background were a yellow beak and small black eyes. We silently agreed to forego this first course and get on with our usual whalemeat. Violet regarded us with more puzzlement than usual, but quickly recovered when she realized that she could have these eggs for herself—and the other three as well. As she had earlier observed, our tastes were unaccountable.

I think it was that same evening that we decided to finish only the midden squares currently under way and then move on to look for a more profitable field. Some of our helpers had told us about a place called Jabbertown seven miles along the coast to the east. They reported "old things" over there, just as here at Tigara. Rainey volunteered to stay and finish the work at Tigara with our native assistants while Larsen and I looked into the possibilities of Jabbertown. Driven over the wet grass of the swales the next morning by a neighbor named Antonio on a sledge pulled by a team of nineteen dogs, Larsen and I quickly reached the long-abandoned Jabbertown. Tests in a grass-covered mound were highly rewarding. Larsen recognized the materials as unlike those from our squares at Tigara but, instead, similar to many of those he had excavated in the Thule sites of Greenland. At home that night Rainey agreed that Larsen and I should excavate at least one house at Jabbertown while he completed the work at Tigara and that then we should all either join in further work at the newly discovered site or pack up our belongings and explore the coast to the south.

The mound at Jabbertown was more deeply thawed than that of Tigara; hence we were able to move earth quickly and expose the lower walls and floor debris of a house. It had been a multi-roomed structure, unlike the single-roomed houses we had encountered at Tigara. The artifacts recovered were closely like those of Thule sites in Canada and Greenland, and on the strength of these resemblances we named the phase "Western Thule," and now date it to roughly one thousand years ago. By the time we finished this house, however, a dramatic turn of events was taking some of the bloom off our new findings. We continued to travel the seven miles to Jabbertown by sledge as often as drizzle or dense fog made the grass slick, but on fine mornings, when the grass was dry, it impeded passage of the sledge almost as much as if the runners were being pulled over sandpaper. Then Larsen and I would walk the first mile or so northward past the mission and over the beach ridges to the edge of the lagoon. There Antonio would meet us with his dogs, harnessed with long rawhide lines to a skin boat. He, Larsen, and I climbed into the boat and the dogs ran swiftly along the gravel beach pulling us through the water to our destination. At the end of the day we again traveled by dog-boat and then walked from the lagoon back to our cabin.

One day we worked very late, eager to get on with the business of exposing a house form not previously described for the western Arctic. It was midnight when Larsen and I, carrying our shovels, began the walk back over the beach ridges from the lagoon to a well-earned dinner of whalemeat. Stopping at one point along our ridge top to look toward the low, red, midnight sun, we observed a peculiar phenomenon. The top of the ridge bore a reticulation dimly outlined along the entire surface. What could this be? "Frost cracks," suggested Larsen; the frost does do strange things in the Arctic. On the next ridge top we stopped again, however, for we saw the same phenomenon. Then we noted that instead of being irregular polygons such as frost creates in moss-covered ground of the Arctic, these outlines all appeared to be square or rectangular. What could have caused them other than man? But no, we assured ourselves, these could not be man-made because no village in the Arctic could have been so large. The markings appeared again on the third ridge and on the fourth, but beyond that there was no trace of the peculiar squares. Curious about them, I made a suggestion: I had nothing to lose, I said, by digging a hole in one of the squares to see what it might contain—if, that is, we could find them again when the sun shone high in the sky. Larsen thought a moment, then said: "Let's all come and try."

The next morning, earlier than usual, Rainey, Larsen, and I, giving our assistants a half-day off, again walked past the mission and retraced our steps of the night before. Diffuse daylight had indeed obscured our illusion, if illusion it had been. Only with the closest scrutiny could we now identify a few of the shallow rectangles. Standing away at a distance we could barely make one out, and then the only way to reach it was to pick out a particular tuft of grass near its center and, never moving our eyes from the tuft, walk toward it.

We felt a bit foolish as we separately laid out three-foot squares in neighboring areas. Unlike excavations in sites nearly everywhere else, there was no trace under the sod of the blackened earth of cultural deposits. We continued, however, to dig ourselves deeper into the ground. At about two feet we each struck a diffuse brownish streak in the gravel that gave some encouragement to go on. Moments later there was a shout. It was Larsen, but neither Rainey nor I ran immediately to see what he had found, for we, too, were striking dark soil, an unmistakable sign of culture. But Larsen was not to be put off. When he yelled again and climbed out of his pit, Rainey and I hurried over to see the small object he held in his hand. It was an ivory hook, about three inches long and stout enough to have been used as a suspension hook rather than a fish hook; at the shank, looking out at us from the curved barb, was a grotesque face with eyes made of two inset discs of jet.

Returning expectantly now to our separate squares, we soon accumulated enough ingenious, thin bifaces of chert and chalcedony, chips of flinty material, and one or two more examples of ivory carvers' art to know that we were digging in an ancient pit house. Furthermore, materials like these, similar in some respects to objects of pre-pottery sites of the Old World, had not previously been found in Arctic America. We felt that we might have here the oldest site in the Eskimo area. Most striking of all, however, was the indicated size of the settlement. If all the dozens of squares we had seen on the surfaces of old beaches the night before were houses, this must have been a phenomenally large village. With these positive tests and in great elation, we turned back toward camp to gather our equipment and hire more Point Hopers for what we had no doubt would be the most important dig in the Arctic.

The site was previously unknown to the villagers and they had no name for it. Reviewing local place names we found one, quite pronounceable, for a sandbar between a small lake and the lagoon. Thus "Ipiutak" became the name of the site and of a culture. During the remainder of the season we excavated nine rectangular pit houses, the floors of which were invariably at a depth of two and a half or three feet. Besides the artifacts, each floor contained quantities of flint chips and bones, showing that the houses had been occupied for many seasons. Both bones and artifacts of ivory and antler were often well preserved, even though the wood of walls, floors, tools, and utensils had long since vanished into a few fibers or a brown stain.

Night after night we pored over the day's collection of artifacts from each house, attempting to see meaningful ties with other sites. The flintwork reminded Rainey and Larsen most di-

35. Engraved ivory piece, Ipiutak culture, Point Hope. Length, about 8⅔ in. (22 cm.). (*From Larsen, 1951*)

rectly of Neolithic flints from the Lake Baikal region of central Siberia, while the elaborate engraving art in ivory, including small, grotesque animal depictions and conventional freehand designs, reminded us more of the art of the Old Bering Sea culture of St. Lawrence Island and certain pieces from Siberia and China (Figs. 35 and 57). If the site were as recent as Old Bering Sea (which lasted from about the beginning of the Christian era until A.D. 500), on the other hand, we would expect it to have more of the most widespread Eskimo traits such as ground and polished slate implements, oil lamps, implements for whaling, and pottery. None of these did we find. Ipiutak was beginning to look like the long-hoped-for ancestral site of Eskimos.

Now that we had more than justified our existence at Point Hope, the time seemed propitious for trying to pry loose from the archdeacon some small contribution from his reported hoard of supplies. Armed with the exciting information that his mission buildings stood on the edge of the oldest village site in the Arctic— one where many secrets of Eskimo origin might be solved—we thought it appropriate to pay him a formal visit. On the way to the mission across the beach ridges one Sunday afternoon, we

discussed our tactics. What we longed for most were cigarettes—
and, according to the Eskimos, the archdeacon had a store of
tobacco as well as reserve supplies of food in one of his warehouses.
We decided, on this social call, to speak softly of our shortages
and ask for nothing more, if the occasion arose, than a carton of
cigarettes. We agreed that Rainey should be the spokesman. Archdeacon Goodman, a very short, stocky old gentleman, greeted us
as pleasantly as he had on an earlier occasion—this time inviting
us into his quarters for a talk. We sat on straight-backed chairs,
Larsen and I attentive while Rainey, casually intense, described
our discoveries. We had gathered from our previous conversation
with our host that archeologists were no more welcome at Point
Hope than were visitors of any other pursuit who might exert an
influence on the natives and thus upset the delicate balance of
power that he appeared to enjoy.

Now, however, we saw him respond with enthusiasm to
Rainey's disclosures. He leaned forward and questioned us with
animation. At length, having brought details of our latest findings
to a sort of climax, Rainey ended his account. After a brief pause,
he went on to praise the people of Point Hope and expressed our
liking for native food. The only serious shortage was tobacco. We
were all smokers, he said, and had long since run out of cigarettes,
which we missed much more than "Stateside" food. The archdeacon
brightened at this, and shook a finger toward us. "Gentlemen," he
said, "I think I can help you." He then pushed a high stool to a
corner of the eating and living room where we sat and, mounting
it, opened the top door of a cupboard. He reached into the recess
and came down with a package in his hand. Anticipating cigarettes,
we were puzzled for a moment by its small size. "Gentlemen," he
said, "I have here a package of bubble gum. Chew it, and you will
forget your longing for tobacco." With this he opened the package,
handed us each a piece, and bade us farewell. As we walked back
across the beach ridges to our house, we wisely kept silent until
we were well out of earshot, our jaws working vigorously the while.

Only a few days later the trading boat arrived, full of supplies
for the store and goods enough for all who had money. By this
time we were quite accustomed to an all-meat diet. Even so, it was
with gusty enjoyment that we supplemented our meals with such
delicacies as ham, beans, bread, coffee, and, especially, an after-
dinner smoke.

When the season ended at Point Hope, Rainey arranged for me to go to St. Lawrence Island to excavate until late in the fall in a search for both datable wood and further traces of earliest Eskimos on the island. I was successful on both scores (pp. 165–72) and the following season I combined my studies of tree growth at timberline with archeology in the Kobuk River valley. Rainey, with his wife, returned to Point Hope in January, 1940, and together they made an intensive study of the Eskimos and their annual cycle of activities. During the summer of 1940 Rainey again excavated at the Ipiutak site with student assistants and a large number of Eskimo laborers. The following summer he and Larsen, with Dr. Harry Shapiro of the American Museum of Natural History, excavated for a third season at the site, rounding out our knowledge of a crucially important aspect of Alaskan prehistory.

IPIUTAK is by far the most extensive and complete one-period archeological site yet discovered and described in the entire circumpolar region. Nearly all the seventy-two excavated houses are of Ipiutak culture, but in addition to these there are more than five hundred other definitely identified house pits. More outlines, less clear, show that the Ipiutak site contained at least six or seven hundred houses, not counting others undoubtedly washed away by the sea. Before the discovery of Ipiutak, nearly all large-scale excavations in the western Arctic were made in mounds rather than in isolated individual house pits. Even when an archeologist is able to identify a house within a large midden mound, he can seldom be sure that the objects collected from it actually belonged to the period of occupation of that particular house. This is because the original builder, in excavating the pit for his house, would have dug out of his excavation any midden deposits left from earlier periods, and, although he might retain them on the roof of his dwelling, they would eventually drift downward again toward the floor after the house had been abandoned. The Ipiutak houses, like those of later and earlier periods at Point Hope, were isolated from one another in almost all cases. This made possible a close comparison of both the contents of individual houses and of the styles from different beach ridges or segments of the settlement.

In a similar way, the excavation of one hundred thirty-eight

burials classified as Ipiutak offers an unparalleled means of studying and comparing the skeletons of these people and tells much
about their burial customs. During his second summer at Point
Hope, Rainey was particularly eager to find Ipiutak burials because he knew the shape of the skull and other bones of the body
would go far toward answering the question of whether or not
these people had been Eskimos. Unsuccessful at finding burials in
random tests, he decided to offer a prize to anyone who could discover an Ipiutak grave—the prize to be a silver dollar. The next
morning, as he later described the scene to us, he glanced out of
his window and was astonished to see dozens of people walking
toward the Ipiutak site carrying makeshift digging tools of a great
diversity of types. Nearly all the villagers had responded to the
incentive of a prize. Sensing danger, Rainey dressed as quickly as
he could and went at once to advise them how to deal with a burial
if one were found. By the time he caught up with them, they had
gone to dig some three miles beyond the Ipiutak site and were
already heading back toward him. An old man—who had discovered
the first grave—held in his hand some "elaborate and fantastic
spiral carvings." Rainey hastened to caution the treasure hunters
that he would pay only for burials located but not disturbed. Much
to his pleasure, more than fifty graves were discovered in those
first days of searching.

The burials tended to bear out legends told by the oldest
Point Hopers—especially one about a weird race of the past that
had eyes of ivory. One of the first burials unearthed gave its excavators a real start as it stared up at them with eyeballs of ivory
inset with pupils of jet. Other skeletons also were buried with artificial eyes as well as diverse trappings of a bizarre kind. One skull
had been equipped not only with eyes but with a sewn-on mouth
cover of elaborately engraved ivory and two nose plugs, each
projecting from the nasal cavity in the form of the head and beak
of some fabulous bird (Fig. 36).

Another time Rainey, brushing sand from a skeleton from the
legs upward, came to a miniature carved caribou hoof of ivory
protruding from the pelvic region. As he followed the stem of this
piece upward it became a thin cylinder, amazingly penetrating
the entire spinal canal and threading together each vertebra from
pelvis to neck. Carefully exposing the ribs and each vertebra and
then the bones of the arms and shoulders, Rainey came to the skull,

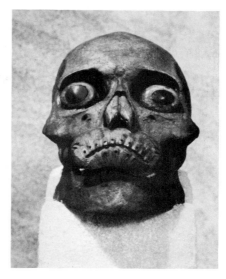

36. Skull from Ipiutak burial, Point Hope. The eye, nose, and mouth cavities have been filled with decorated pieces of jet and ivory.

where the ivory rod emerged from the neck vertebrae, bent slightly forward where the mouth would have been, and protruded as a miniature carved human hand. The most reasonable interpretation was that some magician who was also a skilled anatomist had forced the hooflike tip of the ivory rod somehow into the cervical vertebrae, pushing it through the length of the spinal column. This evidence, together with the sewn-on mouth covers of ivory on several individuals, the nose plugs, and the eyes of ivory, suggests a belief sometimes found among recent Eskimos that the openings of the body should be artificially closed to keep dangerous spirits either in or out of the corpse.

Elaborate composite masks or crests of engraved and sculptured ivory seem to have been placed directly over the body or attached to some undetermined form of tomb cover. The burials were made either in rectangular log tombs deep in the ground or were laid out on the surface, where they slowly became covered with sod. As no time difference could be established, the reasons for these two types of burials have not yet been learned.

Nearly all the burials were accompanied by grave goods. Weapons such as bows and arrows, harpoons, working tools, and other utilitarian objects were included while at the same time many burials contained grotesque objects of no conceivable practical use (Fig. 37). Some were pretzel-like or swivel-like objects somewhat resembling the metal hangings from coats of Tungus shamans of central Siberia. Others were odd and useless travesties of

a) openwork piece

b) pretzel-like object

c) swivel

d) links

e) ornamental chain link;
length, 8 in. (20.3 cm.)

37. Ivory carvings from Ipiutak burial, Point Hope.
(*From Larsen and Rainey, 1948*)

utilitarian objects. An arrowhead of antler, for example, might have some of the barbs pointing in the wrong direction, or be broken in the center by chain links carved all in one piece. These were objects obviously made especially for the burial. All in all, the grave goods and trappings of the Ipiutak affirm an extraordinary emphasis on preparation of the dead and involve an elaborate conception of life after death.

Studies of the Ipiutak skeletons, though not yet complete, indicate that the bones are by no means identical with the best-known and most widespread types of recent Eskimo skeletons but bear, instead, strong points of resemblance to both the pre-Aleut, or earliest skeletons of the Aleutian Islands, and those of recent Yukaghirs, a people living a thousand miles away from Point Hope in Arctic Siberia. Thus, the Ipiutakers appear to have been Mongoloids resembling, in general, recent northern people on both sides of the Strait, but differing in such a way as to suggest that the "Eskimo" physical type may itself have undergone change in recent centuries. The enormous ruined settlement of Ipiutak when first discovered seemed unlikely to be that of Eskimos. Now, after a quarter-century of further research, it still shows curious anomalies of culture and in some ways breaks the continuum we see leading up through time to the modern Eskimos. Nevertheless, from the specific implements and records they unwittingly left, we see the Ipiutak people as more Eskimo than anything else, and leading quite certainly in at least one line of direct ancestry to the modern Eskimos of western Alaska.

THE HOUSES of Ipiutak were of rather uniform size, offering nearly the same living space as do the dwelling houses of recent Point Hope Eskimos. There were no large and aberrant houses to suggest the *kazigis* or men's ceremonial houses of recent times nor were there small dwellings that might indicate some social distinctions between families. In other respects the Ipiutak abode was not arranged like that of Eskimos. To begin with, there was no tunnel, or, if the rectangular pit sometimes found in front of the house floor—suggesting some form of cold trap—really had anything to do with an entryway, it still operated quite differently from the recent Eskimo tunnel. The house was usually square in floor outline but its corners were rounded, as though the roof and

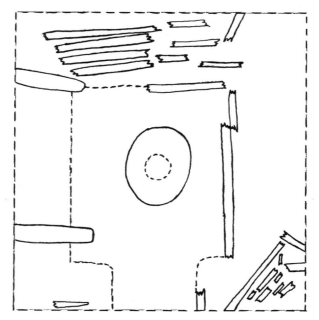

38. Floor plan of Ipiutak House 41, Point Hope. Width, about 13 ft. (4 m.). (*From Larsen and Rainey, 1948*)

walls had been based upon a four-post central construction (Fig. 38). Between these posts lay the hearth, a roughly circular area in most houses where, presumably, the cooking was done and where a fire may even have been kept going throughout all the waking hours, since we find no evidence in Ipiutak of a seal-oil lamp. A man returning to his house may have entered through a hole in the roof, as some of the coastal peoples once did in eastern Siberia. It is likely, however, that at least some of the houses were entered directly from the surface, for the floors as a rule show sleeping benches only on three sides, suggesting that the fourth side functioned as the entrance.

Since there were no signs of pottery vessels, the housewife must have prepared food in more perishable containers. Fragments of sewn birch bark indicate that cylindrical baskets were made and these may have been used in the cooking method whereby heated rocks are placed with food and liquid in containers until the food is cooked. Folded bark baskets have been used thus recently by Indians of the interior of Alaska.

The Ipiutak hunter procured all kinds of seals and many

walruses, both large and small, using toggle harpoons much like those used by recent Eskimos at open leads in the ice. Although boats unquestionably were employed, no direct evidence of them was found at Ipiutak. Hunting devices used with kayaks, in particular, are lacking. A few bones of big whales occurred in the excavations but these could easily have been brought in from carcasses that occasionally washed up on the beach. No whaling harpoon heads, blades, or associated parts were found in houses of Ipiutak culture proper. All these facts convinced Larsen and Rainey that the Ipiutakers had spent a good part of the year away from the sea, hunting for caribou in the treeless slopes and plateaus of the Brooks Range or going even farther into the forests where wood and birch bark might be obtained. The absence of ice-hunting devices such as those used for awaiting seals at their breathing holes, together with the impracticability of heating a house through an open smoke hole in the blizzardy heart of winter, gave strength to the conclusion that coastal residence occurred during the late spring, summer, and early fall, rather than all year round.

39. Knife with inset blade of chert; handle, wood. Ipiutak culture, Point Hope. Length of blade, 3½ in. (9 cm.). (*From Larsen and Rainey, 1948*)

The greatly skilled and meticulous art and technology of Ipiutak, on the other hand, are not easily associated with a highly nomadic people. Arrowheads were made of cylinders of ivory sharpened at the ends and fitted with either thin, triangular end blades or inset, semilunar blades of flinty material. Some of these delicate bifaces showed diagonal flaking on both faces. The manner of insetting side blades both in these small weapons and in knives and elaborate swords departed from any Eskimo patterns then known but conformed to Mesolithic and Neolithic ways of hafting blades in Siberia and other parts of the Old World (Fig. 39).

Engraving art and sculpture more closely resembled that of the Old Bering Sea period of St. Lawrence Island and the Asian coast than of American Eskimos. Animal forms carved in the round, usually of ivory, more often took fantastic and grotesque shapes

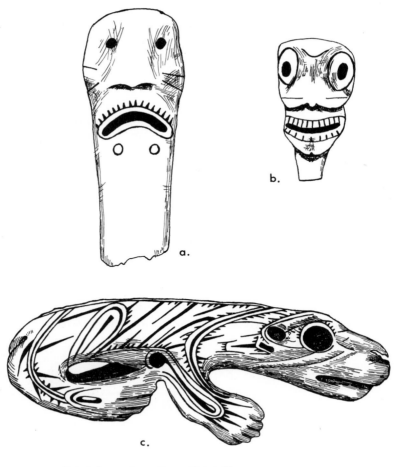

40. Ipiutak carvings from Point Hope:
a) stylized human head, antler; length, 2⅔ in. (6.8 cm.)
b) human face, antler; length, 1½ in. (3.7 cm.)
c) baby walrus, ivory; length about 4 in. (10.4 cm.)
(*From Larsen and Rainey, 1948*)

than realistic ones. The same holds for depictions of the human face or figure (Figs. 35 and 40). Highly stylized and more animal than human, they suggest figures out of a rich mythology. Small death's-heads that fit over the tips of the fingers may have been used as finger masks in some miniature pageantry. In this form of stylization, as well as in the conventional designs used in engraving with fine lines on antler and ivory, Ipiutak resembled Old Bering Sea, but here the resemblance stopped. Most often the designs were quite distinctive from those of St. Lawrence Island,

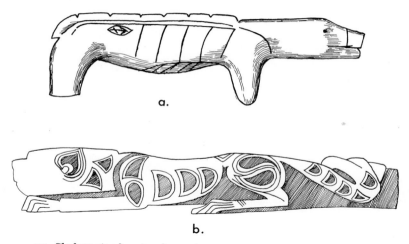

a.

b.

41. Skeletonized animal carvings:
a) Ipiutak polar bear, ivory (*From Larsen and Rainey, 1948*)
b) Asian animal (*From Borovka, 1928*)

though they consisted of curvilinear as well as geometric freehand elements intricately interwoven to cover, generally, the whole surface of a decorated piece. Perhaps the most distinctive of Ipiutak carvings were those of animals. Some had a "life line" leading from the mouth to the region of a heart. These and others were sometimes skeletonized—that is, stressed the ribs and joints, as did some examples of ancient Scythian or Scytho-Siberian art of the region four to six thousand miles away in western Siberia (Fig. 41). Other animals, possibly representing bears, called to mind depictions from the Shang dynasty of China.

After the Ipiutakers of fifteen hundred to two thousand years ago, Point Hope and the neighboring coasts were inhabited by people who hunted whales, cooked their food in vessels of coarse pottery, made their knives and weapon points of polished slate in preference to flint, and dwelt in warm underground houses entered by a cold-defeating tunnel and heated and illuminated by seal-oil lamps. These people Larsen and Rainey named the "Arctic Whale Hunters." If they were descendants of Ipiutakers, the evidence was not clear-cut.

ONE PUZZLING ASPECT of the excavations was the finding of one or two house pits, a series of burials, and a few small midden deposits near to or verging on the Ipiutak site that were clearly re-

42. Point Hope Peninsula from the air. Numerous beach ridges may be discerned.

lated to Ipiutak in culture but differed in enough respects to be considered apart. In these deposits there were definite signs of whaling, though the whaling harpoon heads had been tipped with Ipiutak-like flints. There was also evidence of the use of oil lamps and pottery—items that were missing in the main Ipiutak site— though these were of different forms from those used by more recent Eskimos, and there were a few pieces of rubbed slate along with flints only in part like those of Ipiutak. Calling this "Near Ipiutak," Larsen and Rainey thought that this new body of materials must be intermediate between Ipiutak and the Arctic Whaling culture. Not until many years had passed and the successions of cultures on the beach ridges at Cape Krusenstern were understood did this Near Ipiutak phase fall into its proper place in time as slightly older, not more recent, than Ipiutak.

THE BEACH RIDGES at Cape Krusenstern reminded me from the beginning of those at Point Hope (Figs. 42 and 72). They, also, had broad crests and lay parallel for many miles. Furthermore, at Cape Krusenstern in 1959 we were finding Ipiutak house pits and other signs concentrated on four beaches, 32 through 35, and a check of an aerial photograph of Point Hope showed the Ipiutak concentration there to be on four beach ridges almost identically situated with respect to the stable shoreline to the south. On the northwest side of Point Hope, the spacing between all the most occupied ridges looked remarkably like that at Cape Krusenstern. The main difference between the two localities was that while there were only three or four beach ridges beyond the innermost house pits at Point Hope, at Cape Krusenstern there were seventy-nine. If we were to find at Cape Krusenstern that Near Ipiutak people did not share the same beaches with those of Ipiutak, it should be possible, by searching the older and younger beaches, to learn with certainty where the Near Ipiutakers fitted into the Arctic picture.

(VII)

IPIUTAK BEACHES

A CASUAL WALKER across the beach ridges and swales of Cape Krusenstern would find it hard to believe that a trained archeologist who had been fortunate enough to discover a small village of house pits could subsequently lose it so effectively that it remained lost for two years. Yet I managed to do just that. Only after many a puzzled walk did I happen upon the buried village again, two years after having originally discovered it. When I first came upon the village in 1958, I had left my companions digging the Western Thule House 7 (p. 82) and had walked some distance inland to explore and test for signs of older habitations. I was now walking along Beach 35, the highest crest in that part of the series, scanning the lower ridge tops on either side for signs of house pits. Sometimes one can more easily detect a shallow surface rim from a distance than by walking directly over it. Most of the signs of former digging had proved to be caches and other features smaller than houses but then, looking seaward across some low, neighboring beach ridges mostly covered even to their crests with clumps and continuous patches of low willows, I saw what looked suspiciously like a regular outline of willow growth.

Walking through an acre or so of these willows that reached only to my knees or waist, I emerged in a squarish pit fringed by shrubs. Swinging the long-handled shovel from my shoulder, I cut a square into the thick moss and peat near the center of the pit and, bracing myself, lifted one edge to tip it over. The underside of the foot-thick block carried in its rootlets and fibers the unmistakable chert chips from an old floor. Among the chips were a side scraper and the fragment of a bifaced knife or point. I placed these objects on the upturned sod and turned back through the willows toward my beach-top roadway as there was obviously no need for further testing. Christening it "House 40" in my notebook, I knew that as soon as there was time we must excavate this and the other probable house pits that I saw in the vicinity. They should give us, I surmised from their position on an intermediate beach, a glimpse into the transition period between the Thule and the older cultures. While I might have marked the site with a stake, it seemed needless at the time because the large pit and the neighboring small ones loomed large as I walked among them. They lay on Beach 29 or 30, about half a mile inland from Thule House 7 on Beach 10. That the little village could not be found again that season or the next was due to its position in the lee of the several miles of higher beach crests from which one willow patch looked very much like another.

In the meantime, despite frustrating searches the next summer, 1959, we found enough to do on Beaches 32 to 35 to keep us more than reasonably occupied. It was just twenty years to the week after my first archeological venture at Point Hope in 1939, when we had found the ancient Ipiutak settlement, that I found myself again poised to dig an Ipiutak site, this time on the beach ridges at Cape Krusenstern. Several house pits and more problematical small dents and mounds had been discerned the previous summer, and the objects found in limited tests left no doubt that the only people who had camped, dug, and built extensively on the high crest culminating in Beach 35 were people like the mysterious old Point Hope Ipiutakers. We spoke of this crest, which stood ten feet above sea level, as the "Ipiutak Beach."

Our midsummer landing in 1959 was that inauspicious one from aboard the *Pauline*. Bill Simmons, Sam Friedman, and I had now joined forces with Hans-Georg Bandi, who had flown from Switzerland via the polar route and met us at Kotzebue. Bandi, director of the Berne Historical Museum and author with Maringer of *Art of the Ice Age,* had excavated lake villages in Switzerland, and, on a previous venture to the Arctic, had joined Jørgen Meldgaard in digging a Thule site in East Greenland. After a few weeks he fell easily into the American vernacular that we share with the Eskimos each summer in Alaska, but at first he spoke rather formal English with a strong German accent. The Eskimos, interested as they are in foreign ways, quickly took up not only some of Bandi's strongly accented English but some actual words of his German. Bandi returned the compliment by asking them for Eskimo phrases.

One evening after work we were somewhat startled to see a porcupine walking determinedly westward down the beach just above the edge of the water, stopping now and then to stare in the direction of Siberia. We hastened to the shore, pointing our cameras. The porcupine was not to be easily put off. He paused to draw himself up and spread his quills to impress us with his ferocity, but seemed quickly to give that up as a hopeless job and continued plodding along the beach. Almond and Murphy Downey explained to Bandi that this was a porcupine. Bandi was delighted. He had not seen one before. "*Stachelschwein,*" he said, "that is how we call it in my language." The Eskimos were charmed. They had Bandi repeat the word until he and they became weak with laughter. Meanwhile the porcupine, whose nearest natural home in the spruce forest was at least twenty miles away, was continuing on his way to the point. We toyed with the possibility that he was planning to swim to Siberia or, like a solitary lemming, drown himself in the sea. "*Stachelschwein,*" shouted the Eskimos after the ambling beast until he was no longer in sight.

WORK those first few days suffered from the poor location of our camp—the eastern extremity of the beach ridge series where the *Pauline* had had to deposit us. At first we explored in small teams or singly, hoping to find at this end the same rich spread of sites that we knew to exist on one ridge after another at the western end of the Cape, but we soon discovered that a great deal of walking was required to find a few hearths and other surface features which, when found, yielded little. However, Bandi and I were both eager to excavate large houses of Ipiutak origin to learn more of their construction—which appeared to vary basically from other houses of the Eskimo region—so we were determined to dig something of that culture here before moving camp.

In contrast to the prominent "Ipiutak ridge" farther west along the Cape, the ridge tops here were poorly differentiated, being not much more than wide, gravelly strips separated by deep sphagnum bogs that flattened out near their tips. The sea, evidently having cut back at this point, had built as an outer beach a barrier at least a yard higher than these vestigial ridges. A series of large squares and smaller depressions showing through the sod nevertheless proved to contain flints. We excavated two of the larger sites and found their floors to lie on what had been the original top of the beach ridge. Ancient builders had apparently removed only the sod, stacking it at the walls of their square dwellings. Fireplaces marked by charcoal and ash lay roughly at the center, and a darkened segment of deep floor led from this point toward the sea, indicating that the entrance had been through a simple doorway rather than through a tunnel or storm shed. Nearly all organic material had rotted away, but from the forms of side blades, discoidal scrapers, arrowpoints, and other flints, mainly flaked of blue, gray, and black chert, we identified the site as one of Ipiutak culture. As the shallow pits indicated a little, though not much, recessing of floors, we judged the dwellings to have been reasonably substantial huts rather than simple tents. The sizable number of flinty artifacts and chips lying on the floors indicated that the Ipiutak people must have returned to their same huts over and over during the milder part of each year.

Hoping to find deeper floors bearing materials like those at the Point Hope site, we tested several long, rectangular or slitlike depressions on the surfaces of the same ridges. One of these turned out to be an empty cache pit about five feet long by three feet wide. The decayed logs could be brushed free enough to show that it had been a structure of cribbed poles floored with bark or skin. Since caches most often are disappointing in this area, I expected little more that same day when I cut a strip across another such depression and trowelled down to see if it, too, had an empty floor. Nothing more than sterile gravel met my efforts to a depth of two feet, but I decided to test further with the shovel before leaving the scene. My test, fortunately, was gentle, for the shovel blade grated on a substance neither rock nor wood. Now I called for assistance, and two of us cleared sod from a wide area and began systematically to clean away the gravel in an ever lowering level. Unfortunately, squirrels had been ahead of us during some centuries of the past, removing nearly all traces of another cachelike structure. We could see, though, that the original dimensions of what walls we found were like those of the previously excavated cache. But this one was not empty.

Trowelling brought to view a coffee-colored spot that enlarged upon brushing and then revealed itself as a human skull. Complete with its mandible, this skull was remarkably well preserved in view

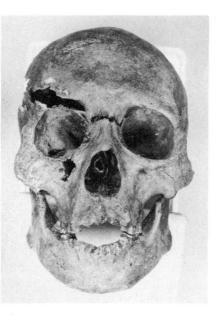

43. Skull of Ipiutak man, Cape Krusenstern, 1959.

of the scattered remainder of the burial (Fig. 43). Most of the ribs, finger bones, and toe bones of the skeleton were missing, but what remained of the bones of the arms, legs, pelvis, and vertebral column indicated it to have been a muscular man of middle age whose teeth, though sound, were worn nearly to the gums, as is often the case with Eskimos who chew gritty food. When we found grave offerings, too, we could be sure this was not a supply cache but a burial. The grave offerings included a fragment of a large, broken lip plug of jet, and leaf-thin, expertly flaked arrowpoints from perhaps a whole quiverfull of arrows. Only one ivory carving was recovered, but this was a large handle, possibly for a drum (Fig. 44), profusely decorated on all of its surfaces with the fine,

44. Incised ivory handle, Ipiutak culture, Cape Krusenstern.

45. George Moore standing beside weasel, which is carrying a boat (top) and motor (right).

curved-line decoration so well known at the Point Hope Ipiutak site.

Not even this encouragement, however, justified our lingering on at the eastern end of the beaches. Almond Downey and his crew had now arrived and I had only to say the word and we would all pitch in and load the boat. As I was preparing to do so, a unique means of moving camp presented itself. We knew something exciting was going on when we saw Ruth Downey and the children come running from camp shouting: "Weasel coming." Remembering the porcupine, I wondered at their agitation. Then the puzzling roar of a motor was heard. It was an unfamiliar sound, like neither plane nor boat. As we looked at one another in bafflement, a huge "thing" rose suddenly from the first beach ridge and lumbered in our direction. It really *was* a weasel!—one of those military tracked vehicles designed for both water and land—and now in sinister fashion it was making a high road of our culture-bearing ridge tops. When it neared, two men jumped out: Dr. George Moore and his assistant, John Cole, who were members of a geological crew employed by the Atomic Energy Commission to study the topography and shorelines of the region (Fig. 45). They had traveled seventy miles from their base at Cape Thompson and soon became as enthusiastic over the possibility of our being able to date beach ridges by the included archeology as we were over getting a geologist's point of view.

First, however, I mentioned our projected move up the coast, and Moore insisted that we employ the weasel. Unloading its "cargo"—a metal boat and motor—and thus freeing both decks of the strange craft, we managed, in two loads, to move the greater part of our camp to the long-anticipated site three miles closer to the tip of the Cape where the tower stands. Relieved now to see the geologists leave their destructive machine for a more minute reconnaissance on foot, the rest of us turned to the Ipiutak beach series again, looking for a substantial winter house pit to dig. The main Ipiutak series, on Ridges 32–5, now lay more than half a mile inland from Beach 1 at the seashore, and we soon found two or three clusters of pits suggesting underground houses and caches.

One of these, now smoothly grown over with firm sod, contained two prominent rims of earth surrounding deep and wide circular pits. Perplexed by the circles, we marked off a rectangular area large enough to encompass whatever lay below. After removing much unprofitable earth, we began to strike pay dirt. Wall logs, first in the form of matted fibers intertwined with rootlets, began to straighten out and point to four definite corners. The farther down the excavation proceeded, the clearer the alignment of these logs became, even though individually none retained a solid or even a rounded form. At last we reached a stage where the matted material took on the consistency and plane of a floor, which was entered into our records as House 17, an arbitrary number, yet showing the house to be farther from the sea than the lower-numbered Thule Houses 4 through 8. Now working with trowels and brooms, we exposed what we thought were the bottom logs of the structure and the last walked-on floor (Fig. 46). Strangely, however, the few artifacts that we now obtained, though definitely of Ipiutak type, diminished toward this level "floor." Neither a fireplace nor irregularities came to view.

Considering the smooth and photogenic excavation one day, Bandi and I concluded that this was indeed a strange house. Nowhere in the floor could we discern the stain of a supporting post. With a flash of belated insight, we turned to our trowels again and began in different parts of the house to scrape squares into the floor. Only a few centimeters deeper we saw the cause of our dilemma. The supposed floor had been no more than the rotted fallen roof and wall logs bound together, as in a felting process, with generations of horizontal rootlets. From here on, all excavation was a bonanza. The artifacts, stone and organic, lay abundantly on a blackened and well-trodden floor. Near each corner we found the molds of heavy support posts (Fig. 47). The original posts had stood three feet or more inside the house, which now clearly measured eighteen by twenty-two feet from corner to corner. The heavy posts thus described a smaller rectangle within the larger one, and now we found, as in nested boxes, a third rectangle at the house center. This was a four-by-six-foot hearth area in which a deep deposit of ash and charcoal testified to many an ancient meal and warm evening at home.

Try as we could, we found no sign of an entryway at ground level. Rather, the house was undoubtedly entered by means of a ladder through the smoke hole in the roof. In the northeast corner of the floor, we found that the now empty space of a rectangle bordered by one of the inner support columns had been boarded over, perhaps as a cover for a storage space under the floor.

46. Hans-Georg Bandi sketching floor plan of Ipiutak House 17, Cape Krusenstern, 1959. The small pedestal of earth (at left in photo) was left unexcavated so that we could observe its soil profile.

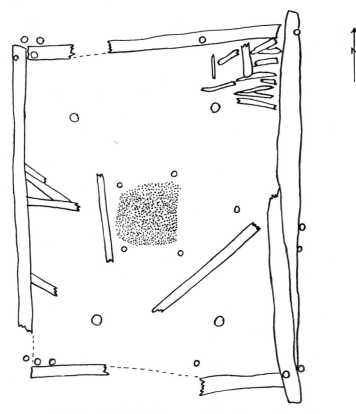

47. Floor plan of House 17, Cape **Krusenstern. Size** approximately 18 × 22 ft.

The house was considerably larger **in floor plan than** any of those at Point Hope (twice as large as **the average one** there— see Fig. 38) yet contained only artifacts of Ipiutak **culture,** showing that the old Ipiutak people had built **their dwellings** in a surprising variety of forms. This and the **shallow houses** we had dug a few miles east promised from the **Cape Krusenstern** Ipiutak beaches something more than a mere **repetition of things** learned at the Point Hope site.

Turning now to the second pit, House 18, **we found** another dwelling of the same outline, though the **precise structure** had been too much damaged by ground squirrel **activity for us to** ascertain minute details of the floor. The smaller **squares and hummocks** in the vicinity of the two large houses **appeared to be** those of summer huts.

48. 1959 camp on first beach, Cape Krusenstern. Chukchi Sea is in background.

OUR OWN new campsite was felicitous indeed. Returning to it singly or in small groups after work in the late afternoon, we could not help but admire the play of sunlight on this bit of civilization that arose from the monotony of the first beach ridge (Fig. 48). Wind gave a gala glitter to the Downeys' clothesline, usually a row of diapers whipping about like a ship's pennants. The large white tents cupped themselves into the wind and bulged to the lee, and the row of small tents, green, blue, and yellow, stretched unevenly away as our suburbs. As we came closer, dogs, who served no useful purpose during the summer but were cared for by their masters until they became important again in the fall with the coming of ice, raised a chorus of welcome, half howl and half song. On good days we washed ourselves in the not too salty sea water at the sandy beach edge and on bad days, when the surf ran high, we washed in pond water splashed hastily into tin basins at the side of the work tent. Cleaned up, we gathered inside the tent to talk over the day's events until Ruth Downey placed pots and platters of steaming food upon our makeshift table. The fare was often mainly from cans—meatballs and gravy, tomatoes, and peas—but we sometimes enjoyed such uncanned staples as potatoes and bread. Occasionally, when the sea had become calm enough to set the nets overnight, we ate fresh salmon or, if the herd visited us and a reindeer could be purchased, we might have as many roasts and steaks as we could eat for a week.

After dinner, some cleaned and marked artifacts while others retired to their tents to read and write in their journals. Now and then Julian Towkshjea, Almond's hunting partner who worked for us that season, would drop in to our tent with his guitar (Fig. 49). Julian, we felt, was a fine musician within his limits, these being that he sang only Western and hillbilly songs. By listening to records, he had learned to imitate to perfection the style and precise intonation of each of his favorite stars, while in ordinary English conversation his accent was as pronounced as that of other Eskimos. Beginning with "Home on the Range," the sounds he uttered were the flawless sounds of the Texas Panhandle. We were fortunate indeed if Julian and Almond together rendered their favorites. Shifting tempo easily from the West to the hills of Tennessee, their accents changed faultlessly. On one memorable evening we reached our musical zenith. While canvas flapped and wind screamed at the tent poles, all of us joined Julian and Almond in a hill song while the baby cried competitively in the adjoining tent and all the dogs, tied beyond, loudly voiced their protests.

AFTER EXPOSING the two big Ipiutak houses, we turned our energies to other kinds of excavation during the rest of the 1959 season, but the Ipiutak problem came strongly into focus again the following year. That year (1960), while Jim traveled with relatives in Mexico, my wife Bets, our two younger children Ann and Russell, and I drove up the Alcan highway to Fairbanks. Bill Simmons, now

49. Julian Towkshjea with his guitar.

a seasoned archeologist of three summers in Alaska, met us at Kotzebue. From there we traveled by small boat with our Eskimo companions of previous years and established camp at the western end of the beach ridge sequence at Cape Krusenstern a mile north of the tower. One final, new member of the expedition was yet to arrive. We intended to excavate within an easy walk of the seashore a whole string of house pits and other features ranging from late prehistoric back to Denbigh times of five thousand years ago. In view of previous samplings and the large collection of Ipiutak artifacts yet to be studied, the Ipiutak beaches were not our primary concern that year.

Before we had started work, a float plane landed three miles away in sheltered water on the south side of the cape. Simmons and I took a shortcut acoss a segment of the Ipiutak ridge, Beach 35, to see if it had brought our new digging assistant from the States. The plane had arrived and taken off again before we reached it, having deposited its passenger—a muscular figure with a sea bag across one shoulder who was now striding toward us over the beach ridges. There is always a little apprehension about welcoming someone we do not know to a dig in Alaska, but a good look at Douglas Anderson dispelled any doubts. Within minutes we were all talking archeology as though we had worked together for years. And showing the Ipiutak ridge to a newcomer is always a privilege. Its disturbances, even though carpeted with sod, are readily recognizable, even to untrained eyes, as man-made eruptions on the surface of an otherwise smooth ridge top.

Pausing in one such area to catch our breath, I began explaining the signs on the ground to Anderson, and as I did so I began to convince myself that we should dig this particular site. More certainly than had last year's House-17 group, this one, a cluster of disturbances, gave promise of belonging together, possibly as a community occupied all at one time. Since Anderson was to continue his graduate studies at Brown University the following years and had excavated both in an Iron Age village of Germany and in Indian deposits along the Columbia River in Washington, I felt that he might well cut his teeth in the Arctic by excavating this site. During the following days Anderson proved to be a careful operator. Working with Murphy Downey and another Eskimo, Robert Lee, he contour-mapped the site and laid out a large square over what we optimistically designated House 30, having skipped several unused numbers. Previously we had assigned the next consecutive number to each house pit as it was tested and found worth digging. Now, though, because of the quantity of as yet untested pits of like age, we began to set aside blocks of numbers to be assigned when tested and proved worthwhile.

At the end of their first day's sod-stripping, Doug and Murphy appeared somewhat disillusioned with their dig. The area exposed was not one of clean sand streaked with an occasional stain of early building logs. Rather, it was a slimy, black and yellow surface of half-thawed charcoal and ash. This was a house that had burned. Far from sharing the dismay of the smudged diggers, I encouraged them to go on. A burned house, if it has not been deliberately fired by its owners—an unlikely prospect in view of the shortage of wood on these shores—should contain in it some of the complete and treasured tools and other belongings of the residents who had been forced to flee their house in panic.

After the first two or three days the digging became less of a chore, and the outlines of the house showed it as large and square. Deeper in the ground, logs of charcoal remained more or less intact, embedded in earth of increasing cleanness. When, finally, the floor was traced to its limits and freed of dirt, we could see that the original excavation, no deeper than two feet below the top of the beach, had included no obvious opening in the wall. The house had been about eighteen feet square, its low benches extending four feet in width from all sides about a large, square central area (the walked-on floor of the house) in the middle of which lay the fireplace. By elimination, we saw that the entrance to this house, like that of House 17, was over the fireplace. We guessed that the old Ipiutak residents descended through a square smoke hole by means of a ladder or notched pole.

We were not disappointed in the preservation by fire. Lying in the floor debris were a few undecayed organic pieces. Foremost among these was a pair of snow goggles—an elaborate ivory carving in one piece (Fig. 50). We marveled at the careful workmanship with which the piece had been fashioned and particularly at the tasteful design covering its whole outer surface. The whittling and chiseling out of this hard organic substance at the inner edges and concavity had been done to fit some particular man. His nose must have been long and straight and his face extremely broad with wide cheekbones—a face, in short, not unlike that of a large Eskimo of today. Where Western Thule goggles (Fig. 24a) had been provided with narrow slits, these had round holes half an inch in diameter, each outlined on the outer surface by engraved concentric circles suggesting the shape of the whole human eye. Whether intended as such or not, a comma-shaped mark at the inner edge of each such "eye" suggested the tear duct. At either edge of the nose channel were similar markings, the dots filled with plugs of jet.

The whole design, while differing from any to be seen in Point Hope Ipiutak carvings, was nevertheless classed as Ipiutak rather than as any other decorative style known in the Arctic area. A meticulous touch was seen in the way the line holes at the ends—for attaching the cord that bound the goggles to the head—were concealed. By grooving into the edge with an extremely narrow instrument, the maker had produced a lip that he drilled for the cord only from the inner side. This kind of grooving might have been done with a tool like the burins of an earlier period. True burins of flinty material seem to have been unknown to the Ipiutak people, although a so-called "burin-like implement"—a thin slab of hard slate ground on both faces to a high polish and provided at the working end with two narrow, ground surfaces meeting to form a miniature cutting edge—did occur in House 30. While such instruments are more common in earlier sites of the region, we

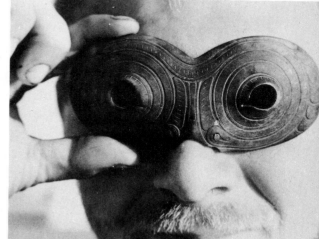

50. Douglas Anderson trying on carved ivory snow goggles of Ipiutak culture, Cape Krusenstern.

51. Burin-like implement, Ipiutak culture, Cape Krusenstern. Tip of hard slate, handle of wood. Length, 4⅛ in. (10.4 cm.).

found one here still firmly attached to its wooden handle (Fig. 51), offering proof that burin-like implements were hafted similarly to recent Eskimo end-bladed iron knives that are used for splitting antler and ivory. Another exceptionally fine implement, without its onetime handle, was a large, highly polished adz head of hard slate, blunt at one end and ground to a sharp edge at the other (Fig. 52).

As Anderson and his assistants were removing the last traces of cultural material from House 30, they noticed that the floor had been disturbed in three large patches. Since these disturbances must have been made shortly before the house had fallen in embers, Anderson began cautiously to excavate what now appeared to be intrusive material that had fallen into one of the holes. A foot deeper he came to a layer of animal bones. He soon comprehended, however, from the peculiar shape of one of the bones, that this was no animal but the skeleton of a human being, quite certainly a child. Now all of us gathered to watch, or take part in, this uncommon excavation. Very gradually, this as well as the other two disturbances were opened out by trowel and brush, exposing a human tragedy of some two thousand years ago.

The first skeleton, at a south corner of the house, was that of a child perhaps six years old. The arm bones and skull lay just under the base log of the house, while the largely decayed remainder of the skeleton lay within the house outline. As the last grains of sand were cleared from the arm bones, we saw that the child had held in its hand the wooden handle of an adz. While the wood left only

52. Adz head of hard slate, Ipiutak culture, Cape Krusenstern. Length, 11 in. (28 cm.).

a dark outline in the sand, the antler sleeve with its inserted greenstone adz blade was intact (Fig. 53). Apparently the child had died while digging a hole under the southeast base log of the house. At the northeast corner a similar pattern unfolded. Again the skeleton, less well preserved than the first, was that of a small child. The head and right arm bones lay under the house corner and another adz head with its greenstone blade lay in a position corresponding to that of the first. The third disturbance in the floor lay at the west side of the house. Here the skeleton was that of an adult, clearly a woman, even though the skull and the extremities were mostly decayed. A third well-preserved adz sleeve and blade lay in front of her as though she, too, had been digging under a foundation log.

We now saw a nearly complete picture of the last minutes of life within House 30. A woman with two children had been somehow trapped inside their home by spreading flames. Perhaps they had slept while the cooking-fire spread; perhaps they had been unable or unwilling to climb to safety through a flaming smoke

53. Douglas Anderson exposing the skeleton of an Ipiutak child, Cape Krusenstern. The skull is beyond his brush, and an adz head is at the right.

hole. Giving each child an adz and taking one herself, the woman had chosen to dig out of the burning house. All three had made some progress before suffocating in the smoke, but even had they been able to dig for much longer they would probably have been stopped by frozen ground, for the deeply excavated house indicated residence during the winter.

But why did the woman not wrap the children and push them through the smoke hole even if she could not escape that way herself? One further clue encouraged us to reconstruct more of the scene. Lying within the discolored earth that marked some decayed bone of the woman's pelvis lay an arrowpoint. While this might have been a flint that happened to fall into the excavation, it might also have been the head of an arrow shot into the woman from above. Until recently, Eskimos of the Kotzebue Sound region maintained a fear of attack by Indians or half-fabulous "Arctic people" who lived somewhere north of the Brooks Range. Elderly Kobuk River men told me in the 1940's how they had been conditioned to expect surprise attacks. An enemy always approached in darkness (which came early in winter), poured burning oil through the skylight, and waited at the entrance for the panic-stricken householders to emerge. Thus, in thinking about the tragedy of House 30, those of us who studied the evidence visualized just such an event—an enemy firing his arrow at the woman he has surprised while she prepares a meal at her fire, then pouring oil into the flames to make sure no one ever uses the house again. We can understand from this what a woman with her children might have felt as she weighed the terror of flames against the greater terror of the enemy waiting outside.

THE SURFACE of the beach ridge for dozens of yards on either side of House 30 was ridged and pitted in the same way as had been the house site itself. The deep moss growing over all the disturbances indicated them to be the same age as the large house. In hope of learning more about an Ipiutak community, we set about excavating as much of the site as seemed worthwhile. Five rectangular areas, much smaller than House 30, had been dwellings of another kind. Small (some no more than ten feet square), they had the same plan as our Ipiutak summer houses of the preceding season. The builders had again merely removed sod within the predetermined house-wall area and stacked it at the margins. Whether pole-roofed or not we were unable to tell, but in at least one excavation a brown stain just beneath the present sod had extended up from the edge of the floor at a steep angle, as a wall might have done. In one of the best-preserved spots of this layer we found hair which our native workers thought was that of a polar bear, suggesting that roofing materials were sometimes made of animal skins. Four of these houses had fireplaces, and lying clustered together near the north wall of one that had burned were the decayed remains of three skulls. Whether or not three more people had been trapped by flames we could not tell.

A short distance southeast of House 30, still on our Ipiutak ridge, Beach 35, we excavated a peculiar, squarish, domed-over area about the same size as the small dwellings but which had had a different use. In it were masses of broken or disjointed bones, mainly from the heads of hundreds of animals. A count of the identifiable bones showed 1,162 of small seal, 338 of the large bearded seal or oogruk, only 4 of caribou, 7 of polar bear, and 3 of walrus. Comparing the fragments to the bones of modern animals, we discovered that the cache held the parts of no fewer than 156 bearded seals and 566 small seals. As to the reasons for gathering so many heads of seals within narrow confines and covering them in such a way as to preserve them from scattering by animals or the elements, we surmised that the cache stood for some religious or magical practice concerning game animals. Recent Eskimos have sometimes returned seal bones to the sea, and the eighteenth-century missionary Cranz might have been describing Ipiutakers when he said of his Greenland parishioners: "The heads of seals must not be fractured, nor must they be thrown into the sea, but be piled in a heap before the door, that the souls of the seals may not be enraged and scare their brethren from the coast." Other mounds containing piles of seal bones, but in far smaller quantities, were identified at intervals along the whole seven miles of the Ipiutak beach sequence.

Not the least interesting small excavation in the vicinity of House 30 was a burial. While we could never be sure that this burial belonged to the house group, since it contained no definable grave goods, the presence of fragments of Ipiutak flints at the base of the sod suggested that it did. A tall man was buried there; he had been over six feet, judging from the length of the leg bones,

54. Skeleton of an Ipiutak man nick-named "Old Smiley" by expedition members, Cape Krusenstern.

yet his square face and keeled skull were more typical of eastern than western Eskimos (Fig. 54). The burial chamber itself was identical to underground caches on these and later beaches. Since the corpse had been strongly flexed at the knees—to fit it into the confined space of the box—we wondered if it had been literally put away in a cache. Frozen ground in winter could have made interment difficult, and a converted cache may have been a satisfactory solution for a burial chamber. The imposing individual whose skeleton it contained may even have been a survivor of the ill-fated House 30 who was eventually buried in his own back yard.

WE NOW had reason to believe that the Ipiutak pattern of settlement at Cape Krusenstern was much more varied than it was at Point Hope, and the excavation of whole communities of large and small dwellings and accompanying structures became a main goal. It was a stroke of good luck, then, while we were still digging in the House-30 group, that I rediscovered the village I had lost two years before in 1958. It happened as I was taking a shortcut from the south beach to camp. A few beaches seaward of the main Ipiutak Beach 35, I found myself walking again through willows and into a large, rectangular house pit. My first reaction was to wonder how we could have missed so obvious a pit in this crucial area. Then I saw an upturned sod block with flints lying upon it and realized that I had finally happened again on the lost village. Scarcely trusting my memory a second time. I built a prominent monument of sod blocks and willow sticks before continuing with the day's work.

A little later that season we began to excavate the re-found site, the House-40 group, on Beach 29 or 30 (it was not always possible to be specific about numbers because in some localities several ridges merged together). Contrary to my earlier hopes that it might furnish a link between Ipiutak and Thule cultures because of its location on a ridge more forward than the known Ipiutak beaches, it turned out to be nearly a duplicate of the House-30 group of Beach 35. Besides a big, deep house with elevated benches, three small sites proved to be "summer houses" like those of the other Ipiutak settlements. A fourth small house lacked a fireplace but contained great quantities of seal bones. The proportions were similar to those of the earlier bone caches except that here skulls were missing.

More than anything else, House 40 was distinguished by its etched pebbles. Ordinarily, when lunchtime came the natives were the first to leave the excavation and begin opening the cans and bags in which we brought lunch to the site, and those of us who kept notes and records paused a moment to cast a summary eye over the day's progress. One day, however, Anderson and I were sitting before a fire of willow twigs waiting for coffee to boil when we noticed that Julian and Robert were still standing in the partially excavated House 40 examining some object and talking briskly in Eskimo. Asked what they had found, Julian called back: "This must be their writing," holding up a pebble. The previous year I had found a flat pebble of about the same size with a bar of geometric design cut into it and had cautioned everyone to look for marked pebbles in these sites, so I reached for this one with some anticipation.

An intricate and balanced design on one face of the flat pebble had been drawn with a fine, sharp point. Its purpose could not have been to catch the eye, as this could better have been done by painting the rock; rather, the lines were so thin as to be seen with difficulty if the stone were not held in a contrasting light. My first impression was that the drawing represented a reindeer covered fore and aft with antlers. Again, I saw it as ferns growing from a table top with small glyphs spread among the fronds (Fig. 55). This was scarcely comparable to the simple, abbreviated design on last year's pebble. It was an elaborate symbol, perhaps representing a complicated idea. An ideograph? Turned upside down, it could have been a character in Chinese writing. I was reminded also of drawings on birch bark made by adolescent Yukaghir. Boys and girls of that Arctic Asian group used, not too long ago—perhaps even now—to construct complex symbols on bark using treelike figures, with intricate hatching, to express oddly detailed romantic ideas. We all gathered round and speculated at some length on this intriguing design.

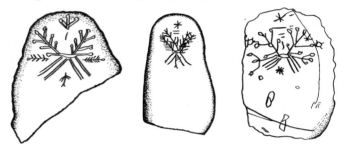

55. Three etched pebbles from House 40, Ipiutak culture. Length of middle one, 1½ in. (4 cm.).

Following lunch hour, all hands began to examine pebbles, and we were not disappointed. Time and again the hard, flat, fine-grained pebbles of kinds common to the beach contained, on one or both faces, the curious basic design of the first, though with infinite variations. All of us tended to orient the pebbles in the same direction—that is, with what appeared to be the two, four, or six legs of a table or an animal pointing down and the branching tree, feather, or fernlike appendages up, as though growing. Sometimes the tree figures held circles or rhomboids at their tips reminding us of light bulbs. The detached elements between branches took the form of short or long dashes, asterisks, or more complex characters like those in Oriental writing. Before the House-40 group was completed, we had recovered more than one hundred etched pebbles, by far the majority from the large House 40 itself. As the season wore on, a few etched pebbles similar in basic design were recovered also from the House-30 group and one or two isolated house excavations elsewhere on the Ipiutak beach. While all at first appeared unique, and I tended to refer them directly to Asia, I soon learned that two had been excavated in houses of the Point Hope Ipiutak site and that there existed a general resemblance between the etched pebbles at both sites and certain Point Hope stylized faces etched in ivory.

At the suggestion of Helge Larsen in a letter to me, we began to turn the pebbles around, causing the "trees" to point downward and the "legs" up. In this position they more nearly resembled the Point Hope ivory objects. While the Cape Krusenstern etchings on stone may thus have had direct ties with Point Hope Ipiutak, they may also have had other relationships. Some strikingly similar forms appeared in the earliest writings of China—in the ideographs etched on the surfaces of "oracle" or augury bones in 2000 B.C. Even farther afield, one sees tree designs on triangular or square bases on certain ancient coins of India. Carved onto rock walls along the Amur River of southwestern Siberia are grotesque faces, the more stylized of which also recall the style of our engravings. But we need not go so far from home. Etched and painted pebbles exist in certain sites of southern Alaska, notably on Kodiak Island and the Cook Inlet sites, and, beyond these, a few decorated pebbles along the Pacific coast of Alaska and Canada lead southward to tree- or feather-like engravings that have been found on pebbles in the Columbia River Basin. Whatever the remote relationship between all these areas, the etched pebbles at Cape Krusenstern probably had local significance, possibly symbolizing prayers or divinations.

Since the House-40 group, by its location on forward beaches, may be the latest Ipiutak settlement at the Cape, the designs of the pebbles appear to have grown in importance through the centuries. Yet, while we have extended our knowledge of Ipiutak culture at the vast uniform site of Point Hope with the series of small communities at Cape Krusenstern, some of which were surely occupied through the coldest time of winter, we are still faced with an important question about Ipiutak culture: why did it lose all its remarkable specializations including its elaborate art and its fine, but old-fashioned, stone technology?

Though we have as yet no firm answer, we do know of the direction of the change. Two house pits at Cape Krusenstern excavated on still more seaward beaches (numbered in the midtwenties) showed an intermediate stage between Ipiutak and Western Thule. The flakeknives, side scrapers, and thin bifaced blades of Ipiutak continued to be used, but the people had now become whale hunters, slate grinders, and pottery makers—in short, their crafts were not so much like those of Ipiutakers as they were like Birnirk people, whose sites were known at Point Barrow and Point Hope and who lived about A.D. 700. Their way of life ultimately changed to the staid and utilitarian Thule culture.

The more important question about Ipiutak culture, of course, is how did it originate? Who were the first to put together the successful pattern of food-getting and the bizarre art and magic that for some centuries at the beginning of our era dominated the coasts of Alaska? In the excellent monograph Larsen and Rainey wrote describing the Point Hope sites, they concluded that while Ipiutak had an antiquated look as compared with the later pottery-making, whale-hunting cultures, and might thus be called "paleo-Eskimo," it also drew directly on the reservoirs of art and style of far-distant central Asia. One difficulty in bringing Ipiutak culture mainly from the interior of the Old World, however, was that it closely resembled in other important respects the earliest known cultures, Old Bering Sea (p. 153) and its preceding Okvik culture of two thousand or more years ago, cultures that did not themselves contain resemblances to those of central Asia.

Whatever its distant affinities, I had begun to doubt that Ipiutak culture could be entirely separated from the older sites that we knew from tests and excavations existed on earlier beach ridges at Cape Krusenstern. In a search for similar flintwork from which Ipiutak pieces might have evolved, we could look in the beaches of sand and gravel paralleling the Ipiutak ridge but farther from the sea. If similar but earlier flintwork were found on older beaches, this might show that there had been no great influxes of new people but that the cultures of the area had changed gradually over thousands of years as they absorbed new styles and points of view from all directions.

(VIII)

WIDENING
HORIZONS

O N NEITHER SIDE of the Ipiutak ridge at Cape Krusenstern did
we find signs either of the Old Bering Sea culture of St. Lawrence Island and neighboring Asia or of the Dorset culture of eastern
Canada and Greenland. Since, however, Ipiutak culture held many
general traits in common with those presumed equally old cultures,
we puzzled over what manner of interchange had brought about the
likenesses. The man who named both the Old Bering Sea and the
Dorset culture was the Canadian ethnographer, Diamond Jenness.
Brought up in New Zealand and trained in anthropology at Oxford,
Jenness joined the Canadian Arctic expedition under Vilhjalmur
Stefansson in 1913 and during the next four years lived with the
isolated Copper Eskimos of the Coronation Gulf region of Arctic
Canada (Map 4) until he was prepared to write in full about
their way of life. Having become deeply involved in the problem of
Eskimo cultural origins, he decided that the most vital area in which
to study language and archeology was the vicinity of Bering Strait,
where the islands and headlands ought to hold the evidence of any
"tribes" that might have "migrated since Pleistocene time from Asia
to America across Bering Strait or from America to Asia."

One such island, Little Diomede (Maps 1 and 7; the other,
larger island, Big Diomede, belongs to the U.S.S.R.) is a flat-
topped mountain of almost solid rock rising 1,300 feet above the
sea like a great chocolate cake. The archeology there, Jenness found
in 1926, had been severely limited by the amount of soil available

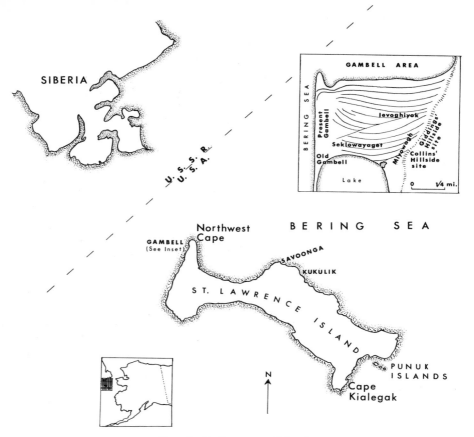

Map 6. St. Lawrence Island

for a village. The present settlement of a few Eskimo families is located on the west side of the island, where a fringe of gravel beach is cluttered with sharp boulders that have fallen from towering cliffs through the centuries. Here, where nearly every open space is the site of construction, present houses often have walls partially of stone. Jenness's excavations of the parts of six houses were sometimes impeded by fallen rocks too large to move. Nevertheless, he amassed a collection of artifacts from the house floors and rubbish heaps that proved the occupation of the Diomedes to have been more or less continuous and with a succession of implement forms.

One object that Jenness watched an Eskimo unearth came as a surprise. This was a harpoon head, triple spurred, slotted for the insertion of a side blade, and decorated with a highly distinctive arrangement of small concentric circles and fine connecting lines (see Fig. 57, p. 158). He had seen two or three other examples of this same style of art in museums of the United States, where they had been obtained by purchase somewhere in the Bering Strait region. Jenness felt sure that he had now hit upon at least one of the stopping places of some ancient Arctic people whose sites had not been precisely located before and whose artistry bore greater sophistication than that of other Eskimos. On the strength of this thin but distinctive thread of cultural continuity, Jenness applied the term "Bering Sea," later renamed "Old Bering Sea," to the archaic culture which he thought might have been superseded by the invasion of northern tribes of Asia that introduced the Thule culture to the region. Until then the only authenticated site in the western Arctic older than communities of patently recent Eskimos was the one examined by Stefansson near Point Barrow, the culture of which later received the name "Birnirk."

During the same summer, 1926, when Jenness was digging among the rocks on Little Diomede and at Cape Prince of Wales, Aleš Hrdlička, a physical anthropologist of the Smithsonian Institution, was surveying the coasts of Alaska. On St. Lawrence Island (Map 6), our American outpost that lies only forty miles from the mainland of Asia, well to the south of Bering Strait, Hrdlička obtained from the natives a number of examples of Old Bering Sea art which here was often engraved on ivory now strongly discolored and presumed to have been buried in the ground for a great period of time.

The steep, rocky cliffs of St. Lawrence Island—a small mountain range about one hundred miles long rising out of the sea—and its brown, treeless plateaus offer little inducement to the casual traveler to go ashore. Nevertheless, the wide gravel bars and series of beaches occurring at intervals have been attractive to many generations of Eskimos who settled here and made a living from the sea. The absence of caribou and the sparsity of other land animals helped give the tools, clothes, and belongings of St. Lawrence Islanders a characteristic stamp. Where in other regions Eskimos dressed in caribou skins, here they depended upon the skins of seals and birds; and where on the mainlands of both Asia and America antler provided the most common hard organic substance for manufactures, the islanders used ivory.

Everywhere on the island near a present village, and at many points in uninhabited coves, the archeologist sees earlier villages in the form of large midden mounds. Seldom concealed, as are the more usual individual houses and caches on the shores of mainland Alaska, these mounds, rich in nitrates, support a dense growth of rich green grass that contrasts with the more dun-colored tundra and proclaims the presence of a site from miles away.

In 1927, the year after the explorations of Hrdlička on St. Lawrence Island, Otto William Geist, a collector associated with the young Alaska Agriculture College and School of Mines at Fairbanks (now the University of Alaska), also traveled the Bering Sea coasts including St. Lawrence Island and made an enormous collection of artifacts. Although he was at first more interested in natural history specimens than in artifacts, he, too, recognized the significance of the old engraved ivory and made plans to return often to St. Lawrence Island.

Geist, who had emigrated from Bavaria before World War I and had no sooner become a United States citizen than he found himself back in Europe with the Expeditionary Forces, was a self-educated man of alternately explosive and sentimental temperament. As short in stature as most of the Eskimo men of St. Lawrence Island, he was readily accepted by them and chose to live with Eskimo families through more than one winter on the island. With the unexcelled advantages of living as an Eskimo villager (he was even adopted as a member of one of the highly esoteric whaling crews), he accumulated rare and valuable firsthand knowledge about these and other Asian Eskimos.

During his first years Geist dug wherever he pleased on the island, but later, between the years 1931 and 1935, he carried out methodical excavations in the huge Kukulik mound. These collections, made with but little expense to the college, were so extensive that they led to the founding of a college museum. As a result of Geist's continued collecting, the museum grew rather more rapidly than did other facilities of the institution, but his materials now form the nucleus of the collections of the University of Alaska's fine museum.

At the same time that Geist was working there, the Smithsonian Insitution in 1928 sent a party of archeologists under the direction of Henry B. Collins to excavate extensively on the island with the particular goal of learning more about the Old Bering Sea culture. Collins and his crew first attacked deep mounds at the eastern end of the island. Immediately beneath the grass in each one they found a continuous kitchen midden encompassing house remains well preserved by ice. A hindrance as well as a preservative, this ice retreated with painful slowness. Frozen objects thaw at varying rates, and it is a trial indeed for an investigator to watch and wait while logs of driftwood, slabs of thick walrus hide, whale bones, stones, and blubber-soaked black earth thaw each at its own rate, interfering with the ideal excavation of sheer walls and level earth shelves.

On one of the small Punuk Islands just off the eastern tip of St. Lawrence Island, another site consisted of a mound 400 feet long by 130 feet wide by 16 feet deep at center. In the course of a season this great depth was plumbed and, disappointingly, found to contain none of the mysterious old fossil ivory with "Bering Sea" carvings. Toward the lower part of the deposit, however, another elaborate form of decoration covered the whole surface of many ivory tools and implements. The lines were deep and straight as though evenly incised with metal tools. Joining them were compass-drawn circles centered about deep, round dots. This bold, geometric form of art, bearing many combinations of long and short parallel lines, some with ticked edges and appended dots, became known to the diggers as the "Punuk" style (Fig. 56), and this led Collins to so name the whole phase of culture subsequently found from one end of St. Lawrence Island to the other and along the shores of the neighboring Asian mainland. Another mound at Cape Kialegak (Map 6) was even deeper and more extensive, yet it too showed signs of having begun to accumulate at the time of Punuk culture.

Punuk people lived in large, rectangular, half-underground houses with long tunnels. The houses were constructed of horizontal logs of driftwood and were flagstoned in part or throughout. The belongings of the occupants were engraved in characteristic Punuk styles and often took unique forms: among them, ivory engraving tools to which iron points were bound; trident-like objects and lyre-shaped objects, probably, as we now surmise, attached to the proximal ends of some forms of harpoons; adz heads with knobs and a "shoe" shape; drum handles; combs with chain links at one end; and a great many small, delicate ivory objects, including long chains made by carving the links from one continuous piece of ivory. Baleen was extensively employed in the making of toboggans, toys, and implements.

Though its limits are still in question, Punuk culture was full-

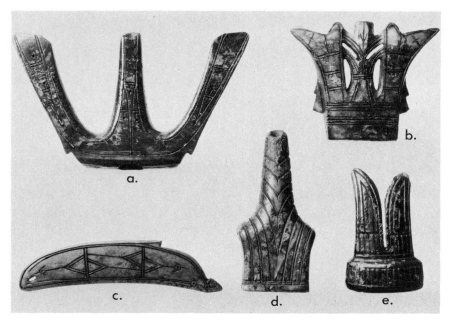

56. Ivory objects of Punuk culture (approx. A.D. 1000):

a) trident-like object, height 2⅔ in. (6.8 cm.)
b) lyre-shaped object
c) handle
d) unknown object
e) wrist guard
f) animal's head
g) unknown object
h) harpoon head
i) headless human figure
j) harpoon head
k) harpoon head

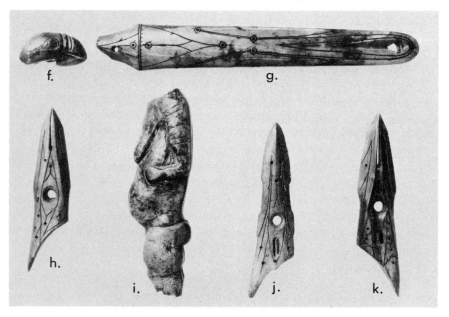

blown at A.D. 1000. But it did not simply end when another replaced it—rather, the testimony of the mounds is that a slow cultural change set in, removing from the culture much of the elaboration it had possessed. Most strikingly, the art and the odd-shaped "ceremonial" objects disappeared, and the artifacts and styles remaining were left looking more and more like those of Thule culture of continental North America. These resemblances had been there all along, however. Mathiassen's "Thule" types of harpoon heads (Fig. 15) were all represented, as were whaling harpoon parts, "winged" and tubular needlecases, side prongs for bird darts, drum handles, combs, and many other objects familiar to both recent Eskimos of Alaska and those of Thule culture.

Armed with this knowledge of cultural trends from Punuk to modern on the island, Collins found he could dip deeper into time by digging shallower mounds at the opposite end of the island. At Gambell, first, he found that shifts of the shoreline outward from the first inhabited slopes had obliged people to move periodically in order to remain close to the sea and their main sources of food. These moves had prevented the middens from growing to the great depths that force archeologists to cut through all the late deposits to find the old. The deposits that might have become deep, loaflike mounds were here more pancake-like and spread out laterally (Map 6, inset). The modern town of Gambell, with its frame houses built on the surface, has accumulated little rubbish, but Old Gambell, partly on an earlier beach, contained the last of the half-underground Punuk houses with tunnels. A nearby mound, Seklowayaget, carried the record a little further back into that period of culture when Punuk most closely approximated Thule.

A quarter-mile or more inland was the next mound in the succession. In this one, Ievoghiyoq, the deep, geometric engraving of pure Punuk culture persisted from top to bottom of a five-foot deposit; then, at the base of a steep slope, on perhaps the first substantial beach to form at that tip of the island, another wide mound, eight feet deep, contained only a capping of earliest Punuk, beneath which lay materials of the fabulous Old Bering Sea culture of 1,500 to 2,000 years ago. The houses of Miyowagh, this oldest mound, were rectangular like those of Punuk culture but smaller, and they, too, had tunnels with a slightly widened forepart to serve as an antechamber.

The Old Bering Sea people decorated their ivory as persistently as did those of Punuk. Their style, though containing similar ele-

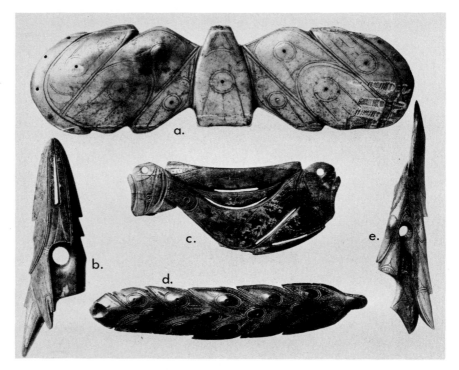

57. Carved ivory objects, Old Bering Sea culture:

a) winged object
b) harpoon head
c) ornament

d) pail handle; length, 6⅛ in. (15.5 cm.)
e) harpoon head

ments such as circles and ticked lines, was art as opposed to drafts-manship. Each line and curve that followed the natural contours of an ivory artifact or a lifelike figure was cut by a forceful or a feather-light hand to produce a design that seems to have evolved as the artist felt out his medium. Incredibly skillful combinations based on free-flowing curves fill whole broad faces of ivory artifacts, combining stylized small elements into a coordinated whole. Where the carvings of Ipiutak often run to the weird and grotesque, those of Old Bering Sea appear more balanced and pleasing, as though their artists led a secure—even serene—existence (Fig. 57). Certain "winged" objects (Fig. 57a) calling to mind birds or butterflies and at first classed as the appurtenances of some unknown ceremony now appear to be the more artistic prototypes of the stiff and formal trident and lyre-shaped objects of Punuk.

The harpoon heads of Miyowagh are distinctive forms, only a few predicting those of Thule. These are often many-spurred and provided with inset lateral blades of chert and agate. Heavy sledge runners of whole walrus tusks and others of whale ribs, together with baleen toboggans, show that these people ranged widely on the ice, hauling their boats to the open leads and pulling home loads of meat as did their descendants of Punuk and those of the present day. Recently found Old Bering Sea whaling harpoon heads show that these people procured their whales by a method similar to that of modern Eskimos—a point at first held in question. While all the decorated objects of Punuk, and some plain ones, can be readily distinguished from those of Old Bering Sea, the two cultures have many similarities, naturally enough since the one most likely grew out of the other.

Certain implements differing in emphasis and technique came to St. Lawrence Island from some outside sources with the end of Old Bering Sea and the beginning of Punuk times, however, perhaps about A.D. 500. These include seal scratchers for attracting seals on the spring ice; parts for the bladder dart; the light harpoon normally thrown from a kayak; the side-pronged bird spear; blunt tips for bird arrows; bow braces, sinew twisters, and wrist guards indicating a new assemblage for archery; and, importantly enough,

58. A suit of armor obtained on the Diomede Islands in the nineteenth century. Of walrus ivory with sealskin cording, it is nearly identical to armor plate of bone made in Punuk times 1,000 years earlier.

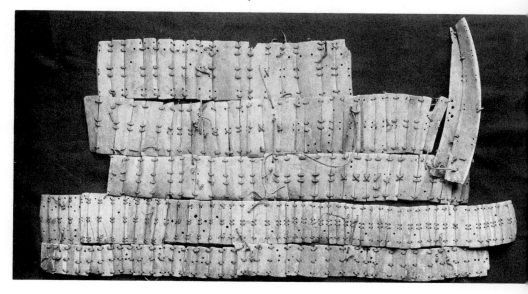

plates of ivory or whalebone that were lashed together to form suits of armor (Fig. 58). These and other innovations, including a great increase in whaling and a better supply of iron for cutting tools, lead us to believe that the island was caught in surges of cultural change based both upon more effective and wide-ranging hunting methods and more open belligerence as the population increased.

Even though Miyowagh is the earliest site at the foot of the hill, an older one turned up higher on the slope, named simply the Hillside site (Fig. 59). There Collins excavated two grassy spots that turned out to be small, flagstone-floored house remains with short tunnels. In the floor of one of these and under the floor stones of the second, Collins found forms of artifacts distinct from those of the Miyowagh mound and with a different style of decoration. This artwork, rare and manifestly early in style, was delicately executed but lacked much of the sweep and flow of late Old Bering Sea art. Flints, too, prevailed in the earlier period, though they scarcely rivalled polished slate in the later.

The story thus seemed complete for the northwest Cape of St. Lawrence Island: the first people had built small houses on the hill-

59. Henry B. Collins and helper excavating at the Hillside site, St. Lawrence Island, 1930.

side, their descendants had moved down to form a village on the
first stable beach, and the generations that followed moved forward
as often as the sea deposited extensive new sediments that formed
new beaches, changing the cast of their culture with the passage
of time.

While Collins and his assistants, including James Ford who
went on to excavate at Point Barrow and write a definitive report
on Birnirk culture, worked out the scheme of things at Gambell,
Otto Geist continued his attrition on the mound of Kukulik part way
around the north coast of the island. This enormous midden mound,
over 800 feet long by 140 feet wide, reached a depth in places of
14 or more feet. A number of half-underground houses had been
built into its present surface; these were the latest in a long series
of houses. In one case, four successive houses had been built with
time intervals between, each facing the sea and erected exactly over
its predecessor. Altogether they spanned perhaps a thousand years.

Unlike some mounds that are still occupied and thus difficult
to dig, and others that were long ago abandoned for unknown reasons, Kukulik is an archeologist's ideal. We know when the recent
town was last occupied and why it was abandoned and we have
more than one excellent firsthand account of what the village was
like shortly after its abandonment. In the summer of 1878 some
fifteen hundred people were living on St. Lawrence Island when—
according to E. W. Nelson, the biologist and ethnographer, and C.
L. Hooper, captain of the United States Treasury Department's
revenue steamer, *Corwin*—some unscrupulous traders sailed in
with an abundant supply of whisky. The men of the island liked
it so well that they continued to drink when they should have been
hunting walruses for winter food, and, as a result, people began to
go hungry early in the fall. By then it was too late to improve the
situation, and as the winter wore on people became ever weaker
from starvation and subject to all manner of illnesses, and, perhaps,
an epidemic disease. By spring, two thirds of the islanders were
dead. In seven of the villages, none survived. Only Gambell remained
a true village, and its population was reduced from six hundred to
two hundred in that year. Kukulik as it appeared two years later in
the summer of 1881 was described by the naturalist and writer
John Muir in his book *The Cruise of the Corwin*. Muir went ashore
with Nelson and Captain Hooper and wrote:

We found twelve desolate huts close to the beach with about two hundred skeletons in them or strewn about on the rocks and rubbish heaps within a few yards of the doors. The scene was indescribably ghastly and desolate, though laid in a country purified by frost as by fire. Gulls, plovers, and ducks were swimming and flying about in happy life, the pure salt sea was dashing white against the shore, the blooming tundra swept back to the snow-clad volcanoes, and the wide azure sky bent kindly over all—nature intensely fresh and sweet, the village lying in the foulest and most glaring death. The shrunken bodies, with rotting furs on them, or white bleaching skeletons, picked bare by the crows, were lying mixed with kitchen-midden rubbish where they had been cast out by surviving relatives while they yet had strength to carry them.

In the huts those who had been the last to perish were found in bed, lying evenly side by side, beneath their rotting deerskins. A grinning skull might be seen looking out here and there, and a pile of skeletons in a corner, laid there no doubt when no one was left strong enough to carry them through the narrow underground passage to the door. Thirty were found in one house, about half of them piled like fire-wood in a corner, the other half in bed, seeming as if they had met their fate with tranquil apathy. Evidently these people did not suffer from cold, however rigorous the winter may have been, as some of the huts had in them piles of deerskins that had not been in use. Nor, although their survivors and neighbors all say that hunger was the sole cause of their death, could they have battled with famine to the bitter end, because a considerable amount of walrus rawhide and skins of other animals was found in the huts. These would have sustained life at least a week or two longer.

The facts all tend to show that the winter of 1878–79 was, from whatever cause, one of great scarcity, and as these people never lay up any considerable supply of food from one season to another, they began to perish. The first to succumb were carried out of the huts to the ordinary ground for the dead, about half a mile from the village. Then, as the survivors became weaker, they carried the dead a shorter distance, and made no effort to mark their positions or to lay their effects beside them, as they customarily do. At length the bodies were only dragged to the doors of the huts, or laid in a corner, and the last survivors lay down in despair without making any struggle to prolong their wretched lives by eating the last scraps of skin.

Mr. Nelson went into this Golgotha with hearty enthusiasm,

gathering the fine white harvest of skulls spread before him, and throwing them in heaps like a boy gathering pumpkins. He brought nearly a hundred on board, which will be shipped with specimens of bone armor, weapons, utensils, etc., on the Alaska Commercial Company's steamer St. Paul.

Half a century later, Geist found the houses somewhat disintegrated but still containing their grim reminders of the tragedy. In one house, thirty-four human skeletons lay on sleeping platforms paralleling the walls while at least thirty-three other individuals were represented by disturbed skeletons on the floor. Besides those in houses, skeletons were found lying on the tundra leading to a nearby burial hill, possibly the remains of some who had attempted to leave their houses and go to the burial ground when they felt death near.

After he had dug beneath the surface of the mound and the recent houses, Geist found a regular succession of cultural materials extending deep into the ground. Halfway down appeared Punuk art and artifacts, and, deeper still, an earlier phase of Punuk; then came Birnirk; and, finally, at the bottom, a thick deposit of cultural leavings of the later phase of Old Bering Sea culture. People of the earliest Old Bering Sea phase—that of the Gambell hillside—do not seem to have lived at the site.

The archeology of St. Lawrence Island, represented by collections of artifacts that are bountiful as compared with other localities in the Arctic, now seemed to be thoroughly outlined. One other important phase of culture remained to be described, however. Geist learned in 1931 of an ivory bonanza discovered by natives who were accustomed to making lengthy trips to the Punuk Islands for "fossil" ivory to use in their ivory-carving trade. In looking over the collections made by some of his friends, Geist recognized at once that harpoon heads and various other items were decorated in a curious new design. Though it basically resembled Old Bering Sea forms, this engraving ran more to straight lines and deep, freehand gashes.

At the end of the 1934 season of digging at Kukulik, Geist and Ivar Skarland set up camp on the outer of the Punuk Islands and proceeded to mine in the vein that the Eskimos were so zealously exploiting. The reason for the site's having been overlooked earlier was that it was clearly only the edge of a village site, probably a mound, all but this edge of which had long since been washed into the sea. They found, however, that by cutting in from the sea-washed bank they could accumulate quantities of artifacts in the now thawed ground. They carried on this work to advantage, although life was not always ideal. Skarland recalled one blustery evening when he and Geist had finished supper and were relaxing with books on their cots on either side of a roaring camp stove when, without warning, a powerful gust of wind lifted their tent from its moorings, leaving them staring upward into the glowering sky and driving rain. Despite such interruptions, they continued to work late into the fall.

The remarkable carvings of this assemblage and its other, more mundane artifacts, which subsequently received the name Okvik, became a prime focus of interest when Geist and Froelich Rainey examined them again at Alaska College. Rainey, who had been working in sites of the Caribbean, joined the Alaska faculty in 1935 to inaugurate a program of anthropology and especially to help organize and write up the tremendous collections made by Geist. Cases of artifacts now overflowed from a temporary museum and hallways and completely filled a large sheet-iron warehouse that had been built to ease the strain. In 1936 Rainey finished a monograph with Geist that described the collection, but to understand better the conditions under which such excavations are made he went to St. Lawrence Island in the summer of 1937 and completed a section of his own through the middle of the Kukulik mound. Late that season he encountered Eskimos returning from the Punuk Islands and purchased from them a few additional pieces of the then rare Okvik art that was made by people on those islands from shortly before until shortly after the beginning of the Christian era.

TWO YEARS LATER, in 1939, after the successful season Rainey, Larsen, and I had spent at Point Hope (Chapter VI), we found passage southward on a Coast Guard ship. Revelling in the luxury of a cruise through Arctic waters and the fine food served in the captain's and warrant officers' messes, we found ourselves the center of attention as we told about our fabulous findings at the Ipiutak site. From this the subject turned, naturally enough, to St. Lawrence Island where I was to be dropped off, and to the wealth of ivory to be found on the island. The ship's personnel became intrigued— especially with Rainey's account of the elaborate fossil ivory carvings still washing out of the beach on one of the Punuk Islands. We hoped, he told them, to reach Savoonga, the village near Kukulik mound, just at the time the ivory hunters would be returning with their year's take from the Okvik deposits so that we could acquire some of this fine material for the museum's collections.

Before long the ship anchored off Savoonga and the three of us prepared to go ashore in the first boat. The officers, who also planned to go ashore, explained to us, however, their apprehension about landing civilians until they had made sure the shores were safe. We watched them head toward land and saw with relief that their boat reached Savoonga without incident. After a surprisingly long time, the boat returned, and our brave hosts greeted us with the welcome news that the natives had indeed returned from the Punuk Islands—and that they, the officers, had managed to purchase valuable souvenirs to take home to their wives and children. Our congratulations may have lacked the full ring of sincerity as we saw Okvik-decorated dolls, harpoon heads, and winged objects displayed in the hands of our benefactors. Nevertheless, we went ashore and salvaged what we could.

WHILE LARSEN and Rainey continued south, I remained on the island from early September to mid-November of that season, catching the last ship out just before ice closed in. While my main objective was the collection of driftwood timbers with which to supplement my chronology of tree-ring dates, I was also urged by Rainey to keep my eyes open for other Okvik materials, and particularly to look for an Okvik site that could give us information about all those aspects of life that a mere collection of artifacts cannot furnish. Engaging a small crew of Eskimo men at Savoonga, I planned to dig at Kukulik for a few weeks.

Though I had read about the site and had for some years followed the news of Alaska College field trips with interest, I was still unprepared for its enormous size and remarkable facilities. During his first years on the island, Geist had used every cent he could scrape together to hire native laborers and make purchases, but as the importance of the mound became recognized and funds became available, the college built for him one of the most palatial archeological headquarters in the far north. The frame building was large enough to house twenty or thirty individuals in all comfort. It had a large living room with a wood stove in the middle, a kitchen, a dining room, a storage and utilities room with more than adequate cupboards and shelves, and, on two sides of a long hallway, a map room, a radio room, and living quarters for the leader of the expedition and his assistants. My two Eskimo helpers and I luxuriated in space. We spread our small supplies thinly in many shelves and cupboards and took for ourselves the best of the beds, chairs, desks, and pictures that abounded in the vacant rooms.

Next morning, as we prepared breakfast, a young girl materialized from off the tundra. She had walked over from Savoonga, explained one of the men—her father—to be our cook. Remembering Point Hope, I suggested that she show us how well she qualified by preparing lunch. Her father passed this word along, showed the girl where to find our provisions, and joined us at the site. At noon, hungry, we walked back to headquarters and sat down to bowls of what I at first mistook for soup. A taste quickly dispelled that notion. Our cook had spent her morning boiling the entire season's supply of dried apricots, mixing them, obviously, with great quantities of sugar. Observing that my companions were spooning up this dish as though it were indeed a fine bouillabaise, I held my questions and waited for the next course. But there was no other. Fortunately for me, the other men also still seemed hungry as we passed a box of crackers. What was apparently a servant problem resolved itself when the girl disappeared before dinner; as we all joined in preparing our meal, the father explained that his daughter had never cooked before and had now learned that she did not like it, so had gone back to help her mother and sisters pick berries on the tundra.

After gathering a good supply of datable wood by extending previous excavations at the edges of cuts through Kukulik mound, I went to Gambell to secure wood from structures at Ievoghiyoq and Miyowagh and then to search, as instructed, for any trace of Okvik culture. Alaska College still owned a sparsely furnished, small, one-room frame house in Gambell, and in this I made headquarters for whatever length of time should remain before some means of transportation back to the mainland appeared. It was, in fact, quite a while after the departure early in September of the last supply ship from the States before I saw another American ship, and I wondered a little if, indeed, I might not be left on the island all winter. Ironically, the open lines of communications were with Siberia rather than with the rest of Alaska. Groups of islanders in skin boats made repeated trips across, and at least one or two families visited the island from Indian Point, the nearest Siberian village. Pipe tobacco and long Russian cigarettes, lengthened by cardboard tubes as mouthpieces, were cheaper for a while than American tobacco. A flourishing trade took place between Gambell and Indian Point, even though this was strongly discouraged by the Russians.

One day that fall, two years before the 1941 attack on Pearl Harbor, Gambell's two schoolteachers, many of the Eskimos, and I, looking seaward, were sobered at seeing an Asian manifestation of an unexpected sort. A large gray ship, seemingly a freighter with extensive passenger accommodations, slipped out of the fog and cruised slowly by a short distance offshore. Lacking flags or any insignia that we could see, the ship steamed past while men but poorly concealed in ports and passageways stared at us, some with binoculars. The faces we could discern looked oriental. A short time later the ship returned, moving even more slowly and deliberately, within calling distance of shore. Yet not a sound was heard above the throb of its motors. That night the schoolteachers, checking by radiotelephone with Nome and other mainland points on the teachers' wavelength, failed to learn of any ships known to be operating in that vicinity. We decided, no doubt with justification, that the ship was Japanese, and observed that if war should break out for any reason at that moment, we were closer to the Russians and the Japanese than to our own countrymen.

After that season I understood quite clearly why the Eskimo speakers of St. Lawrence Island looked different from those of Alaska to the north and practiced a variant culture: because they were Eskimos of Alaska only by virtue of a sharp bend in the International Dateline. Geographically, they belonged to Siberia and, as far as I could learn, so did their history and their culture for hundreds, perhaps thousands, of years.

At Gambell I engaged new helpers, one of whom, Paul Silook, introduced himself in surprisingly good English almost the moment I arrived in the village (Fig. 60). The teachers had told me that Paul was a good worker and was the "literary" man of Gambell, and it took me only a few hours to learn why he had this reputation. He had learned English by working for the missionaries who had lived there when he was a child. Learning to read from mission books, he had absorbed biblical terms, which he used both in ordinary speech and in the interpreting he did for me when I recorded ethnographic accounts from the oldest people in the village. We had

60. Paul Silook, 1939.

no sooner begun to dig at the edges of older excavations at Miyowagh than I realized I had been chosen by the right man. Paul had worked with the Smithsonian group and he indicated, no doubt with some reason, that he knew better than I how we should go about procuring buried timbers for my tree-ring dating. Conversation occasionally became strained between us when he pointed out that I was not measuring and digging precisely as Mr. Collins had done. Paul was so clearly an archeologist at heart, however, that we soon compromised in our methodology and freely talked, to my great benefit, during each digging day.

Then one evening after work Paul came visiting and brought with him two of his most prized possessions. One, as I recall, was a thick Department of Agriculture report; the other, I gratefully and avidly observed, was the volume I would have chosen were I to be a castaway on this particular island with only one book. It was the *Archeology of St. Lawrence Island, Alaska* by Henry B. Collins, and on its flyleaf was written a gracious message from the author to his former assistant. Promising to keep the book wrapped except when I read it in my cabin, I borrowed it for the duration of my stay on the island.

I learned the names of many people at Gambell and occasionally visited them in their homes, but the family I came to know best was that of the Silooks. Evenings after work I would take my notebook and pencil and walk past several huts, each buzzing with a swarm of children. Each also had dogs, tied to a post, who watched my passage with curiosity or mistrustful snarls until I came to the small rectangular house in which Paul and his family lived.

If the day were cold, or wind whipped around the corner of the house, I hastened to push open the small, square door, the sill of which was two feet above the ground. Bending to avoid striking my head, I climbed over the threshhold and emerged in a large, dark anteroom with an earthen floor where all the household supplies and hunting gear were stored. An inner room was partly raised by a wooden platform. This was partitioned from the front of the room by a flap that hung like a stage curtain from the low ceiling. Someone within, hearing the noise of the outer door, would lift a corner of the flap, and I would doff my parka and crawl quickly under the curtain and into the warm inner section. Here the length of the room was the width of the house, perhaps fourteen feet, but there were no more than ten feet between the curtain and the rear wall. Skins of walrus and bearded seal were sewn together and used to cover all walls, ceiling, and floor, effectively locking out any drafts or stray breezes. With ventilation carefully regulated through a small hole in the roof, the family sat about in the light and warmth of a large seal-oil lamp, some clad only in abbreviated trunks and short, soft-soled boots. We usually sat for a while in silence. Then Mrs. Silook, having boiled water in a kettle over the flame of the lamp, would pour tea. Children and adults, including usually Silook's ancient father, would suck the liquid loudly through their lips, some holding sugar in their mouths, Russian fashion.

When the time came, I would ask the old man, Daniel Ouotalin (patronymics were not a part of the old naming system of these Eskimos) if he had remembered something new to tell me about the old days on the island. He might then begin to talk in Eskimo with Paul as his interpreter. My shorthand notes now give Ouotalin's account a biblical ring because of Paul's mission-learned English. Hearing his recollections of the big plague year of 1878 when nearly everyone on the island died, I judged him to be about seventy-five years old. He remembered well the period of slow starvation when a combination of bad weather ("wind all the time") and thin ice kept hunters ashore even when the seals could be seen out in the water. Because they had not hunted earlier in the season and now had no food in the caches, they simply stayed at home watching the seals swim by, until disease overcame them and they died.

By the steady white light which Mrs. Silook regulated by trailing oil and fire along the rim of her pottery lamp, I wrote, and the small children played or listened quietly to the sometimes dramatic words of their grandfather. The furnishings in this house were scant. Besides a Sunday School picture or two on the walls, there were rolled-up sleeping bags in the corner, a drying rack for boots and mittens above the lamp, and two urine tubs in the middle of the floor just forward of the curtain. While Silook was now in the minority of people at Gambell who still preferred to live in the old way, he pointed out to me that his neighbors who put linoleum on their floors and sealed their walls with plasterboard found the houses so drafty they were obliged to spend a great deal of money for coal with which to keep themselves warm. He, on the other hand, lived by the seals he caught, rendering from them all the oil he needed for heating, lighting, and cooking, and using their skins for the house interior, effectively locking out drafts.

One day, while we excavated at Miyowagh and I wondered how much longer the weather would allow me to accumulate sections of the buried logs, I began also to speculate about the old Okvik people and where they might have camped if any had inhabited this end of the island. Turning to the steep slope behind the mound, high upon which we could see the luxuriant grass that had flourished for ten years since Collins's excavation of the hillside, I concluded it could be only there that we might find traces of the earlier culture. Suspending work in our Miyowagh squares, we turned to the hillside some distance north of the old excavations. Here each of my helpers and I laid out two parallel lines leading from the beach upward along the slope. Between these we excavated rapidly, looking for signs of culture. Almost immediately the experiment paid off. In place of the polished slates that were found in quantity at Miyowagh, here were only chips and occasionally an artifact of flinty material. As the trenches deepened slowly into the slope I concluded that most of the hillside, not simply the small area in which Collins had found his two houses, had been occupied.

Now impatient of sleuthing with narrow trenches, I attempted to short-cut the process. About a third of the way to the top of the slope I saw the suggestion of a bench or terrace, so began a series of test pits there in the hope of finding a hidden dwelling site. I had not far to go. Below sod in the first test were bits of rotten wood and, lower, chips of flinty material in rocky soil. At a depth of about two feet appeared the definite signs of structural remains. Here I threw caution to the winds. It was already October and winter would surely not delay much longer. Suddenly fearful of having to cease work before I could learn more, I trowelled fever-ishly to find the bottom of this man-made layer. Soon my trowel struck stone, this time not a sharp fragment but a large flat stone from the beach. Lacking the patience to widen the test properly, I lay on top of the ground and reached a full arm's length to clean the stone with a trowel, thus exposing a second stone—this one a slab standing upright. Before the limits of the test were reached,

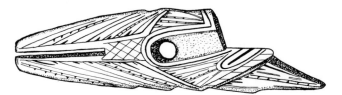

61. Harpoon head of ivory from St. Lawrence Island, probably dating to the beginning of the Christian era and intermediate in culture between Okvik and Old Bering Sea. Length, about 3⅜ in. (8.5 cm.).

three upright stones that formed a small chamber could be seen rising out of what was clearly a broad, flagstoned floor. Then I saw wedged between one of the uprights and a flat floor stone a brown ivory object decorated with a lacework of fine etched lines. Gently prying it loose with the tip of my trowel, I found it to be a harpoon head with curious winglike structures accentuating its sharp basal spur (Fig. 61). I had seen the style before yet I could not remem-ber where. Surely it was not the classical kind of Old Bering Sea decoration. Was it like objects from Collins's Hillside houses?

By then it was late in the day. First explaining the discovery to my assistants, who immediately shared my enthusiasm for the new dig, I excused myself and hastened back to my house to unwrap Silook's copy of Collins's report and search the more than eighty photographic plates for the harpoon head that I felt I had seen before. Turning the pages, I failed to match my specimen to any of those from either the Miyowagh or the Hillside site, but just as I was ready to despair there flashed into sight three heads nearly its duplicate. Eagerly checking to see what part of St. Lawrence Island these illustrated specimens had come from, I found that they were not excavated on the island at all but had been acquired by Collins on Little Diomede Island in the Bering Strait.

When the next few days' excavations showed me that we had hit upon a large house floor with no trace of squareness about the walls, I could contain myself no longer. Prevailing upon the teachers to send a message to Nome to be relayed to Fairbanks via the Army Signal Corps, I addressed Froelich Rainey. Weighing my words carefully, for we operated on restricted funds, I said "Have dug large circular house Gambell Hillside, evidently new phase Old Bering Sea. Six heads like Collins's Plate 27, Diomede 5 and 6. Designs on wood, black pigment on red. Fifteen pounds small stone tools, flint predominant; ten pounds flint chips. Perhaps important your report." However exuberant Rainey may have felt over this disclosure, he too kept within the fifty-word limit. His immediate reply was: "Heads are Okvik type B. You must have pure Okvik. This is marvelous. We need dope on house construction, bone refuse, burials, wooden implements, and follow it up if you find additional deposits. Good going. Don't get stuck out there. Congratulations again."

Following this exchange of messages on October 6, I proceeded to enlarge the excavation in spite of the fact that by now the temperature remained almost steadily below freezing, dipping to zero or lower some nights. We could excavate only by breaking through a frozen crust, removing this to the edge of the cut. In the evening we spread canvas over the excavation and, on top of this, an inch or so of earth to maintain our thawed ground. Going to work next morning we lifted the canvas with its burden of now frozen earth, and sometimes an inch or so of snow, before proceeding with the dig.

The last ship of the season, the leaking old *M. V. Boxer* of the Alaska Native Service, did not arrive until November 16. No transatlantic liner could have been more welcome, however, now that I had the plans and collections of the first house of Okvik culture. Within two weeks I reached Alaska College with all of the collections intact, to my great relief. Upon examining the more than nine hundred artifacts from the round house, Rainey decided that while there were differences, these more nearly resembled artifacts of Okvik than of Old Bering Sea. Hence, although no final report has yet been written on my Hillside excavation, it is still the oldest structure yet excavated on the island and it represents a phase of culture related to both Old Bering Sea and Okvik that is probably intermediate between the two.

Except for St. Lawrence Island, practically no archeology was done along the coasts inhabited by the mainland Eskimos of Asia until 1945, when S. I. Rudenko made excavations in a number of mounds from East Cape southward to the shores of Anadyr Sound. From these studies we see that the mainland bears the same general phases of culture as does St. Lawrence Island, ranging from Okvik forward to the present. Within the last few years another Soviet scientist, M. G. Levin, and others returned to the region, finding ancient burials, most of them of Old Bering Sea times, but some containing Okvik and others containing more recent objects as grave goods.

While the final dating of the Okvik–Old Bering Sea sequence on St. Lawrence Island and Siberia and that of Ipiutak on mainland Alaska must await more tests before we are able to place each of the phases in a precise time scale, the dates thus far accumulated show that the Okvik through Old Bering Sea phases, in the main, parallel the range of Ipiutak culture. Thus we have arrayed on the two sides of the Strait, from about the beginning of our era and lasting some five hundred years, the peoples of two traditions, whose art forms, though distinguishable in each individual piece, nevertheless display many of the same elements, an over-all distinctiveness, and equally high artistic ability. Even so, the differences are many, not the least being that all the Asians pursued whales in open boats while the mainland Alaskans of Ipiutak culture seldom did.

Our questions about why Ipiutak culture seems to have reached past the western coasts of Bering Strait and on into the heart of Asia for its most striking relationships are only partly answered by a close examination of the early St. Lawrence Island cultures. We learn that close resemblances did, in fact, exist between the engraving art of the two neighboring regions. Both the Ipiutak and Okvik–Old Bering Sea artists covered their ivory implements with freehand curvilinear designs, employing many identical elements. Yet Ipiutak design tends to stress the grotesque and the bizarre, while Old Bering Sea is more benign and pleasing. Resemblances are harder to find in stone technology. Here one sees little evidence of strong influence from one region to the other. Each seems strongly rooted in this respect to its home ground, where it has drawn sustenance from deep and separate sources thus far hidden from view.

After the disappearance of the distinctive Old Bering Sea and Ipiutak ivory styles, there appeared the Punuk style on the Asian side and the Western Thule style on the American, both slowly losing their engraved decorations as the centuries passed and taking on the utilitarian look of more recent Eskimo styles. Apparently Bering Strait served, through these two thousand years, as an effective barrier to the displacement of either group by the other while at the same time it encouraged trade and the communication of ideas between the two continents.

The situation differs at the eastern end of Eskimo country. There, on the coast of the Atlantic, from Newfoundland north through the island passages and around a large part of Greenland, lived during the same period and earlier a succession of people whose culture, the Dorset, differed basically from that of the ivory carvers about Bering Sea. Their background, indeed, points to the beach ridges at Cape Krusenstern, where behind the main Ipiutak ridge of Beach 35 lies the next successive series of beaches containing a still older culture.

(IX)

Norton Beaches

ONE SENSES a contrast in terrain as soon as he crosses the Ipiutak ridge at Cape Krusenstern and continues down its inner side and on to the deeper, wetter moss of the more ancient beaches. Here frost action has formed small ridges and gullies between wider-spaced, large frost cracks, and a walk on a continuous ridge is frequently interrupted by these breaks in the hard ground as well as by swamps and small ponds. However close this ground lies to the Ipiutak ridge, the flints we find here are different from those of Ipiutak culture.

Vegetation, too, is different; there is more variety, especially in the sedges, water plants, and typical waxy-leaved heath that forms on peaty soil. Small birds fly up ahead of the walker— yellowlegs and sandpipers from the gravelly rim of a pond, and multi-colored phalaropes, at first swimming rapidly away like miniature ducks, then twirling on the surface before taking wing, orderly again, in a swift flight to a neighboring pond. Large gadwalls and an occasional teal leave the ponds and nervously circle the area in which their eggs or young are concealed, but old squaw mothers with their pointed tails and thin necks urge their young to dive and stay under water until the danger has disappeared.

In 1959, the summer the *Pauline* had left us at the eastern end of Cape Krusenstern and George Moore's "weasel" had helped move us to a better location westward, we next dug the two big Ipiutak houses, House 17 and House 18 (pp. 134–6). When they were finished, Bandi, Friedman, and I were walking one day in a reindeer path that had cut through the moss of one of these older, farther inland ridge tops when Bandi paused to pick up a brownish

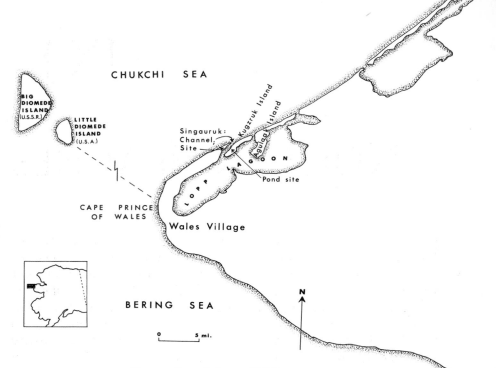

CHUKCHI SEA

BIG
DIOMEDE
ISLAND
(U.S.S.R.)

LITTLE
DIOMEDE
ISLAND
(U.S.A.)

Kugzruk Island

Agulga Island

Singauruk:
Channel;
Site

L A G O O N

Pond site

L O P P

CAPE PRINCE
OF WALES

Wales Village

BERING SEA

N

0   5 mi.

Map 7. Cape Prince of Wales

object. As we inspected what he had found, we instinctively backed away from the area to avoid causing damage. His artifact was a thin piece of pottery, the outer surface of which had been stamped all over with small, evenly spaced rectangles. Not a trace of pottery had occurred in any of the Ipiutak sites at Cape Krusenstern or elsewhere, and recent pottery was a thick, coarse gray or black ware.

Kneeling and carefully lifting patches of moss, we freed an area wide enough to give more details. A large number of pieces showed that one large cooking pot of this check-stamped ware had been broken and discarded by some ancient campers (Fig. 62). Although no hearth or other artifact was found just then, we felt that one more segment of beaches had borne out our suspected sequence of cultures, for pottery of this type was typical of Norton culture which we knew to be older than Ipiutak. Why the art of making and using pottery was known by Norton people, and before them, Choris people of three thousand years ago, but was bypassed

62. Potsherds with check-stamped design from Norton culture beaches, Cape Krusenstern.

by Ipiutakers, only to be taken up again by more recent people, is still one of the unfathomables of Arctic archeology. So far only the Ipiutak people themselves know why they resisted the use of pots in any shape or form. At any rate, not long after that first piece of Norton pottery was found, numerous hearths and tent floors on that and neighboring ridges (Beaches 36–44) defined for us a long period of occupation by people of several phases of Norton culture.

NORTON WAS at first the name applied to the remains of houses and artifacts found in 1948 in the middle levels of a deeply stratified site at Cape Denbigh and in three other localities of that northern Bering Sea region. Later, on our 1958 reconnaissance of Kotzebue Sound, we learned that the culture was widespread and quite certainly older than that of Ipiutak. There were even strong indications that the Near Ipiutak of Point Hope was a late phase of Norton. Furthermore, earlier that present 1959 season before we returned to Cape Krusenstern and found the broken pot, some of us had found and dug Norton sites at Bering Strait, one hundred seventy miles to the southwest.

We had begun the summer by investigating beach ridges at Point Spencer, forty miles south of Cape Prince of Wales, and then in mid-June we had set about moving to the Cape itself and Wales village (Maps 3 and 7). Sam Friedman remained with the bulk of our equipment at Point Spencer, while Bill Simmons and Chester Topkok, a native of Teller, took a small boat up along the shores to look for signs of early archeology, with Wales village their destination. I engaged a small plane to take me to Cape Prince of Wales, where I planned to pick out a camping place near Wales village before being joined by the others. Aerial photographs showed series of beach ridges at this Cape much like those at Cape Krusenstern, and I confidently hoped to find another succession of cultures here at this crucial point where skin boats had been plying between Asia and America for at least two thousand years.

I sat next to the pilot, heading toward Bering Strait, the plane taxed to capacity with my camping gear, including a small sheet-iron stove with its pipe rattling about on top of the load. Dark clouds lay ominously overhead and I anxiously scanned the cliffs and rocky shores below for a place to land at Cape Prince of Wales. Less than five miles from Wales village the pilot, noting that the clouds were now pressed down almost to the top of the sea, regretfully said that a landing would be impossible and he would have to turn back southward. As he did so, however, we saw an opening in the clouds beyond, past some cliffs and up a narrow green valley. Not wishing to return to Point Spencer with the chance of being stranded there, I suggested that we turn up the valley, climb through the clouds, and try to land on the far side of the village. The pilot was willing, and after climbing for a few minutes until the clouds parted, we looked down upon a mountain ridge and the flat lands and lagoons beyond.

The cloud bank lay like a mushroom over the Cape to the south, and when we dropped lower we kept as close as possible to its north margin. Observing that streaks of sand lay parallel to one another at wide intervals for a mile or more back from the edge of the coast, I asked the pilot to drop me off wherever he could land. He suggested an outlet where Lopp Lagoon opened to the sea. We were low enough to see a boat tied along a protected bank of the channel and three people moving about on shore. After circling a time or two we set down on a long strip of level sand at the ocean beach. The pilot, fearing the soft, moist ground in which his wheels settled, helped me unload and then took off before we could speak to the people who were running toward us.

Once again, as so often happens in Alaska when one travels the Arctic coast, I knew that I must explain myself, and I began formulating my answers to the inevitable question: "Why are you here?" The men rushing forward in their tattered fur and denim garments looked as if they were about to repulse an attacking horde.

Unscathed a moment later, though, I walked back with them, each one helping to carry a part of my load, and was soon their guest at a primitive meal. Behind their shelter—a low windbreak of sticks and canvas, more a protection for the Coleman stove than for men —I learned that they were hunters from Wales who had come here in their boat two days before and had found it impossible, in the fierce wind, to breast the waves of either the sea or the lagoon, and had thus been unable to return. They had brought with them neither tent nor food—only tea, depending for nourishment on whatever they could procure with their shotguns. In their boat lay piles of ducks, geese, and brant, and in split-open gasoline cans were the eggs of ducks and geese they had gathered from a small island in the mouth of the lagoon.

While we ate a boiled brant, the feathered head and brown feet of which I ignored as I dug into the steaming pot, I began with some misgivings to explain my reasons for landing here on the beach. I need not have felt concern, however. Phillip Kugzruk, Jonah Tokeinna, and a third man whose name I do not recall, all nodded enthusiastically at my mention of old things in the ground. I ceased to simplify terms as they spoke knowingly of "archeology" and "artifacts" and asked if I had a digging permit, and I realized that I had dropped into a land less wild than it appeared—one in which I must again be initiated to archeology by those who had worked with Henry Collins and James Ford. The situation worsened considerably when my companions assured me there was nothing out here on the old beaches and decided among themselves that I must go back to Wales and dig in the old village mound which, they said, was still full of ivory and all manner of excellent artifacts.

Having failed to explain my search for sites on earlier beaches, I expressed thanks for the food and turned inland to see for myself. I did not go alone, however. My friends, still skeptical but having nothing better to do, fell into step. On a beach only a short distance from the shore I found traces of a campsite some hundreds of years old, to judge from the coarse, broken pottery, and a weapon point or two. Beyond this the ground became thickly covered with a spongy, tundra-like sod. The occasional wide beach ridges we walked over, though of sand beneath, exposed no soil to view. It was nearly a mile to a particular sandy beach ridge that I had seen from the air. By the time we reached it, I, too, had become doubtful and heartily wished I were alone to search unhurried, win or lose. My gloom vanished quickly, though, when I found that with rare good luck I had come to just the spot on this old beach where there had once been a large campground of the very old Denbigh Flint people. Seeing microblades on the ground among characteristic fire-cracked pebbles, I knew my beach ridge approach to archeology had worked once more.

I prevailed upon my companions to leave the site undisturbed until I could come back with equipment, and then continued along the ridge of sand that stretched before me. Another site soon became obvious. This time, however, it was not one of Denbigh flints but contained, I saw at a glance, the white quartz flakes and scrapers, crude worked slabs of slate, arrowpoints, and thin, brown pottery of Norton culture. Here, as at Cape Espenberg farther to the north and east where the ridges were once rows of shifting sand dunes, more recent people now and then walked back to the older beaches to make camp. My future task would be to find exposed beach crests between this ridge and the sea and to learn what limits forward in both space and time existed for the older, Denbigh culture. Jonah and Phillip were impressed by my demonstration and on the way back to camp they offered to work for me as long as I wished. They would take me to Wales in their boat, they said, and then we would come back here to search and dig. That night, when the wind died down, I accepted their invitation to travel, and after three hours of seafaring I was able to set my tent between two colonies of howling dogs on the beach at this westernmost settlement of mainland America.

Early next morning the plane bearing Friedman landed him on this same beach and we spent some hours becoming acquainted with Wales (Fig. 63). A black headland of granite, Wales Mountain, had emerged from the clouds, and we saw that it was still spotted with snow. It would have been a prominent landmark for primitive navigators, even those starting out from Asia. And it would have seemed very near at hand from the Diomedes, for we, looking westward, clearly saw details of rocks and shore on those two big, flat-topped islands. How different, we felt, would have been the result of Bering's voyage had he passed through the Strait on a clear day.

Wales lies on the ample crest of the forward beach. Frame houses, with cache platforms of poles at their sides, range in either direction from a town center of post office, store, and meeting hall.

63. Village of Wales, Alaska, June 1959.

A stream off the mountain cuts a channel behind the village and breaks through the forward beach at its north end, isolating a few native huts and some military installations now largely abandoned.

Phillip guided us to the post office early the first day to meet Dwight Tevuk, postmaster and mayor of the village. Tevuk closed his establishment to take us home for coffee, introduced us to his pleasant wife and daughters, and leaned back in his chair to tell us about his own experience in archeology. He, too, had worked with Henry Collins in 1936, excavating part of the large mound across the "river" from the village. This mound, I had observed, lay on an earlier beach ridge that, presumably, had been on the ocean-front when it was first occupied.

The conversation then turned to more serious matters. Tevuk, as mayor, would like to see our Interior Department permit. As this was the first time in twenty years of digging that anyone had expressed so keen an interest, I took pleasure in spreading the document before him. He turned to us at length and said that while our papers seemed in order, we must understand, of course, that we needed the permission of the town itself to excavate in its vicinity. I began to feel vaguely apprehensive. "We have a Reservation here at Wales," said Tevuk. I had not realized that either, but I knew that if, indeed, the village stretched all the way up the coast to where I wanted to dig, I must bow to whatever restrictions its officials might impose. Tevuk was not certain where the "Reservation" began or ended. Neither he nor I knew if it exceeded the bounds of the dwellings themselves; so, as he pointed out, since we did not know, it would be up to the town council to decide whether I could dig anywhere in the vicinity, since the town limits might later be found to extend to those points. It was fortunate, he said, that the council had some business to transact that very evening, and he could arrange to have my case heard at the same time.

I could not help but fear that our plans for the first half of that season, expensive and vital to our research as they were, might actually be jeopardized by the decision of that town council. We were to meet in the village cooperative store, which, as expected of a trading post, was provided with benches in front of the counters on three sides and heated by a more than adequate oil-drum stove. My presence had been anticipated, for as I entered the store with my papers and rolls of maps, women and children hastened out of the door past me with what I interpreted as uneasy looks, and I stepped in to see benches full of grim-faced village elders. Not even my friends Jonah and Phillip ventured a smile of welcome. Tevuk, on the other hand, graciously made room for me at the center of one of the longer benches and sat down beside me. No voice was heard for a full five minutes while I sat under the scrutiny of the examining board. Then Tevuk began to talk in Eskimo. His address was lengthy, and I detected from some familiar words that it concerned me. At length he turned and said in English: "Now we will hear you."

I shall never know how well my speech was understood, but I have seldom had occasion to be more eloquent and persuasive. I described the work we had done in the past, and how we hoped, by excavating the camps of their ancestors, to learn the unwritten history of Wales. I spread out my maps and photographs, explaining in detail what we had found on the shores of Kotzebue Sound and how sure I felt that we could find even more here. Leaving nothing to chance, I explained how we would dig and where the materials would be housed—that we were not interested in recent skeletons but would like to find the bones of ancestral ones to learn whether they had been Eskimos or not. I may have continued for an hour before summarizing and resting my case. Now any interest my documented lecture had brought to the faces around me disappeared, and I looked again at a bank of stolid countenances. Tevuk thanked me for my talk and said that the council must now enact its business and would I mind waiting outside until they could get around to my petition.

The cold wind blew as I paced back and forth in front of the trading post under the eyes of a gathering crowd of villagers. Fleetingly I wondered if I had misunderstood the occasion and had, in fact, been on trial for my life rather than for the right to dig. At last the door opened and Tevuk invited me in. Again we sat for a minute of silence, and then Tevuk turned to me agreeably and said: "The council has decided that you may dig wherever you please on the Wales Reservation." With this the stoical faces became comradely again, and everyone went out to the beach, where women smiled, children played, and we were all the best of friends.

SIMMONS and Topkok soon arrived by boat, having found no old sites along the rocky shores, and our sizable crew now included not only them, Friedman, Jonah, and Phillip, but also the mayor who was simply going along for the ride. On June 20 we launched two boats in a light surf and, with powerful motors, turned northward paralleling the shore (Fig. 64).

Getting to work was not going to be as simple as this, however. First things came first. We had no sooner passed far enough out to escape the sandbar that stretches northward from Wales than a whale spouted nearby. It was a large baleen whale and we had on board neither harpoon guns nor adequate weapons. The thrill of the hunt was too great, nevertheless, for the Wales men simply to admire the beast and continue along. We must give chase. The artillery comprised two .30 Springfields suitable for caribou; two .22's, which we normally reserve for rabbits, ptarmigans, and ground squirrels; and a shotgun. Whenever the whale emerged, a fusillade was fired from all of these weapons toward the great black head, back, and waving flukes. The men would slow the motors, calculating the next point of emergence, and then rush ahead to fire again. The whale did not seem overly disturbed by all this attention, but continued on its way until we found ourselves far from land and out of ammunition. Our pursuit had clearly run its course. We were late

64. Launching boat from Wales village. Sam Friedman is in foreground. In background are Diomede Islands in Bering Strait, halfway between the United States and the U.S.S.R.

reaching the inlet where we intended to establish camp and the gasoline supply was low, but all agreed that it would have been a splendid thing to return to Wales towing so great a beast behind our boats.

We set up our tents on an island near where I had first met my friends at the old goose-hunting camp beside a sheltered channel—the middle one of three channels that fill and drain Lopp Lagoon with the daily changes of tide. This large island was called Agulaak (Map 7). A smaller island, two miles long, less than a mile wide, and bounded at the far end by Singauruk channel, had no name. We remedied this and honored Phillip at the same time by calling it Kugzruk Island. It was on that island and on the south bank of Singauruk channel that we found a succession of sites representing phases of Norton culture. On the forward beaches, which were still unstable lines of shifting dunes, there were signs of more recent peoples that we chose to ignore.

The old beach ridges of sand found intermittently all the way from Cape Espenberg to our sites near Wales are frequently difficult to follow because the original dunes were leveled off by wind and water before they had time to become heavily carpeted with sod or swamp. Along the banks of Singauruk channel, however, the current had acted as a dissecting tool to expose cross sections through ridges and swales. By walking along the shore at low tide, we found it possible to see not only artifacts that had been washed like nuggets in the shallow water of a miner's pan but even, occasionally, streaks of early floors in the banks themselves.

In three such cross sections representing old beach crests some hundreds of feet apart, we found an interesting succession. The thawed portion of the bank and the sloughed sand lying at the foot of the bank each contained a portion of a house floor. A few items recovered from the crest nearest the sea and, therefore, the youngest, were closely similar to objects of the Old Bering Sea culture of St. Lawrence Island, the most striking artifact of which was a fragmentary but typically decorated whaling harpoon head of the later Old Bering Sea style (see Fig. 57). The next older site (farther from the sea) and another beyond that contained only the stonework of Norton culture. With these clues to succession on the beach ridges and two large Norton culture deposits on Agulaak Island, our trip to this area was surely worthwhile. There remained, however, a mystery and challenge to pursue.

Several of the older people at Wales, on hearing that we intended to work at the farther end of Lopp Lagoon, were reminded of a story. Somewhere out there, they said, on one of its islands, one might look down into a pond and see, shining on the bottom, stone knives and mammoth ivory. Tevuk said that other archeologists had gone hunting for the pond but without success. Some time later Phillip, returning from a quick trip to the village, reported talking to a man who had actually seen the pond and who said it lay in the middle of what we now called Kugzruk Island. Fired by this encouragement we left our current excavation and, taking one boat and some shovels, set about scouring the island.

Most of its two or more square miles of inner reaches were difficult to traverse because of swampy swales and innumerable ponds. Now and then, however, a ridge top showed itself in the form of more solid ground or an occasional patch of bare sand. We methodically walked back and forth on the old shoreline, then criss-crossed the island for good measure, looking into the edges of all ponds. Discouraged at having found nothing, and tired of walking through the soggy terrain in the unceasing wind, we finally gave up and returned to our boat. Because of the rough sea, we had tied the craft at the shallow lagoon side of the island, and when we reached it, the tide had retreated, leaving it nestled in soft mud and no more than an inch or two of water. Anticipating an hour's pushing and poling to float ourselves free, we decided to fortify ourselves with a cup of tea. A fire of twigs was soon blazing and a pot set to boil. Sitting partly sheltered in the lee of the lagoon bank, I found myself turning now and then to scan the level ridge tops that came nearly in a line with my vision. Two uneven places, probably distorted by the lack of contrast, could be seen on the horizon. Idly curious as to whether they were a hundred feet or a half mile away, I stood up and noted with interest that they remained visible even though they were several beach ridges over. Further observing that each of these small mounds had an exposed, sandy top, I asked my companions to save some tea for me while I walked back to investigate.

Though they were hardly mounds at close range, the first of the bald features rewarded me with the sparkle of flint. Someone had camped there. Perhaps, even, human effort had in some way built the low eminence. Wind rippled the surface of a pond a few feet away and, through the habit formed during earlier hours, I walked to its mossy edge. The pond was perhaps two hundred feet long and a fourth as wide, and it was shallow, as I could see from objects lying on its sandy bottom. Then, with a flash of recognition, I saw not mere stones but objects of flint and bone. Stepping into the foot-deep pond edge in my water-resistant shoe pacs, I rolled up one sleeve and reached in to dredge with my fingers. The objects were all archeological: slabs of slate chipped into blades at the edges, flinty projectile points and fragments, bones of seals, birds, and caribou, and fragments of pottery stamped with lines or rectangles. The entire end of one side of the pond seemed to be coated with clean-washed artifacts, bones, and even fragments of wood. I fished out a polar bear skull to show my friends and, raising it high with a shout, hastened back to assure them that the old story was true after all.

"Underwater archeology" occupied us for the next three days. Fortunately the pond was no more than knee deep throughout the area in which artifacts were exposed. Even so, we could only stand in the icy water retrieving sticks and stones by hand for a short time before sloshing to shore to wave and stamp warmth into our extremities. A small fire helped considerably. Another less satisfactory way of retrieving artifacts was to dredge slowly with shovels, lifting each load carefully so as not to dislodge objects of light weight. Studying the surrounding land, we could see how the pond had received its deposit. Unfortunately for romance, this had been no sacred well into which worshippers threw their treasures. Rather, during the 2,400 years since the site was occupied a small pond had slowly enlarged its banks, cutting, eventually (not very long ago) into the frozen bulk of a winter house ruin. The bases of a few posts indicated where the tunnel must have been, and in the east bank a few bones, perhaps once tossed out the roof hole, marked the outskirts of the original mound. Fortunately objects both heavy and light remained on the firm, sandy bottom, none, as our tests showed, having become buried deeper. The mound must have remained frozen for many centuries before melting away into the water, for the wood as well as bone and ivory was far better preserved than it usually is even in very recent sites.

The fragment of a side prong of a salmon spear of spruce wood still had a sharp barb made of a sliver from a caribou leg bone bound in its tip with baleen fiber (Fig. 65d). One object of antler became a special prize because it was both well preserved and a key type. This was a harpoon head, unique in itself but carrying the marks of workmanship that tied it to more than one early culture (Fig. 65a). It was unusually broad and flat and consequently its socket was extremely wide. In these respects it resembled some specimens of Near Ipiutak and other Norton phases of culture; but it also called to mind certain Canadian and Greenlandic Dorset specimens in having a line hole in the form of two long slots on one flat face, these joining to open as a single slot on the opposite face. Long slits like those on artifacts of Ipiutak culture were grooved into the two narrow edges for the receipt of long, thin blades designed to protrude only enough to continue the forward cutting edge of the antler projectile heads themselves. Both faces of the specimen were decorated with long, narrow, parallel lines, three of which were deep gashes pointed at the ends.

A fragment of an arrow or spearhead formed from a long, cigar-shaped piece of antler had a parallel slot grooved deeply at either end (Fig. 65c). Such slots were meant to contain a stone point at the tip and to join a shaft at the base. A gash with both ends pointed, like those on the harpoon head, embellished the opposite sides. This kind of heavy projectile head is different from the thin ones of Ipiutak and later cultures but appears to be the prevalent form in all of the earlier Norton sites.

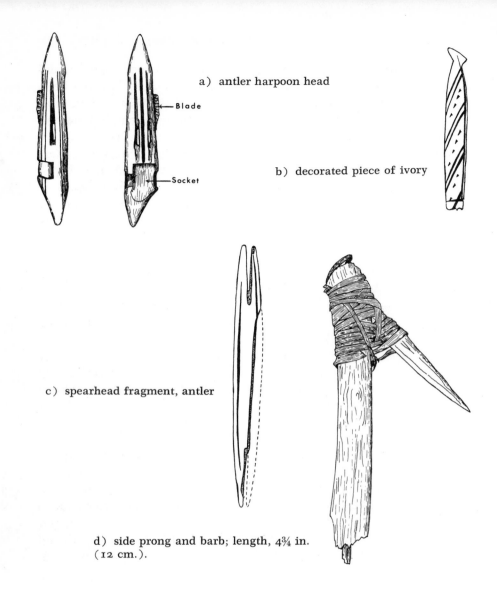

a) antler harpoon head

—Blade

b) decorated piece of ivory

—Socket

c) spearhead fragment, antler

d) side prong and barb; length, 4¾ in. (12 cm.).

65. Artifacts nearly 2,400 years old, recovered from a pond near Wales.

    A few objects showed examples of engraving, which included diagonal straight lines with rows of small triangular nicks between (Fig. 65b), large opposed triangles, and, especially, double-pointed gashes like those on the harpoon head and the spearhead. Flintwork was much cruder than that of Ipiutak, though some chert side blades and end points for projectile heads were elegant in design.

The most distinctive stonework appeared in the many knife blades and weapon points crudely flaked from a kind of hard silicified slate that separated into flat slabs along crystalline planes of cleavage. These "slab knives" ranged from a size easily hafted for use as whittling knives to large ones the size of a butcher's cleaver. Some of the medium-sized ones were presumably hafted in antler handles like the handles we found with wide slots along one edge and an open end.

Pottery lay everywhere on the pond bottom, all of it either check-stamped (see Fig. 62) or linear-stamped on the outer surface. Though thicker, it resembled Norton pottery in its flat-based forms and surface treatments.

While we were still dredging the pond we detected two shallow pits a few yards to the north. Though obscure on the surface, they could only mean the presence of squarish underground houses with entrance tunnels. We took on their excavation, too, and from the two areas once or twice a day we removed as much earth as had thawed. One house thawed more rapidly than the other, particularly in the main room, and there we began to expose a floor near the center while the tunnel and forward corners were still irregular with ice masses. One evening as we were leaving the site I noticed that the melting was proceeding more rapidly than usual, for in the deepest part of the house, where we had laid bare a central fireplace and the remnants of wood flooring, a small puddle appeared. By next morning, to our dismay, our excavations were but two pools of water. The ground we thought perennially frozen had contained, instead, only the winter's ice, now thawing from the bottom as well as the top. We had already found enough artifacts, chips, and bones, though, to show that the two houses were the same culture as the pond-site house. Radiocarbon dates for the shore houses indicate that they were built about 600 B.C., while wood from the pond house dates to about 350 B.C. Since the close similarity of stonework in the three houses leads us to think that they may have been part of a contemporary settlement, it is possible that one set of samples had enough impurities to give a date that was "off" by a few centuries.

The combined information from the scattered small sites near Wales adds up to a picture of long occupation by expert seal hunters whose livelihood depended mainly on walruses, bearded seals, and, especially, small seals during most of the year. They hunted caribou less persistently. Like all Norton people, they lived in rectangular houses with short entrance passages, the houses heated by fireplaces and seal-oil lamps. Their artifacts, though differing in some types and details from those of other sites of Norton culture, nevertheless fit into its pattern. Common to all Norton people was their almost haphazard work with soft slate. Roughly scratching it into shape and polishing only its edges, they produced but few types of blades. From flinty materials, on the other hand, they flaked a great variety of projectile points, knife blades, and the like, though these contrast with implements of Ipiutak in being useful without elegance. They seem thus to have taken little pride either in their stone edges or, judging from the few organic specimens recovered, in their finished products of antler and ivory.

Numerous net sinkers (small, flat beach pebbles, notched at the ends) show that Norton people fished a great deal, and a quantity of fine, polished grooving instruments, adz blades, and drill bits mark them as accomplished woodworkers. While we do not yet know which sex wore them, enormous labrets of stone, bitumen, and jet (that must have filled a long slit cut into the lower lip) speak for strong pride in personal appearance. Despite these specialties, though, when we compare Norton technical skills and workmanship with those of the earlier Denbigh and later Ipiutak people, we decide that Norton people were more practical in their outlook, less burdened by the demands of religious and artistic excellence, and, in many important respects, more directly in line with the uncomplicated Eskimos of recent centuries.

BEFORE we generalize too far, however, we must consider an early ceremonial aspect of Norton culture that came to light the following year, 1960, at Cape Krusenstern. Doug Anderson was just finishing work on the Ipiutak house with the skeletons of the family that had been unable to save themselves from their burning home, and the rest of the crew was hard at work on an older beach well back from the sea, when a period of rare good weather for the Cape came along. We had been waiting for such an opportunity, so Doug, Almond, and I quickly traveled by boat fifteen miles up the coast to examine a site we called Battle Rock. The Eskimo word for the site was actually more explicit: *Ochrorurok*, but this was difficult both to transliterate and to pronounce. It could

66. The author digging at Battle Rock site.

mean "oily" or "slippery rock," but what it really implied was that the gray, rounded outcropping slopes of storm-beaten limestone resembled a slab of whale blubber that had been exposed to the elements for some time. Since the rounded, sod-coated eminence at the top of the rock was the legendary site of a great fight between the shamans of Point Hope and those of Cape Krusenstern, we chose to christen the site, more simply, Battle Rock (Fig. 66).

I had been intrigued with the place for some time and once, when flying over it at a low elevation, had observed several piles of stones partly covered by sod. Doug, Almond, and I now found shelter for our boat in a small creek mouth, walked to the base of the rock, and climbed to its domelike crest. The small piles of stones that I had seen from the plane strongly suggested burials, but we decided to delay testing them until we learned something of the ordinary ground on top, where campers down through the centuries might inadvertently have left some record of their visits. We began to strip sod from a relatively flat expanse, greener than elsewhere and not unlike a clipped lawn. Within moments we knew that the site was a rare one. Light-brown objects glistening in their dampness were artifacts—not mere animal bones of a long-ago feast. Furthermore, these were weapon heads of antler, larger than any I had seen, and of an ancient style, despite their fresh appearance and place just beneath the sod (Figs. 67 and 68). I recognized

67. Weapon heads as they were uncovered just beneath the sod at Battle
Rock site, 1960. Made of antler, they
were used about 600 B.C.

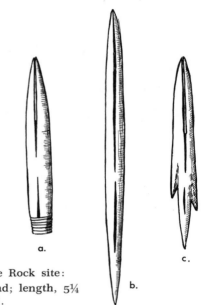

a.

c.

68. Antler weapon heads from the Battle Rock site:
a) socketed head   c) barbed head; length, 5¼
b) double-pointed head   in. (13.2 cm.).

b.

the form as similar to that of the heavy, cigar-shaped weapon head
from the pond site near Wales (Fig. 65), but these were a third as
long again, slotted at only one end, and differently engraved.

Resisting the impulse to take up the artifacts at once, we continued to strip sod, uncovering an incredible number of similar
pointed objects together with a few artifacts of other types and a
few small bones. None of the objects were localized on the surface,
and since they formed no pattern to foretell the form of a structure
deeper in the ground, we could not guess at first what manner of
excavation we ought to make. After more digging and testing, the
area in which the artifacts appeared turned out to be roughly
circular, with a diameter of no less than fifteen feet. As we dug
deeper, the tops of large stones began to emerge, and lying at all
angles between were the points and bases of projectile heads.

Slowly, as our excavation deepened, we saw that the perimeter in which artifacts and bones were found decreased in size as it deepened. Also we observed with interest that none of the scattered bones were those of seals. Among them we soon identified the heel bone of a human being—and then discovered that they were, in fact, *all* human.

At first the stones made no sense as a grave, but after sketching their location and removing the top ones, we saw that the heavier ones beneath described a large rectangle, originally of upright slabs and more capacious than an ordinary burial. More speculative excavation presently solved the curious nature of the deposit. Some of the long arrowheads and spearpoints lay parallel to one another and in a line, as though laid out at an angle from the tomb to some distant part of the surface. All other explanations failing, we thought of our traditional enemies at Cape Krusenstern, the ground squirrels. Though none now lived in the site, they had undoubtedly burrowed for decades or centuries through and under this stone-lined grave, attempting from time to time to remove the prickly objects in their way by dragging them through their circular tunnels. When one arrowhead and then another and another became jammed in their path, the beasts had undoubtedly abandoned that exit and dug a new one.

Our excavation when completed was an inverted cone, its vertex four feet below where the floor of the tomb must have been and its wide perimeter at ground level. Human bones as well as artifacts were equally distributed throughout, and we learned from the bones that no fewer than three individuals were represented, all apparently adult males. While a large proportion of the smaller bones of their bodies were recovered, not one jaw or skull fragment remained. An incisor tooth, shovel-shaped as expected in an Eskimo or other person of Mongolian stock, furnished the only evidence that the bodies may have been whole when buried. We still speculate about how even a trained team of squirrels working together like so many stevedores could have removed skulls from such a deep burial without leaving a further clue.

The projectile heads took three main forms. First were the cylindrical ones, long, drawn to a point at the extremities, and provided either with a slot for a flint end blade or with one or two slots for long slender side blades (Fig. 68b). Second were very thick and short heads with an end slot or with barbs; these seemed more likely to have been spear than arrowheads (Fig. 68c). Third were other thick forms often decorated with a series of rings about the flat base into which a socket was deeply drilled for shaft attachment (Fig. 68a). Presumably these weapon heads were attached to their shafts when placed as grave goods in the original burials. As all but a few rotten fragments of the wood that seems to have floored the grave had long since disappeared, any shafts also would have rotted away.

At first we thought the weapon heads might have been put into the graves unfinished, but in a few of them we found broken bases of end points or side blades of flint. These seemed to have been ripped out hastily in preparing the grave goods, perhaps a form of "killing" the object so that its spirit could follow its dead master's spirit into another world, a custom widely practiced among American Indians and tribal groups in other far-flung places. Many of the flints extracted from the weapon heads must have been allowed to remain in the grave, however, for we recovered enough to show the range of points and side blades that had been used.

Other goods from the same burial included the head of a splitting adz, side prongs for bird or fish spears, a barb for the tip of a fish spear, a flaker handle for flintwork as well as two tips to be bound into the handle, a two-hand scraper, a long sharp awl or pin of dog leg bone, and other organic objects. A few

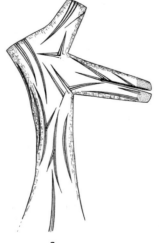

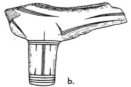

69. Engraved antler objects, Battle Rock site:

a) Only half this convex piece is shown; its full length is 13½ in. (35.5 cm.).

b) Parallel lines and gashes mark this carving, which is 4¼ in. across (10.7 cm.).

sherds of thin gray pottery, fiber tempered like some of the Norton and all of the Choris pottery—the latter being the earliest found on the Alaskan coast—bore either a linear stamp or cord marking; the surface treatment was too obscure for certain identification.

The most remarkable pieces recovered from the site were well-preserved examples of engraving art. One such large segment, of antler, appeared at first to represent an animal's head (Fig. 69a). This resemblance was fortuitous, however, for the object was apparently designed to fit some unidentified frame or wider surface. The basic elements of the design, which covered the whole face of the piece, were long gashes brought to a point of spider-web thinness at either end. These double-pointed elements were combind with half elements in a variety of pleasing ways and were essentially the same as the design on the sides of most of the projectile points. Another object that was covered with these long, deep, double-pointed gashes was a segment of antler grooved on the base with parallel markings (Fig. 69b). Though double the size, the gashes on these Battle Rock pieces resembled those found on the harpoon head from Kugzruk Pond. They suggested, too, some of the decorative elements and motifs found on Okvik culture objects, though the Battle Rock pieces were ten times as large.

Some other decorated pieces from the Battle Rock grave suggested brow bands and, at the same time, snow goggles—yet if they were "brow bands," they had a space, as for the bridge of a nose, but no eye openings; and if they were "goggles," they had hollowed channels on the under surface as though for fitting over a nose, but again lacked provision for sight. They were probably designed for attachment over the faces of the dead, a custom similar to that practiced by Ipiutakers several hundred years later who, in some of their burials, placed thin plates of antler over the mouth and nose and replaced the eyes of their dead with ivory eyeballs (see Fig. 36).

The old Battle Rock burial thus seemed to anticipate the burials of Ipiutak in the deep interment, abundant grave goods, and the provision of decorated face masks to cover the eyes. In other respects, however—the rock-lined tomb, the forms and large size of implements and weapons, and the expansive and unique style of decoration—this site is set apart from all others in the Arctic. Whoever these men were, they were treated with exceptional

70. A Western Thule man who was buried in a stone-lined grave at the Battle Rock site.

respect by their friends and relatives. Their weapon heads alone numbered more than two hundred fifty, nearly all in a good state of preservation. Added to the other organic pieces and flints, more than three hundred artifacts were recovered from this single burial.

As to its date of occupation, we might have guessed Battle Rock as halfway in time between Denbigh and Ipiutak if it had not been for the close similarity of its flints to those of certain Norton hearths and other features on the surfaces of beach ridges at Cape Krusenstern. From its flints we knew that it must be classed as the earliest aspect of Norton culture, about 600 B.C.

A side light to the excavation of the old rock-lined tomb was the exposure that same summer of three nearby, half-buried rock piles that we had earlier puzzled over. Each proved to be the burial of a man, with sparse grave goods, probably dating from Western Thule times. The bodies had been placed in a rectangle of upright stones and each tomb had been sealed with stone slabs (Fig. 70). The surprising thing was that stone-lined graves were known for Thule people of eastern Canada and Greenland, but Western Thule people elsewhere had buried their dead in log tombs. These Battle Rock Western Thule interments must have been much like the centuries earlier Norton burial that we had first dug. Only further searches can tell whether or not rock-lined graves such as these persisted for a long time in the western Arctic without our having noticed them before.

. . .

BUT TO RETURN to the summer of 1959: after Bill Simmons, Sam Friedman, and I had been permitted by the village council of Wales to excavate in the vicinity and had retrieved the many Norton-type artifacts from the water of the pond, we met Hans-Georg Bandi in Kotzebue and all went to Cape Krusenstern to dig the beaches there for the rest of the season. It was that summer that Bandi found the piece of pottery on a ridge top behind Beach 35 (the Ipiutak ridge) that led to the finding of other pieces of the broken pot of Norton culture (Fig. 62). After that, we walked and rewalked those older ridges hoping to find some obscure house to excavate or, failing this, any feature at all that would add to what we already knew of Norton culture.

At first the discoveries were few and far between. Then we learned to prospect by studying the color of the ground where patches could be glimpsed through the moss. A reddish hue in the sand or a red, fire-broken pebble usually led to an old hearth. The hearth in turn was often the center of a larger area marked by cooking rocks, charcoal smears, flint chips, potsherds, and even artifacts. Many such areas—perhaps most—were once the sites of tents. This was indicated by the limits to which flint chips and broken rocks extended—the limits being those of the former inside walls of a circular or oval tent.

While it was obvious at once that the artifacts from such sites were not those of the Ipiutak people of A.D. 400 or the Denbigh people of 3000 B.C., it was sometimes difficult for us to detect whether they belonged to a phase of the intermediary Norton culture or some other. This could better be determined after examination and study in the laboratory at the Haffenreffer Museum. After a winter or two of close scrutiny and cross-comparison of the materials from these hearths, we can now draw upon both the field discoveries and analyses to know that nine beach ridges at Cape Krusenstern, 36 through 44, present a panorama of some six hundred years of Norton culture.

Ridges 36 to 39 could be identified and counted only toward the less rich eastern end of the beach ridge sequence. Farther toward the west they were long ago removed by sea action and covered over by the Ipiutak "crest" of several ridges, but Beach 40 paralleled the Ipiutak ridge for some miles and contained a relatively large number of hearths of Norton culture. On this ridge one day

71. Cache of arrowpoints found on Norton Beach 40, Cape Krusenstern. They date to about 200 B.C.

that same summer, Bill Simmons saw a glint of light between the leaves of a carpet of crowberry plants growing directly out of the gravel. Approaching with caution so as not to destroy a possible hearth, he found no mere chip but a handsomely flaked projectile point. Carefully cutting away the berry plants, he then exposed a site such as one is seldom lucky enough to find. His first point, a broad and very thin triangular biface, was only one of many specimens overlapping each other like the scales of a fish. Careful though he was in lifting and cutting the dense branches with his pocket-knife, he was unable to keep the entire cache intact for a photograph. Yet nearly all the objects had lain together as shown by the few in Fig. 71. Only three or four had been scattered, possibly by a reindeer's hooves, before the present ground cover had formed.

Of the forty-six points, undoubtedly of arrows, thirty fragile specimens were whole. Of the fragments for which no completing parts were found, thirteen were bases; two, tips; and only one an unmatched mid-section. This imbalance suggests that a few fragments were lost but shows clearly that all belonged together, probably as the products of a single flintworker who most likely had used them in a day's hunt. From the broken specimens, the prevalence of bases suggests that the hunter had gone out with a quiverful of arrows, had broken thirteen, but had not yet removed the bases of these from their shafts. Why so much valuable equipment was left intact we can only guess. Perhaps the hunter had some reason to hide his bow and arrows in the grass or under a bush and then, as bewildered by the sameness of the beach ridges as we are now when trying to return to an unmarked spot, failed to find them again—or perhaps he met with some mishap. At any rate, the arrowheads of his cache show that he lived during a late phase of Norton culture, about 200 B.C.

On Beaches 40 to 43 nothing was found that did not correspond to Norton culture at Point Hope (where it was called "Near Ipiutak"—p. 126), Cape Denbigh, and Wales. On Beach 44 in a large hearth area, side blades and the base of a large point turned up that were identical to points in the Battle Rock burial. Since Beach 44 contained two distinct types of surface features—one related to Battle Rock, an early phase of Norton dated at 600 B.C., and the other to Choris, which preceded Norton—we felt that on this single beach ridge, which fronted the ocean for at most a few decades, we could pinpoint the change that took place between the culture of Choris and that of Norton.

At least on this part of the coast of Alaska, Norton culture began earlier than 600 B.C. with a Battle Rock phase originating we know not where, and this was followed by centuries of occupation by a people of changing Norton culture that culminated in the Near Ipiutak phase of about 100 B.C. If the Battle Rock people overwhelmed those of Choris, we are left with no evidence of a conflict but only of change. The possibility of armed clashes cannot be ruled out, however, in this area where the folklore of Eskimos is replete with accounts of killing and vengeance and where for a number of recent centuries men provided themselves with heavy armor made of bone (see Fig. 58). Whatever the causes of change in culture at Cape Krusenstern, we are certain that the beaches, if ever abandoned at all, were abandoned for only the very shortest time.

(X)

CHORIS—POTTERS AND VILLAGERS

Those of us who try to see the greater picture at Cape Krusenstern by walking its surface sometimes feel we are fleas examining an elephant. On the older ridges where there are Norton, Choris, and even earlier sites (Map 2), it is easy to lose the beach crest we are following when it is cut across by a pond or what appears at first to be a limitless lake. In other places, the ridges are cut at irregular intervals by long, canal-like ditches often terminating southward at the imposing Ipiutak ridge but sometimes slicing through it. On first seeing these ditches at close range, one assumes that they are man-made—some swamp-draining federal project of the Great Depression, perhaps. On second thought, though, what conceivable reason could there have been to create such strikingly regular ditches for the benefit of a few coastal hunters or a herd of reindeer?

They are, of course, neither the waterways of ancient boatmen nor the drains of government engineers, but are made by frost action. Unlike the small frost polygons marking the ground of oldest beaches, these are nearly all rectangular and large, their margins cutting (dozens or hundreds of feet apart) at right angles across the beaches or, at even wider intervals, parallel to the ridges. On the lower ground these frost cracks become canals leading from one pond to another. Presumably they have influenced the formation of the larger ponds and lakes in the older parts of the beach ridge sequence. All this becomes clearer as we take to the air in a slow

72. Aerial view of beach ridges and ponds, Cape Krusenstern. Frost cracks can be seen cutting across the ridges in the foreground.

plane (Fig. 72). The greater frost cracks then seem limited by time, for the full network stops short at Beach 35 which began to form only about two thousand years ago.

WE HUNTED repeatedly on the older ground at Cape Krusenstern, behind Ipiutak Beach 35 and Norton beaches 36–44, for the oval depressions that would indicate Choris-period houses. All surface signs that looked like house depressions proved barren, however, being instead sink holes caused either by ice in the ground or quirks of current and sea encroachment during the time when the beaches were formed. Once reconciled to the dearth of houses, we learned to recognize Choris sites of another kind—namely camping places, presumably tent sites, just under the sod. Moreover, we saw that implement types changed from beach to beach, attesting to a long period before Norton times when people of Choris culture dominated this coast of Alaska. These new forms promised to add materially to what we had learned of Choris culture at Choris Peninsula (Map 3).

There, in 1956, the discovery of the first big oval house pits had been quite startling. My companions that season were Almond Downey, whom I had met in Kotzebue and hired as boatman, and two graduate students, Robert Ackerman from the University of

Pennsylvania and Melvin Reichler from Brown University. On our way to investigate the shores of Eschscholtz Bay and the banks of the Buckland River, we had set up a temporary camp on the east side of the long Choris Peninsula to wait out a wind storm. Making the most of a bad situation, we explored the local beaches on foot.

Our longest hike took us slogging upward through deep tundra for several hundred feet to the crest of the whale-shaped peninsula. We then walked briskly down the west slope until it became a steep embankment, where we lowered ourelves slowly through dense willow thickets to the base near the sea. There each of us chose one of a series of parallel old beach ridges that filled a mile-long embayment and proceeded along looking for flints or house pits.

My ridge was the most clearly defined inner one, wide, and covered nearly everywhere with a well-developed sod. Having found no sign of habitation until halfway along, I was gratified, finally, to see a depression ahead—and no ordinary depression at that! Stretching forty feet across the beach ridge crest and twenty-five feet from side to side, it was neither the rectangle of a house nor the circle of a bomb crater but an even, elliptical hollow, shaped like some gigantic serving dish. Surely this was not an aboriginal dwelling site! Could it have been the work of nineteenth-century explorers who had sojourned here? No, not that, either, for the slow-growing heath that covered it was as well established at the rim and inside the pit as on the surrounding ground surface. Signaling to my companions on their several ridges, I ranged more widely on mine while they approached. Fifty yards farther, I saw a second oval pit, somewhat smaller than the first but still much larger than any other Eskimo ruin of which I knew. Fifty yards again beyond that, as though the three had been purposely spaced at equal intervals, was another, the largest of the three.

We walked about marveling at this strange discovery and saw that small, shallow depressions lay at irregular intervals near the large ovals and that in front of each was a deep, smaller oval no more than twelve feet long. While we were not fully equipped for excavation, each had his shovel and trowel, and with these we set about cutting a test trench across the first-discovered pit. The sand and gravel immediately beneath the surface were sterile, containing no artifacts, but as our tests progressed, brown stains appeared, suggesting roof layers of disintegrated houses. Still deeper in one square, we found signs of a floor, now a dark bed of gravel

73. Choris potsherds showing linear stamping. Sherd at lower left is about 2 in.   Compare design with that of Norton and Western Thule pots (Figs. 22 and 62).

two or more inches thick, that contained both flint chips and fragments of slate.

Then a special kind of artifact came to light. This was the fragment of a clay pot, stamped on the outside with a linear design (Fig. 73). Unlike the early Norton Bay pottery, which had a gritty texture, this specimen had been made of clay mixed liberally with something organic, possibly the down of ducks.

By the end of the day we had exposed enough of the floor to show that numbers of people had lived in whatever kind of structure this was. They had eaten many a meal here, feasting upon caribou as liberally as upon seal, an unexpected circumstance if the site were of Norton culture. Additional artifacts—the basal fragments of two bifaced blades, probably spearpoints, and a complete stemmed spearpoint flaked diagonally and serrated at the edge—told us definitely that this house was not Norton.

That evening, tired but exhilarated with our discovery, we climbed back over the hills through sodden tundra, almost unmindful of the lashing rain. When we reached camp, the storm had beaten at our tents until two of the small ones had broken loose from their guy lines and now lay like wrinkled oysters on the beach. During the night the sky cleared and the wind died as suddenly as it had risen. In the morning, still fascinated with our discovery, we debated about whether to move camp to the seaward side of the peninsula to start digging the new site or to go ahead first with exploring for other sites, our main purpose that season. We decided on the latter.

WHATEVER local deities controlled our good fortune those first days at Choris in 1956, they cast no favor on our subsequent moves. Eskimo gods are sometimes troll-like creatures, placing obstacles in the paths of men and rolling in laughter when their tricks succeed. The first day out, we examined Chamisso Island (Map 3), feeling that we were climbing its rocks almost in the footsteps of von Kotzebue, Beechey, and other early explorers. The island held nothing of appeal, but from its heights we could see broad beaches on the southeast mainland of Choris Peninsula, so we headed in that direction before entering Eschscholtz Bay. Still finding no early sites, we turned our boat northward again later the same afternoon and were at once buffeted by wind which churned up such waves that we progressed hazardously at only half speed. At this point an emergency struck.

The sight of game of any kind triggers a reflex in the male Eskimo, and there on the peninsula parallel to us were a pair of caribou. Rolling and pitching with our boat, I turned to see Almond reaching for his rifle. Unquestionably we were in for it! Our navigator would surely shoot first and only then consider the danger of tipping over. Glancing at the rough water ahead, and then back to the stern, I was somewhat relieved to see Almond continue to steer with one hand as he passed the rifle forward with the other. The .30–.30 went to Mel, who lost no time in passing it like a hot potato to Bob. With distress, I saw the weapon continue on its way to me in the bow. Clearly Almond wanted me to shoot a caribou from this pitching boat at a distance I would never have chosen even had I been on solid ground and equipped with a telescopic sight.

There was no opportunity to debate the point, however, nor did I mistake my role. Like the harpooner in a whaling crew, my duty was to strike. I caught the rifle, braced myself as best I could, and pointed it in the general direction of the fleeing deer. It was no use. The boat bucked the waves and then wallowed in the troughs. The barrel one moment pointed high into the blue sky and the next into the gray water. I made a gesture of futility toward the stern of the boat, but my companions waved their arms excitedly toward the beach and all yelled: "Shoot!" Once more I aimed, and when the barrel seemed to be dipping from the sky over the tops of the moving dots, I fired. Incredibly, one of the dots hesitated, leaped into the air, and fell flat to the beach. I assumed that it had stumbled on a rock, but Almond turned the boat shoreward at once. We all crouched as the boat, with motor roaring, mounted the crest of a wave, and was carried high onto the sandy beach. In an almost continuous movement Almond had dashed off with the rifle, leaving the rest of us to secure the boat. That done, we followed along, I considering myself only a surrogate hunter and expecting to see Almond standing jubilant beside his prey.

Instead, when we arrived his face was blank. With a total lack of emotion, he said: "Looks like he's got a tag on." Glancing down with misgivings, I saw the glint of a metal band looped through a hole in the animal's ear. We had not killed a wild caribou from the hills—we had killed a reindeer buck that was someone's property. Abashed, we gathered about and contemplated the fat beast. How a reindeer happened to be on this coast we could not guess, for the nearest herd of which we knew was forty miles north at Kotzebue. Nevertheless, there was the tag, except for which we might have remained carefree travelers with a boatload of meat, welcome wherever we went. After a fleeting thought of destroying the offending ear with its message, we decided to shoulder the blame, search out the rightful owner, and make recompense of whatever sort might be required. In the meantime, we assured ourselves, we would not be hung higher if we helped ourselves to reindeer steak.

After a day of exploring the south shore of Eschscholtz Bay, we entered the mouth of the Buckland River, a stream forested in its upper reaches. I had hoped to take growth samples in the form of cores from spruce trees for tree-ring dating and had thought we might also find datable house pits along the banks of the river here as I had along the forested Kobuk River. By the time we got as far as the first straggling trees, however, the river had become so shallow that it seemed doubtful for a while that we could reach even Buckland village thirty miles upstream. Nevertheless, after a hard day's travel we reached the town that evening (Fig. 74). Only a few families lived in this village of log cabins arrayed on either side

74. Buckland village, 1956.

of the Alaska Native Service Cooperative Store, and they regarded us with interest. Visitors rarely came here, and our efforts to set up tents on the riverbank met with many suggestions from the townsfolk. Small children, especially, were almost too eager to help, and a dozen or so husky pups inquired into everything.

We still had the reindeer on our consciences, and at the first opportunity made inquiries. Its owner soon appeared. He had only recently received a herd of his own from the government stock near Deering, and while he had not missed any animals, he was certain that the two we encountered had strayed the thirty miles or so from Buckland. The estimate of worth that he placed on our reindeer was high, and though I calculated the cost of our steaks and stews as outlandishly expensive, I nevertheless gave him what he asked. This made Almond once again the legal possessor of a boatload of meat and ready to do what any self-respecting hunter likes best—share his catch with his neighbors. With our consent, he distributed all but one hindquarter of the carcass among his new-found friends and relatives. As things turned out, we might as well have given away all our meat, because the dogs got into our boat while we slept and carried away what little we had kept. With the minor gods so clearly against us, it is not surprising that we became eager to leave the all-too-young archeology of the Buckland and get back to the mysterious and intriguing oval houses at Choris Peninsula; yet, before this there was time for one more joke at my expense.

On the morning after we arrived at Buckland I asked where I could find the oldest man of the village, and all agreed that I

75. Mrs. Handley and some of her descendants, Buckland village, 1956.

should walk up the trail to John Handley's cabin, where, they said, the old man would be glad to tell me about the early days. Handley was at first reluctant to turn off the shortwave radio on which he was getting pre-election news of the 1956 presidential race in the States, but at length he settled down to tell me of his life as a reindeer herder and the ways of his people. From his recollections, I calculated him to be in his early seventies. He was a good narrator with a memory still keen. But after a while we reached an impasse. This had to do with the life of women in the summer camps while the men were away procuring deerskins for winter clothing. John admitted that he knew little about this and could not answer some of my questions.

"Well," I said, "if you don't know, I guess no one does, because they tell me you are the oldest man in the village." "Yes," he said, "I am the oldest man—but you could ask my mother—she lives over there across the river and she knows all about those things." It was true. They thought the old woman was over a hundred, and I had no doubt she was as I tried in vain to coax her into telling me the story of the oldest woman in the village (Fig. 75).

After sampling spruce trees at Buckland with a tubular borer, we turned back down the river and soon reached Choris Peninsula, where we set up camp on the ocean beach. I was eager to uncover the story of one of the Choris houses here, because their large size

76. Excavation of a Choris house, Choris Peninsula, 1956. The oval outline of the house can be seen around the cuts.

and oval shape seemed to be unique in Alaska. As we had already learned from the test trench, the problems of excavation at Choris were special. Whatever wood had been used in construction was now wholly rotted away or was represented only by brownish pulp with occasionally a flattened bundle of fibers. The house may not even have been floored with wood. The thickness of its cultural layer, and the fact that artifacts were scattered unevenly throughout instead of lying flat as they would have had the surface been floored, suggested that people had simply laid their beds directly on gravel at the bottom of the excavation. When this is the case, such things as bones left over from meals, shavings from whittling and chopping, chips from flintwork, and other carelessly dropped objects inevitably become trampled haphazardly into the gravel.

It seemed impractical to expose the floor of this enormous house all at once and expect it to remain intact. Rather, it would be better to pare down a series of strips and pie cuts, leaving untouched sections or walls standing between (Fig. 76). By this means we could carefully watch profiles (the steep faces of such excavations), noting from the stains they left where the roof and walls had lain, or where ground squirrels had burrowed. Slowly the pattern emerged. This was a house without corners—a great oval excavation, originally protected at the edges by a low wall of wood. The stains of post holes in two curved rows down the center of the floor showed that the roof had probably been formed by slanting poles from the ground to long rafters. Between the rafters would have been a flat strip of roof. We envisioned the whole house as a mound of earth with a hole at its summit for light and ventilation.

House 1, this first excavation, had no clear-cut fireplace, though a charred area near one end contained fragments of charcoal. Nearby was a large stone lamp. The floor was thirty-four feet long by fifteen feet at the widest—tremendous by Eskimo standards. If the areas between the rows of posts and the outer walls were sleeping places corresponding to those in Eskimo houses, this dwelling might easily have accommodated thirty people. Trench as we might around the periphery of the house, we could find no trace of an entrance passage below the original ground surface. It seemed likely that entry to the house was through the same hole in the roof that provided light and air, a feature apparently shared with the later people of Ipiutak.

The small oval pit that lay thirty feet diagonally to the left of House 1 looking toward the sea had rounded edges and a basin-like floor in which no signs were strong enough to indicate its function. Unduly large and deep for a cache pit, it may have been a sweathouse like certain small ones used recently by Bering Sea Eskimos. The smaller and shallower circular pits resembled recent cache holes. Another depression, near the south wall of the house, contained in its shallow floor many sherds of broken pottery as well as burnt bone and charcoal and may have been a sheltered cooking place.

IT WAS NOT until two years later, in 1958, that we excavated the other two houses at Choris Peninsula. That was the year we made a reconnaissance of the whole Kotzebue Sound area (Chapter 2), digging these houses before we headed for the beach ridges at Cape Krusenstern in August. The remaining two Choris houses had the same oval plan as House 1, though House 2 was shorter (twenty-six feet) and House 3 longer (thirty-nine feet). The rows of the molds of central posts in Houses 2 and 3 were less distinct, but both houses may have had parallel rows of posts rather than paired arcs. House 2 had a well-defined central fireplace, while House 3 had none.

Like their successors (the people of Norton culture), the people of Choris boiled their meat in small, round-bottomed pots of clay impressed over the outside with fine parallel markings left by a striated stamp or paddle (Fig. 73). They used some slate for knife blades, polishing only the edges and leaving the other parts coarsely scratched as by scraping with flint edges. Other Norton-like articles used by Choris people were grooved stones, thought to be shaft smoothers; stones for pointing the tips of antler and ivory implements; and both flaker tips and flaking hammer heads for flintwork.

The resemblances of Choris objects to those of Eskimo cultures are perhaps due mainly to the plainness of many familiar tools. Among these are blunt bird arrowheads, barbed dart heads, knife handles of antler, spoons, and plain adz heads. Unlike later Eskimos or even Ipiutak or Norton people, however, the people of Choris flaked adz blades of flinty stone, setting them, unpolished, into antler heads.

For their hard organic materials the Choris people chose to use mainly antler. Their extremely fine needles were of bird bone, with eyes so small as to receive only the thinnest strands of sinew, this speaking for excellence in the sewing of skin clothing. Nothing remains of their work in wood, but their rare pieces of ivory show they were expert artisans and decorators. Their barbed dart heads were like those used by recent Eskimos for hunting seals, yet had a distinctive style of their own. Curiously enough, the Ipiutak people, between Choris and recent Eskimos in time, knew nothing of such barbed dart heads. One of the Choris specimens, carved of antler, has its two upper barbs slightly asymmetrical but joined by a curve that makes the upper segment appear to have been pierced by the point of the lower. A slot crossing the end of the upper segment contains, still firmly wedged in, a blade of amber-colored chalcedony (Fig. 77a). The tip of an ivory dart head of the same kind has the curve of its upper barbs set off by a series of minute drilled dots.

Most of the ivory objects have become eroded from long entwinement by roots, yet with a magnifying glass and a shift of lighting one can make out on a carved bust of a human figure traces of lines leading across the face from the corners of the mouth

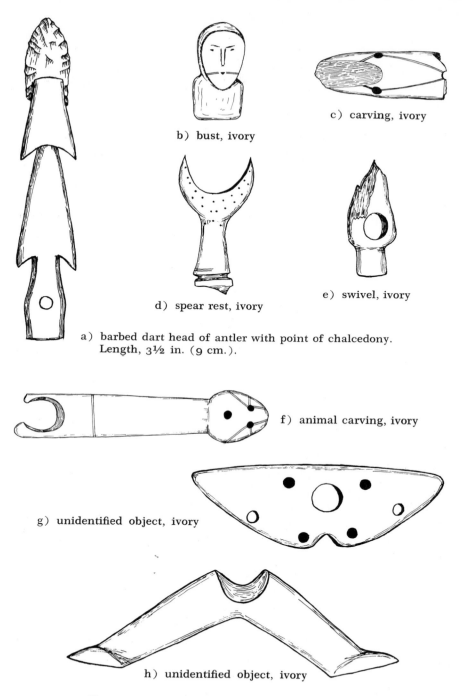

b) bust, ivory

c) carving, ivory

d) spear rest, ivory

e) swivel, ivory

a) barbed dart head of antler with point of chalcedony.
Length, 3½ in. (9 cm.).

f) animal carving, ivory

g) unidentified object, ivory

h) unidentified object, ivory

77. Choris artifacts of about 1000 B.C., Cape Krusenstern.

(Fig. 77b). These lines were made with an extremely fine-pointed instrument, as were similar decorative lines, always in pairs and executed with a uniform lightness of touch, on a number of other objects.

Large drilled dots appear on two carvings (Figs. 77c and 77f). These are interconnected by parallel lines and were most likely inset originally with jet or another dark substance, reminding one of Okvik and Punuk designs (see Fig. 56), yet the combination of their large size and the almost invisible parallel lines makes the Choris carvings unique. One of these decorated pieces (Fig. 77f) has light lines arranged in such a way as to suggest a face with tattoo marks about the eyes, and when the piece is turned sideways a still different face appears.

Some of the ivory objects may not presently be identified even though they seem to represent swivels of some kind, "rests" such as might be placed on the deck of a kayak to hold spears, or bow-string guards such as northern Indians have used recently to protect their hands and wrists (Fig. 77d, e, g, h).

Shoulder blades of caribou were also lightly engraved by Choris people. One or two had paired lines, as on the ivory carvings, while others were more coarsely treated, one even showing part of a painted design. In examining the bone collection further, we noticed that these scapulas far outnumbered other caribou bones. Since there would be no particular reason for bringing into the house more cuts of venison containing the shoulder blade than those containing, for example, marrow, we set about studying these pieces in detail. Soon it appeared that nearly all the scapula fragments shared one point in common: they had been cracked on the wider part of the blade as though from exposure to fire. Indeed, a smudge on one or another side bore out the probability that they had been cracked by heat.

This phenomenon might have been more puzzling had we not known of the practice of scapulimancy, or scapula divining, a form of fortune-telling practiced by peoples on both sides of Bering Strait. Known from archeological evidence some thousands of years old in northern China, where sheep bones were used, and from recent tribes including the Chukchi of northeastern Asia, this practice apparently bypassed recent Eskimos but cropped up among the Athapaskan Indians of Alaska and continued as a custom across the continent to the Algonkian Indians of the Atlantic seaboard. Did this mean that the Choris people, so different in culture from those of Ipiutak, represented a wave of Asians into America or a wave of Indians to the Arctic coast? Intriguing as this thought is, we still must note the basically Eskimo-like nature of most of the antler and ivory pieces from the Choris houses and the evidence of Choris skills at hunting seals as well as land game.

The bones from Choris Peninsula posed another question, too. All animal bones from the three houses were taken to the laboratory for study, and more than three thousand were complete enough for measurement and precise identification. The proportions were quite different from those of most Arctic sites similarly located on a coast of the mainland. An Ipiutak site, for example, had 53 per cent small seal bones, 12 per cent bearded seal, 23 per cent walrus, only 10 per cent caribou, and 2 per cent miscellaneous. Choris contained 20 per cent small seal, 5 per cent bearded seal, no walrus, 54 per cent caribou, and 21 per cent bones of beluga, birds, and a few other animals. The proportion of caribou bones from Choris was thus inordinately high. Why should this be so? Choris Peninsula has not been an exceptionally good caribou hunting place in recent times.

In measuring the distinctive parts of all of these bones, we found another anomaly. Those of caribou were considerably smaller than the bones of present-day Alaskan caribou. Furthermore, in comparing the bones of Choris caribou with those of two domesticated reindeer skeletons we had procured—presumably of Siberian origin—we found that the Choris ones were as small as or even smaller than those Old World animals of today. Did this mean that all caribou at the time of Choris were considerably smaller than modern caribou? One bit of evidence, all too slight for so important a conclusion, did appear. A single astragalus—the blocky joint bone in the leg—was larger than all the others and proved to be identical in size to those of modern caribou. Since this bone also came from a Choris house floor, it seemed to indicate that caribou of the present variety as well as a much smaller one coexisted in western Alaska and were both hunted by Choris people.

Still another answer was possible, however. According to theory, domesticated reindeer originated somewhere far in the west of Asia and only slowly penetrated eastward, arriving in the Chukchi area but a few centuries ago. While the arguments for such a distribution have never been seriously questioned, they appear to be based on something less than archeological proof and seem grounded in assumptions about the spread of tribes across Asia— assumptions that themselves bear re-examination. Our heretical question is, were those aberrant deer of Alaska not caribou at all but reindeer of the time, domesticated, and introduced to the coast of Alaska by some herding groups from the Chukchi Peninsula? Present reindeer were brought to Alaska in the late 1800's without much trouble—they were merely hobbled, lifted into small boats, and brought ashore. Why, then, could not people with big skin boats have transported animals, even by the dozens, across Bering Strait whenever they wished?

If our Choris people were, indeed, deer herders rather than hunters, then their great communal houses, their scapula divining, and their pottery (apparently introduced from Asia) are easily understood, for the people were pastoralists who looked after and depended upon their own herds, supplementing their diet with the meat and fat of seals. Impossible though it is just now to pursue the idea further for lack of sites of comparable culture and age in Asia and Alaska, I sometimes visualize the Choris village as that of three extended families, each with several men as herders and enough others to go out in boats to procure the sealskins and ivory that they fashioned into Eskimo-like clothing, weapons, and implements.

Whatever the evidence from the animal bones may prove to mean, the flintwork of Choris related most readily to very ancient and distant flaking skills in both Asia and America. Microblades appear to have played no part in this flintwork. On the other hand, large, parallel-edged blades, most of which, unfortunately, were broken (Fig. 78a), appear identical with those of the blade-and-core industry of the European Paleolithic of 50,000 years ago. Other large flakes used for scrapers and coarse tools (Fig. 78d) as well as for the first step in producing smaller tools such as burins (Fig. 78c) resemble Old World techniques that preceded those of the blade-and-core industry. Most of the earlier cultures in this same Arctic area lack these specialties, and we have as yet no insight into how or why these ways of working flint were passed along from very early times.

More immediately puzzling was the presence in each of the houses of fragments of large stone spearpoints that, in details of shape, were like some of those used to kill now extinct herd animals in the Great Plains and Rocky Mountains of the American West. These pieces were mainly the basal fragments of points (Fig. 78b); they were perhaps already broken when taken home, where it would have been easier or more convenient to unlash them from their shafts. Then, perhaps, they were discarded in the loose earth of the house floor. All showed excellent, parallel, diagonal flaking, concave bases, and edge grinding like those of their protoypes in distant and more temperate lands.

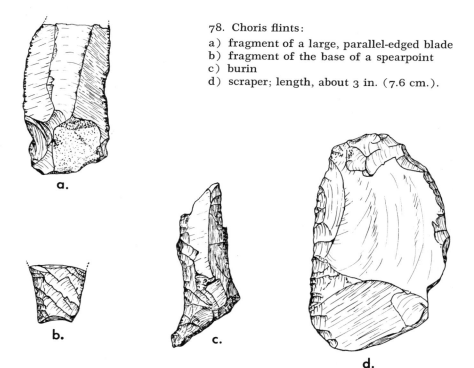

78. Choris flints:
a) fragment of a large, parallel-edged blade
b) fragment of the base of a spearpoint
c) burin
d) scraper; length, about 3 in. (7.6 cm.).

HERE, THEN, was a village that existed before Norton times— a village of caribou hunters and seal hunters who lived about 1000 B.C. on the coast of Choris Peninsula in large communal dwellings of unique form, whose stonework retained vestiges of the flaking done in the distant past in both Asia and America, and whose tools and designs were later adopted by the Eskimos and Chukchis.

While no Choris houses other than those original three have yet turned up, at least two other localities possess sites that show the Choris occupation to have been long, and its culture changing. One of these, Trail Creek, excavated in 1949 and 1950, lies back from the coast about thirty miles south of Deering on Seward Peninsula (Map 3). High in the hills, Helge Larsen and his companions investigated a series of caves and fissures in this limestone country, and in two seasons obtained a wide range of artifacts, flakes, and bones from various depths of the deposits. Larsen found that hunters had sought shelter in the caves during at least four cultural periods. By the latest of these, when the floor had been built up by the accumulations of generations, there would have been little headroom left for a person sitting before his fire.

At the top of the deposits were arrowheads and flints of Western Thule and later cultures. Buried just beneath these were arrowheads, side blades, and end points of Ipiutak culture. Midway down in the deposits, at levels where the caves would have been more commodious, came another kind of cultural material: obliquely flaked spearpoints that brought to mind points used by ancient hunters of the American Southwest just at the end of the last Ice Age. Some of these Trail Creek points had been broken and their broken edges given burin blows. Others had apparently been designed to fit into slots at the ends of long, thick, cigar-shaped spearheads of antler. Deeper still, in the very bottom of one or two caves, were found other kinds of arrowheads and flints—those, probably, of two phases of the Denbigh Flint complex.

For the moment, though, we are concerned only with the middle levels and the thick spearheads and diagonally flaked points (Fig. 79). These Larsen at first thought to be very old, perhaps even as old as the Early Man points of the States (shown in Fig. 133). But with the discovery of the Choris site a few years later, he saw that, instead, the old flaking techniques had simply persisted and had become the usual ones in that Trail Creek–Choris culture. Not only were the large, diagonally flaked points from Choris Peninsula and Trail Creek closely similar, but broken fragments of these points had been used at both places for the making of crude burins. Since no other forms of burins and no microblades were found in the middle levels at Trail Creek, which would have indicated affinity with earlier cultures of the region, it seemed clear that people of Choris or their close relatives had repeatedly used the

79. Diagonally flaked Choris points from the Trail Creek caves. The point at lower left is about 3 in. (7.6 cm.).

Trail Creek caves for shelter while hunting caribou in the highlands.

Now that we had learned this much about the habits of Choris people, the beach ridges at Cape Krusenstern less than one hundred miles away seemed an ideal place where they might have settled in their big oval houses for the winter. In 1958, then, after we had dug Houses 2 and 3 at Choris Peninsula and finished our reconnaissance of Kotzebue Sound, our final investigations were made at Cape Krusenstern. But neither then nor in the succeeding two summers spent on those beach ridges did we find house depressions made by Choris people, though we searched the miles of beaches with all diligence.

Choris surface hearths, on the other hand, occurred at frequent enough intervals on the older beach tops (Beaches 44–51) behind those once occupied by first the Norton and then the Ipiutak people to give us a sequence not only of the same kinds of stone artifacts found at Choris Peninsula but of earlier ones more nearly related to those of Trail Creek. The hearths were most often found by accident. A flake lying in a reindeer path led to the careful uplifting of the thin moss or thicker sod in which it lay. With luck, underneath would be the site of a temporary camp containing Choris artifacts.

The hearth usually contained a scattering of broken, fire-discolored pebbles, small to medium in size, spread over an area from three to six feet in diameter. In that area and beyond for another three or four feet were strewn the flint chips and an occasional stone tool left by the people who built the fire and presumably sat around it in some form of circular surface dwelling. The width of the fire-rock area may have had little to do with the size of the cooking fire built in the tent. Rather, it seems most often to have been the area in which boiling stones were scattered after they had been put to use. These stones would have been placed in the fire and, when sufficiently hot, lifted with tongs to soup-filled baskets or wooden buckets. Stews were prepared in this way in recent years by Eskimos of western Alaska and Indians of the forested interior.

Boiling with hot stones was not the only cooking method known, though, for in some of these Choris camps lay bits of broken pottery, undoubtedly cooking pots, which would mean that food was boiled in them directly over the coals of a hearth. The pottery was marked on the outside with a stamped or paddled design of either plain, parallel lines or twisted cords. Linear stamping, as shown in Fig. 73, appears to be more recent than cord marking in the beach ridge succession, while the check stamp of Norton culture (see Fig. 62) does not appear in any of the Choris sites at Cape Krusenstern.

As at Trail Creek and Choris Peninsula, there occurred in Choris sites at Cape Krusenstern large, leaf-shaped blades thicker than those of Ipiutak; fragments of large, diagonally flaked knives or spearpoints; discoidal scrapers shaped like thin mussels; large tongue-shaped flints, probably used as the heads and blades of adzes; and, occasionally, a burin (see Fig. 78). These last, unlike the small burins of the Denbigh Flint complex, were most often made on broken projectile points, as had been the case in the Middle Trail Creek deposits, but one or two were large enough to be held comfortably in the hand, in this respect resembling the large burins of the Paleolithic of Europe.

Bit by bit during four seasons at Cape Krusenstern, from 1958 to 1961, we learned of the long time span during which the pottery-bearing Choris culture had held sway. On the older beaches, 48–51, the earlier phases of Choris contained burins, corded pottery, and large spearpoints related to those of Middle Trail Creek; on the more recent beaches, 44 to 47, we learned that Choris culture had not changed so much by slow acceptance of new ideas as by a sharp transition to full-fledged Norton culture. This was especially evident on Beach 44 which contained sites of both Choris and Norton cultures. Even though this much was clear, our evidence for Choris culture was scantier on the Krusenstern beach ridges than elsewhere because the artifacts were fewer and often fragmentary.

Then one day toward the end of the fourth season one of those rare strokes of archeological luck left us suddenly opulent. That was the summer our group consisted of Douglas Anderson, then in his second season of Arctic digging; Paul Dayton and Robert Stewart, students from the University of Arizona and Brown University respectively; the Downeys; and Dr. and Mrs. Helge Larsen of Denmark. Larsen, slated soon to take over the responsibilities of Kaj Birket-Smith who was retiring as head of the ethnographic and archeological section of the Danish National Museum, was pleased to have one more field season before his new duties began.

Toward the end of the season he and I, eager to find a few more links in the chain of cultural connections, left the pits where others were digging to hunt the beach ridges of the particular segment containing both Norton and Choris cultures. Like trains chugging past on adjacent tracks, we traversed neighboring ridges, back and forth, one heading east, one west. At length we drew abreast and paused to check our findings. Larsen had been luckier than I. "Here is a gift from a ground squirrel," he said, holding out an object in the palm of his hand. It was the base of a large, diagonally flaked point of light-gray chert shot through with dark streaks. Larsen explained that he had seen this flint lying on a pile of dirt freshly kicked out of a squirrel burrow. Was there any sign of a house or a hearth? Larsen thought not. Should we then dig a test trench anyway?

While we thought about it, we became aware of two figures plodding toward us from the northeast. As they climbed from swale to ridge top and down again, we could see that they were Murphy Downey and Paul Dayton. The shovels they carried and their packsacks told us that they had finished the job they had been doing and were essentially without work for the rest of the afternoon. Here was our answer. We asked them to mark off a cross a meter wide on the surface, its center at the squirrel hole, and, beginning there, dig out the arms of the cross far enough to make certain nothing lay in the ground.

With this plan under way, Larsen and I proceeded in opposite directions along our separate ridges. Engrossed in my search, I walked farther than I had intended, spent some time uncovering a minor hearth, and then, aware of how far I had strayed, turned back, realizing that I would be late for dinner.

As I approached camp, no clairvoyance was needed to tell me that something was afoot. Murphy "happened" to be wandering about between me and the first tent and, farther away, I could see nearly everyone in camp regarding my approach with studied nonchalance. Reaching Murphy first, I made the expected inquiry: "Did you find something in the squirrel hole?" "Maybe," he answered, falling into step with me. "Let's see it, then." Murphy reached into his pocket, felt around, and at length brought out a broken flint. It was indeed a prize, for enough remained to show, from its size and expert diagonal flaking, that it was the larger part of a spearpoint which if found in Colorado would have been classed without question as an Angostura point, originally known as a "diagonal Yuma" (see Fig. 133d, p. 330). While I had bases of points like this from Choris Peninsula and Larsen had whole pieces generally similar from the Trail Creek caves (Fig. 79), this one measured up in every respect to the ancient forms associated with extinct bison in the southern Great Plains.

"Did you find anything else?" I asked. "Maybe," replied Murphy. Now fully absorbing the fact that my role as the sitting duck would not be quickly over, I suggested we go into the tent to examine whatever other treasures they had. My companions eagerly began to ask what I thought of the point, and, while sliding onto a bench at our makeshift dining table, I had no trouble showing the expected enthusiasm for their find.

"Now let's see the rest of it," I suggested. Murphy hunted again through his pockets and soon found something else. This time the piece was a complete Angostura point, each flake scar as sharply rippled as though removed by a jeweler. Again I expressed amazement at our good fortune and asked if this were all. But their expressions showed that their fun was just beginning. One after the other Murphy and Paul searched their pockets like the well-rehearsed members of a vaudeville team, producing each time a flint quite as dazzling as the previous one, if not surpassing it in beauty. I soon ran out of superlatives and simply reached with a grin for each new specimen. Handsome, perfect Angosturas continued to emerge from their hiding places and were lined up side by side on the white oilcloth of our table. The complete haul contained forty such whole pieces and fragments plus a single notched point; a stemmed point; one long piece similar to stemmed points of the Great Plains of the United States and two fragments of the same type; thick, small, leaf-shaped points, perhaps for the tips of arrows; a scraper or two; and a whole series of long bifaces, diagonally flaked, though more crudely than the others and of coarser material.

When a long pause finally came, I counted nearly seventy of these remarkable pieces. Now I expected things to relax. No words

80. Stemmed blade from Choris cache. Of black chert, it is 6⅞ in. long (17.5 cm.).

were left to express my admiration for any conceivable flint that might cap the ones lying before me. Drawing on reserve strength, however, I asked again: "Is there anything else?" Now the panto-mime became burlesque, calling forth howls of laughter as Murphy slapped at all his pockets and sides, watching my face the while. At length, having played his role to the hilt, he reached into some hidden recess of his jacket and slowly drew forth the *pièce de résistance*. Whatever I said was surely inadequate. Murphy held in his hand a gigantic stemmed blade of glistening black chert, deep flake scars paralleling one another diagonally across the whole face of the implement. At the same time Paul held forth the two halves of another such object. None had seen the like before. Diagonally flaked on both faces and possessing enormous serrations at the edge as compared with the little saw teeth of the smaller points, these objects fitted no known pattern but stood alone, as they still do, as supreme examples of a style and form of American flintwork (Fig. 80).

Now the tension released itself in laughter, questions, and the many-voiced recounting of how the cache of flints had come to light.

There had been no problem of excavation. The squirrels down through generations had seen to that by removing all traces of the organic matter that must once have surrounded the flints. The artifacts had lain within six feet of one another, most of them at or near a level about three feet deep, where they had probably been deposited by some long-dead owner who had surely never intended to lose them.

This cache of flints is of great value in showing that, in all probability, one man at one time used this array of weapon tips in the course of his pursuit of game both at the seashore and in the mountains. We imagine that he stored his weapons in a boxlike cache in the ground and then, for one reason or another, failed to return. Whoever he may have been, he used both large and small weapons, the coarser pieces probably as skinning knives, and made his pieces diverse enough to fit his needs. What he could not know was that the patterns he used were the same as those employed at different places thousands of years before, when similar implements were used to slay or butcher animals now extinct—a time long before his beach ridges had even come into existence. From radiocarbon dates of a still earlier culture—the Denbigh Flint complex—and other bits of evidence, we know that our Alaskan hunter launched his handsome weapons at seals, whales, caribou, and bears about 1000 B.C.

Later, as we scoured those older beaches adjoining the one on which the cache was found, I think we each suffered a little disappointment at finding nothing further, for we imagined quantities of beautiful implements buried beneath the ridges and known only to our rivals, the ground squirrels.

(XI)

OLD WHALERS

Life at Cape Krusenstern the summer of 1960 was sometimes as precarious for us as it must have been for another group of people whose homes we found on a beach that now lies a mile from the sea. The people were "Old Whalers," and their village is on Beach 53, a few ridges back beyond the Choris ridges (Map 2). Douglas Anderson worked with a small crew primarily on the Cape Krusenstern Ipiutak beach that summer, while Bill Simmons, Almond and Murphy Downey, Bets, and I concentrated our early attention on this buried village that was twice as old as Ipiutak and, consequently, much farther from the present seashore.

We had found it hard to travel by small boat that spring. Ice remained fast against the shores until mid-June, and we had no more than reached the Cape and put up our tents when ice closed in again, opening at intervals between winds only long enough for the native hunters to push their boats among the floes to hunt for bearded seals (Fig. 81). Even though we had occasional clear days when we could see that the sun did not set, we shivered most of the time in the fog that blew off the ice, doubting that summer had really come. Rain blew into our sleeping gear, and we began to sneeze and relay colds. Now and then one of us stayed home with a fever for a day or so, and all the time the blue and white masses of ice floated slowly back and forth off the beach. Despite the bad weather and our occasional ills, we carried on the excavations with enthusiasm and were soon learning much about this new section of the beaches.

Often as I walked back across the many ridges at Cape Krusen-

81. Launching a boat among the ice floes during seal-hunting season at Cape Krusenstern, June, 1960.

stern I speculated about the people who had lived in this particular area. Their summers, like this, would have been cold at best, and the winters formidable. Since earliest times they would have occupied themselves mainly with the quest for food, giving attention too, of course, to the essentials of keeping warm: adequate shelter and clothing. The procurement of food, for us, was little more difficult than a trip to the store at Kotzebue for canned meats, dry milk, or beans; but early dwellers on the oceanfront at Cape Krusenstern were entirely dependent on their success at trapping, snaring, shooting, harpooning, or netting whatever was available to fill their caches or food racks—unendingly, season after season. While food would have been their primary concern, ceremonial gatherings or periods of recreation must have given occasional pleasant changes. And from all of the people who lived on these beach ridges, sharing similar problems and hardships, there emerged through the centuries the Eskimo of today: a careful, watchful, fun-filled individual—crafty, brave, and enduring.

On Beach 53, even before we began looking for houses, we noticed the uncommon number of whale bones there and decided that the people of its day had hunted the greatest game of all—whales—and these must have cruised by not far from shore. Today they do not, and no whaling is done at Cape Krusenstern. With the whale bones as inspiration, we began looking for houses, but these were slow to make themselves known. During our first season at the Cape in 1958, Bill Simmons had returned to camp one evening with the news that on one of the very old beach ridges a mile back from the sea he had seen three shallow but large oval depressions that he felt might be houses of Choris culture. He and I took shovels and hiked two or three miles along this beach (later numbered 53) to a place on its broad crest where three depressions between a willow-covered swale to the south and a long, deep pond to the north might, indeed, have been small versions of a Choris house. On sinking test holes more than two feet deep in their centers, however, we found nothing but clear gravel. At two feet we struck ice, preventing any deeper testing just then. Concluding from past experience that a house pit would carry at least some darkening of the soil above this depth, I judged these to be only dry ponds or the sink holes from former ice pockets in the ground.

The next season, 1959, Bill, on walking past the same depressions late one afternoon, thrust his shovel again into a hole we had dug. Finding that the frost had retreated, he quickly removed the old sloughed gravel and enlarged the hole. With one of his shovelfuls of earth he brought up a streak of telltale charcoal. Alert to its significance, he enlarged the hole and trowelled rapidly, finding in

82. Beginning to strip sod from the site of Old Whaling House 21 at Cape Krusenstern. Dark object in right foreground is an overturned whale vertebra.

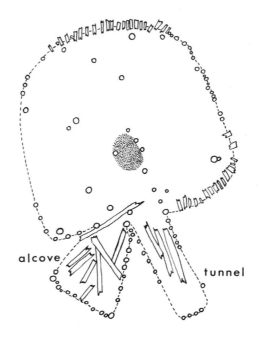

alcove

tunnel

83. Floor plan of Old Whaling House 21 on Beach 53.
The length from the tunnel entrance to the rear of
the house was approximately 26 ft. (8 m.).

the bottom a thick, black culture layer containing both flint chips
and animal bones. Hurrying back to camp with this news, he announced triumphantly that he had at last found a Choris house.
Expectations soared, and on the following day we began the momentous excavation of the pit house given the number 21 in our continuing series (Fig. 82). We found during the rest of that season
that it was not a house of Choris, but of a new form of culture with
artifacts not previously known in the far north.

In digging it, we opened a considerably larger oval area than
that in which we expected to find the house floor. First leveling off
a wide space, we pared away the gravel until an oval stain identified
the topmost traces of wall timbers well within the excavation.
Digging still deeper and learning that the timbers were so badly
rotted that we would have to support those still standing by leaving
them partially embedded in their gravel matrix, we resorted to
brushes to expose the outer walls at the edge of the floor. The back
of the house was rounded, similar in this respect to the Choris houses
found at Choris Peninsula, but otherwise the construction was quite
different (Fig. 83). Small spruce poles, their bases packed into a

trench outlining the original excavation, had leaned inward against a structure of some kind. Since the lower segments of all the inward-sloping wall logs were still decipherable, we learned that the front of the house was more complicated than the rear, for at the right, the walls turned inward to form rounded corners, then turned forward again to describe the right wall of a short tunnel; on the left, the wall of a somewhat triangular room opened into the main house by a portal next to the inner one of the tunnel.

As we trowelled and brushed down toward the floor of the main room, we came first to the impressions of fallen timbers—those so rotted that, on drying, they tended to blow away. They represented fallen parallel wall and roof logs (Fig. 84) and the crossbeams of a basically square framework, posts of which encompassed a deep deposit of charcoal and ash of a long-used hearth. Nearly all the artifacts lay under these impressions of fallen timbers on the floor and benches of the house, its side room, and its tunnels. Contrary to the practice of most Eskimos, dwellers in this house appeared to have stored or dropped little on the roof. Removing the above-floor traces, we found the floor itself deep black and rich in artifacts and chips. Probably because of their depth and long preservation by frost, such organic materials as ivory and animal bones were quite well preserved. Tools or utensils of wood, on the other hand, could be determined in only a few instances where the objects had left a

84. Bill Simmons exposing the fallen roof logs of Old Whaling House 21.

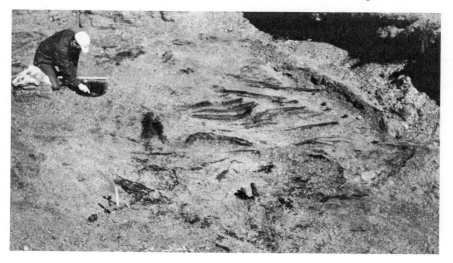

mold. This meant the wood of the object had both decomposed and become compressed until only a paper-thin tissue remained to outline the original shape. The object, through the years becoming filled with earth or gravel and now still bearing a thin skin of discernible wood, was like a mold (Fig. 85). By cautiously clearing away the earth or gravel, then brushing away the mold with a soft paintbrush (most molds are so fragile as to blow away in the slightest breeze), the nature of the original could be discovered.

House 21 was large, about eighteen feet across the front of the room and another eighteen feet from the tunnel door to the curved rear wall. A deeper floor deposit that lay within four feet of the edge of the fireplace suggested that a low bench, four to five feet wide and extending around three sides of the hearth, had served as a seat and sleeping platform. Signs were that this bench had been supported by retaining logs held in place by vertical pegs. The fireplace also may have been boxed in, as it remained compact and as much as a foot thick in spite of obviously long and intensive use. Along with charred wood, bone, and antler in the fireplace, there were many flint chips and a few broken artifacts, suggesting that house cleaning, rare though it must have been, was largely a matter

85. The mold of a burl bowl from an Old Whaling culture house.

of throwing debris into the fire. To one side of the hearth lay a whale vertebra, forming so excellent a seat that we used it as such while trowelling the floor.

The short tunnel, only eight feet long, continued the thick deposit of the house floor, but inside the forward room we found neither the remains of fire-building, such as would have been present had the house been of Thule culture, nor a thick floor, though artifacts lay abundantly distributed in a single layer throughout. This may have been a hard-floored room for storage or for sleeping. Perhaps, on the other hand, it was a room for the confinement of girls at puberty or for women made spiritually dangerous by childbirth, for Eskimos of the neighboring forests and Indians of the interior often constructed separate huts or arranged partitions within their houses for such purposes.

One of the first artifacts found in House 21 was a startler. My immediate reaction to it was that it was a hoax planted by someone with a warped sense of humor—a Piltdown man type of thing—but a glance at my companions dispelled this notion. The object was a chert arrowpoint (Fig. 86a), its sharp tip and parallel edges distinguished by two opposed notches in the edge near the base. Now, a side-notched point would seem common enough if found in the eastern part of the United States, for there it was characteristic of early, pottery-making Indians, but here in Alaska I could count such notched points on my fingers. They were simply not known in the area, though, remarkably enough, we had picked up one of a different shape just a few days earlier on the mountainside across the lagoon to the north. Still, until this moment the notched point in Alaska was an anomaly with no definite cultural significance. We soon saw, however, that this point could not have been dropped accidentally by some itinerant hunter on his way to or from some distant land, but, rather, notched-point makers had long lived at the site, for other such points soon turned up with surprising regularity. Some were small enough to be arrowpoints, but others were heavy, thick, and long—the probable tips of spears and lances (Fig. 86c).

Another form of flintwork caused us even more excitement, however, than did the notched points. A very thin but broad and long point of gray chert had the dimensions of a harpoon blade, but its size was much greater than flint blades we knew to have been set into harpoon heads for walrus hunting in, for example, the

Ipiutak culture. This one, four inches long and nearly as wide, never-theless appeared to be the blade of a whaling harpoon head (Fig. 86b). Its dimensions were practically identical to some of those made of polished slate and used in recent years by the whalers of

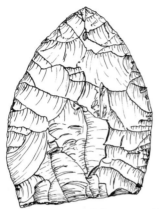

a) side-notched arrowpoint, chert

b) harpoon blade, chalcedony

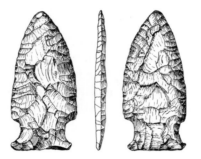

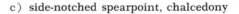

c) side-notched spearpoint, chalcedony

d) lance blade, chalcedony; length, 8¼ in. (21 cm.).

86. Old Whaling artifacts dating about 1800 B.C.

Point Barrow and Point Hope. Yet this one of flint had been chipped from a very large flake and then treated with bold pressure retouch.

We had hardly begun to speculate on what these proofs of whaling in so early a site would mean to archeological theory when

a large bifaced lance blade turned up (Fig. 86d). This was of chalcedony, with parallel edges and a straight base, but though over
eight inches long it measured less than two inches wide. My first
thought was that it was no Arctic specimen but one transplanted
from Neolithic sites of North Europe or Egypt. This one, again, suggested no other implement of flint in the region, yet its shape and
size were closely like the blades of polished slate used by recent
Eskimos for killing and flensing whales.

FOR TRAINED CREWS of Eskimos or northern Chukchis, the
hunting of whales is still a serious enterprise (Fig. 87). Though
harpoon guns and iron lances and knives now take the place of
weapons and tools of stone, the hunt until recent times was con-
ducted much as it was centuries ago. Eskimo whaling crews consisted, usually, of eight men: six at the paddles, one at the helm
with his steering paddle, and a harpooner in the bow. After preparing themselves spiritually by communing together in the ceremonial
house and observing with great care the omens brought forth in
winter and spring ceremonies, the crewmen, avoiding their women,
stood continuous watch together for some days before the whales

87. Eskimos hauling their boat (*umiak*) on a sledge over the ice to open water
for a whale hunt, Point Hope, 1940.

were expected. They huddled in new fur clothing at the ice edge, ate little, and watched the sea between catnaps until one day in late spring the whale they awaited at last appeared at the far end of an open lead. Knowing that the whale's great wish was to be captured by them, and depending upon their women at home to be living by certain magical rules that attracted whales, they slid their large skin boat into the water and paddled slowly to the spot where the great black beast was expected to emerge again. As it rose to blow, the paddlers pulled with all their strength, lifting the boat's bow high in the water while the harpooner made ready to strike.

At the moment their craft rose over its quarry, the harpooner thrust his heavy weapon with all his might into the beast's back. The head of the great harpoon, piercing through the tough outer hide to the soft blubber, came loose and turned, forming a toggle through the skin of the whale. As the whale then sounded to escape and the harpoon line drew taut, the men watched apprehensively to make sure that, freed of its shaft, the line snapped clear of obstructions over the gunwale, dragging with it a series of inflated sealskins. Once the whale was fastened to the end of the line, like a fish on a hook, it would eventually tire and become short of breath from dragging the floats through and under the water. Paddling swiftly again and chanting their magic songs, the men would try to anticipate the shorter breathing intervals of the beast, and if other crews were waiting nearby, they, too, would join in the kill. At last, when the whale was exhausted, a boat was pushed onto its head, into which the harpooner, now turned lanceman, would again and again thrust his long, heavy lance with its sharp cutting blade of stone. The boat was then thrown clear; and, with luck, the whale was thus tormented and wounded to death and could be towed triumphantly to shore in front of the village.

For some years most scholars believed that Eskimo whaling by this method was not known before Punuk culture of A.D. 1000, but then large harpoon heads decorated in Old Bering Sea and Okvik style (Figs. 57 and 61) turned up along with other evidences of whale hunts in those oldest St. Lawrence Island cultures. On the American side of Bering Strait, similar signs appeared in Near Ipiutak sites at Point Hope, showing that whaling was at least two thousand years old in its present form. Were we now confronted with a settlement of whale hunters twice as old?

.   .   .

WE CONTINUED to speculate on the significance of objects from House 21 the following summer of 1960 and intended to excavate the whole settlement of houses, however large it might prove to be.

Camp, that cold, rainy summer, was set up on the seacoast as close to the ancient village site as we could go by boat—a spot north of the tower near the west end of the Ipiutak ridge and less than a half-hour's walk from the digging place (Map 2). Our tent village was sizable. The Downeys' tent and our big cook tent stood on the first beach crest overlooking the sea. Murphy Downey (Fig. 88), Raymond Lee, and Julian Towksjhea slept in a smaller white tent, just forward of the Downeys' tent, on a patch of bare gravel. Staked downwind from them were the eleven dogs of Almond's team, flourishing on spare seals and fish. To the north of the mess tent were Doug's blue pyramidal tent and Bill's green mountain tent. My family, less for exclusiveness than for shelter against the excessive wind, pitched its orange-colored umbrella tent and a smaller green one on a broad but dry swale.

Looking back toward camp as we walked to work in the morning, we could see our various children silhouetted against the sky going about their business of daily exploration. Ann and Russ Giddings were eleven and nine. The Downeys' Lydia was eight; Percy, six; Mary, three; and their baby of that year, Joe, was still carried about in the back of his mother's parka (Fig. 89). Despite their age differences, the older children found a variety of things to do together. Percy and Russell spent many hours trying to outwit ground squirrels with traps and slingshots. Lydia and Ann, watchful of

88. Murphy Downey repairing a motor.

89. Ruth Downey with children, Mary and Percy.

small Mary, might stop a while to build a brush hut in which they would light a small fire and play house. Again, the four older children, leaving Mary with her mother, would pack lunches and walk far away down the beach, exploring the tide wrack for glass net floats, fish skeletons, and other treasures.

The one pastime we discouraged was that of climbing on the stranded, half-floating clusters and spires of ice rising to heights of eight or ten feet along our waterfront. Kettle holes in the ice contained fresh water, though, and in spite of our ban, thirsty children frequently turned to them for a drink. By early July, we had all become so familiar with the ice that we no longer thought to caution the children about jumping aboard or climbing the slopes of the tilted blocks and turrets.

Early one evening, Mary and Ann, clad in their waterproof breeches and quilted parkas, found an exceptionally good sliding place on a cake of rotten ice in the lee of an up-ended slab (Fig. 90). Here they happily climbed and slid until suddenly, without warning, the slab of ice broke loose and fell against Ann, crushing her to the slope. Russ and Percy, hearing Mary's cries, rushed to get help. By the time Bets arrived, Ann lay white-faced and dazed on the gravel, while Ruth and Almond stood beside her, looking out to sea. They had brought her ashore and now, stunned by the disaster, were immobilized.

It was clear that launching our boat could do no good, for, although an open lead occurred off the shore, ice lay solidly packed farther around the Cape as far as the tower. Beyond that, the sea was clear, and fortunately for us, visiting geologist friends had left their boat and motor at the tower, so that by the time I reached camp a few minutes later, Almond and Bill had already begun a memorable dash to Kotzebue for an airplane to take Ann to the hospital. Toward midnight, less than five hours after the accident, we knew our emissaries had succeeded in crossing the Sound, for we heard the welcome hum of a plane's motor. The veteran sixty-eight-year-old pilot, John Cross, was an old friend and accustomed to such emergencies. He soon landed on a flat stretch of beach ridge less than a mile from our tents, and within minutes Ann, on a home-made stretcher, and Bets were aboard the plane. At Kotzebue, where a single doctor served the coast between Nome and Point Barrow, Ann was allowed to enter the Alaska Native Service Hospital as a

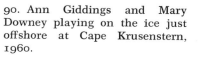

90. Ann Giddings and Mary Downey playing on the ice just offshore at Cape Krusenstern, 1960.

special emergency case and there she received excellent care for a minor form of broken hip. Two weeks later she was back with us on the beach again, and throughout the remainder of the summer, with flattering attention from all the crew, she relearned first to crawl, and then to walk, as her bones healed, and her attentive friend Lydia provided all the care and solicitude of a private nurse.

DESPITE such emergencies and the dismal weather, the old village on Beach 53 continued to emerge. The culture of these people had been quite distinct from both the earlier and the later cultures here at Cape Krusenstern, and by now we had named it "Old Whaling." The oval surface appearance of the first excavated house had not accurately predicted what we would find. The house floors and walls were exceptionally deep, the floor lying three or more feet below the surface. We had failed to see cultural signs in our test hole partly because the walls and roofs of these houses apparently were not covered with sod as they were in nearly all other coastal areas and periods. Rather, the framework of parallel poles seemed to have been overlain by a membrane of skin or bark over which was heaped clean sand and gravel from the original excavation.

As the 1960 season wore on, we located a deep house floor under each of the two other ill-defined depressions, and two more as well. The main room of each house turned out to be shaped much like the one in House 21. In other respects, however, each had its own plan and style.

House 22 lay directly ahead of House 21, its entrance tunnel reaching to the lip of the beach ridge. Again the tunnel was short, its floor at the same level as the house floor, but in place of a single lateral room this house had two, both of them squarish with rounded walls. Just forward of the fireplace and to the left of the inner tunnel door we carefully brushed away a dark, hemispherical stain—a mold—that represented the remains of a wooden bowl a foot and a half across at the mouth, probably carved from a burl such as occasionally appears on spruce trees in this region (see Fig. 85). In all major respects the construction of this house was the same as that of House 21 (Fig. 83).

Under the third depression, which was very shallow and unpromising, we struck pay dirt again, unearthing House 23 with three appended rooms and a tunnel. This exhausted the surface signs, but in testing whether a house lay behind House 23, as one had behind House 22, we discovered an elongated house we numbered 24. The main room had the usual rounded walls, but through a doorway with a sill in the floor it opened into a rear room almost as large again. The tunnel, a foot or two longer than those of the other houses, also had a door sill halfway along its length, where those passing through stepped down a few inches into a small lateral room. In this house, as in House 21, a small whale vertebra formed a seat alongside the fireplace.

Now we began to dig systematically a series of test holes, for there seemed no other way to determine what lay beneath the surface of the ground. In this way we discovered the deepest house floor of all, lying toward the front of the beach and between Houses 22 and 23. Having used up higher numbers of the twenty series elsewhere, we designated this last deep house of the group House 20. It, too, had two small forward rooms opening into the main room on either side of the tunnel and another small room at the left rear.

Continuing with our test holes, we found no other underground structure. However, thirty feet along the crest of the beach ridge beyond House 23 and only a few inches below the surface, we found a whale's skull (Fig. 91). It appeared to have been buried intentionally by residents of the village, and a few flint flakes lay about its base. Part of one ear bone and another segment of bone had been removed as though needed for manufactures of some kind.

Elsewhere on the same broad crest of Beach 53, we continued testing humps and ridges on the surface of the ground and found them to be the vertebrae, ribs, or jawbones of whales. This beach was singularly favored by the presence of such bones; they could scarcely have been washed all the way up to its crest but must have been hauled there by men. The contemporary houses of this small village, then, indicated a settlement of hunters who effectively pursued whales—and on no small scale. Each house may comfortably (by Eskimo standards) have housed ten to fifteen people, not counting any who may have lived in the appended rooms.

A puzzling aspect of house building in the Old Whaling site was that the dozens of spruce poles used in constructing the walls were of a nearly uniform size. Other coastal houses that I had excavated or examined had been built of whatever driftwood had lodged on the beach. Even if driftwood of spruce were chosen over poplar and birch, the logs would have been of varying sizes. The best explanation seemed to be that the villagers obtained their wood along the banks of the Noatak River, where spruce of uniform size could probably as easily have been procured then as it can today. From there they could have rafted the wood to the seacoast and floated it to Cape Krusenstern by means of towlines pulled by walkers along the beach.

Late prehistoric Eskimos of the Kobuk River, in contrast, found it easier to use driftwood for their building than to chop down trees with their inadequate tools; for until iron axes were introduced into the Arctic, Eskimos had never known axes of any kind. This made the collection of quantities of small logs of uniform size by Old Whaling people the more impressive. Early Arctic people did, however, have adzes with stone blades, and they used wedges of wood, antler, and ivory, and mauls of wood or stone for splitting dry logs into the slabs and planks they needed for construction or the making of utensils. Though no obvious ax blades appeared among the

91. Eskimos Bobby Lee (left) and Frank Norton (right) excavating the skull of a whale found on the crest of Beach 53.

flints of Old Whalers, means could no doubt have been found to fell trees in one way or another.

If the Old Whalers did exploit the forest edge, they seem not to have ventured far up the Noatak River or into the hills, for besides fish bones, which occurred frequently in hearths, the only bones of food animals were those of seals. Whale bones would not have become kitchen refuse, of course, no matter how much whale flesh were eaten. In contrast to the quantities of caribou bones in house pits of later cultures, the entire Old Whaling site yielded only a few broken marrow bones of these animals, further stressing dependence on the resources of the sea. Whether by preference or from fear of alien dwellers farther away, the Old Whalers did not even procure antlers for making tools and weapons. A sealing harpoon head and a few worked fragments are the sole antler specimens found. Nearly all implements, weapons, and utensils were made of wood. While the wood was not well enough preserved for us to obtain whole artifacts, we brushed away at the stains of wooden shafts in several places on the floors of houses, thus getting a last look at the piece before it disintegrated. One such stain led to a large notched point of chalcedony, evidently the tip of a heavy spear or lance, a weapon more appropriate for whales than for other game. While it might have been used for bears, there was no evidence of such use.

Weapons such as this probably fell to the floor when the house collapsed in ruins, but other objects, like bones, chips, and flints, had been trampled into the loose, dry, gravelly earth floor while the house was lived in. Who knows why the occupants left their house one day and never returned? Whatever the reason, they probably intended to come back, for they left favorite spears and other belongings suspended from the roof or stuck into the interstices of the pole walls, where they would be straight and safe until needed again. The possible disaster that overcame the house residents is our good fortune, for the fine specimens thus left enable us to envisage a more complete picture of life in those days.

EVIDENCE that the Old Whalers spent their entire year on the coast came with the discovery of another part of their community. While exploring Beach 53 on either side of the village and learning in the process to find whale bones by cutting with the tip of the shovel into suspicious small ridges or humps on the surface, we dis-

covered five hearth sites just under the sod of the beach in an area
about a hundred yards from the edge of the winter village. These we
took to be either outdoor fireplaces of the village itself or spots where
residents dumped debris from their houses. The latter probability
became slight when we saw how little reason there would have been
for the winter householders to remove their trash far from the house
entrance when they allowed so much of it to accumulate in the
house floor itself.

In late summer we turned from the nearly excavated winter
houses to see whether these surface hearths were really those of
Old Whaling culture. We removed the sod in three-meter strips that
exposed the entire hearth and soon learned that they were not only
planned fireplaces but integral parts of surface structures of some
kind. The hearths were thick, six inches or more in depth, and contained the same mixture of charcoal, bone fragments, and flint chips
as did those of the houses. Unlike the house hearths, on the other
hand, these contained, in and about them, quantities of burned
beach pebbles. Beyond each hearth, blackened earth containing
flints outlined a large, oval floor. The artifacts—notched scrapers,
large semi-lunar blades, chalcedony objects (half of which, when
held to the light, turned the color of honey or clear caramel), and
even the presumed blades for whaling harpoon heads—proclaimed
these dwellings to be of the same culture as the neighboring winter
houses. A thin bone needle containing an extremely fine eye attested
to excellence in skin work and to sewing like that of recent Eskimos.

By trowelling and brushing but more often using a broom to
clear post molds and the mark of the floor edge, we turned up
enough evidence in the first excavated lodge to show that it had been
oval in form with a fireplace slightly to the rear of center and a
peculiarly offset entryway at the front. Residents apparently had
entered the house at the left front, which projected two or three feet
beyond the right front as one faced the sea. This feature gave the
floor plan of the lodge a curious imbalance. It was a large dwelling,
eighteen feet long by fifteen feet wide, with a light structure based
upon four substantial central posts enclosing the hearth and lighter
posts close to the base of the wall. As there was no indication of a
sod cover, which would have left a peaty deposit on the floor, we
sought for a solution as to how the structure might have been enclosed and in a second lodge found the answer.

There, in a well-defined floor edge, a slight trench filled with organic stain represented the base of the wall cover. Just inside it were occasional marks of pegs or light posts. As seen in profile, a stain rose from the trench to a thin wall—perhaps once a membrane. It appeared, however, more substantial than that from the hide of seals or walruses, more nearly resembling the decayed spruce bark sometimes encountered in river sites. The most probable reconstruction of these structures is an elliptical dome built of bent poles or lathes supported by a few internal posts and roofed over by bark, like the wigwams of Northeastern Indians of the United States. Such use of bark, too, would strengthen our theory that the Old Whalers rafted spruce logs to their oceanfront beach from the valley of the Noatak River. These dwellings, too, would have late historic and modern equivalents in summer huts, shelters, and fish caches of the Kobuk River Eskimos, who peel the bark off spruce trees in long strips, flatten it to dry, and use it for both roofs and walls of temporary structures.

While we excavated these surface houses and it became evident that they represented the same culture as that of the winter houses, we began to see a striking correspondence in the community plan. The lodges, like the deep houses, were clustered into a compact group, three toward the front of the beach and two behind. In view of the similar layout we could not escape the conclusion that people of the winter village simply moved into these other, summer, houses when melting ice flooded the floors of their winter homes. The order and regularity of this two-part village became the more remarkable as we considered comparable evidence from other parts of the Arctic.

Nearly all Eskimos who maintain half-underground winter houses on the coast or in the interior spend the greater part of their time elsewhere during the summer. In such modern villages as Point Hope and Point Barrow, it was customary until a short time ago to move from winter houses, at the advent of good weather, to summer tents along seacoasts, rivers, or wherever seasonal fishing and hunting were profitable. A Point Hope family might move its tent many times in the course of a summer while exploiting a wide variety of natural resources. The whaling station of Shesualek (described on p. 15) is another such case.

Where later tent sites on the beaches at Cape Krusenstern were invariably meant for short-term occupation, certainly no more than a season, those on Beach 53 were houses occupied again and again, for debris had accumulated in their hearths and floors to an extent comparable to that of the winter houses. It began to look as if the Old Whalers, living through the winter in one compact cluster of houses and through the summer in another, might have banded together on this wide, long, and spacious beach as much for security as for communal effort in the whale hunt. But whatever enemy, real or imagined, may have lurked in the interior, they made a good living from the sea, and their probable forays to the sources of living wood and bark indicate a background not wholly free of forests.

ALL THESE FACTS and inferences, involving as they did new tools and techniques, gave us reason to look in all directions for origins. It was obvious that this culture had not originated in any of the known older cultures of the American Arctic. Nor was it similar to cultures that followed it on later beach ridges at Cape Krusenstern: Choris, Norton, Ipiutak, or Western Thule. Its contents contrasted as sharply as we could conceive with the minuscule remains of the older Denbigh Flint culture on Beaches 80–104. Whaling seemed to afford the clearest insight. The kind of whaling indicated by the bones, the toggle harpoon heads, and the large harpoon blades and lance blades, was precisely that known from St. Lawrence Island and north around the Arctic Sea coasts of a small part of Asia and much of America—the kind of whaling described on pages 231–2. Such whaling was usually carried out from permanent villages of long-maintained houses and by trained crews operating, several together, as a community.

Whaling in the Aleutian Islands and other North Pacific localities had been of a different sort, so far as is known from written records and archeological evidence. There, in recent centuries, hunters went out in two-man kayaks (bidarkas), the forward man throwing a slate-tipped spear at the middle of a whale's back. The poison of a plant, aconite, smeared on the detachable tip of slate caused the animal to sicken and, later, to die. The hunters then merely waited at home in hope that their whale—or one poisoned by other hunters—would wash up on their beach.

Sharply in contrast was the aforementioned Arctic pattern of planned interception of a whale between ice floes, its capture by direct and dangerous contact, and its subsequent towing to shore. Whatever the origin of this type of whaling, we saw that it had persisted for nearly four thousand years, starting in Old Whaling days about 1800 B.C.[1]

ON MANY OCCASIONS while we toiled in the Old Whaling houses, we asked our Eskimo helpers for their opinions about the site. Even though Almond and his friends understood our search for series of beach ridges, they never seemed to visualize fully the physical situation of a site at the time it was occupied by some unknown people of the past. Rather, they were prone to think of the Ipiutakers or the Old Whalers as people like themselves who, though bizarre in some of their practices, would have responded in the same ways to their environment. The large numbers of whale bones on Beach 53, however, impressed upon all of us, including the natives, the fact that the ocean had been close by when the site was occupied, for it was inconceivable that the heavy ribs, jawbones, and skulls of whales would have been transported any distance like the mile that now separates the sea from the beach.

Our Eskimo helpers also realized that the arrangements of the houses and the kinds of artifacts in this village did not conform to the styles they had come to expect. We sensed at times a speculative and puzzled reaction to the things we found here, as though the mystery of these remote people were of a different order and a greater subject of awe than were the ruins of the tent sites, caches, and houses of other people who had inhabited the beach ridges. Our questions about the Old Whaling people seemed to cause a certain unease, similar to that caused by our excavations of burials on more recent beaches. An older generation of Eskimos would have believed that working with such things as these might bring on spiritual ills that could only be counteracted by the strength of one's personality, his spirit helpers, and the power of his *angatkoks*—priestly go-betweens with the spirit world.

Nevertheless work continued, day after day, that cold summer of 1960, though not without stresses. In August unusually strong winds blew, giving a hint of winter to come. The consequent rough seas prevented our getting supplies from Kotzebue on time and, as though unwilling to face another winter, Almond's motor died of some internal ailment and could be revived only by the purchase

[1] Radiocarbon dates indicate Old Whaling culture to have fallen between 1800–1500 B.C.

of a part from some distant factory at some unpredictable time. Almond could as easily have spared an arm as his motor, and he brooded over its loss. Attempting to overcome his bad luck, and with my reluctant consent, he began a campaign of borrowing boats from relatives. To do this he twice made his way to Kotzebue, once catching a ride in a passing plane that stopped to bring greetings from a scientific party working at Cape Thompson. On both occasions when he borrowed boats in Kotzebue (before he finally bought a new motor to return our program to an even keel), he tipped over in a too-strong surf, narrowly escaping with his life. The second time, just in front of camp, his overturned boat, lifted by a wave, fell upon him, severely bruising a shoulder before our men could drag him, unconscious, to safety.

Despite the winds, driving rain, and threat of an early fall, we finished excavating the Old Whaling village and, in a period of welcome calm, safely removed our valuable goods from the beaches to Kotzebue using Almond's restored boat. By then we knew we had surmounted the odds of lowering skies and angry spirits and escaped with all of the records and belongings that the beaches seemed to hold of the vanished people who had hunted whales almost four thousand years ago.

Unlike all the other cultures in western Alaska, from that of present-day Eskimos to Choris, to the much earlier Denbigh Flint culture, the Old Whaling culture showed no strong signs of continuity. The Denbigh people of 3000 B.C. had handed down certain traits to the Choris people of 1000 B.C. and these traits could be seen again in the more recent Norton and, especially, Ipiutak cultures. Why, then, did the Old Whalers of 1800 B.C. have no ties with their successors or their predecessors on this series of beach ridges at Cape Krusenstern?

There were, on the other hand, close parallels between Old Whaling notched points, large and small, and notched points of archaic peoples who lived four or five thousand years ago in the region of the Great Lakes and the eastern part of the United States and Canada. There were parallels, too, between Old Whaling houses and certain aspects of houses of recent Eskimos of the forested interior, between the Old Whalers' catching of seals and whales from boats with toggle harpoons and the methods used by Thule and later hunters in the sea, and between Old Whaling summer lodges of bark or skin and those of Indian tribes in faraway regions. Yet, as an assemblage of traits, we found it hard to understand where the Old Whalers had come from and how they had broken the chain of events on the beaches at Cape Krusenstern. To the present day we can only speak of the Old Whaling culture as one might of a strange plant that suddenly appeared in his garden and then, after becoming firmly rooted and strong, disappeared one day without a trace.

LATER THAT FALL, after returning to Rhode Island, I received brief letters from Almond on one matter or another, and, in one such letter, written at the end of October 1960, after speaking of a sum we owed one of the Shesualek men for the use of his motor, he went on to say that he had almost recovered from the injuries received when the boat hit him. He was able to hunt and work, but could not yet lift heavy things. Ruth and Murphy, he said, were out hooking trout through the ice, where they sometimes filled two sacks in a day. Then came a paragraph at the end: "Sorry to say Lydia is drowned and her girl friend. We did not know they play in a river. And get to a thin ice."

Returning to Alaska and Cape Krusenstern the following season, I observed that the weather was good and that the Downey family had been successful in their spring beluga and seal hunting and were in excellent spirits. They did not speak, the day we met, of their lost daughter, but later in their tent Ruth took the new baby, born that spring, from the perch in the back of her parka, and she and Almond replied to my question with pleasure: "Her name is Lydia."

(XII)

DENBIGH BEACHES—
THE OLD WORLD
ENCROACHES

THE FIRST MEN to walk the very earliest beaches at Cape Krusenstern were the Denbigh Flint people. When they arrived, some
five thousand years ago, most of the glaciers had melted, and sea
level since has never risen enough to destroy their sites. The beaches
where Denbigh camps are found near the northwestern tip of Cape
Krusenstern now lie well inland—a mile and a half from the sea if
one sets out from recent beaches near the United States Geological
Survey tower (Map 2).

Our first look at the craftsmanship of these meticulous flintworkers was at an extensive site at Cape Denbigh that we excavated
between 1948 and 1952 (Maps 1 and 8, pp. 2 and 278), and in our
subsequent years at Cape Krusenstern we were pleased to find that
Denbigh people had been here too—on the now most inland ridges.
In this windblown but mosquito-free location, they erected windbreaks and tents along the sea edge waiting for seals to swim past,
and they left as evidence a litter of hearths with oval patches of charcoal, fired pebbles, and flint chips. The small size of their charred and
flint-strewn ovals which we uncovered just under the moss brought
to mind the low, skin-covered, dome-shaped huts that are still used
occasionally in the caribou-inhabited passes of the Brooks Range
and along neighboring rivers.

We pictured their family—parents and children—gathered inside a small enclosure where they kept warm by sitting close to a conservative fire of twigs rather than a generous hearth of flaming driftwood. At night, the toolmaker in the family faced the firelight as he flaked new weapon tips. In the wider oval beyond the flame lay cracked, reddened beach pebbles among which glistened the black, red, gray, and tan of cherts, jasper, and chalcedony and, occasionally, the glassy gleam of a flake or implement of obsidian. In these simple surroundings the Denbigh artisan pressed his antler flaker tip repeatedly against small flinty stones, turning out the burins, scrapers, microblades, and marvelous miniature arrowpoints and edging blades that we recognize at a glance as the hallmarks of Denbigh culture (see Figs. 102 and 103, pp. 263–4).

As we excavated these surface sites on the beaches of Cape Krusenstern during the summers of 1960 and 1961, we wondered why the first discovery of Denbigh flints had not been made in a place such as this, rather than deep in the frozen earth of a terrace between the rocky cliffs of Cape Denbigh. Until 1948, however, when we settled down to digging at that North Bering Sea peninsula, no trace of the Denbigh Flint complex had previously come to light. That year I particularly wished to find archeological sites on the shores of Norton Sound where people might have exploited both the growing spruce and birch trees and the plentiful driftwood that was regularly deposited along those shores by currents from the Yukon River mouth. I could thus try to extend my existing tree-ring calendar further into the past and at the same time learn whether or not Eskimo culture in this other forested region had differed as sharply from the culture of the barren coast as had the Kobuk Valley culture. While an archeologist is never without hope of finding traces of the earliest people in the region, my plans that summer were no more ambitious than to learn whether or not Ipiutak culture had existed on the shores of the Bering Sea, for few archeological investigations had been possible during the war years, and nearly ten years had now passed since Larsen, Rainey, and I had dug the Ipiutak site at Point Hope in 1939.

With my wife, son Jim, aged one, and two students from the University of Alaska, Wendell Oswalt and Walter Arron, I expected to traverse the shores from the mouth of the Yukon River northward around Norton Sound to Nome, settling down for a protracted dig or two wherever we might find propitious signs. Norton Sound is well south of Cape Krusenstern, and beach ridge archeology had not yet been thought of. Late in the spring, while making plans for our flight from the University of Alaska, I received a letter from John Newcomb with most enticing news. Newcomb, who had assisted me in excavations along the Kobuk, was now teaching with his wife in an Alaska Native Service school at Shaktoolik, a village in the heart of the area we planned to visit (Map 8). He described a neighboring site, Nukleet, a midden mound high on a slope of Cape Denbigh, where a limited test had yielded harpoon heads of Thule types and pottery covered on its outer surface with impressed concentric rings. These clues, coming together, told both Newcomb and me that the site must have levels as old as our oldest house pits along the Kobuk River. I would not need to look further for a site to expand our knowledge of forest-dwelling Eskimos.

After persuading Arron and Oswalt, the latter having worked with me the preceding season in the Kobuk area, to do the coastal survey, I took a plane with Bets and Jim straight to Shaktoolik. A day or so later, after visiting with the Newcombs, we proceeded by boat fifteen miles to the Nukleet site on the east side of Cape Denbigh near its tip. With us went two Eskimo men who were uncertain as to how long they would stay with us. Neither had previously worked directly for wages, though both had spent years apprenticed to a native chief herder with a large, privately owned reindeer herd that formery ranged near Shaktoolik. Consequently our new companions were exceptionally strong and agile. The first, Lewis Nakarak, took with him his wife and three young children—his second family, after his first wife had died. He explained that they would lay in a supply of birds' eggs and wild greens before going back to the village. The other, Saul Sokpilak, was a small man, noncommital in English but full of humorous pageantry and good nature. As things turned out, Nakarak, his family, and Sokpilak stayed with us throughout the entire season and, having come under the spell of archeology, became dependable assistants during three other seasons at Cape Denbigh (Fig. 92).

NUKLEET contrasted sharply with other Eskimo sites. Easily identifiable as a former village by the dense growth of grass covering several acres between patches of willow, poplar, and spruce, it seemed to overflow a slope of the little mountain range of Cape

92. Saul Sokpilak (left) and Lewis Nakarak (right) with his young son sitting before their tent at Cape Denbigh, 1948.

Denbigh and, like molasses, to ooze part way over a rocky bluff sixty feet high. We found that the gravel beaches on the east side of the Cape were narrow, tending to disappear at high tide. This accounted to a certain extent for the high perch of the site. Not wishing to be a great distance from our boats, we made a precarious camp among fallen boulders on a shelf beneath a steep alder- and spruce-coated slope. Climbing to the site by pressing aside the tenacious branches, we emerged on a splendid lookout from which we could see deep into the blue and black water on either side.

One reason our Eskimo friends wished to camp near Nukleet became evident at once. A small group of harbor seals foraged in the water directly below, occasionally rising to breathe and scan the landscape, and a pair of white whales ten or twelve feet long moved lazily about the base of the cliff to our right, now and then taking alarm and plunging away in a straight line toward the open sea. A supply of food was thus within easy reach.

After the first day of reconnaissance, we laid out a projected trench leading from a thicket downhill one hundred eighty feet to the steep slope at the edge of the bluff. This trench, opened in six-by-ten-foot sections, after a few weeks provided us with a cross section of the site and thousands of artifacts. Directly under the deep sod lay the last ground surface before the site was finally abandoned some two hundred years ago. Those upper layers, though latest, were poorly preserved, no doubt because they alternately froze and thawed each season while the deeper deposits remained solidly frozen.

While I worked with my two Eskimo assistants and, for a short period, with Jack Newcomb and two or three other men who came to Shaktoolik to make a few dollars before returning to their regular food-getting pursuits, my wife, with Lizzie Nakarak and her children, set about exploiting the beaches and slopes, gathering a variety of greens, stems, and roots that could be boiled or used fresh as salads. These, along with netted fish and large squares of white and amber beluga skin drying on hastily constructed racks, soon showed us how modern residents of Cape Denbigh may live handsomely with but little expenditure for food.

LATE one calm evening two boatloads of men, women, and children—visitors from Shaktoolik—dropped by our camp. After talking loudly in their native language and sampling the *muktuk,* or whaleskin, served by the Nakaraks, they suggested we join them that very night in an egg hunt at the southern tip of the Cape. Why not? In short order our three boats were churning noisily past the bases of ponderous cliffs, setting off echoes against the rocky corridors. We paused at one place to collect herring eggs from among the rocks. A few days before, enormous schools of herring had followed the shoreline from the north, rounding the Cape and depositing their eggs and milt in the water on the east side. By what scheme such a migration had evolved, so that the fertilized eggs clung in a thick coat to the short seaweed growing to the height of normal tide along the rocks, I shall never understand, but now that the tide was low we paused to gather bushels of this tasty food, stowing it away in wooden crates. Once on our way again, Sokpilak and Lizzie boiled a pot of hot water over the Coleman stove in our boat, while Nakarak steered, and before long all of us were dipping stalks of seaweed into the boiling water and popping them into our mouths. Like peanuts, one bite and it was impossible to stop. There seemed no end to the quantity of egg-covered leaves we could eat.

Near the tip of Cape Denbigh, the motors were slowed to meet the short waves caused by the longer ocean swells that broke around the point. Here were the nesting cliffs where hundreds of sea birds

93. Eskimo men gathering birds' eggs from the cliffs at Cape Denbigh. The men stuff their shirts with eggs until they can carry no more, then nimbly descend.

laid their eggs on every conceivable ledge. The Eskimos slapped the palms of their hands against the sides of the boats, producing sounds like rifle shots, and dozens of birds—puffins and guillemots —came hurtling down toward us, catching their weight with beating wings and soaring away again close to the water. The sea gulls, less easily frightened, simply took wing, squawking and circling us in swarms before returning to their long, green, brown-specked eggs. Once through the rougher water, we entered a small cove on the south side of the Cape at the base of a chimney of rock through which we could look directly upward between almost sheer walls from three to five hundred feet high. Having timed our approach to low tide, we found here a precarious amphitheater floored with white sand. Overhead, birds wheeled, their amplified, reverberating cries suggesting a cave of pterodactyls in a long-past era.

The men and older boys immediately began scouring the cliffs (Fig. 93). One of the first on the rocks was Nakarak, nearly sixty-five years old. Wearing soft-soled skin boots, he leaped to a narrow ledge and, hands clutching at cracks in the rock, half ran from one shelf to another, up and up the side of the cliff, to the very heart of the nesting area. Now tightening his belt and getting a grip with one hand, with the other he began to transfer eggs from their perches on bare rocks or on minute patches of straw to the inside of his shirt. He continued this way from one ledge to another until it seemed improbable that he would return safely or his burden remain unscrambled. Other hunters were exploiting ledges above and below, but it seemed to us that Nakarak was the most nimble of the group.

At length he returned, never having missed a step, his glasses steaming in the cool of the late night and his shirt bulging dangerously with unbroken eggs. He explained that he had climbed these cliffs since childhood and knew all the footholds and handholds on the rocks of the Cape. Though in earlier days, he said, men had sometimes dropped rawhide nets from rock platforms high on the slope for protection, he had always preferred to trust his own balance and footing. When the others had also come down from the cliffs, their eggs filled the containers in the boats to capacity and there came next a great feast of boiled eggs. I noticed with satisfaction that, this early in the season, no eyes or beaks stared out at us as we broke the shells.

ON ANOTHER calm day, Jack Newcomb, Nakarak, and I made a ten-mile trip around to the west side of Cape Denbigh to examine the only other archeological site known to exist in the vicinity. Rounding the Cape once more in a rain of diving sea birds, we continued around the west side, crossed a long bay to a distant point, and beyond it entered a small, protected bay at the end of which lay the site that Nakarak called Iyatayet.

Here the slopes of two sides of a small creek were covered with partially frozen, thick tussocks of last season's grass that reached in places higher than a man's head. To the left of the creek the grass covered a steep bank forty feet high and, at that height and above, part of a spacious bench or terrace (Fig. 94). Where the slope again increased, the grass disappeared and fifteen-foot-high thickets of alder and willow flourished. To the right of the creek, at the base of a steep slope, grass covered only a low mound a few feet above the elevation of the creek mouth itself.

Climbing with a pick and some shovels to the terrace edge on the left side, we attempted to dig a test hole into whatever deposit

94. Iyatayet site from the air. The grassy area seen on the hillside to the left is the archeological site.

there might be, but with little success, for the tussocks had thawed only an inch or two. We managed to find a few more deeply thawed spots among the grass roots, though, and from the objects found there, judged the site to have been occupied no earlier than the other site, Nukleet. Among the objects found, first of all, were many chips of flinty material—basalt and chert predominating. Other artifacts were a thin, narrow side blade, much like those of Ipiutak, a piece of jade, some well-preserved wood, and an arrowhead dating no earlier than the seventeenth century. I decided that the Nukleet site would be the more promising of the two to dig.

BACK AT NUKLEET, then, that summer of 1948, where each day's thaw took us deeper into our long trench, we reached bottom at the upper end of the slope. Toward its middle the trench deepened in two places where it crossed pit houses that had been built into the slope. The floors of these held material obviously earlier and more Thule-like than the fairly recent upper levels. Still farther down the slope, where the deeper deposits were thoroughly frozen, we found preservation excellent, but because of the frost progress was slow. Bones sticking out of the walls of our trench delayed us, too, but at last bedrock was reached in the deepest part of the site.

95. Iyatayet site and camp from the sea, 1948. To the left of the stream are the Eskimos' tents and to the right, ours.

As we looked over the artifacts from these excavations, we puzzled over one thing. Here at Nukleet hardly a flint flake had come to light. The stone-cutting and piercing tools were nearly all of polished slate, the only exceptions being a side scraper or two. At Iyatayet, on the other hand, chips of flinty materials had been everywhere. Why should Iyatayet hold so many flints? Could there be, at the distant site, beneath a veneer of late occupation, the leavings of some people who, like those of Ipiutak, had preferred flints to slate? To find out, as soon as our test trench was completed at Nukleet, we moved camp to Iyatayet, though without Newcomb who had to return to Anchorage.

Choosing a suitable patch of gravel above high-tide line on the right side of Iyatayet Creek, Bets and I erected our tent; Nakarak and his crew placed their tents in a corresponding position on the left (Fig. 95). Before us stretched white gravel in place of the jagged rocks of Nukleet, and farther along the beach was a long stretch of white sand on which a stroller might find starfish, shells, and clusters of mussels lodged among seaweed and driftwood. One evening when Nakarak came visiting, he said: "Now I cross the river," and he jumped over the clear stream. Henceforth, Iyatayet Creek became our "river," and our two sets of tents became neighboring villages. Our young Jim was just learning to walk, so we built him a corral of driftwood, and over this fence the Nakarak children would lean for hours as though studying a prize animal at the county fair.

Up on the terrace, we began at once to clear six-by-ten-foot rectangles and a larger area to encompass the depression that I thought would cover a late-period house and tunnel. Once the sod was removed, the earth underneath thawed from one to three or four inches a day. The house, because of the texture of its soil, thawed more rapidly, and I decided to clear its floor before concentrating on other areas. Besides, a period of rain and wind had set in and it was more pleasant to work on the comparatively level surface of the melting house pit than on the slope, where objects slid downhill across the ice as they thawed. Also the walls of the pit gave a little protection from the wind.

At length we reached bottom, finding the edges of a wooden floor under grooved base logs that had held walls of split poles. Though rotten, the floor was discerned to have been made of driftwood poles split in half and laid flat side up. In the middle of the floor was a fireplace of gravel on which lay a deposit of ash and charcoal. Just forward of this was the entrance to a tunnel. A departing householder would have lowered himself two and a half feet through a hole in the floor and then crept forward on hands and knees past the front wall of the house and on to the end of a ten-foot passageway where he would have emerged on the brow of the terrace. Among the artifacts definitely belonging to the house were a large, round, shallow lamp of clay blackened inside from long usage, a jade adz blade, and many other objects that indicated the house to have been occupied no earlier than A.D. 1600.

When the floor had been cleaned of its debris and was sketched and photographed, I found myself alone one day with the enticing work ahead of removing the floor planks. In another kind of site where a house pit had been dug into virgin sand or gravel, there would have been less anticipation. But in the first days of this excavation I had seen enough flakes and fragmentary artifacts of flint to know that something must lie below. Leaving the flattened base logs intact, I began at the rear of the house and with trowel and shovel stripped the wet and half-rotten floorboards from the earth underneath. When I had cleared a space three feet wide stretching from side to side of the house, I began to trowel with keen anticipation. And I was not disappointed. During the two or three days it took to clean the house floor, the 60° late summer temperature had helpfully penetrated several inches into the ground below. At once I saw that none of the materials were like those of

96. Whetstones of shale, Norton culture, Cape Denbigh. The left one is 2½ in. long (6.3 cm.).

the house and upper segments of the midden. Rather, the soil, a fine-grained loam darkened with organic inclusions, yielded a whole range of objects that we had not found at Nukleet and none that belonged to its culture.

Here were thin end blades and side blades of chert, jasper, and chalcedony of types more closely resembling those of the Ipiutak site at Point Hope. But there were variant forms, including some with sharply serrate edges, and many of these blades were made of local basalt and silicified slate rather than of the finer flints. Some of these thin blades were ground along the center of one or both faces. Short knife blades with a strongly curved edge reminded me of similar blades of Dorset culture in eastern Canada. Thick flakeknives and side scrapers again reminded me of Ipiutak. Other more common objects did not: the ovate adz blades of silicified slate, and very small, thin whetstones of shale, grooved on one or more surfaces from constant use (Fig. 96).

The most unexpected elements were the fragments of stone vessels, apparently lamps for illumination rather than for cooking (Fig. 97), and numbers of sherds of a thin, brown pottery stamped over the entire outer surface with minute squares or rectangles (similar potsherds are shown in Fig. 62). This pottery, in particular, was a source of excitement because it outwardly resembled some of the earliest pottery from the southeastern United States and also some from Japan. Though it was probably not as old as southeastern pottery, in 1948 no other early pottery was known throughout the great coniferous forest of the interior of North America from western Alaska to Ontario, and the possible cross-ties of this ware with pottery of other cultures in remote parts of the world could not be overlooked.

Most of the wood and other organic material had disintegrated in this "middle" level, yet here and there an animal bone or the fragment of an artifact of antler or ivory was preserved. Streaks of black seen in profile were, I found by trowelling through them, remnants of salt-water mussel shells—evidence of many a tasty meal. Only the chitinous covers of the shells, paper-thin, remained for identification. The advanced state of disintegration in this level was in sharp contrast to that of the upper deposits and the entire midden at Nukleet. I could not resist interpreting this as a sign of age and, despite the resemblances to Ipiutak culture, wondering if these were not older. The aggregate of their artifacts was given the name "Norton," and Norton culture sites are now known in other coastal areas, including the beaches at Cape Krusenstern (Chapter IX).

The middle (Norton) layer under that first house floor at Iyatayet proved to be two feet thick. As I penetrated deeper into the gray and black soil of the deposit, pleased that the rain had now ceased to make a quagmire of the excavations, I realized that there were few signs here of regular stratification. Rather, the lower part of the deposit seemed to have been often mixed, as if it had been soft mud into which heavier objects were dropped and stirred.

97. Stone lamps from Iyatayet site, Cape Denbigh. They are of Norton culture, about 200 B.C. The lamp at upper right is approximately 6 in. long (15 cm.).

The streaks of mussel shells too often turned from a level and curved downward through some inches of the soil to allow firm assumptions of increasing age with increasing depth.

Then one day my trowel cut into soil of a different texture, a sandy silt, clean, uniform, and apparently untouched by human feet or hands. It was a satisfying feeling to have reached bottom, the virgin soil upon which the first of these early pottery makers had established camp. Tests thus seemed complete. Sterile soil was exposed all the way across the bottom of my cut, which now bit into two feet of earth beneath the rear of the house.

Although it seemed obvious that I had reached the lowest cultural deposit, I did not at once take a shovel and scoop hurriedly through whatever of this coarse soil might be thawed, but from long habit knelt with the trowel and scraped away a level as if I were working in the finest midden. Now and then I poked down to learn where frost lay and where this sandy soil might rest on the bedrock of the slope. Then, just as a snipe might sense from its flexing beak a meal beneath the lakeshore sand, I felt with my trowel tip a harsh and grating resistance unlike that of any soil layer thus far encountered. Another probe or two told me that indeed a layer of gritty material lay less than an inch below. Turning the trowel blade on edge, I described a small square, pressing the edge each time to the resistant layer. Now, at the fourth edge of the square, I angled the blade slightly inward and lifted. As I expected, the sandy loam of the sterile earth parted cleanly from the layer below, so that I could tip it intact and thus remove it safely.

The surface I saw could not have been more breathtaking had it been covered with gold. Glistening there with hardly a grain of fallen soil to mar them lay countless flakes of chert and obsidian and, unmistakably, the prismatic facets of microblades like those of the Middle Stone Age of Europe. Trembling with excitement at this rare disclosure, I continued to remove the sterile soil until I had exposed a glittering floor a yard across. Now I could see that all the objects were small—the chips ridiculously so. A leaflike flake or two turned out to be side blades fashioned by the removal from their surfaces of incredibly small, parallel, ribbon-like flakes (see Fig. 7). This accounted for the minute facets of light that glinted upward. A test with the trowel showed that none of these flakes or artifacts stood at an angle, but all lay flat on a surface of clay as though purposely placed there to form a mosaic.

Now lifting an obsidian microblade on the trowel, I took it between my fingers, wiped it clean of the clay, and held it to the light. Like other microblades that I had examined from the Campus site of the interior and in collections of European Mesolithic artifacts, this had been struck. That is, the maker, taking a block or core of obsidian only an inch or two long, struck blows at one end to remove long, thin flakes, one after the other. When finished with his core, five or more facets ran its length between parallel edges

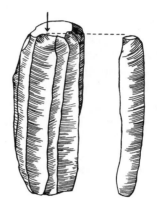

98. A microblade (right) that has been struck from a core (left) with a quick, sharp blow. (*From Oakley, 1959*). The blade was often further worked by sharpening its edges and tip, as shown in Figs. 1 and 137.

showing that at least five blades had been struck, each having left a thin scar (Figs. 98 and 102). One such blade I held in my hand.

Only then, after making sure that the bottom layer was no delusion, did I call Bets to the scene. Needless to say she fully shared my excitement, and before long all the others, attracted by our enthusiastic cries, had gathered so closely about the edge of the cut that I feared the walls might collapse and the whole revelation become buried again. Although the Eskimos never quite understood the old level as a whole, even they were impressed by the small size of some of the artifacts and the meticulous workmanship that had produced them. We worked in the aura of discovery for the remainder of the season, and although I allowed none but myself to expose this oldest layer, we all continued to examine each recovered artifact with amazement and delight.

The stratigraphy of the site in such hard and fast levels as these was extremely rare in the Arctic and gave us much satisfaction. I felt that perhaps no other culture in the region was as deeply buried and sharply defined over such a wide area as was the one in the lowest level of our cut, and I now named it the Denbigh Flint complex.

However widespread the interest in succeeding months after those 1948 findings, the best discussion of the dig took place shortly after we left the field and returned to our log house near the University of Alaska. Helge Larsen and Erik Holtved were in Alaska that season, having come from Denmark to excavate in the Bristol Bay region of the southern Bering Sea. We had talked over our prospects in the spring, and now, together once more with our scores of prize artifacts spread before us, we entered into a session as animated as that between medieval navigators who had discovered new continents. The Danes, too, had found sites of Ipiutak-like flints complete with house pits, and in some of them—those least resembling Point Hope Ipiutak—they too had found check-stamped pottery, stone lamps, stone sinkers, and many other cultural leavings similar to those from the middle levels at Cape Denbigh.

In that single summer we had not only extended the knowledge of pre-Thule cultures for nearly the whole length of the Bering Sea region, but at Cape Denbigh had found the known cultures stacked one on top of another and had found a culture earlier than all the others—the Denbigh Flint complex—that recalled both the earliest known archeology of central Alaska and findings from the Gobi Desert of Asia. Our talk and excitement continued long into each night, and to nonarcheological visitors who dropped in briefly from time to time, our self-centered and explosive conversation was like shaman talk in an unknown tongue.

Our strongest point of agreement was that new horizons were opening in Arctic archeology and we must get back into the field as soon as another season began. Thus early the next summer, 1949, Larsen flew to Deering in Kotzebue Sound to investigate the series of limestone caves (the Trail Creek caves described on p. 216) high in the hills of Seward Peninsula south of Deering village, and I returned to Cape Denbigh to work at Iyatayet with a crew of Eskimos, arranging for Wendell Oswalt and his wife Helen to continue excavations for me at Nukleet.

The high point of that season was the finding of three or four spearpoints so closely resembling certain ones of paleo-Indian sites of the early Western Plains that some kind of connection between the two regions could not be ignored. Each of the points was found in place in the Denbigh Flint level, and each drew from me such enthusiastic cries of admiration that my Eskimo friends may have had some concern for my judgment.

The most remarkable was a broad spearpoint of chalcedony from each face of which a wide channel flake had been removed (Fig. 99). This parallel-edged object thus had a fluting down the middle of each face that thinned it centrally, as though to fit easily into the pincers of some large shaft tip. Though one part was now broken away, the lower edges of the point had been parallel, each with a projection that bordered a concave basal edge. However attractive the point in its own right, I recognized it as a short variety of the fluted points that were widespread between the Rocky Mountains and the east coast of the United States. Such points when found in place in deep deposits in those more southern locations were often associated with the bones of wide-horned bison and other species of animals now extinct. This was only the second

99. A fluted spearpoint of chalcedony (the lower left tip is broken). This is from the Denbigh Flint complex at Iyatayet. Length, 1¾ in. (4.5 cm.).

100. Angostura-type point (broken) of chert from the Denbigh Flint complex, Iyatayet. Such points were used by the Denbigh people from about 3000–1000 B.C. Length, 2⅞ in. (7.3 cm.).

fluted point known in Alaska, the first having been picked up by a geologist two years before on the north slope of the Brooks Range.

The fragment of another long, slender point, also with parallel edges, was distinguished by narrow diagonal flake scars paralleling one another the entire length of the piece on both its convex faces. Even without its base I could see that this was identical in every respect to points then known as diagonal Yumas (now called Angosturas), associated, in Colorado at least, with extinct animals (Figs. 100 and 133d).

Along with these points were a graver or two—small, scraper-like objects with a sharp, flaked tip projecting from the edge (Fig. 101); these also seemed to be tied directly to Early Man sites farther south.

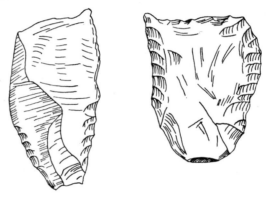

101. Two chert gravers, Denbigh Flint complex. Length of right graver, 1½ in. (3.8 cm.).

Most of the other techniques of flintwork found in the Denbigh level were well known in the Old World, either in the forested sites of Siberia and the steppes of Mongolia or in the Meso-lithic and Paleolithic periods of Europe. Microblades and cores, for instance (Fig. 102), were characteristic of those in the so-called Neolithic sites of Siberia, where they were associated with bifaced flint edges known to have been set in series into slots along the sides of weapon points—a fashion better known from European Meso-lithic sites.

Another group of objects, burins (see Figs. 6 and 109), did not seem to stem from either the Neolithic or the Mesolithic but from a much earlier archeology found mainly in Europe (where

102. Two microcores (top left) and eight microblades that are struck from such cores. Denbigh Flint complex. The larger core is 1¼ in. (3.1 cm.).

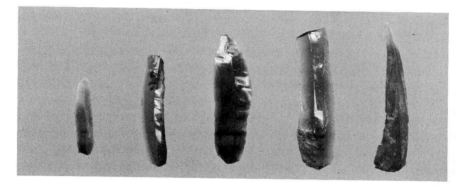

they are sometimes called gravers). These little pieces, only an inch or two in length, at first seemed to be specialized tools purposely roughened for some unguessed-at purpose; perhaps they were hafted and then drawn along bone or antler objects to make parallel markings. There were so many of these burins in the Denbigh level, however, that I decided to turn my attention to the tiny flakes that had been struck from them. These, it turned out, occurred in far greater numbers than the burins themselves. Soon it became obvious that the thin, narrow, four- or three-faceted flakes called spalls (Fig. 103), some not much larger than a spruce needle, had been created intentionally by a skilled technician, and I began to believe that they had been the ultimate objects sought, the burins being only the rejected cores from which the thin spalls had been struck.

That fall I continued studying the Denbigh materials at the University of Pennsylvania. Though miniature in comparison with those of the European Stone Age, they ran through nearly the whole range of types known in the Aurignacian period of some 40,000 to 30,000 years ago. Whatever the function of the large burins made on unifaced blades of the Paleolithic, these of Alaska had been used for grooving and splitting hard organic materials— antler and ivory—into thin pieces basic to the making of arrow and spearheads and a variety of pointed tools. We then saw that the polished instruments thought to have had the same function in the Okvik culture and in the middle, or Norton, culture of Cape Denbigh were those of an intermediate stage in evolution between the Denbigh burin and the Eskimo grooving knife of steel that is still in use.

Some further months of work with the specimens led to parallel assumptions about the burin spalls. Though these were no doubt often removed to sharpen the knifelike tip of the burin, many of the opposite ends of the thin spalls had been retouched in such a microscopic manner as to make them surely among the world's

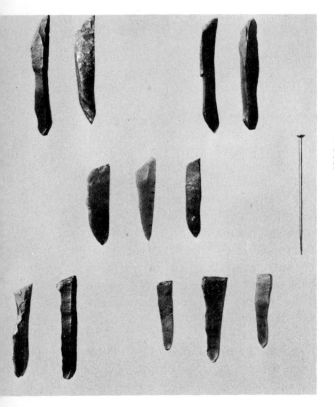

103. Burin spalls. For sizes, compare them with the common one-inch pin shown at the right.

104. The tip of a burin spall enlarged twenty times. The spall is the one shown at the extreme lower left of Fig. 103.

most minuscule implements (Fig. 104). Their use had been as tips of engraving tools, not unlike those employed by modern artists; in later cultural periods they were replaced by rodents' teeth and then by styluses of metal. When these burin spall artifacts— bifaced small side blades and weapon tips minutely flaked diagonally over their whole surfaces—are looked at under magnification, one cannot help but be amazed at the precision and meticulous workmanship of the old Denbigh craftsmen.

While we were still in the field, however, our Eskimo helpers never considered these to be parts of weapons or knives used by people like themselves. Rather, they recalled Nakarak's legend of the dwarf chief and may seriously have envisioned a whole tribe of miniature people swarming over the slopes of Iyatayet. If such matters were puzzling to the Eskimos, however, so too were some aspects of our behavior, the most perplexing of which, perhaps, came in our third season at the site.

DURING THAT SUMMER of 1950, Froelich Rainey, Helge Larsen, and I planned a cooperative course together, as we had done in 1939. Larsen was to continue excavating the Trail Creek caves, Rainey was to explore the western shores of Seward Peninsula, and I was to continue the work at Cape Denbigh. Two graduate students from the University of Pennsylvania, Gerald Henderson and James VanStone, accompanied me. After a survey of neighboring capes and shores around Norton Bay, my party settled down at

Iyatayet to continue exposing as much as possible of the Denbigh Flint complex layer. On one side of our mighty trickle of a "river," Henderson, VanStone, and I often sat before our tents discussing archeology, while Nakarak, Sokpilak, and their respective families and friends sitting on the other side a few feet away conversed in Eskimo.

On one such occasion, while we waited for our supper (the all too familiar pressure-cooked beans and bacon), Henderson, Van-Stone, and I were discussing early primate forms, recalling certain lectures by Professor Loren Eiseley at the University of Pennsylvania. There was always the question of which were closer to the line of human descent: lemur-like, or tarsier-like creatures of the Eocene period?—and, before these, tree-shrews, or even some precursors of the more lowly modern shrews? From this, talk turned to the tiny shrews themselves that fell with some frequency into our test pits and, becoming hungry because of their amazing rate of metabolism, fought and ate each other until but one remained. The thought suddenly struck Henderson and VanStone that an amusing and useful gift for Professor Eiseley would be the mounted skeleton of an Alaskan shrew.

After dinner, my companions set about putting their plan into effect. They would find a newly dead shrew in one of the test pits and boil it until the fur and flesh fell away, then mount the articulated bones. The evening was calm and relatively mosquito free. I sat reading a book in front of our mess tent a little later and only half noticed when my friends returned. Henderson was holding a ball of brown fur by the tail and walking gingerly ahead. The rather incredulous interest from our neighbors across the river attracted my attention. Old and young alike ceased their activities and began to watch intently. The students, absorbed in their project, moved to the next stage in their operation. VanStone walked a few yards to a strand mark on the beach where he picked up some dry twigs. These he formed carefully into a miniature cone and set ablaze. Henderson, meanwhile, put an inch or two of water into an old coffee can and then joined his partner squatting before the small fire. They placed small slabs of rock around the flames and put their miniature kettle on top.

By this time, Nakarak, unable to contain his curiosity, slowly sauntered across to our beach. Trying to appear as oblivious to the fire makers as they were to him, he nevertheless edged closer until the two students looked up, startled. Reacting at first as though they should explain themselves, they seemed to decide otherwise, and both turned back without a word, Henderson still holding the shrew by the tail while waiting for the water to boil.

At length Nakarak spoke. "Making soup?" he inquired. Aware of the futility of an explanation, the two shrew-boilers simply nodded and went on with their cooking. Nakarak, having learned our odd tastes, rejoined his group, all watching with unflagging interest until the shrew was boiled.

WHATEVER the Eskimos may have thought of these supposedly dwarf Denbigh men and their tiny flints, we were becoming more impressed daily by the great skill of these ancient flintworkers, and learning their date of occupation became a matter of consuming interest. Levels so firmly stratified were most remarkable for the Arctic, and we wondered if the lowest layers might not be the oldest so far discovered on the Alaskan coast.

The profiles of our cut permitted a view of the different layers as clearly as would a slice through a many-layered cake. The topmost levels contained the leavings of a Western Thule-like people, here designated "Nukleet." In the middle levels were the artifacts of Norton people; and at bottom, the Denbigh Flint complex. Not only were the Denbigh artifacts vastly different from those of the two cultures above, but they lay much deeper, separated from the others by a sandy soil containing no artifacts. Throughout the world, the deepest layers in a site, or mound, are the oldest; here, the question was *how* old?

In the 1950 season, a nonarcheological find that we hoped might help answer our question turned up in the Denbigh layer. This was something that a geologist could best interpret, and it was my good luck that Dr. David Hopkins, a specialist in Pleistocene geology for the United States Geological Survey, made a special trip to Iyatayet to study our stratigraphy. His geological knowledge and analyses of the soils, together with our archeological findings, soon told us we were viewing a five-thousand-year-flashback into history.

The special find that Dr. Hopkins so competently described is a rather common Arctic phenomenon called a solifluction lobe (Fig. 105). Such lobes are formed under steep slopes whose subsoil

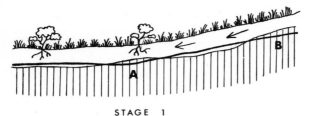

STAGE 1

STAGE 2

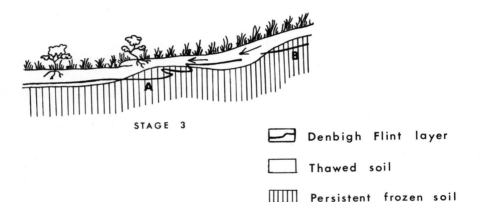

STAGE 3

Denbigh Flint layer

Thawed soil

Persistent frozen soil

105. Development of a solifluction lobe at Cape Denbigh.

Stage 1: The upper ground thaws in the late spring, but frozen ground remains below. The Denbigh culture layer thaws in most places but stays frozen at (A) and (B).

Stage 2: The saturated surface layer creeps downslope, forming a soil lobe. The thawed part of the Denbigh culture layer overrides the frozen part (A), and a gap is formed upslope.

Stage 3: During spring thaw another year the front of the soil lobe advances, overriding the surface turf (note the tilted shrub with roots trailing upslope). Additional folds are formed in the Denbigh culture layer and the gap upslope widens where the culture layer is missing. (*From Hopkins and Giddings, 1953*) generally remains frozen; yet in some summers, enough warmth penetrates here and there to cause patches of ice to melt under the grass cover. If such a spot is clay, which becomes slippery when wet, it tends to slip forward down the hillside until it comes to the obstruction of an area still solidly frozen. There it slowly inches over the top of the icy block, pushing up the sod as it bulges forward, until both clay and sod fold over atop each other.

This is what happened during a long span of time on the steep slopes of Iyatayet. Gradually in later years the folded part consolidated itself, as the turf rotted away, into a thin, tough, elastic layer that now lies folded underground, holding the tiny chips and tools of the Denbigh Flint workers.

Using our geological and archeological knowledge—and later obtaining radiocarbon dates from small bits of charcoal off the site —Hopkins and I before long were able to reconstruct the sequence of climates and peoples here on the hillside. The first residents were the Denbigh Flint people, who came some 5,500 to 4,500 years ago. Undoubtedly they found the site covered with sod, for we could conceive of no camper who would have set up housekeeping on clay, which in dry weather powders one with finegrained dust, and in rain mires him in mud. The fact, too, that Denbigh artifacts are found lying flat shows that they were not ground by footsteps into mud or dust, setting them at all angles and depths, but must have been dropped onto a deep sod, though this had long since rotted away, as had all traces of organic artifacts.

The climate in Denbigh times was probably milder than it is today. Then, after Denbigh men disappeared, a thick layer of coarser dirt accumulated over their leavings—a kind of soil that indicates a wetter, colder climate, probably colder than that of today. Ice then penetrated the hillside, and during the summers the time was ripe for the formation of solifluction lobes. Gradually this colder climate warmed again, a layer of peat was laid down above the Denbigh layer, and the weather became much like that today.

When Norton people arrived on the scene, about 500 B.C., the climate had moderated to one of few extremes. The site by then was again vegetation covered (had it been bare, it would long since have been cut away by erosion or dug into by ravines) and over the centuries the Norton people left deep middens of trash outside their front doors on the slope. Most of their perishable materials have now decomposed, turning into black mud.

The more recent residents of Iyatayet, as seen in the stratified layers, were the Nukleet (Western Thule-like) people, who first set up their camps on the steep sides of the bluff in the twelfth century A.D. They, too, must have found the land covered with vegetation, probably sodded with the same kind of thick, deep grass that grows there now. Their occupation lasted several hundred years, and their legacy to us is a thick layer of debris containing wood, ivory, and other organic objects such as Eskimos accumulate in and about their camps. This, then, was the composite picture of Iyatayet; but it was the oldest, Denbigh Flint layer that continued to intrigue us the most.

SINCE ONLY the faintest traces of bony material were preserved in the old Denbigh layer, we had no way of knowing whether the animals pursued by the ancient hunters had been like those of today or not. Then one day I listened with renewed interest to a story Nakarak was telling. The legend was about a kind of animal called *kelyegivuk*. These beasts had long ago burrowed underneath the earth, much as a ground squirrel does, emerging now and then into the open air. They were immense creatures with "ivories in their heads." Nakarak thought the English name for them was "maskotus," and it suddenly occurred to me that he was telling the widespread aboriginal tale of burrowing mammoths. This legend, in many forms, is shared by northern Indians and Eskimos as well as their Siberian neighbors.

When asked if he had seen any signs of these beasts himself, Nakarak answered that he had—that we could easily take a boat and go to a place just to the north side of Cape Denbigh where he frequently went when in need of ivory for the manufacture of certain implements. Since Nakarak was more than willing to go, he and I took advantage of the first fine weather to travel to the *kelyegivuk* place. This turned out to be an old Pleistocene bank of silt and ice masses covered by a four-foot-thick layer of tundra that was being eaten away continually by storm and tide. Anchoring our boat in a few inches of water and sloshing through a wide shoal to the exposed beach, Nakarak and I immediately found bones of a variety of fossil animals. Among them were hooves and bones of Pleistocene ponies and horn cores and skull fragments of extinct forms of bison. Here and there were huge mammoth bones and a variety of smaller bones and wood, all thawing and being washed out of the muck bank.

I became even more interested when Nakarak pointed out the end of the *kelyegivuk* burrow, the place where these creatures had once emerged into the open, for as we drew near there was no doubt as to what I saw: part of an elephant's skull with one of the tusks intact, still frozen solidly in its resting place. When Nakarak had picked up enough small segments and splinters of ivory to suit his purposes, as well as two or three mammoth teeth to use, he said, as sinkers for the end of his set nets, we turned away from the area, not having discovered so much as a chip of worked stone showing the presence of man, to my great disappointment.

WHILE IT WAS CLEAR that the whole Denbigh Flint complex did not appear as such in any of the known sites of Asia, although its microblade ingredients did, we soon discovered a broad path of its spread eastward across Alaska and Canada. In 1949, Ralph Solecki of the Smithsonian Institution, traveling with geologists on the plateau north of the Brooks Range, discovered prepared cores and microblades in two localities. The following year, a geologist of the United States Geological Survey discovered prepared cores and two fluted points in the same general region, and, that same year, another geologist and William Irving, a student from the University of Alaska, working in the Anaktuvuk Valley of the central Brooks Range, separately discovered cores and microblades, burins, side blades, and end scrapers similar to those of the Denbigh Flint complex. Taken together, these proved that the Denbigh people were capable of living far from the sea, presumably depending upon herds of caribou inland.

Since then, in 1954 and later, R. S. MacNeish has unearthed a large deposit of Denbigh artifacts from a site of many occupations on the Firth River of Canada a few miles from the Arctic Sea. Little change is to be seen between the artifacts there and those of similar type at Cape Denbigh, although some of the Denbigh forms are not present at Firth River. Still farther east in Canada, Denbigh-like combinations of microblades and burins were found by Elmer Harp of Dartmouth College along the Coppermine River, and by Jørgen Meldgaard of the Danish National Museum on old raised beaches up to 175 feet above sea level in the Iglulik area of northeastern Canada and the Arctic archipelago.

Perhaps the most surprising discovery of Denbigh-like material was that of Count Eigil Knuth in Pearyland in the extreme northern part of Greenland. There men lived but a few dozen miles from the north pole while securing their food with implements not at all unlike those of the Denbigh Flint people. Count Knuth of Denmark (Fig. 106), a tall, blond man of many talents—sculptor, musician, and explorer—first found some of the oldest Greenland artifacts in 1947, but considered them to be of Dorset culture until after the discovery of the Denbigh Flint complex in Alaska. Subsequently he returned to the area and isolated a number of sites in that north Greenlandic slope inhabited by caribou and musk oxen, showing that people lived there at least 4,500 years ago at former sea edges that have since become raised plateaus. They used burins, burin spalls, microblades, and other artifacts remarkably like those of the Denbigh Flint people, and they lived in oval, surface dwellings. Their culture he named "Independence I" (Fig. 107).

106. Count Eigil Knuth excavating at Midsummer Lakes, Pearyland, Greenland, June 1949.

107. Independence I artifacts from Greenland: points, burins, spalls, micro-blades, awls, knives, and scrapers—all of shapes similar to their counterparts in the Denbigh Flint complex. Length of lower right point, 2¾ in. (7.1 cm.).

Whether or not these were the first men in North Greenland, they appear not to have abandoned the region but rather to have gradually adopted over the years a more Dorset-like culture. Recent discoveries by scientists from Denmark, Canada, and the United States working in the Dorset culture area seem to show that the Dorset culture as such did not originate in the west but grew in some as yet undetermined way out of a Denbigh-like base in North Canada and Greenland.

From large sites excavated by Henry Collins on Southhampton Island in North Hudson Bay (Map 4), by William Taylor on Ungava Peninsula, by Moreau Maxwell on Baffin Island, and by Elmer Harp in northern Newfoundland, as well as by Meldgaard, Larsen, Mathiassen, and others in Greenland, we now see that the Dorset culture lasted from at least 1000 B.C. to around A.D. 800, when Thule culture began, maintaining the "small tool" inventory while at the same time accumulating such new elements as polished slate knives and points. Each summer, Danish, Canadian, and American archeologists are working in the far north of Greenland and eastern Canada to fit together the interrelationships between the cultures found there: Independence, Sarqaq, and Dorset. I anticipate exciting new discoveries about these microblade cultures, but for the present I shall hazard a guess that however close to Denbigh some of these cultures may be, they are abstracted, rather than evolved, from it, for they lack the extremely fine flaking and many of the specialized point and tool forms found in Alaska.

SINCE 1956, evidence has been growing that the Denbigh people, known to be capable hunters along the caribou passes of the interior, were also exploiters of the sea. We could not be sure of this at Cape Denbigh, which is at the forest edge where they might have depended upon caribou and smaller forest game primarily, and only sporadically on seal. But in 1956 and early 1958 when we explored the beaches from Cape Prince of Wales around Kotzebue Sound to Choris Peninsula and in subsequent seasons when we sampled the Krusenstern and nearby beaches, we learned emphatically that Denbigh people had lived at the ocean edge throughout this entire area and would surely have been adept at making the most of the sea's resources. Many of the broad, thin points found at these coastal sites, but not in the interior, offer as much proof as can be expected from stone tools alone that these people lived in spring or summer tents while pursuing seals and walruses with toggle harpoons essentially like those used by modern Eskimos.

Neither at Cape Denbigh nor at Cape Krusenstern did the Denbigh people leave signs of having lived in dwellings more permanent than tents. Their temporary surface dwellings were indicated by oval or circular areas, containing chips and artifacts, surrounding small hearths littered with cracked beach pebbles.

AT CAPE KRUSENSTERN (Map 2), hunting for the hearths and tent sites of the Denbigh people was far more difficult than looking for surface disturbances made by people who dug houses deep into the gravel ridges. The first discovery of a hearth was in 1958 in the area of Beaches 102–4, and it was made partially because the sod cover happened to be thin in that particular region. After a few distinctive Denbigh pieces had been found we searched more diligently, and when a chip was discovered, we crawled on hands and knees pulling up the moss until we located concentrations. Excavation then consisted mainly in lifting the thin cover of moss roots with trowel and fingers while attempting not to disturb the gravel underneath. At last, having cleared an area, we trowelled carefully, finding both artifacts and hearth remains practically at the surface.

In the 1961 season when the Larsens, Doug Anderson, Paul Dayton, and I diligently searched the Krusenstern ridges for signs of Choris and Norton cultures, we learned to spot a hearth by no more of an indication than a slightly discolored or reddened tinge to bits of soil showing between moss stems. In this way I happened upon a line of small Denbigh sites running in a discontinuous area seaward from Beaches 104 and 105 where they trended almost north and south. Once the hunt by discolored soil was mastered, I found it simple to move along a beach crest spotting many hearth signs from the surface and then investigating the mossier areas between.

While I was thus occupied on what later proved to be the youngest Denbigh beach, 80, Helge and Gerda Larsen discovered another similar string of hearths more than three miles away to the east. By mentally projecting the beach ridges past their points of erasure, we found that the Larsens' discovery was almost certainly on a continuation of the same ridge on which I was working. Analysis later showed that the materials from these hearths, so widely separated, more closely resembled each other than either of them resembled materials in older hearths on the earlier beaches, 102–5.

Some of the objects on the later beaches not found in the same form on the earlier ones were large crescentic side blades much like those of Ipiutak, very narrow but relatively thick microblades made from wedge-shaped cores, one or two crude burins anticipating those of Choris beaches, and at least one arrowpoint polished lightly on both faces. Otherwise, however, the culture of Beaches 102–5, presumably the most populous time of the Denbigh period, was nearly identical to that of Denbigh sites elsewhere on the coast of Alaska.

Why the population at Cape Krusenstern was so sparse for seven hundred years between Denbigh times and the era of Old Whaling culture, we still do not understand. Certain it is, though,

that the highly distinctive Denbigh culture, with its jewel-like precision and miniature forms, came to a rather abrupt end in that
region, being followed much later by cultures such as Old Whaling
and Choris of quite different origins. In Greenland, on the other
hand, it seems a fact that Denbigh-type artifacts continued to be
made for a much longer period. While it is possible that the Denbigh people themselves moved, their mastery of both the interior
and the coast suggests instead that their flint forms, rather than
they, drifted across the Arctic, and hunters living farther east and
north took up their ways of living and making tools after such
practices had become obsolete on the coast of western Alaska.

(XIII)

THE INTERIOR—
INDIAN OR ESKIMO?

KNEELING into the wind to avoid the dust of trowelling while digging the Denbigh hearths at Cape Krusenstern, I sometimes pondered the contrasts between life on these barren shores and in the neighboring forests. Along the coast, where Denbigh people camped some five thousand years ago, wind blows almost continuously. A northwest wind generally brings fair weather and clear skies, but the sea ice is never far off even in summer, and if one removes his head covering and outer garments, the chill soon penetrates to his very bones. Wildlife rustles about in the grass— field mice and lemmings, ground squirrels, and small, seed-eating birds. They enjoy a little warmth only on sunny summer days, and the eggs of sparrows, sandpipers, and even ducks concealed in nests hollowed among the plants must incubate quickly in the short season of comparative warmth.

When a small bird flies, there is always the wind to fight, and if it soars high, it is buffeted from its course and preyed upon by hovering pigeon hawks and jaegers. Red foxes lie sprawled in the sun, panting, while their pups fight and play in the lee of a low mound that contains their burrow. Larger animals and men, going about their business, cannot remain in unprotected spots for long and are continuously ruffled by the steady blow. Loose flaps of clothing are whipped about, and tents and cache covers, if the lashing becomes slack, are quickly worn to shreds. If the wind changes to the east, rain often follows. No longer as steady, the new

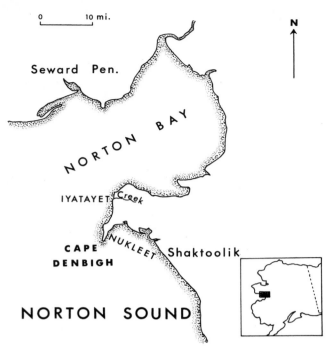

Map 8. Cape Denbigh

wind drives moisture into seams of clothing and shelter, making indoor fires a necessity for dryness and warmth.

Frequently during the day a round head pops up from the water close to shore as a seal surveys the horizons of beach and sea. In days gone by, an Eskimo seal hunter might have made his way out among the ice floes and leads of the sea in a well-equipped, efficient little skin boat and, approaching to within twenty or thirty feet of a surfacing seal, hurled his harpoon at the animal. Or, in the very early spring, he might have landed cautiously on the far side of an ice floe, approached to within a similar distance of a seal basking in the sun, and then cast his spear at his prey. This latter skill took long practice at stalking, for the hunter might approach the wary animal only if it believed him to be another seal. Hours of lying prone, wriggling, scratching, and sliding sideways toward the napping animal were needed to come finally within striking distance.

Early in the summer at Cape Krusenstern, the ever-watchful hunter sees herring swim past, attracting small white whales which, in turn, attract killer whales, accounting for the occasional huge black fin that moves by. After midsummer, individual char and salmon break the surface. Late in the evening, a black bear and her cubs pad along the forebeach just above the waterline, sniffing at dead fish and examining many things, even driftwood, that they cannot possibly use, through sheer bearish curiosity. Sensing a human camp, they draw up without haste and turn back in dignity.

When the wind is not too rough in summer, boats forge past. On rare occasions, even now, a skin boat may hoist a sail, but the more usual craft are flat-bottomed, wooden boats propelled by powerful outboard motors. Formerly, perhaps even in Denbigh times, there would have been groups of paddlers in skin boats or bark canoes visiting back and forth, exploring unoccupied stretches of the shoreline, or perhaps planning a communal attack on an unfriendly tribe. In either wind or rain, summer life on these beaches is nearly mosquito free, and the shoreline is a great open highway of never-ending interest to those who read its signs.

In winter, of course, the scene changes completely. The winds blow as strongly as before, but now they whip grains of ice and hard snow into long drifts behind crags of ice on the sea and behind each obstruction on land, and an eastward-extending ridge thus created over a dome-shaped winter hut may extend for hundreds of yards. The families or bands who live on the coast throughout the winter usually do so by preference. Most available food is now under the sea ice, but Eskimos have special and ingenious ways in which to exploit their frozen surroundings and capture fish and seals.

Winter sealing among the more northerly Eskimos, in particular, depends on the help of the animals themselves. Seals must surface for air, and when ice begins to form late in the year the seals push out certain spots of thin ice, never permitting it to become solid or deep in these areas. As the temperature over the water continues to plunge, a seal's job becomes ever harder, and eventually his "blowhole" becomes cone shaped, with only a small opening at the surface. Still, it is enough for the seal—and for his pursuer. Sometimes aided by his dog who sniffs through the covering of snow to locate a blowhole, the Eskimo carefully scrapes away all but a few inches of snow from over the top, leaving the cover of the hole undisturbed lest the seal take alarm and not rise to breathe there. Dressed for warmth in skin clothing of many layers, equipped with an efficient, long spear, and having considerable knowledge of the seal's habits, the hunter is prepared for the long wait that is an inevitable part of his life.

Through the snow into the water the hunter pushes an indicator stick, leaving the top high enough so that he can watch for its slightest movement. When a movement comes, he knows his seal is at the narrow hole beneath the stick and he thrusts down mightily with his spear alongside the indicator, stabbing the seal. A line is attached to the head of the spear, and the hunter quickly fastens the other end of the line about his leg or sled as anchor, next using his ice pick to cut away the edges of the breathing hole until it is big enough to allow him to lift the huge animal out onto the ice. Sometimes the hunt is carried on with his neighbors at a number of nearby holes, thus ensuring the capture of any seal who is unlucky enough to pop his head up for a breath of air.

PREDECESSORS of Eskimos, too, seem to have lived throughout the winter on the coast, for at Cape Krusenstern and other nearby sites the deep houses of modern and Thule cultures, the great square ones of Ipiutak with their central fire pits, the snug huts of Norton, the large oval dwellings of Choris, and the deep, multiple-roomed houses of Old Whaling give firm evidence that these shores were not abandoned even in the heart of the cold season.

On the other hand, nowhere on the earliest beaches from Cape Prince of Wales around Kotzebue Sound are there signs that the Denbigh hunters ever dug their dwellings into the ground for the insulation that would have protected them from the icy blasts of winter. Since Denbigh flints occur in the mountain passes of the interior as well as on the coast, the Denbigh people may have differed from most others in that they had a winter culture adapted to the rivers and mountains of the interior and only a summer one adapted to the seacoast.

Despite the recent finding of Denbigh sites at Cape Prince of Wales, a hundred miles from the nearest timber, we cannot overlook the fact that at the Cape Denbigh, Cape Krusenstern, and Brooks Range sites, Denbigh people camped at, or fairly close to, the forest edge. And the known microblade sites of the interior—those of the Campus site near Fairbanks, and others at Kluane Lake in the southern Yukon Territory of Canada and along parts of the Alcan Highway (through the land of Athapaskan Indians)—all lack the most distinctive object of Denbigh workmanship: the burin. Hence, there seemed good reason at first to think that the Denbigh culture would not be found deeper in the forest than its edge.

In recent times, life on the tundras and seashores surrounding the Arctic forest has been predominantly that of Eskimos rather than Indians. This terrain roughly parallels that occupied long ago by Denbigh people, and I began to speculate on this and wonder if in the Denbigh people we might not have a five-thousand-year-old foreshadow of Eskimos, even though their adaptation to the sea was incomplete. Could the clever-fingered Eskimos we know today have inherited some of their skills and resourcefulness from Denbigh ancestors?

IN 1953, I made a direct test of these assumptions. In order to study the Arctic treeline (the latitudinal limit of cone-bearing trees toward the region of cold), I traveled to a part of this borderline between Indians and Eskimos where it reaches the west shore of Hudson Bay (Map 4). I intended to collect samples of timberline spruce growth for tree-ring dating to learn more of how tree growth relates to extremes of climate, and I also hoped to find signs of people earlier than Dorset or Thule. My first destination was Churchill, in the northeastern corner of Manitoba. There, according to my map, I would emerge both from the land of Chipewyan Indians and the spruce forest onto a treeless coast occupied only by Eskimos.

The latter part of my trip—from the town of The Pas to Churchill, six hundred miles—was on a slow train called the "Way Freight" that made frequent stops on its three-day journey, giving me the opportunity to sample trees and talk with Chipewyan Indians along the way (Fig. 108). Timberline characteristics scarcely showed in the trees until within a few miles of Churchill the spruces became strongly twisted in grain, stocky in trunk like upended carrots, and covered with short limbs down to the ground, as are timberline spruces all across Arctic America (see Fig. 114, p. 287).

After taking core samples from many spruce trees and learning how difficult it would be to find open ground on which to look for archeological sites, I arranged to make a trip two hundred miles farther, into the Northwest Territories, where I hoped to find the means of traveling inland to another timberline area bordering

108. Chipewyan Indians, Manitoba, Canada, in 1953. They were waiting to collect their annual "treaty money" from the Canadian government.

on the country of those Caribou Eskimos called Padlimiut. On the evening before leaving, however, I met Mr. and Mrs. Irwin H. Smith who had something to show me.

A short time before, Mrs. Smith had acquired a handful of small flints from an Indian who lived west of Churchill on the North Knife River (Fig. 109). She was apologetic as she unknotted a handkerchief in which the small flints jingled, explaining that there were only one or two complete arrowheads among the broken

109. Some of the flints in Mrs. Smith's collection. They are, left to right, part of a bifaced point, a bifaced point with a concave base, a side blade, and a burin.

fragments and chips. Expecting little from such a chance collection, I could scarcely trust my eyes when objects of white chalcedony and pink agate scattered across the tabletop. Mixed with double-pointed and concave-based arrow tips were burins and bifaced side blades not previously reported from the region. Although more crudely chipped, they were strikingly like those from Cape Denbigh. Where had they been found? The Smiths did not know, and, search as we did in the Arctic daylight of that late evening, we could not locate the Indian who could tell us. Assured by my friends that they would look for him during my absence, I decided, somewhat reluctantly, to go ahead with my plans for travel.

North of the village of Eskimo Point on Hudson Bay (Fig. 110), I engaged four Padlimiut men who spoke no English and with them, in a borrowed boat with a rented motor, started up the Maguse River hoping to cross from its headwaters by foot to the treeline limit near the Hudson Bay post of Padlei. My companions were a far cry from the resourceful Eskimos I had expected to find. Biding their time with their families at a mission near the mouth of the river, they had been living on a few fish, dwelling by custom in unheated tents, and waiting for autumn when the caribou were expected to come again from the north. I had been

110. Some Padlimiut Eskimos at Eskimo Point on Hudson Bay.

assured by the missionaries that we would see no caribou on our trip, since the Padlimiut were firm in their belief that none could be found. We had traveled no more than a few miles up the swift stream, however, when a pair of caribou were silhouetted on the bank. We beached the boat, and one of the men leaped ashore with our one, borrowed rifle. He climbed to the top of the bank and, crouching, ran across the tundra in full view of his quarry. At length a shot rang out and one of the beasts was felled. Within a short time we were sitting around a fire of heather waiting for tea to boil and the leg bones of the caribou to heat enough for extraction of the marrow (Fig. 111). Meanwhile, my companions ate raw the tongue and other choice morsels.

We traveled on for four days, and it was well that there was game about, for on the first day out these enthusiastic companions discovered and ate all my week's food supply except for a little sugar and coffee that I held on to and doled out with care. Along the banks of the river we searched for signs of archeology, and we had occasionally to portage around rapids and a waterfall (Fig. 112); finally, despite all efforts, we found ourselves no stronger than our

111. Padlimiut Eskimo butchering the caribou he shot. Maguse River, Canada, 1953.

112. My Padlimiut companions preparing to portage our boat and supplies around the rapids called "Bloody Falls," Maguse River, Canada, 1953.

faulty motor which, unmindful of our patient coaxing, would take us no further and forced us, because my time was limited, to turn back to the coast. All around were caribou—we had a suspenseful few moments when our boat was surrounded by a large herd swimming across the river—yet on the last day my companions shot only one on which we gorged ourselves, and then for reasons that I cannot yet fathom, returned empty-handed to their families and children and to the kind missionaries who had furnished us with both the rifle and the ammunition.

The few flint artifacts recovered on that trip bore no resemblance to those I had seen at Churchill, and we had not been able to reach the treeline. Yet I considered the trip a success of another kind. The men with whom I traveled, in their fatalism and earthy humor, their carefree approach to leaving home equipped only with what I possessed or we had borrowed, and their almost childlike pleasure in the caribou kills and enormous meals of pure meat, stood out in sharp contrast to other Eskimos and Indians I had met, and I regarded them somewhat as vestiges of an era long past.

BACK IN CHURCHILL, I learned that the Smiths had found their Indian, whose name was Thomas Jawbone. Though Jawbone and his friend Peter Bussidor (Fig. 113) could secure leave from their

113. Chipewyan Indian friends Peter Bussidor and Thomas Jawbone on the North Knife River, Canada.

jobs at the local air base for only three days, I persuaded them to set out with me at once in a canoe with a motor for the site, Thyazzi, meaning "sandy place," where they had found the flints—a day's travel up the North Knife River. In contrast to the treeless Maguse River, the North Knife, though equally swift, cut through forests of spruce and poplar. We saw countless geese and ducks swimming with their young, fish making slow progress against the current, and along the shore, bears. Thyazzi proved to be the windblown bank of a long, rock-strewn lake on the edge of a plateau a mile or so inland from the river (Fig. 114). Walking slowly over the white sand exposed by wind between patches of dense muskeg and thin sod, we collected dozens of chips of the same materials as those shown me by the Smiths, and a variety of stone artifacts.

The burins and burin spalls, end blades and side blades, scrapers, and other forms all reminded me of the Denbigh artifacts of Alaska. Though they differed somewhat in style from their Alaskan counterparts, they had far more in common with Denbigh artifacts to the west than they did with the Dorset culture flints we then knew from shores to the east. The main point of difference between this site and either of the others, though, was the absence here of long, thin microblades. Even so, I thought it significant that once more I had found small, delicately worked, Denbigh-like objects at the edge of timber—this time at a spot some two

thousand miles distant from the original site. As though to comple-
ment my success in archeology, the tree borings from the vicinity
of Churchill later proved as valuable in recording summer temperatures as had timberline spruces in western Alaska; they seemed,
in fact, to crossdate with one another, offering the possibility for
the future of compiling a climatic chart for the whole treeline area
between Hudson Bay and western Alaska.

Did ancestors of either Jawbone and his fellow Chipewyans
or the Padlimiut of Maguse Mission have anything to do with the
trail of burins we were beginning to see along the northern treeline? The Athapaskan tongue is spoken by all the forest tribes south
of the treeline from Hudson Bay to western Alaska (Map 4). To the
north of this treeline are Eskimos. Eastward across Hudson Bay, the
Naskapi and Montagnais, Algonkian speakers, meet the Eskimos at
treeline similarly. The stern, sometimes warlike, opposition of these
forest people to the Eskimos of the barren grounds and tundras
over most of the range seems to be long-standing, and suggests that
the early spread of Eskimo language and culture over most of the
continent followed, but did not penetrate, the northern treeline.
Since the range of most Denbigh-like flints is within the present

114. Thomas Jawbone and Peter Bussidor collecting chips at Thyazzi site near
the North Knife River, Canada, 1953. The spruces in the background are
typical of those found at northern timberline.

Eskimo country, we find it easy to envisage a Denbigh-age spread not only of flints but of speakers of the Eskimo language.

The different way of life of Indians along the northern forested rivers from that of Eskimos on the barren coasts and tundras is not entirely a matter of chance. Rather, the forest environment places certain strictures on the people who dwell there. In summer most of this sheltered region is dry and calm. Impervious frost in the ground, except on slopes and thawed river banks, supports a cover of wet muskeg and a terrain riddled with ponds and lakes. In the calm air, clouds of mosquitos surround all living things (Fig. 115), tormenting unmercifully those poor men or beasts who at any time must expose bare skin.

Except during rainy seasons, the sun, never setting for weeks above the Arctic Circle, makes temperatures rise as high as 90° Fahrenheit in the shade. Vegetation is lush compared with that on the tundra and barren grounds, and there are many kinds of edible roots, stems, and berries. The use of bark canoes and baskets throughout this whole region attests to the serviceability of forest

115. Mosquitos on Eskimos traveling up an Arctic river on a windless day. Here the Eskimo has pulled mosquito netting about his head, but he may lower it over his face for fuller protection.

116. Snowshoes made and used by present-day Eskimos and Indians of interior Alaska and Canada.

materials to which the Arctic Eskimos seldom have access. Deer, bears, and smaller fur animals are plentiful, providing meat as well as materials for clothing and trade. The only true migrants in the interior are caribou, some of which travel in large herds from their winter forests to their summer habitat on the northern treeless slopes. Moose, on the other hand, are home-loving animals, moving swiftly from one valley to the next when occasion arises, yet often spending their whole lives in some small territory near a lake edge where they wade and feed on a succession of succulent leaves and winter bark. Similarly, the smaller creatures tend to have a limited territory within which they achieve a balance of population with their food and their enemies.

In winter the contrast of this inland country to that of the tundra is probably greatest. Snowflakes leisurely fall like feathers through the trees of the forest, drifting softly down through freezing air and remaining loosely packed. So long as the temperature remains well below freezing, this softness of the snow prevails, and men and animals sink deep, floundering helplessly if forced from beaten trails into the surrounding white fluff. Human mobility in the area has thus come to depend upon snowshoes. Theorists have even proposed that the forests could not have been occupied before the invention of netted snowshoes, whenever that may have been (Fig. 116).

Hunting, too, differs here from that in the barrens where the tracks of animals are quickly obscured by changing drifts. In the forest, the tracker may persist until he finds one or another of the animals whose prints he has followed, for trails are indelibly impressed until a new snowfall, and individual tracks are obscured only by the trampling of later beasts over the same paths. Nor is the ice fishing the same here as in Arctic seas. No seals live in the fresh water under the ice, and winter fishermen of the interior deal with stable populations of lake trout or the slightly more migrant fish of the creeks and rivers (Fig. 117). The family fire is far more easily controlled in the calm of the woods than in the gales of the Arctic coasts, and indoor fires rather than oil lamps are the usual means of heating and illuminating woodland tents and lodges. House construction, too, differs, for houses need not be deeply excavated where few winds blow. Archeologists rarely find pits in the ground of the interior that lead them to earlier Indian habitation sites.

The tribes living just south of the treeline all the way from Hudson Bay to the delta of the Yukon River speak Déné languages of Athapaskan stock. Though closely related in structure, these tongues are more than dialects, affording the main distinctions between Chipewyan, Yellow Knife, Dog Rib, Hare, Kutchin, and Ingalik Indians. Culturally, all these people, living winter and summer in nearly identical fashion, share not only methods of exploiting the land but similar tribal organizations, myths, and views of life.

117. Eskimos of the interior fishing through winter ice on the Noatak River, Alaska.

Physically, although there are blends—as toward the mouth of the Mackenzie River where Eskimos and Indians frequently meet to trade—these northern Indians, especially the men, are usually distinguishable from Eskimos by their taller stature, longer legs, shorter trunks, straighter-sided faces, and more craggy features.

Thus, for one who travels from the Atlantic seaboard along the northern forest edge of Quebec, the Northwest Territories, the Yukon Territory, and then across most of Alaska, there is little reason to doubt the northern latitude treeline as a natural divider between Indians and Eskimos. Knowing this as I dug the Denbigh hearths in the wind at Cape Krusenstern, I nevertheless remembered how near were the spruce forests of the Kobuk River, where, well before the trip to Hudson Bay, I learned that Eskimos had long been living comfortably in the forested interior. Indeed, were it not for the questions raised in my mind during the three earlier seasons of work along the Kobuk, I might not have turned to beach ridge archeology for answers.

(XIV)

ARCTIC
WOODLANDERS

THE THOUGHT that Eskimos long ago might have lived in the woods had come up repeatedly during the summer of 1939 when Froelich Rainey, Helge Larsen, and I dug the first Ipiutak house pits at Point Hope. We wondered where the Ipiutak people came from and why their ways differed so much from those of early St. Lawrence Islanders who had lived about the same time. Their use of birch bark and indoor fireplaces along with quantities of caribou bones and artifacts of antler all pointed inland, but no one knew whether or not inland archeology existed in Alaska anywhere north of the Yukon River. Thus, while Rainey returned to Point Hope in 1940 for another season of digging the old site and Larsen flew back to Denmark for an uneasy year in the shadow of World War II, I returned to the wooded Arctic on a quest in which all three of us were vitally interested. Many a summer was yet to pass before beach ridge archeology was begun and the beaches of Cape Krusenstern explored.

As well as looking for inland archeology in 1940, I hoped to find answers to some other questions. Previous tree-ring work in the interior of Alaska had shown that trees recorded climate best at timberline on the mountain slopes. Would not the forest edge at lower elevations, where it reached the limits of Arctic cold, show a similar contrast of thick and thin rings—possibly the same, in fact, as at the upper elevation of spruce growth? I intended to work from the Yukon River drainage system over a pass into the Kobuk River valley and thence down toward the Chukchi Sea to the limit

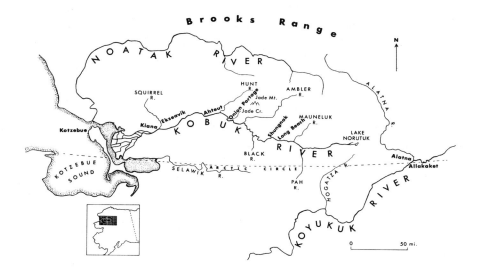

Map 9. Kobuk River area

of trees, taking samples at short intervals along the way. If the trees proved to be good climatic indicators, and thus datable, could not borings taken from timbers used in Eskimo pit dwellings near the treeline also be dated, giving us firm information about their time of use?

On one or two previous occasions when I had proposed such a hiking trip along timberlines in search of tree-ring materials, the president of Alaska College, Charles Bunnell, had doubted the wisdom of anyone's traveling alone in uninhabited country, and I had let the matter drop. Yet it continued to intrigue me. A party of investigators, I felt, would have been needlessly costly and, in my view, even encumbering. I preferred to travel light, resting when I pleased, day or night, and accountable to no one. I began making more definite plans to take the trip alone, and when next I told the president of this, he merely cautioned me to keep an exact accounting of all expenses and said he hoped these could be refunded to me by the college at the end of the season.

In early July 1940, then, I flew to Allakaket, an Indian village on the Koyukuk River (Map 9). Only a few hundred yards away was another village, Alatna, made up largely of Eskimos from the Kobuk River who had moved to the Koyukuk as a result of the gold rush of 1898. In that year, a thousand or more gold-seekers, having mistakenly stampeded the Kobuk, brought the Kobuk Eskimos sudden acquaintance with the outside world. When the rush ended, as swiftly as it began, some bedazzled Eskimos of the Kobuk moved to the Koyukuk where gold had been found and where white men's goods could be earned. There they had remained ever since.

Talking with both Indians and Eskimos of the villages, I learned that none now traveled between the two rivers in the open season. Some communication did exist in winter with Shungnak, a town 130 miles away downriver on the Kobuk, but this was possible only when the ground was frozen and dog teams could be used. At any rate, no trail or markers now existed. My large-scale map of the region showed a blank space of some fifty miles between the Koyukuk and the Kobuk Rivers, and my only means of crossing it, in summer, was by foot with a compass as guide.

Hearing of my plans, the local missionaries objected strenuously, pointing out that the last man who had attempted such a trip in summer had not been heard from again. I took their concern lightly and assured them I would do nothing rash. Next day I waved good-bye as an Indian took me across the river in his boat. What I did not know was that the missionaries were so in earnest that they mailed a letter to President Bunnell urging that an airplane search be made if I did not return to Allakaket within a reasonable time.

With only a forty-pound pack, most of which consisted of a waterproof tent with a sewn-in mosquito net, a featherweight down sleeping bag, rain gear, a change of the heavy underclothes one must wear as mosquito protection, and my .22 semi-automatic rifle, I felt more than adequately prepared to stay out the remainder of the summer if necessary. I carried little food as I planned to live off the land.

For the first few days I walked at a leisurely pace on the shores and ridges parallel to the Alatna branch of the Koyukuk, pausing at intervals of a few miles to break away the dead lower branches of an older spruce tree and remove a core with my increment borer. The cores of ten or more trees sampled in each stand were put in envelopes inscribed with the details of collection, and these I placed in a metal case in my packsack. As a core is little thicker than a matchstick and only a few inches long, they were no additional burden.

On the fourth day, turning due west from the river, I adjusted my pocket compass and began the tedious business of traveling a straight line across unmarked territory. The ordeal of the following three days made me keenly aware of the difficulties Indians had long faced in hot interior summers. For hours at a time no breath of air disturbed the cloud of mosquitos that surrounded me. Although I wore my head net continuously, I nevertheless had to plug the airholes in my hat and anchor the net securely to the front of my shirt to prevent the buzzing, probing insects from finding every weak spot in my armor. If I sat to rest, so that the insulation of clothing tightened over shoulder or knee, some few of these small swordsmen unfailingly managed to thrust their weapons deep enough to draw blood.

Walking hour after hour with or without the hot July sun, I perspired until my entire soggy costume grew saturated. This in itself gave some respite in the cooling of evaporation, but deterred mosquitos not the least. Small gnats, "no-see-um's," and larger ones, "bull-dogs," found a way into, under, or through my head net, biting at leisure or flying blindly into my eyes. When I paused to light a cigarette, I puffed as rapidly as possible to create a smoke screen until the net could be cleared and fastened again.

Small flying things were only the expected annoyances of a summer trip across the muskeg, however. What I had not counted on was the prevalence of forest fires. Somewhere not far to the south, one of those great fires raged—too large to be coped with effectively in such an uninhabited area, and certain to spread unstemmed until it had burned from river to river or was doused by rain. One, two, and then three days went by during which the smoke so thickly covered the terrain that I could see only a few hundred yards ahead, while overhead the sun looked like a great coal glowing in the sky.

There had been enough ducks and geese along the Alatna to supply me with food, but now in muskeg I had little opportunity to secure a proper dinner, though each day yielded at least a spruce hen or a small, brown tree squirrel. These morsels I would set to boil over a small fire at the edge of a pond while I retreated to the mosquito-free luxury of my netted tent. It was perhaps near midnight on the third day of this smoky journey when I came to a sizable stream, a branch of the Hogatza River, flowing south across my compass trail. Here, just above the Arctic Circle where there is no July darkness, I arranged my shelter before indulging in a long drink of the cool, clear water. Stepping to the edge of the stream and looking down, I saw silhouetted against the white sandy bottom of a deep pool quantities of fish. I lost no time in affixing a Royal Coachman to my line at the end of a willow pole and cast this lure hopefully to the surface of the water. Immediately a trout struck and I had a moment of struggle as it thrashed about disturbing all the other shadows in the pool. Having landed this fish, enough for an ordinary meal, I found the excitement too great to forego. Nearly every toss of the fly in the stream brought a slashing strike from trout or grayling.

When I had as many fish as I could possibly use, I built a sizable fire, the smoke of which held the mosquitos at bay; and boiled my catch in relays, eating as much as I could manage and then preparing for meals to come. Making fillets from the fish, I added salt and pepper and packed them into a coffee can. They would be a tasty treat as well as a source of quick energy throughout the following day. My good luck continued in other ways, too, for that night a thunderstorm blew in from the north, swaying the big spruces above my tent, blowing away all vestiges of forest smoke, and deluging the parched shrubs and heather with cold, cleansing rain.

Next morning my compass took me up a slight but steady slope where soon, above the level of the stream-bank trees, I could see to the north the rugged mountains of the Brooks Range, patches of snow still lying in their higher valleys. If my calculations had been reasonably good, I should now be nearing the far end of the blank space on my map, where, in bright blue, was shown a wide lake called Norutuk. No more than an hour later I reached another height of land and was elated to see ahead a great expanse of blue water at the foot of low gray hills. This was indeed the lake, and my course had been true. There remained only to round it and enter the valleys beyond to have my first glimpse of the Kobuk River.

On the north side of the lake was a trapper's cabin and its cache—a little house on stilts—and a row of dog huts, now obscured by the thick green grass. Clearly the cabin was occupied only during the winter months. To the west a small stream drained the lake, and, as I walked past, I noted a midden-like quality in the soil where the bank was cracked at the edge of the encroaching stream. Lacking a shovel, I made a note of the spot, a good fishing place, where like as not some people of the past, Indians or Eskimos, had camped.

I was then at the height of land in the low pass between the Yukon drainage system and the Arctic slopes. Walking on down the creek some ten miles, I reached the gravelly bank of the Kobuk, here in its headwaters a wild river made up of many tributaries slicing from the north through sharp, steep-walled mountains. I came upon the stream at a rare spot where the water ran deep under a deceptively placid surface.

Intending as soon as practicable to build a raft in order to travel unburdened through this scenic country, I set about gathering poles of driftwood. As I had neither ax nor hatchet, I planned at first to find logs of suitable size and bind them together with willow roots and stems, but before I did so a different method occurred to me. Gathering up as many dry poles as I could find and placing them parallel to each other on the shore, I laid atop them a few small poles to serve as crosspieces. With the tree borer, I drilled holes for fastenings at all necessary points. Though the holes were small, I found that I could drive a pencil-thick whittled pin through one pole into the next, using a stone as hammer, and thus fasten all the poles to the crosspieces.

Pleased with my discovery, however flimsy the craft might prove to be, I was hard at work doweling when, with a change in the direction of the breeze, I became aware of a deep and distant roar. It seemed to come from downriver. Curious and somewhat apprehensive, I went to investigate. Around a bend, the gravel banks grew narrow, and, still farther on, they disappeared. I mounted the left bank above a wall of rock and came to the edge of a cliff, where I looked down to see the whole of the river now gathered into a narrow gorge and plunging, white with foam, over a rapids and waterfall. Unnerved by this revelation and vividly picturing the short cruise I would have had on my raft, I gave up the idea of boating and continued for another day to plod through the riverbank thickets and along the gravel beaches until the Kobuk widened to dependable safety. There I built a second raft.

The weather held good and for nearly three days I sampled trees, fished in creek mouths, and gorged on blueberries between periods of drifting with the current. This was not an inhabited part of the river, and I did not search vigorously for sites of early camps, but on the third day of such floating past flocks of young ducks and geese and black bears annoyed at having their salmon fishing interrupted, I began to wonder where I might encounter the first people. By the time I approached a bend around which my map showed the mouth of the Mauneluk River, my hastily constructed raft had become so waterlogged that, except for a small platform of short sticks near center that supported me and my packsack, most of it lay beneath the surface of the water. When I stood to pole free of treacherous side channels, the water rose to the leather edges of my rubber-soled shoepacs. Now seated on the packsack and facing forward, I drifted with the five-mile-an-hour current rapidly around the great bend and saw the Mauneluk mouth exactly where it should be. But even more exciting, I caught sight of two white patches in a clearing just below the tributary stream. They were tents, and the moving objects in front of them were my first Kobuk River people.

Eager to make a good impression and to land with the decorum that befits a traveler on these northern rivers, I threw back the hood of my rain parka and stood up as the raft drifted closer. But dignity was not to grace my landing. In a moment, my craft was caught in an eddy formed by the current of the Mauneluk as it entered the Kobuk; it was whirled once about, and then again, and I realized that I must pole my way back into the mainstream. The water was deep, however, and push as I might, the raft made little

118. Roxy and Maude Douglas with their family in front of their tent on the Kobuk River, 1940.

119. The Eskimo family of Henry Stocking. Suspended from the bark-roofed shelter are lines of drying fish roe.

progress. In fact it continued to spin slowly with the pool until at last, in desperation, I resorted to splashing the pole as a paddle, and only then managed to work my way out of the little maelstrom.

When I became reoriented, I continued poling toward the tents, but now none of the people—men, women, or children, who had surely all been standing there before—were to be seen. They had not been imaginary, however, for I saw by the frequent agitation of the tent flaps that they had only retreated indoors. Somewhat disconcerted, I managed a landing, tossed my packsack ashore, and proceeded to tie up my raft as if it were a fine river boat. Two men then emerged from the tents, walking slowly toward me, hands in pockets. The first, Roxy Douglas, shouted a greeting in English. The second, Henry Stocking, who spoke only Eskimo, came forward and pumped my hand once briskly up and down before relinquishing it. The ice was broken. The women and children of the two families then emerged from the tents and hurried down to meet this unexpected visitor (Figs. 118 and 119).

Roxy later explained that they had not known what to conclude when they first saw me approaching on the river. No one lived above them, nor did visitors ever come from the east. They had decided, finally, that I must be a downed aviator, though until I landed they were unable to see by what means I stood on top of the water.

Though both families possessed tents, they seemed to place greater reliance on their permanent structures at this summer camp to which they returned season after season. A log cache, roofed over with wide slabs of spruce bark, stood on ten-foot posts, each post with a guard of old gasoline cans to prevent bears and other creatures from climbing to the platform. Next to this was a larger building with a similarly gabled roof of spruce bark and with sides loosely walled with upright spruce poles. Inside, series of poles stretched from wall to wall ready to receive the sun-dried salmon that would hang here protected later in the season until ready to be put in bales and used as human and dog food over the winter.

Serving both families was a third bark-roofed building, only two sides of which were walled with poles. Beneath its overhanging roof the daily work could go on shaded from the sun and protected from summer rains—and here, after a few words had been exchanged, I was invited to sit and have a meal. Before fish came a great bowl of freshly picked blueberries and, as a special treat, sugar from a nearly depleted container, and canned milk. Since the women collect their berries by beating the low bushes against the edges of specially constructed birch-bark baskets, many leaves had fallen in with the fruit. At first I picked out some of these, as well as small twigs, but then I noticed that the others did not bother, and so it was that I learned to eat a leafy garnish with the bright purple berries. A one-legged sea gull, a family pet, hopped in and out at our feet, picking morsels from the earthen floor.

Questioning these families about the ruins of old houses, I learned that they knew of several in the vicinity, some of which I had already passed. They described these as square holes in the ground with a long "storm shed" in front. After I had spent an hour or two taking notes on their summer life and surroundings, I explained that I would like to add a log or two to my raft and continue down to the first village, Long Beach, where I could buy a shovel and supplies and look in earnest for archeological sites. Roxy insisted, instead, that I run down by boat, to save time and to play it safe. They had no faith in my raft. Henry Stocking lifted a partly decked, flimsy little craft, locally called a kayak, and placed it in the river with only its bow resting on the bank (Fig. 120). He would paddle

120. Henry Stocking putting his kayak into the river; its deck and sides are canvas covered.

me to Long Beach in short time, Roxy explained, and I could pay him something if I wished. The prospect of riding two together in such a small boat seemed far more precarious to me than reboarding my raft, but in view of my hosts' determination I lifted my packsack and walked to the kayak.

The boat was like an eggshell and scarcely wider than a man's seat. Its frame was of birch withes and the floor of thin laths ran lengthwise. I sat with my back to the wooden brace across the center as Roxy placed the packsack on my outstretched legs. Then, pushing the boat out, the heavyset Henry climbed in, facing forward. He lifted the paddle to brace the boat and prepared to shove off into the current, but with the shift of the boat the bottom caught on a snag and water began to gush through a hole in the thin canvas. We scrambled out, little the worse for the damage, and I felt secretly relieved that I could now continue on my own devices. But no, motioned Stocking. He turned the boat over, placed it on the grass, and at once his wife approached with needle and thread, quickly sewed a patch of canvas over the torn spot, daubed it with warm resin, and we were ready to travel again.

Stocking was indeed a phenomenal paddler. The small craft had no weight of its own and leaped forward at each pull of the paddle—one, two, three strokes to a side, then shift, and three again. Stocking kept up this rhythm for a full hour before he pulled to shore for a short rest. Now and then as we traveled, he spoke a few words in Eskimo, pointing to something on the bank, to which I could only grunt an affirmative. I am not sure that he ever learned that I spoke little of his language. In less than four hours from the time we left his camp, he had paddled the fifty miles to Long Beach with an average speed as great again as that of the current.

STOPPING a night or so at Long Beach with Harry Brown, a trader of the early days, and his half-Eskimo family, I learned a great deal about life along the upper river. The women of Long Beach were in the midst of their salmon-fishing season. Formerly, I was told by one of the two or three very old men who remained in the village at that time of year, all the able-bodied men and older boys would leave the womenfolk early in the summer and climb up into the mountains where, in passes and on rocky plateaus, they would hunt both caribou and sheep for their pelts, eating well the while but staying away from their families until the salmon season was over. Meanwhile, the women, who alone were thought to attract salmon all the way up the river, worked as a team. Though times had changed, even now I was allowed to watch only if I kept my distance and stayed well out of the way.

All the women sat in front of their separate tents (in earlier days these would have been hemispherical, bark-covered huts) and waited for a signal from their lookout, a gnarled little old woman who stood on a sandhill with her eyes turned downstream. Then I saw her give the signal. Raising an arm and shouting commands, she galvanized the community into feverish activity. Two women dashed down to a light wooden boat in the bottom of which lay a folded net. (Earlier, birch-bark canoes would have been used.) Quickly launching the craft, one woman paddled swiftly toward the middle of the stream as the net paid out upstream. Her partner held the wooden stretcher against the shore. As the boat and far end of the net began to drop swiftly downstream with the current, forming a large arc to the end on shore, all the other women placed themselves along the near shore at short intervals to receive the net.

Now I could see frothy ripples rising from the water nearly encompassed by the net.

The women in the boat reached the far shore, jumped out to secure their craft, and at the same time pulled shoreward on the stretcher at their end of the net. As the net surrounded the churning mass of fish, all the women not holding onto its ends waded as far as possible into the river, plunging a hand and arm in the water shoulder deep to catch the weighted bottom of the net. With their other hand, each grasped the top of the net with its bobbing floats and, pulling together, dragged the net and its contents slowly to the shore. At this point, all the younger girls dashed into the edge of the water, catching salmon by the tails and throwing them on the beach as high as they could. It was not until this time that the old man, my informant, picked up his short-handled wooden club and rushed down to do his part along with the women and children. Their job was to strike each salmon's head, dispatching it, or, at any rate, preventing it from flapping back into the stream. I estimated that hundreds of three-foot-long salmon had been caught in this one haul.

Of course, great numbers of fish must have been swimming upstream every hour of the day, but neither the aged lookout nor any of the others glanced again at the river. I learned that they would fish no more until the whole of this catch had been properly cut and strung on rows of fish fences to dry in the sun and wind. The fish were soon apportioned to the women of different households and thrown, heads inward, into pits previously dug and lined with fresh, full-leaved willow twigs. Then the cutting began. Each woman knelt beside her pit and deftly wielded a wide, half-moon-shaped knife called an *ulu* (Fig. 121). After chopping off the head with a powerful blow and tossing it into a container, she freed the orange meat from the backbone with two long slices. Chopping swiftly but lightly she divided the flesh into short segments, each held firmly to the skin. Girls now took the fish and hung them to dry over a rail of the long, willow-poled fence (Fig. 122). Nothing was discarded. Clusters of roe were also dried in the sun, and the intestines were thrown into a metal pot to be boiled for their oil. Still later, the half-cooked intestines were taken across the river and fed to the dogs straining at chains that held them to their posts.

·　·　·

121. Beatrice Mouse, an Eskimo woman of Long Beach, cutting salmon.

I OUTFITTED myself with digging equipment and some luxury foods, such as even the most common staples in Mr. Brown's small trading post now appeared to me, and for ten dollars I bought a kayak in which to enjoy my further travels down the river. At Shungnak, a "large" village built on a hillside with its imposing school building at the top of a high bank, I learned from natives the location of old pit houses in the vicinity. Quite certain by this time that I should find archeological sites of importance somewhere along the river, I tested these only enough to learn that they were so recent as to contain glass trade beads of the previous century.

My first successful Kobuk River dig was at Black River, a small stream flowing into the Kobuk a few miles below Shungnak. Here, on a birch-covered sand ridge, with the help of a few Shungnak men I excavated two of several pit houses with short entrance tunnels, each of which contained features unlike any of those that I had seen the previous year on St. Lawrence Island or at Point Hope. The house floors were long rectangles at right angles to the tunnel. Two benches, each about six feet wide, rose half a foot above the central floor and were retained there by the remains of a log. The floors offered little more than foot room about a big oval fireplace. While these houses contained no signs of trade goods (neither iron nor beads), surprisingly enough they held no polished slate, either, which had been plentiful in the coastal site at Point Hope. Among the arrowpoints, scrapers, and drills of chert, there were, on the other hand, many implements of polished green nephrite, the local jade. While the houses of these Black River people were no older than those of the slate-using people on the coast, the Black River natives, in their use of jade—a much harder material than slate—had learned both new ways of shaping tools and new kinds of tools as well. Big slabs of sandstone with a circular groove worn inside showed that adz blades and larger jade objects had been ground and fashioned by repeated rotation.

My companions on one occasion pointed to a mountain across the river, saying that the creek flowing from it carried both pebbles and huge boulders of jade. They also told me of another mountain, a day's journey downstream by kayak, where jade occurred in slabs that could be pried loose from the walls of ravines. Their ancestors, they had heard, used to go there and camp near the mouth of Jade Creek at a place called *Patitakh,* or Onion Portage. From there they walked to the mountain, procured as much jade as they wanted, then returned to camp, where they cut the material

122. Fish cut up and hung to dry beside the Kobuk River, 1940.

with stone "saws" and ground it into weapons and tools while waiting for caribou to cross the river.

Now that summer was speeding by and I knew from the Black River houses that my venture was a success, if only in showing that the Eskimos of the Kobuk were not newcomers from the coast, I traveled on alone in my kayak, examining sites, testing a few pit houses, and making plans for the coming season. Pulling ashore at Onion Portage, below the mouth of Jade Creek on a grassy, shaded plot of high ground in the lee of a birch-covered ridge, I noted with great satisfaction that house pits, some apparently older than those of Black River, were scattered here and there over the river-bank and slopes. A small test in one indicated that this site also contained jade. In the days following, it became clear as I pulled ashore at creek and river mouths and scoured the ground beneath the willows and alders that someone had lived in pit houses at one time or another in nearly all such localities.

WELL BELOW Onion Portage, at a great bend of the river called Ahteut, I made an even more striking discovery with no help from legendary sources. Paddling swiftly with the current, I had almost passed a riverbank stand of trees when I realized that it had an unusual appearance. Looking again, I saw tall, dark-green spruces, big birches, and poplars, with the usual underbrush of alder and willow. Feeling, nevertheless, that the place was unique, I pulled ashore to learn why. I climbed a sphagnum-covered bank into a bramble of wild currant and rose bushes, emerged in open and leafy woods through which the sunlight shone in shafts, and saw at once what had struck me as unusual. The birch trees here were of enormous size, a foot or more in diameter, as I had not seen them since leaving the upper river. Birches, I had observed before, had become increasingly small and scrubby below Black River, hardly large enough for making baskets, much less the canoes that formerly plied the Kobuk. These birches, as well as some excep-tionally thick spruces, must obtain uncommon nourishment. Then I saw that the uneven, mossed-over surface was not pitted by ordinary erosion. Extremely deep pits identified themselves as houses and caches—all of such a depth as I had not seen before on the river or elsewhere. Each tunnel was clearly revealed, but in place of the expected single tunnel per house, several of these pits also had an opposite passage, as though to make entrance and egress possible from either side.

The pit I tested revealed slate artifacts but no jade, and it also turned up fragments of a clay pot decorated on the outer surface with impressed circular designs that were then new to me. This site with so many deep house pits, whose decaying refuse fed outsized trees, when further studied should add greatly to our knowledge of times long ago on the river.

CONTINUING DOWNSTREAM, I came to the town of Kiana, a village built on a steep bank, picturesque enough during dry weather, but a mass of mud during protracted rains. The native houses, mostly log, nestled in small ravines just above the line of flood rush of a spring thaw or were perched on precarious edges of steep banks, where their front yards were being gradually cut away as the seasons passed. The burly owner of the town store, W. R. Blankenship, had been a dog musher for the United States Army at old Fort Gibbon on the Yukon and, before that, a dog and boat man for the United States Geological Survey on an exploratory mission to the north slope of the Brooks Range. After his discharge from the Army, he married an attractive half-Eskimo, the daughter of a white trader, and now he himself enjoyed the good life of a trader. He was a substantial member of the community, well liked, and not only owned his own store but also a freighting boat and barge. Frequently he took his two growing daughters by boat or sledge to the exciting town of Kotzebue, eighty miles downriver on the seacoast.

In talking with the older people of Kiana, recording their recollections and legends, I learned of a place named Ekseavik on the Squirrel River that flows into the Kobuk. Ekseavik means "the place where people are afraid." What they had been afraid of was that their traditional enemies from the Noatak River might invade the headwaters of the Squirrel, drop down to Ekseavik, and kill them all in their sleep. Once, when an attack finally did take place, the plight of the villagers of Ekseavik somehow reached the ears of a pair of twins living somewhere near the head of the Squirrel. Twins, in Eskimo folklore, are magical beings considered to be very powerful even though, as in this case, they may be so small as to drink from the skulls of chickadees. The twins lost no time. Each armed himself with a bow and arrows, slipped on his headband with its upstanding feather in front, and dashed away to the rescue. Just as the Noatak invaders were about to attack (the villagers being too stunned to defend themselves), the twins burst upon the scene and with swift arrows quickly put the enemy to rout.

At Ekseavik, said my informants, one could even see the bones of the dead people, including shoulder blades pierced by the flint-pointed arrows. Did anyone know where Ekseavik had stood? I asked. They nodded quick assent. The place was only a few bends up the Squirrel. It took little time for me to hire Oscar Henry with his boat and motor (and friend Tommy Jackson) to take me up the river to the site of Ekseavik. The "few bends" were longer than I had anticipated, but by late morning we were able to tie the boat up and walk the half mile through alders and willows along a shallow pond, formerly a slough of the river, to the sandy bank that was Ekseavik.

Though it was lunchtime we were all too curious to delay the search. Try as we might, however, we could find no human bones in the wide space where wind whipped the sand bare from old patches of ground surface. At length, disappointed that the legend seemingly had no substance, we decided that at least we could satisfy our appetites. Opening our lunches in the shade of some tall willows and setting a pot of coffee to boil over a fire of twigs, we began with a can of sardines. When the can was empty, Tommy or Oscar threw it over his shoulder into the bushes. The unusual clatter that resulted caused me to look around, and I saw that the can had dropped into a depression in the midst of some willows. Rising to investigate, I found the unmistakable outline of a pit house. After lunch, we turned to with ax and shovels and quickly cleared a patch in the willows where, even though the ground was solidly frozen in the midst of the depression, we were able to excavate enough of a house to retrieve a number of objects, some beautifully carved of ivory. This was certainly no ordinary house, for its people had taken pride in their workmanship and had possessed implements for coastal hunting even though they lived in the forest a considerable distance from the sea.

Finding this house seemed to be the stimulus we had needed, for other pits soon turned up in the close vicinity of the first. There were eleven in all, all of the same age. Though none contained the bones of friend or foe, this may well have been the legendary village of Ekseavik.

An even more stimulating fact about Ekseavik emerged after our second day of excavation of the house. Though most of the lower levels were still solidly frozen, there were enough thawed fragments of building timbers, especially those of support posts and wall poles, to allow me to test them for tree-ring dating. After timbers had been sawed into segments, each section was carefully split from center to outermost ring, then an edge of the exposure beveled with a new razor blade to a forty-five degree angle. I marked out decades with the point of a pin, and indicated the relative widths of rings in a "skeleton plot" on metric-ruled strips of paper. One after another, these sections of old spruce wood recorded the same pattern of thick and thin rings. All the longer records, especially those of trees that had grown slowly, cross-dated without difficulty, showing that most had lived at the same time and that some had ceased to grow in the same year (Fig. 32 illustrates tree-ring comparisons). This indicated that the trees had been cut or collected in the same locality—undoubtedly a neighboring stand of spruce—for the express purpose of using them in building the house. Another careful check showed that none of these buried samples cross-dated with the 350-year record of living spruce that I now had from the same general region, so the Ekseavik houses had to be considerably older.

BACK AT KIANA, I caught a ride to Kotzebue on Blankenship's boat. The town had changed since I had spent a winter there six years earlier, but part of the change, I realized, was caused by the season. Now, in August, people from all the surrounding countryside were gathered in canvas tents and windbreaks on the periphery of the village along the waterfront, expanding the permanent population of about three hundred to perhaps a thousand. As soon as I arrived at Kotzebue, I sent a telegram to President Bunnell notifying him of my safe arrival. He later told me that the urging of my friends the missionaries at Allakaket together with his own misgivings had convinced him that an air search should be made. Instead, with my telegram at hand, he had been able to write a letter of appreciation to the missionaries, pointing out that I had arrived in Kotzebue in plenty of time to return to the college before the opening of the new semester.

The chances of finding significant ruins in the region about Kotzebue seemed poor. Most archeologists and other students of Eskimos working in western Alaska had visited the locality at one time or another, and none had reported sites. Nevertheless, one clear though typically windy day, I walked out past the town's one roadhouse, its last wooden huts, and the long string of white canvas tents of visiting Point Hopers and Diomede Islanders, hoping to find a house pit or other sign along the wide and stable waterfront beach crest. Rewarded here and there by a deep pit from which posts and even planks protruded, I recognized half-buried Eskimo dwellings of the late nineteenth and early twentieth centuries.

About three miles past Kotzebue in this westerly direction, I came to the steep bank of frozen Pleistocene muck in which the townspeople have dug their large, communal ice cellar for the storage of meat. From there I headed back toward the village along the second or third beach crest. Skirting ponds and patches of low willows, I noted the firm coat of moss and heather that contrasted with the more grassy first ridge. In a more undulating part of one of the beaches, I came upon a group of girls and women picking berries (Fig. 123). Stopping to speak to them, I suddenly realized that the depression in which they found the most berries was a house pit. No X-ray eyes were required to see the rectangular outline and tunnel impression under the shrubbery. Pointing this out to my puzzled onlookers, I soon forgot both berries and people for the exciting vista that lay before me. Reaching off for hundreds of feet on either side I could see numbers of other similar depressions in the sod. This was undoubtedly a large village of some remote time when these beaches stood near the waterfront. For more than two miles into the village itself, I found the pits of these old houses. Estimating at least a hundred, I saw signs that some might be older than others. For sheer volume, they promised to add appreciably to the information that I hoped to gain from work along the forested river. Test excavations during the next two or three days showed a basic resemblance between this coastal archeology and that of the river and offered, as well, frozen, solid, and very promising timbers for the construction of a long tree-ring chronology.

123. Blueberry pickers near Kotzebue. Summer tents line the shore of Kotzebue Sound in the background.

.   .   .

THERE WERE two more full seasons of digging along the Kobuk, broken by the war years, before I was able to write the archeology of the region. None who worked in the Arctic in those days could hope for unlimited funds. Usually neither archeologists nor their students thought of drawing pay, but considered themselves fortunate if their universities provided the bare expenses of a summer's dig. Nevertheless, late in May of 1941 I left Fairbanks with the pleasant knowledge that I might pay four dollars a day to each of several Eskimo laborers and the encouragement to believe that both my own expenses and those of a student assistant, Simon John Newcomb, would be refunded by the college at the end of the season. We shared a plane as far as Long Beach with Froelich Rainey and Dr. Harry Shapiro of the American Museum of Natural History. Both were headed for Point Hope—Rainey for his third season at the Ipiutak site.

Expending a few dollars on a river kayak and a leaky old rowboat, Newcomb and I with a crew of four Shungnak natives ranging in age between eighteen and twenty-seven set out downriver from

Long Beach. First excavating house pits at several creek mouths, including four additional ones at Black River, we then set up a more permanent camp at the mouth of the Ambler River. On an island where the Ambler joins the Kobuk there seemed to be a one-period village, which we set about digging. In one house floor after another we soon found specimens of the distinctive stonework that sharply distinguishes the upper river sites, especially the later ones, from those of the seacoast. Three kinds of stone had been used extensively: sandstone, or sandy schist; flinty rock, mainly gray and black chert; and nephrite, the local jade. The flints had been used in nearly the same ways as had those of the coast. Heavy flint arrow tips with diamond-shaped sections and parallel edges, often strongly serrate, had short, T-shaped stems meant to be set into barbed arrowheads of antler. Also of flint were various drills, scrapers, and knife blades, almost all in forms familiar from elsewhere.

In contrast to coastal sites, Ambler Island had no ground slate like that found at Black River the year before. It had, though, many implements of jade—knife blades, chisels, adz blades, hammerheads, spatulate and pointed implements, and other objects—all shaped by using abraders of sandstone. Although these Kobuk jade workers of 250 years ago did not seem to have made a special effort to choose the most green and translucent material, they must nevertheless occasionally have admired the emerald to almost white light that passed through a thin specimen when held up to the sun.

So far as we could reconstruct the jade industry from conversations with the oldest Eskimos and from our own findings, the raw material was either picked up as river cobbles or taken from a source high on Jade Mountain. The sections or cobbles of jade were cut with slabs of sandy schist. A long slab drawn back and forth, sawlike, could cut a groove into the jade, after which it could be broken into pieces of the required size. Grinding a jade adz blade or knife on a broad, thick slab of sandstone must have required many times the hours needed to prepare a similar implement of slate, and the irregular grain of this tough material often gave a curious twist to the finished product. The grindstones showed that a circular motion had been maintained, for all the well-used larger ones we found had a circular channel about a central hump.

Legend has it that the maker of a large adz head would tie his unfinished piece to a branch of a willow tree that overhung the stream, letting it dangle against a boulder of sandstone in the swift water. The movement of the jade over the rock, caused by the current and the resiliency of the willow, would slowly flatten a face or sharpen an edge. Intriguing though this account may be, most jade workers undoubtedly used the more rapid, if more laborious, method of fashioning their weapons and implements directly on grinding slabs.

The fifteen house pits we excavated at Ambler Island all conformed to a single plan (Fig. 124). Each main room was square to rectangular and had a fireplace at center. A short tunnel, or entrance passage, led out on the same level as the house floor. On either side of the fireplace were the remains of two stout posts, evidently the main supports of the roof, enclosing between them at the top the window which served as a smoke hole when open. Just behind these posts on both sides poles had been placed on the floor, in the same direction as the entrance passage. Earth had been heaped between each set of poles level with their tops and about five and a half feet wide, making benches, or low sleeping platforms. These

124. Excavated floor of a house that was occupied about A.D. 1700 at Ambler Island. The circle of stones rimmed the fire area.

were said by old Eskimos to be identical with the benches of their childhood in which many people had been able to sleep, parallel to each other, heads to the center of the room. The remains of matted willow twigs on some of the beds indicated the recent practice of overlaying the earth with willow branches before spreading the skin bed coverings.

Rectangular slabs of sandstone or conglomerate were hollowed out to form lamps, and some cooking had been done in plain pottery vessels. An old man who visited us while the dig was in progress explained that before the coming of iron stoves, the occupants of dugouts such as these made use of the fireplace only during the day, when women stayed home to boil the soup and roast meat over large wood fires until the men came home from hunting. At the end of the day, the coals were tossed with a pair of wooden tongs through the open skylight, the remaining embers extinguished, and the window of animal membrane placed over the smoke hole. The lamp was then lit for evening light and heat. Most of the warmth of the houses, though, came from radiant heat stored in the ground during the day.

The dating of the site by the tree-ring method was hindered by poor preservation of wood in the relatively warm, upper river climate. Nevertheless, the record from some few logs in the house pits showed, by comparison with the record of very old living trees, that the site had been occupied mainly between A.D. 1700 and 1750, although a house or two had been built a few decades later.

The sand in which this large site lay made digging easy, and our enthusiasm continued, for we were finding things few had seen before, and I was accumulating data on a hitherto undescribed Eskimo way of life. The one discouraging factor was the rain. The early showers in the heat of June were welcome, but when they turned to a slow, enduring drizzle often driven by east winds, and when for hours the drizzle turned to steady rain, our spirits dampened. Responding to its heavy nourishment, the river rose steadily.

ON LEAVING Ambler Island in 1941, we built a large raft of spruce with a tent as cabin, placed the kayak on the side deck, and towed our leaky rowboat behind. As if pleased at our leaving, the sun came out. For a few hours we luxuriated in warm, lazy river travel, cooking a meal on the camp stove set up inside our floating palace

125. Rafting down the Kobuk River, 1941.

and stopping here and there as we went downriver to explore for sites (Fig. 125). At Onion Portage, the wide gravel beach of the previous year was now only a narrow strip, but in the fine sun we felt that the offended gods who had sent the rains to us at Ambler had relented, and we could enjoy good working weather. Alas, these hopes were dashed our very first night when rain began again, more earnestly than ever.

Weather notwithstanding, we laid out the bounds of excavation within four house pits around the slopes, choosing ones that seemed older than those upriver. The pits were frozen, as I had hoped they would be for good preservation of artifacts, but in this case the frost proved no blessing, for the daily rate of thaw in the cold rain was so slight that progress was delayed and the wood was no better preserved than elsewhere. Day after day for more than a week we labored under weeping poplars and birches in the steady rain, trowelling away the day's thaw from the four house pits. The artifacts obtained were undoubtedly older than those from Ambler Island; yet a puzzling difference occurred between the materials here and most of the more recent ones of the jade workers of the Kobuk and the slate workers of the coast. This was the prevalence of flints.

By the time the four houses were cleared completely, the river had risen to an all-time high, and our morale had dropped to an all-time low. I decided that we would leave the place as soon as we had thawed to the floors of each of the houses and cleaned them of their belongings. Digging in House 1, the lowest in elevation and the only pit to have been dug into the yellowish loam of a gentle, grassy slope beneath the poplars, I was intrigued in particular by four flints (Fig. 126). Three of these were wedge-shaped cores from which small microblades, then called "prismatic flakes," had been struck. The only other cores of this type in Alaska of which I knew were those of the Campus site of Alaska College (the Denbigh Flint complex site, noted for such cores and blades, was not discovered until 1948). But the Campus site had held none of the ordinary Eskimo artifacts that were so common in this site and others of western Alaska. What could it mean? There seemed no reasonable explanation except that this supposedly ancient trait had persisted here in the forest for thousands of years after it was thought to have disappeared. If this were the answer, our Arctic archeology would be related to that of the Old World, and these small cores would be a vestige of the Mesolithic period of Asia; for there, between eight and twelve thousand years ago lived a primitive people who were adept at making just such tiny tools—microliths—from cores very like these from Onion Portage. The mystery of the Onion Portage microcores was to plague me for years and finally to lead to important new discoveries there; but that summer of

126. Three microcores and a microblade found at Onion Portage in 1941. The microblade, at right, is 1¼ in. (3 cm.) long.

1941 we rather precipitately left the site on our raft, fleeing the wrath of the rain gods.

LANDING TWO days later at Ahteut, we had far more agreeable prospects. The sun was finally out, the river rose no higher, the salmon were beginning to arrive in such numbers as to be frequently snared in our net, and the archeology promised to be considerably older than any we had thus far examined. The deepest houses, we found upon excavation, had actually opened in two directions as promised by surface depressions (Fig. 127). One opening led to a deep tunnel, a cold trap for winter, through which people could enter their underground dwellings some distance away. Climbing down a ladder to a depth four to six feet below the ground surface, they crawled through this narrow tunnel and emerged, like beavers to their lodges, at the higher floor of a warm room. The floor of the rear tunnel, on the other hand, was level with that of the house. One such tunnel had a small room opening to one side. We felt that these rear tunnels might have been used for storage and also as emergency exits in case of fire or attack by some enemy.

Here at Ahteut we found the emphasis again on local products: spruce and birch bark, beaver teeth (as whittling tools), and antler. These houses, too, had large, central fireplaces. No datable wood was preserved, but large pieces of charcoal from one of the hearths

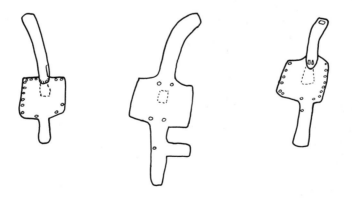

127. Floor plans of Ahteut houses showing tunnels at front and rear. Entire length of house at right is about 35 ft.

could be cross-dated, and this subsequently helped in determining the age of the site. We now know that Ahteut belongs to a later phase of Western Thule culture, dating about A.D. 1100 to 1300. Then, however, it was the oldest Eskimo culture recorded up to that time in the interior, and although it lacked jade it was clearly antecedent to the other Kobuk River archeology.

The remainder of the summer we spent excavating at Ekseavik and Kotzebue. At both these localities preservation was excellent, and cross dating between the sites soon established the fact that the houses of Ekseavik had been contemporary, while those of Kotzebue fell into two main periods, roughly 150 years apart. Since my earlier tree-ring calendar had not yet been tied in with the living trees of the Kobuk, it formed a "floating" chronology allowing the three sites to be cross-dated to one another, though the specific years were still not known. At the end of that season, interest in the prospect of a dated inland archeology had widened, and I looked forward hopefully to continuing my work another year.

Back at the college, however, an event took place that changed my plans, as well as those of many thousands of others. Helge Larsen, who had left Europe a few months earlier with his wife and young son, was now living in Fairbanks to work over the Ipiutak collections. One morning as I sat in the coffee shop before meeting my first class, he approached, white-faced and shaken. The date was December 7, 1941. "You are in the war, too," he said. "The Japanese are right now bombing Pearl Harbor." Within a few hours our complacent little community, which had hardly known the Great Depression and considered itself safely removed from most crises of the nation, was in line of direct threat as the Japanese began to move into the outer islands of the Aleutian chain.

The following spring, just before and during the spring "break-up" of the river, while on a mission for the U. S. Army Engineers, I had a last look at the Kobuk River before joining the Navy and spending most of my wartime months, ironically enough, on the Equator, in the Southwest Pacific area. Not until 1947 did I get back to the questions of the forest Eskimos and the dating of their predecessors.

Returning to the Kobuk in that year with three students from the college, by then become the University of Alaska, I concentrated again on the sites of Ekseavik and Kotzebue. Because of their proximity to the sea, the summers there are shorter and colder, and frost—the best possible preservative for organic materials—remains perennially in the ground. Artifacts of ivory, antler, and even wood emerged from the thawing ground as fresh as if just made. Such things as wooden bowls and snow goggles could well have been put to use again after their centuries of burial. The houses and their contents seemed to be intermediate between those at Ahteut and Ambler Island, but this did not long remain a matter of conjecture for the dating of all the Kobuk sites became dramatically possible that season through the large number of logs and poles we dug in fine condition from house walls and floors.

One evening, by the light of a gasoline lantern in the tent, I again went over the patterns of thick and thin tree rings that marked the date of abandonment of the more recent Kotzebue site. One sequence of rings looked familiar. Turning to the chronology previously made at Kiana and checking through skeleton plots, I found the identical sequence in the record of an exceptionally long-lived tree that had been used as a log for one of the oldest cabins in the present village of Kiana. The rings recorded in my boring of that old log showed the tree to have lived over 350 years. Its latest rings overlapped by a few decades the earliest rings from logs of the Kotzebue site.

Feverishly I checked the earliest rings in the Ambler Island chronology. Again the dating was confirmed. The more recent Kotzebue site (called Intermediate Kotzebue, to distinguish it from the modern town) had existed until about A.D. 1550. The other sites then fell into place as part of the already existing "floating" chronology. Ekseavik and Old Kotzebue both dated to a few years beyond A.D. 1400, and Ahteut, if I could judge from the rings preserved in fragments of charcoal from a single house, to about A.D. 1250. Surely the excitement of the bridging of these two chronologies was as great to us that evening as was the triumph of A. E. Douglass, pioneer dendrochronologist, many years earlier, when he found in the floor of a Hopi kiva the key log that linked his whole Cliff Dweller sequence to the Christian calendar.

At last both goals of my first trip along the Kobuk seemed successfully attained. Dating of timbers had been accomplished, and we knew a good deal about the present natives of the river as well as their ancestors who had dwelt along its shores for the past seven hundred years. All seemed to have lived well, comfortable in their warm, underground houses. While the upper river people depended upon goods that utilized products of the luxurious birch and spruce forests, and, in later years, specialized in jade work, there were obvious similarities between the upper river sites and those of its mouth at Kotzebue. Not all these could be easily tied in with the coastal Eskimo pattern found on islands and peninsular points. There seemed a remarkable interdependence between the people not only of one culture period but of all who lived within the valley of the Kobuk, and I pondered much about this.

Old Eskimos pointed out that formerly men were always on the move. While women fished for salmon during the summer, husbands and sons roamed the high mountains amassing pelts for winter clothing, bedding, and tents. In autumn, whole families traveled together to the lakes and slopes where caribou habitually crossed, then returned, later in the fall, to rebuild or refurbish their winter houses. Home, for these people, was not a single spot but an area within which they moved during the course of a year. Some few men of the upper Kobuk attended the trading fair at Kotzebue in late summer, distributing, upon their return, goods from the coast —seal oil, whaleskin, amber, and metal goods. Then in midwinter most of the river people, including those of Kotzebue, traveled some distance for an annual festival of trading and gift-giving.

Though it seemed likely that the language spoken earlier was Eskimo, as it is today, I could not discount the strong emphasis on inland products and the resemblances of many practices to those of neighboring Athapaskan Indians. Present and recent people of the river might be called Eskimos because of their language, yet their culture had been different enough to warrant their not being categorized by so fixed a name. Instead, thinking of all the older and continuing cultures of the river, varied as they were in content and based upon the contiguity of high mountains, lakes, inland forests, food-giving rivers, and a branch of the sea, I called these people the "Arctic Woodlanders." We had found many of their obvious sites, yet these must only have scratched the surface, for it was hard to conceive of any time since the glaciers when people living anywhere in the region of Bering Strait would not have found and exploited the Kobuk or neighboring forested streams.

YEARS LATER, in trowelling the Denbigh hearths at Cape Krusenstern between 1958 and 1961, I saw no reason to exclude the

varied phases of culture on these beach ridges from the Arctic Woodland continuum. The present hunters of Kotzebue often camp at
Cape Krusenstern for seasonal hunting and gathering, just as they
camp at other times in the woods of the lower rivers. The Western
Thule people used scrapers of schist and beaver-tooth knives, the
Ipiutakers employed birch-bark containers and built open fires in
their winter houses, and the Denbigh people seemed to have spent
the harshest months of the year back in the interior. Most likely,
the beach ridges seemed to say, all who have camped here have also
been at least partly at home in the forests, their lives enriched by
the great variety of food, scenes, and climates offered by their surroundings. The Denbigh people, no less, must have exploited the
Kobuk River country and adapted their culture to the Arctic treeline
—and perhaps from this area their culture spread across all of
Arctic North America.

By the end of the 1961 season at Cape Krusenstern we felt we
had acquired a wealth of information about the ancestors of Indians
and Eskimos. Yet the more we learned, the more we needed to know
to fit our cultural pieces into the jigsaw puzzle of Arctic prehistory.
Could we learn where the Denbigh people themselves had originated
—or might we find an even earlier culture? Though we sampled as
thoroughly as possible all 114 beaches at Cape Krusenstern during
our years there, we finally felt that little new could be learned from
them. The oldest beaches—those bordering the edge of the lagoon—
had no leavings of anyone earlier than Denbigh people. Now it was
time to cross the lagoon to look for ancient sites on the rocky banks
and cliffs of the mountain that was our beach ridge backdrop.

(XV)

BEFORE
BEACH RIDGES

T HE AFTERNOON sun playing on the gray mountain of limestone
across the lagoon from the beach ridges at Cape Krusenstern
creates shadows of undulating reds, yellows, and purples on the
sheer cliffs that are called The Palisades (Fig. 128; Map 2). Rising
to a flat top high above the sea, the Palisades site doubtless attracted
early travelers along the coast before the beach ridges began to form;
and, in an even earlier period, when the sea was lower and the
present Kotzebue Sound was a great, flat plain, possibly it attracted
the hunters of Pleistocene herds. Many people, at any rate, have
camped there over the years. This we learned from scouring the surface and picking up their weathered flints. Yet judging from the
workmanship, none had been the familiar flintworkers of the beach
ridges: neither the Thule Eskimos, nor the pottery makers of Choris,
nor the skilled flintworkers of Denbigh. What we found on the
Palisades was puzzling from the start.

On a windy August day of 1958, Bill Simmons, Almond Downey, and I had tied our boat and paused to boil coffee near the
easterly base of the Palisades where we had arrived after threading
our way through the devious channels that led through the beach
ridges to the lagoon. Intending to camp at the far end of the lagoon,
seven miles away, we stopped only to fortify ourselves with food and
a hot drink before entering the shallow, choppy body of water; yet,
curious about our surroundings, we decided to take the time to investigate some of the rocky exposures above. The way was difficult,

128. The Palisades—a limestone outcropping back of the beach ridges at Cape Krusenstern. The sea, which probably lapped at its base six thousand years ago, now lies some three miles distant.

through bristling alders, but the striking view of the beaches and lagoon made it worth our trouble.

Pausing to enjoy the breeze on a bare ledge part way up, about two hundred feet above the sea, we noted the patches of open ground that appeared like bald spots between the low bushes. Rough, white-crusted flakes of limestone shingled these patches as they did patches higher up the mountain. No obvious signs of camping met our initial scrutiny—not even the more or less ubiquitous spent rifle shells. The place seemed to merit closer inspection, however, and when we examined the rocks more carefully a few flint chips turned up, telling us that we were not the site's first visitors.

Among the first pieces found was the fragment of a microblade. Off now on this trail of bigger game, we knelt closer and poked at the surface with sticks and trowels. This was no ordinary chipping place, we soon learned. At least one in ten flakes proved to be a microblade or fragment. Had we found another site of the Denbigh Flint complex? It seemed quite possible as we continued to expose these sharp, thin objects. Yet the proportions differed. Elsewhere in a Denbigh site, we would expect many thin bifaces among the microblades, not to mention burins and their spalls. But here the re-touched artifacts were all made from the microblades themselves.

129. View from the top of the Palisades. A packsack (right foreground) lies on a bed of flaking limestone that contained archeological chips and artifacts.

Graver tips, like minature drills, were drawn from the edges of micro-blade fragments, and other microblades displayed ragged sides possibly indicating that they had been inserted into the edges of weapon tips.

Inspired by this success on our first climb, we decided to go to the considerably higher, flat top of the Palisades. After a walk across spongy ground we came to a dry slope, and from there picked a trail through a mossy chimney, up past a gigantic twig pile—home of a hawk—and hence up to the flat, windblown surface at the top. The view was superb on this clear day; we could see for miles in every direction (Fig. 129). What we hoped to see, though, were flakes or other objects, and these did not at first appear. Often archeological finds are matters of faith. One who does not truly believe may pass over a site giving it but cursory glances and never knowing what treasures are near. An archeologist, on the other hand, who envisions early men on every rocky ledge, will not quit a spot until he has exhausted every possibility.

Possessing faith that first day on the Palisades, we inched forward, bent over like grazing bison, and were soon rewarded. Flakes began to appear but, unlike those of the first site (later designated Lower Bench), none were microblades. A scraper or two offered little cultural information, but then a more distinctive piece turned up. It was a projectile point of obsidian with a notch on either side near the base, fresh looking and unaffected by weather (Fig. 130). It was an admirable object, glossy black until held to the light when it became a piece of smoky glass—but especially unique because of its notching. Altogether it was an artifact so rare in the western Arctic that its presence would have been perplexing had I not, some years earlier, excavated one almost precisely like it in a house pit at Black River in the upper Kobuk Valley. The Black River houses were no more than four hundred years old, and I had attributed that first obsidian point to Indian intrusion into the Eskimo area. By the same reasoning, this second point seemed to date the flints of the Palisades as recent—too recent to detain us further, and we quit the site in some disappointment.

130. Notched point of obsidian from Palisades site. Length, 1⅛ in. (2.7 cm.).

Over the winter, however, I had reason to question my judgment about this notched point from the Palisades. To begin with, the chips and artifacts of flinty material accompanying it, excepting only those of obsidian, were either patinated to some degree or encrusted with lichens and lime, seeming to indicate great age. Flints from the Lower Bench were less patinated, and did not look as old. If the obsidian pieces from the Palisades were the same age as the objects of chert and chalcedony, might not their lack of weathering be attributable to their being natural glass?

Furthermore, some (though a very few) other side-notched points were on record in the western Arctic. Besides mine from Black River, I had seen one purported to have come from St. Lawrence Island and knew of a few others from northwestern Canada and one from Cook Inlet farther south in Alaska. An increasing number were turning up in Dorset and related sites of the eastern Arctic, but there notched points were more to be expected, for Indians of the Archaic period of the eastern United States and Canada, from about six thousand years ago until nearly the beginning of the Christian era, had produced notched points in great variety. Finally, on our way back home at the end of that 1958 season, I had seen two collections made from south of the Alaska Range, one by William Irving and the other by Ivar Skarland. Both contained side-notched points and both, though undated, had come from deposits that appeared to be old. The notched points from the Old Whaling culture of the Krusenstern beaches nearby (Fig. 86) lay still unknown in their buried house on Beach 53 and were not found until the following season.

When we returned to Cape Krusenstern in midsummer the next year, 1959, one of our more important aims was to give the Palisades another try, but so many projects occupied us on the beach ridges that we did not get back to the mountain-top site until fairly late in the season. Then one fine day in August, Bandi, Simmons, Friedman, and I from our crew, together with a visiting friend, Henry Staehle, of Rochester, New York, walked the four miles from our camp on the beaches to the shore of the lagoon where a small boat was waiting. We quickly crossed the water to the foot of the mountain and set about exploring the sites on its slopes.

Again the Lower Bench yielded microblades, a small bifaced point, and gravers, confirming the previous distribution but adding nothing new. High on the Palisades, however, where each of us staked a claim like rival prospectors, we examined inch by inch the floor of harsh, gray, flaking limestone that covered the ground. Between the native rocks we again found chert, chalcedony, jasper, and obsidian chips and artifacts that had been left there by unknown men of the past. Among the artifacts was the unquestionable fragment of another side-notched point. This was not of obsidian but of red jasper, and we noted with great interest that its surface was weathered to the same extent as were most of the other artifacts and chips of the site. Returning to camp that evening, we examined our finds by lantern light and agreed that, however short the time remaining, more work must be done at the Palisades. Bill Simmons volunteered to go back, camp on the high ground, and learn whether we had missed anything or not.

After three days of being continually blasted by wind-driven dust as he scraped at the rocks and camped in a pup tent with a one-burner gasoline stove, Bill returned, looking as weathered as the flints he poured out of two cloth bags. The site had been by no means depleted, for here on the table before us was spread quite an array of chips and scrapers. Some of the flakes showed burin blows on them, and we counted five more notched points. By then, also, we had found the notched points (though of a different kind) in the Old Whaling culture, where they were a main ingredient of that nearly 4,000-year-old village.

Surely these patinated and lime-encrusted objects from the Palisades, asymmetrical and crude in conception when compared with those of Old Whaling, were much older. We began to feel that side-notched points must have a significant, if not vital, place in the early development of flintwork in the Arctic. Perhaps, indeed, a more than tenuous thread connected the side-notched points of Cape Krusenstern to their counterparts of the Late Archaic in the temperate eastern part of the continent.

Whatever elation Bandi and I, in particular, felt over the first batch of artifacts before us, we failed to feel for the second. We saw a collection of flakes so rough that we at first doubted that they were man-made. But then we discerned an axlike implement similar in execution to a complete piece I had collected the previous season and considered to be a hand-held chopper. Then Bill made an interesting observation: while these did not at first appear to be "flints" but some less flakable rock, none was of limestone, the basic rock of the mountain. They appeared, rather, to be deeply weathered stones, now much too coarse-grained to be attractive to a flint knapper, but at the distant time when he chipped them into tools they must have been of flinty texture.

On closer examination we found that while they were undoubtedly flaked for a purpose, none showed the removal of small chips by the technique of pressure retouch—a relatively advanced technique. Originally flakes were used just as they were, after being knocked off, or struck, from a core. Then a more skilled people learned to carefully press off small chips at the ends or along the edges of the flakes to make them sharper. These from the Palisades were not so retouched, and they were a remarkably primitive-looking group of flakes and tools. Most of the large flakes had been struck by a single blow, leaving a prominent bulb of percussion on the broader face. Many had been treated by the process known as hinge

fracture, in which a blow driven into the mass of the rock detaches
a flake that hinges over at its end, leaving a jagged scar on the piece
from which it has been removed (Fig. 131). The hinges on the
choppers and fragments in particular appeared to have been intended—they were an integral part of the flaking process.

Before long, Bandi and I were inclined to agree with Bill that
at least two peoples had inhabited the Palisades, and that they had
been separated by a time long enough to allow one set of rocks to
change chemically, weathering perhaps throughout, while the other
had changed hardly at all. This prospect was intriguing. Could these
be the crude implements of primitive Pleistocene hunters who had

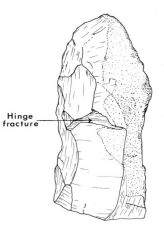

131. A worked implement from Palisades I showing a hinge fracture.
Originally of smooth, flinty material,
it has been changed by chemical
action into rough stone. Length, 4⅞
in. (12.3 cm.)

Hinge
fracture

somehow managed to survive in the Arctic long enough to become
the ancestors of American Indians? My own views of Early Man in
America hardly allowed for a people whose tools were as crude as
these. To endure the extreme cold of the Arctic, sharp missiles were
needed to kill the larger food animals, and effective knives and woodworking tools would have been essential for fashioning clothes and
building houses.

Though pressure flaking and fine retouch could not be seen in
this collection, there was one noteworthy bifaced knife or projectile
point, the tip and base of which were broken away (Fig. 132). This
was as old as the other flakes, to judge from the weathering, but it
had been in the form of a leaf, stemmed by the removal of one side
of the base. The outward resemblance of this piece to the Sandia
point (Fig. 133a), one of the first Early Man weapon tips of the

Southwest, might, we thought, be more than coincidental. The prospect became even more exciting when David M. Hopkins, a geologist, visited our site and expressed the view that some, at least, of the weathered collection were transformed cherts. When pressed for an estimate of the time required for chert to change as this had, he could only guess that "a long time" had elapsed since these had borne a freshly flaked appearance.

Later, during the winter, I found that one of the choppers was of quartzite. Under magnification, the sand grains looked the same as in fresh, milky-white quartzite that has been recently flaked but the cementing material, usually translucent in quartzite, had so changed chemically that the piece had taken on the look of well-weathered sandstone.

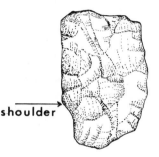

132. Bifaced, shouldered projectile point base or knife fragment, Palisades I. Length, 1⅝ in. (4.1 cm.).

shoulder

In two more pilgrimages to the Palisades before the end of August that summer, we collected more of both kinds of artifacts and chips, designating as "Palisades II" the younger assemblage containing the notched points, and as "Palisades I" the very old, chemically changed flints. Then slowly, during the winter following, I accepted the idea that while the beach ridges at Cape Krusenstern seemed to outline the prehistory of Eskimos, these earlier materials of the mountain slopes were more related to the problem of when and how the first men came to America.

SCHOLARS have puzzled at least since the time of Columbus over the origin of American Indians. At first they were less concerned with the length of time required for the Americas to receive a large population than with the need to know that the New World was seeded with the progeny of Adam and Eve. But as the view of

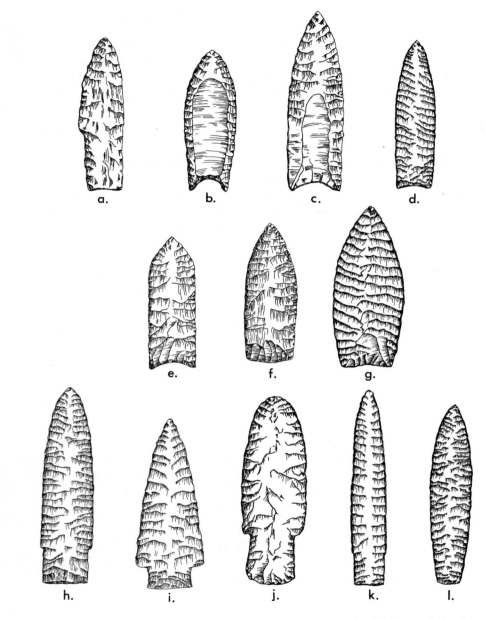

133. Some of the weapon points used by Early Man in the Plains and South-western United States. (*From Wormington, 1957*)

a) Sandia   d) Angostura   g) Brown's Valley   j) Alberta
b) Folsom   e) Plainview   h) Scottsbluff, Type I   k) Eden
c) Clovis   f) Milnesand   i) **Scottsbluff, Type II**   l) Agate Basin

the world widened in the seventeenth century with the discovery of many new seas and lands, questions about the connection and distribution of the earth's animals and people were often addressed to the hazy area between the Pacific Ocean and the "Frozen Sea" as the crucial region where people might first have entered America. Some debated whether the ancestors of Indians, whom they thought to have been Scythians, had ridden into the New World on horses or, as modern Tungus of Siberia ride, on the backs of reindeer. For a long time some form of entry into America through the cold regions of Asia was taken for granted. Then gradually theorists acknowledged that it was not known whether North America was joined to Asia by a solid bar of land or was separated by either a narrow strait or a broad sea. For those who believed in the separation by water, there was either a first invasion of America by people across the sea or an autochthonous growth of Indians from some special creation. An over-enthusiastic Darwinian view in the last century even had the Indians descending from American monkeys.

After Captain James Cook in 1778 discovered and named Bering Strait, there could be little question that this region of the Arctic Circle was a point of ingress to America from Asia, but still no one knew how early mankind had been clever enough to cross the Strait as Eskimos have recently done. By the end of the nineteenth century the Pleistocene glaciation was well enough understood to remove the last doubts that men could have migrated from Asia to America. Bering Strait was shallow, and more than once during the Glacial Age the waters of the world had lowered enough to allow the expanse between Asia and America to emerge as a broad belt of dry land upon which even the most primitive man could have found the means of moving himself and his goods into the New World. (All the Bering Sea and Chukchi Sea areas shown on Map 1 were part of this land mass.) For at least a century now few have doubted that the Bering Strait region was the primary gateway from Asia into America.

So obvious a passageway did not, on the other hand, encourage theorists to look too closely at the Bering Strait region itself for evidence as to how and precisely when the first Americans arrived. Rather, having agreed that men could and did reach America from the Old World by the land route, they looked for evidence of the nature of these earliest men not in the crucial corridor itself but in the more comfortable and populous regions of North and South America. By the early years of this century enough had been learned from the Indian tribes, temple mounds, buried cities, and other archeology to show that men had been in both Americas hundreds and even thousands of years. The rapidly developing archeology of America divided itself nearly everywhere into two parts: one concerning the first people on the continent; the second, the continuities of American Indians and Eskimos back through time. The latter never stretched back far enough to reach the first people, however, which left a gap of centuries between the two studies, and seldom were they determinedly connected.

Nor were the datings suggested for either study likely to bring the two together. On the one hand, Early Men were thought to have stalked the hairy mammoth and other Pleistocene game animals into North America across a "land bridge." Artists painted scenes of brutish men, half-clad in bearskins, plodding with their lumpish weapons through the snow, women clutching their babies following behind, and mammoths leading the way. This would have occurred in the remote time, then usually reckoned to have ended more than 20,000 years ago, when glaciers still covered a large part of the land surface.

The archeology of Indians, on the other hand, clearly held connections back through time, whether in the dry Southwest where Hopi and Zuni pueblos continued the ways of much earlier "Cliff Dwellers" or in the Andes of South America where descendants of the Incas and even earlier city dwellers still built in stone. The estimate of greatest age for one or another of the American Indian culture centers was seldom more than some hundreds of years. The void between these Indians and Early Men thus became a zone of time and culture difficult to enter, yet easy to bridge by the assumption that once a few Early Men had learned to settle down and cultivate plants, they had prospered and populated most of the New World.

The gap widened even more after A. E. Douglass's dramatic application of tree-ring dating to the dry-climate conifers of the Southwest in the 1920's. Dr. Douglass's studies showed that the most continuous sequence of cultures—that of the Southwestern Indians —did not date back four thousand years, as first thought, but only two thousand. Nearly all American archeologists now tightened up their undated sequences to fit well within the same time span.

Then, while Douglass negotiated with Pueblo chiefs to obtain samples of roof beams and floors, resorting on one occasion to their own magical method of placating house gods with gifts of turquoise, other Early Man archeologists found indisputable evidence at Folsom, New Mexico, that man in America and an extinct form of bison had been contemporary. The fluted stone weapon points at Folsom (Fig. 133b), in direct association with fossil bones, showed that Early Man was a clever technician and hunter some 10,000 years ago. It was no wonder that as other flints came into view, many also associated directly with extinct animals, they were dated with an eye first to the Folsom deposit and only rarely with reference to recent Indians. Not long after the Folsom point was found in association with an early postglacial fauna, still older fluted points, called Clovis, were found (Fig. 133c). The shouldered Sandia point (Fig. 133a), though it has never been so firmly placed in time as either the Folsom or the Clovis, offered the possibility of a still earlier American bifaced projectile point.

WHY CERTAIN STYLES of stone tools have caught the fancy of whole populations, across wide spaces, irrespective of tribes or language, and have lasted unchanging from one generation to another over hundreds and even thousands of years, not even archeologists can say. Such was the case in the Old World with certain styles of hand axes in the Lower Paleolithic and with handsome bifaced missile points in the Upper Paleolithic, to single out only two popular objects. Such was also the case, fortunately for those who wish to trace continuities, with fluted points in Early Man's North America. And, though more limited in time, such was the case with a succession of Early Man points of the period immediately following the end of the last glaciation, perhaps 10,000 years ago: the Angostura (Figs. 100 and 133), the Plainview, the Milnesand, the Brown's Valley, the Scottsbluff, the Alberta, the Eden, and the Agate Basin, to mention only those of the western plains and plateaus.

ALL THESE STYLES of spearpoints were first recognized in America far south of the Arctic Circle. It is no wonder that after the Folsom discovery of 1925 archeologists assumed that the same weapon forms would be found in Alaska and, ultimately, on the opposite side of Bering Strait in Siberia. Few suggested, however, that the American forms might have originated in America. It was easier to assume that these large, handsome bifaced points would prove to be related somehow to similar ones in the well-known European sequences. Yet nothing very early had been found in eastern Siberia, and artifacts from the few known late Paleolithic sites of western Siberia did not resemble closely those found in America. Nevertheless, those who thought they knew what kinds of flints the migrants might have lost on their treks across the Arctic reached their conclusions mainly by projecting those earliest-known flints in America back along an imagined migratory trail stretching all the way to western Europe. Only to those who actually dug in the Arctic were the trail signs dim.

IN THE 1930's, the young department of anthropology of Alaska College and its museum, interested in questions about Early Man, began to receive both information and flints from miners working in the Territory's placer gold fields. In these ancient deposits, the bones of extinct mammals washed up regularly and the miners soon began to recognize flints and to donate them to the college. Froelich Rainey made the first exhaustive report of these findings in 1939.

Among the collections of artifacts were nondescript scrapers that might have been of any age, but also three or four long, broad bifaces resembling unchanneled Clovis points or later forms. Two slender bone points, not at all the least intriguing of the objects, were also found in the muck deposits; one was eleven inches long and closely resembled points found in New Mexico in direct association with mammoth bones.

From the same sources, however, Rainey was also obliged to report a few polished slate implements, quite obviously modern, and three side-notched points that were so far out of line with the expected Early Man flints as to be discounted by most who examined them or their photographs.

A difficulty with all the finds from the silt deposits was that almost nothing, no matter how solidly frozen, could be considered as truly "in place"—that is, on the ground just where it was dropped by the man who used it. The deposits have been too often thawed, re-formed, and refrozen down through the millennia. For the same reason it is rare indeed to find two bones of the same skeleton of an extinct animal still articulated.

In 1933, long before most American archeologists thought much about cores and blades, Rainey came upon a small collection of polyhedral cores and blade implements at a site near Alaska College. He could in no way date it with the early American sequences, but from his knowledge of European and Russian archeology he equated it in time with pre-Neolithic sites of Siberia.

With the building of the Alcan Highway during World War II, new, virgin territory was opened up to archeologists, and other microblade sites were soon found between Fairbanks and the Rocky Mountains, vividly suggesting a migratory trail of men into America thousands of years before our own generation followed their path. Since these flints were not associated with the bones of extinct animals, however, they were not placed in time with the Early Man points of the American West.

The Denbigh Flint complex appeared upon the scene in the late 1940's as a possible Early Man candidate just when Willard Libby's radiocarbon laboratory at the University of Chicago was inaugurating—as had A. E. Douglass's dendrochronology—a revolution in dating that would soon envelop the archeology of every land. All living things accumulate radioactivity during their lifetime, slowly losing it for thousands of years after their deaths. Libby showed that certain materials, among them wood, charcoal, and tooth enamel, could be processed and placed before a sensitive geiger counter in such a way as to measure their rates of radiation. These measures, when compared with a scale derived from the rate of radiation of carbon of known age, make possible the approximate dating of many archeological materials. We soon learned from the radiocarbon dates of charcoal from the Denbigh site that despite its technical relationship to Old World sources, the Denbigh Flint complex belonged to a period four to six thousand years ago.

DURING THE 1950's several archeologists went to work in the virtually unknown northern interior of Canada and in the Brooks Range of northern Alaska, while others sought new information from the Aleutian Islands and other points along the north Pacific coast. In the Canadian region of the Mackenzie River valley and neighboring British Columbia and the Yukon Territory, a vast archeological vacuum existed, and there R. S. MacNeish carried on investigations for the National Museum of Canada. Most of his earlier sites contained microblades and produced radiocarbon dates of four or five thousand years ago, while some undated sites throughout the range yielded fragments and occasional whole specimens of bifaced spearpoints vaguely recalling one or another of the Early Man types.

Even more striking finds of this kind were made by others working in the Anaktuvuk Pass region of the Brooks Range only a few dozen miles from the headwaters of the Kobuk River. First, a series of microblade sites, some closely related to those of the Denbigh Flint complex, were found by William Irving of the University of Alaska and Ralph Solecki of the Smithsonian Institution. John M. Campbell, then a Yale University graduate student, announced the recovery of a large number of handsomely flaked bifaces from just below the surface at the height of the Pass. Most of these resembled either the Angostura or the Agate Basin type of Early Man Point. At first uncertain whether these spearpoints, which he called Kayuk, belonged with a body of antler objects he regarded as an inland phase of Ipiutak culture, Campbell later decided that they did not, and expressed a belief that they should be roughly cross-dated with their early parallels in the Great Plains, which would presumably place them at 10,000 or more years ago. He also found in the Pass a site of notched points like those of the Palisades, together with microblades, all of which he guessed to be more recent than Kayuk and Denbigh, mainly because of their resemblance to points of the eastern Archaic period.

In 1960 when I reported both in talks and in a written article on the two notched-point horizons at Cape Krusenstern, the one (Old Whaling) more recent than the Denbigh Flint complex and the other (Palisades II) older, a question about Palisades II was put to me by skeptical colleagues. Since notched points were plentiful in the later Archaic period, say four thousand years ago, in eastern North America, and since, though scarce, notched points appeared more recently in sites of northern Canada, why should I regard them as so much older at Cape Krusenstern? Some of my critics voiced the opinion that the Palisades II phase of culture was not actually old at all, but was related in time to the Old Whaling culture, which began about 1800 B.C. Such a view made it easier for them to place such spearpoints as the Kayuk variety further back in time than all other notched points or all Denbigh-like forms, and thus in the Early Man category of the Western Plains, the forms of which they resembled.

I could answer these questions best with more facts. During the 1961 season at Cape Krusenstern, we made a special effort to determine whether or not notched points had anywhere preceded the Old Whaling culture of Beach 53. We scoured those beaches behind the Old Whaling ridge with all diligence, but nowhere on the older beaches, 57 to 78, did a notched point turn up. Beaches 78 through the remaining oldest ridges contained only leavings of the Denbigh Flint people, surely the first occupants of the beach ridges, and their flintwork differed as much from that of both Old Whaling and the Palisades as we could imagine. Certain then that no final proofs were to be had on the beach ridges, I returned several times to the Palisades to search for more evidence. Each visit strengthened my conviction that the Palisades flints were all older than those on the beaches.

If, though, the Kayuk points of Anaktuvuk Pass and the less definitive ones of MacNeish's sites of Canada were not as ancient as Early Man flints, despite their similarities, how might we explain them? Here I thought again about the distinctive and by now well-known flintwork of the Choris beaches and Trail Creek caves (pp. 214–16; Fig. 79) at Cape Krusenstern and elsewhere around the Kotzebue Sound area. All these sites had contained spearpoints and fragments even more remarkably like those of the Early Man points of the western United States than were the ones reported from eastward across the Arctic. Many of the Choris specimens from the beach ridges at Cape Krusenstern were closely similar to the Angostura points, though some lacked a grinding of the lower edges. Others were stemmed, as in the Scottsbluff or its "Alberta" variant, and still others had convex bases as in the Agate Basin variety (Fig. 133). Yet these Choris flints unquestionably belonged to a period between the Norton and Old Whaling cultures, making them roughly 3,000 to 3,500 years old—more recent by several millennia than the Early Man points to the south.

Then too, a fluted point had been found in the Denbigh Flint complex—in place in the old layer at Cape Denbigh—and fragments of others had been reported in Denbigh-like collections from the Brooks Range. Fluted points, though not exactly like those of either Folsom or Clovis, were thus an element of the Denbigh Flint complex. And in the Old Whaling site we had two or three examples of spearpoints or knife blades shaped almost precisely like the distinctive Brown's Valley variety. I suggested that neither the Kayuk nor most other such spearpoints of the far north were very old, but that most belonged within or near to the Choris–Trail Creek span of time! To this, Henry Collins added that the Choris–Trail Creek points might be an example of "Arctic retardation," a sort of lagging in time of styles once prevalent in other parts of the world simply because the Arctic had not caught up with the advances of more populous regions in both the New World and the Old. He cautioned, though, that *some* Arctic points might be not retarded from, but contemporary with, their southern counterparts.

WHERE MIGHT we go to solve this question of age for the two groups of Palisades flints? There seemed no better means of isolating cultural phases through time than on a series of beach ridges such as we had before us at Cape Krusenstern. Yet all these and the other beach ridge successions of which I knew in Alaska seemed to have divulged their basic information—and none appeared to extend further back in time than the Denbigh Flint complex of 5,000 or so years ago.

Then I remembered, as I had many times in the past two decades, the three microcores and the microblade from House 1 at Onion Portage, far back in the Kobuk River valley (Fig. 126). By now I was convinced that they had not belonged, culturally, where we had found them, but had been either collected by the residents of that no more than seven-hundred-year-old house or displaced from an earlier deposit into which the pit house had been dug. I compared the Onion Portage microcores with those of the Denbigh sequence at Cape Krusenstern and concluded that the Onion Portage ones were much like the more recent Denbigh varieties. We would expect to find similar ones around Beach 80 at Cape Krusenstern rather than on the older ridges.

What a revelation it would be if we could return to Onion Portage and find a site in stratigraphy that contained the leavings of Denbigh people—or perhaps even their ancestors! Thus far we knew only that the Kobuk River had been populated some hundreds of years. If a site or buried level of culture as old as Denbigh could be found there, it would be exciting indeed, even if it did little more than project the Denbigh Flint complex inland to this river site and show that its practitioners had been quite at home in interior forests of spruce, poplar, and birch.

In the fall of 1960 when I worked up a proposal for another season at Cape Krusenstern, I included plans to travel for a few days to the Kobuk River to follow up various leads, particularly those at Onion Portage. Thus, early in the 1961 season, as soon as plans were well under way at Cape Krusenstern, I asked Helge Larsen and Douglas Anderson to take care of things there while I set out with keen anticipation to learn more about the mysterious microblade and cores at the inland river site.

(XVI)

ONION PORTAGE

THE MAKEUP of the cultural site at Onion Portage, we have learned during several summers there, is vertical, while that at Cape Krusenstern, in contrast, is horizontal. On the beach ridges at the Cape, we seek out the older campsites by walking inland from the sea across ridge after ridge of former beach fronts. When we stop to examine one, no matter how far along it we walk in either direction, chances are that we shall not encounter a single object left by man that does not belong roughly to the time when that particular beach lay next to the ocean. As the oldest beach was camped on by men of its generation, so was a newer beach by a newer generation, and thus on forward, up to the beach currently forming, used by people today, at the ocean's edge.

At Onion Portage, on the other hand, the archeology of one level is not older the farther back we go from the river, but only older the deeper we dig downward. Many former ground surfaces lie buried in this site where generations of people have camped, and as we clear one level to expose the flints of the ancient culture it contains, we are reminded of a particular beach ridge at Cape Krusenstern that held similar types of flints. We contrast how the blackened hearth of an ancient Onion Portage family has, over the years, become buried by a covering of earth—while the hearth of an equally old coastal family has become remote from the sea because of the forward growth of new beaches.

If credit is to be taken for recognizing the stratigraphy at Onion Portage (Map 9), I can claim it only through persistence; of foresight there was none. It was in 1940 that I first saw the site—on that solitary journey down the Kobuk River by raft and kayak. Then in 1941 I returned to the Kobuk with John Newcomb and some Eskimo assistants, and at Onion Portage excavated four house pits, but the continual rain and slow thaw that summer caused us to leave the site early, and we never guessed what lay deeper in the ground: many cultures, we now know, displayed through tens of layers, spanning thousands of years. That summer, though, we would have been content with the discovery of a layer only a little older than the pit houses!

Through the years after 1941 my certainty grew that the microblade and cores excavated from the floor of House 1 had some meaning that extended beyond the archeology of recent Eskimos. At length, twenty years later, came the opportunity to go back and see. Leaving the rest of my party digging Norton, Choris, or Denbigh sites on the beach ridges at Cape Krusenstern, and traveling in a rubber kayak that I had transported, neatly folded, in the plane that landed me upriver, I reached Onion Portage on the afternoon of July 5, 1961. Hauling my craft onto the familiar gravel beach, I walked up the slope to a site now dry and pleasant, sharply contrasting to the rain and cold of the summer when I had last been there. Little change had taken place over the years. Sunlight filtered through the grove of tall poplars onto the grass below and I saw at once the T-shaped pit of House 1 (Fig. 134). The rim of back dirt now had a thin turf of its own, but as I looked down into the pit through a sparse growth of wild roses I saw the flat floor, the low benches, and a hearth outlined by stones, just as we had left them.

For a moment I had misgivings. I remembered how well we had cleaned the floor and the deeper tunnel in front and how little reason we had then to expect anything more in the frozen ground below. But I was here and the old questions nagged, so I lost no time lowering myself into the pit, slashing at the briary stems of the roses, and heaving the weighty hearthstones aside with my shovel. Having cleared the deepest part of the floor, where the hearth had been, I then pressed the shovel into the ground to see whether below lay more dark streaks or only virgin sand. Before it had gone full length the blade grated against resistant material that was neither clay nor gravel, and when I lifted, I saw that it contained a mixture of black charcoal and white bone: an unusual combination.

As I broke apart the sample with a trowel, my puzzlement increased. The charcoal and even the abundant small flint chips in it might occur in coastal hearths or recent ones of the river—it was

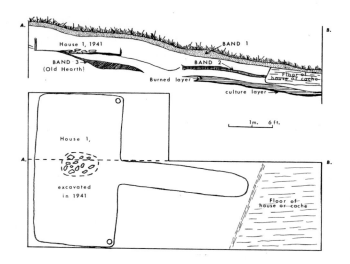

134. Onion Portage excavations, 1941 and 1961.

the bones that seemed strange. They were not gnawed bones carelessly tossed into a fireplace after a feast. Rather, they were small
fragments of leg bones of caribou and possibly other animals that
had been broken into pieces of an almost uniform size and then
burned. At this point I recalled a description by Douglas Leechman,
Canadian anthropologist, of "bone chips" that he had found in
Athapaskan campsites in the Porcupine River region of Arctic
Alaska. There and in neighboring country, Indians extracted oil
from caribou and sheep bones by breaking the bones with stone
mauls into manageable size and then boiling them. The sludge that
remained after oil and soup had been made became bone meal.

With the bones, chips, and charcoal as evidence, I knew that
earlier campers had indeed preceded the Eskimo dwellers of House 1
at Onion Portage, and they must have enjoyed many a meal of
hearty soup, afterward throwing the cracked bones into the fire,
where they became white with burning.

In 1941 the ground had been solidly frozen beneath the house
rectangles, but now in 1961 it was thawed a foot or more below the
floor of House 1. With the burned bones of the older hearth as inspiration, I set about excavating a wider area to learn whether the
more recent House 1 had been erected atop the floor of another
house or was merely built over this earlier hearth on the natural
incline of the hillside. Trowelling every inch, I cut away the sand

and soon exposed the top of a widespread slope containing wood, charcoal, and whitened bone fragments. The fireplace deposit with the bones was deepest (six to ten inches near center) close to the point I first tested with the trowel, under the hearth of House 1 (Fig. 134), and it spread over an oval area about four feet long by three feet wide. Around it lay blackened earth, an occasional bit of bone meal, and an increasing number of flint chips, the last ground into the earth at the hearth's edge. Farther toward the walls of the original excavation for House 1 the layer became thinner, until in profile it resembled only a pencil line about the margins of the cut. Here and there I struck patches of frost in the ground, indicating that I would not be able to dig much more deeply until enough hours or days had passed to allow the warm air to penetrate the ground.

By this time, though, I had uncovered a tantalizing group of artifacts from this level, scarcely resembling those of Eskimo sites, yet testifying to a well-established phase of culture—possibly Indian. Among the objects were a number of pieces made of obsidian: end scrapers with part of the cortex (the rough surface of the original pebble) left on; coarse, drill-like objects; and the fragments of stubby, thick bifaces, possibly skinning knives. Many scrapers, mainly of black chert, fragments of other bifaces, and coarse flakes used along one sharp edge, perhaps as knives, failed to correspond to groups of artifacts found along the seacoast. Bones were rarely preserved except in a charred condition; yet I found one artifact— a skin scraper or large woodworking tool—made of the split leg bone of a moose.

The distribution of artifacts about the hearth suggested that some kind of lodge might have been erected over it, even though the surface was not flat, as in later houses, but conformed roughly to the gentle slope of the hill. The depth of the hearth deposit seemed to indicate numerous fires. On the other hand, though, if the site were simply the fall gathering place of a group of people who found themselves with a plethora of caribou to cut and eat, the deep hearth might have resulted from a continuous process of oil-rendering solely at the times caribou periodically crossed the river.

ONION PORTAGE, I learned by talking with old men of both Shungnak and Kiana, is a point where families still gather for both fall and spring caribou hunts. Its intriguing name results not only from the fact that wild onions abound, but also that it is truly a portage—a shortcut from one part of the river to another (Fig. 135). According to my informants, herds of caribou returning from the Arctic slopes far to the north in late August and early September walk determinedly by the thousands down past the slopes of Jade Mountain onto the high ground leading to Onion Portage and cross the Kobuk River mainly near the mouth of Jade Creek, but in smaller groups at Onion Portage itself. Near where I dug, I noticed parallel trails leading from the riverbank up through the birch- and spruce-covered slope—trails such as are made by strings of animals follow-ing a leader. The caribou move in this fashion down the slope in the fall to cross the river on their way to distant lichen pastures; then, in spring, they come back on the ice or in the newly awakened river to follow an instinctive urge of northward migration.

Pegliruk, a Kobuk man in his seventies who had talked to me in 1940, told of life as he remembered it at the caribou crossings before white men came to the river. The men and older boys of a group customarily spent the summer away from their women hunt-ing in the high mountains for the pelts of sheep and young caribou. Returning to their homes in early fall when the women were just drying the last salmon of the season, the men joined their women-folk and began a journey up the river by boat to their customary

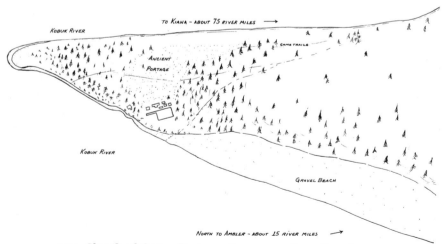

135. Sketch of Onion Portage site as seen from the air.

rendezvous with other families at a caribou crossing. Those who lived below Onion Portage would come there, while those farther upstream would go to one of the lake outlets nearer to the head of the river.

Once established in their new camp at the caribou crossing, the men built or repaired diverting fences to lead the caribou down slopes and into the water where they might be slaughtered with spears from one-man bark canoes. As soon as the animals began to appear, men, women, and children all took part, urging the caribou along until they plunged into the stream where the spearsmen waited. I could visualize the brown-gray herds pouring rhythmically over the bare slopes between the mouth of Jade Creek and Onion Portage, the splashing of paddles in the boats, the plunging of spears and knives into the demoralized swimmers, the spurts of blood mingling with the rush of the blue Kobuk water, and the dead and dying animals, held afloat by their buoyant coats, drifting with the current to the gravel beach at Onion Portage.

According to present villagers, the fall caribou hunting camp lasted until the needs of all participants had been met and the meat skinned and partly dried. Then the camps would break up as everyone returned in small family groups to their winter houses downstream. As I reached the limits of my small excavation, I knew that I had found the record of an early meeting place at this traditional caribou crossing, though the bone meal suggested that the campers might have been Indians rather than Eskimos.

CONFIDENT NOW that my test amply justified more digging at the site, I gathered up the materials I had excavated and paddled downriver to Kiana where I caught a plane back to the beaches at Cape Krusenstern. When work there was completed, toward the end of the summer, Helge Larsen went to Point Hope for a nostalgic visit and to look for hearths of Near Ipiutak culture, Douglas Anderson briefly explored the archeology of the Noatak River, and the rest of our crew—Paul Dayton, Robert Stewart, the Downey family, and Tommy Lee, a Kobuk River man who had worked for me in 1941— traveled in small boats up the river to Onion Portage. Once there and established in a comfortable camp stretched along the gravel beach, we proceeded to strip the thawed sod and soil from three different rectangular areas that were to be test cuts down to at least the old Indian-like deposit which, for lack of a better name, I referred to simply as the "Old Hearth" culture.

We had no sooner removed blocks of sod from the three excavations than we saw in each, roughly matching one another and paralleling the surface of the ground, streaks of black, gray, and yellow earth. Our three test cuts were some dozens of feet apart, yet each looked like the other, with many-hued layers of soil, and this told us at once that the earth was stratified—a condition we would not have discovered so soon, at least, had we merely widened the ancient pit house excavation.

Quite promptly, and only a foot beneath the surface in one of the test cuts, we came to a layer containing flakes of coal-like obsidian (volcanic glass so dense that no light could pass through) and curious obsidian artifacts. I realized that we would not have to dig as deep as the Old Hearth layer to find something new in Arctic archeology. Somewhat incredulous, I sank a limited test cut and found to my elation that there was no limit to the neatly stacked layering of old surfaces. Furthermore, the differences in nature and style of the flinty material in one after another of these charcoal-bearing layers showed that they were not simply the occupation zones of closely successive visitors. Rather, these strata suggested that unconnected peoples of the past, each with a distinctive flintworking technology, had lived on these various levels at the time they formed.

Now certain of stratigraphy, we extended our test pits until they joined at one level, and then we scattered ourselves over this layer to expose its entire surface and separate its contents before all moving down an inch or two to the next stratum. At this time, too, I began numbering each layer as it was exposed. Where several layers grouped themselves together because of their inclusions or arrangement above or below wide sterile layers, they were assigned "band" numbers. Thus, layer 1 of Band 1 was the topmost layer, just under the present sod. In it were glass beads of the last century intermixed with bottle glass, marbles, and tin cans of recent decades. Layer 2 of Band 1 came next below, well within the grass roots, and containing well-preserved antler and even ivory objects of late prehistoric Eskimos who had camped there. Below this top sod there were no other signs of European trade goods. Other Eskimo-like objects, similar to late Western Thule implements of the coast, appeared down to a depth of a foot or more in Band 1 and then disappeared (see Fig. 134).

Beneath that, in a level I designated layer 1 of Band 2, came the curious, opaque obsidian objects, In this layer, too, hearths were encountered that, unlike hearths of more recent people, contained bone meal from burned bone fragments precisely like that in the Old Hearth layer further below.

The next deepest layers of Band 2 contained more familiar flints. These were in two or three distinct layers and were more related to phases of Norton culture of the coast than they were to the opaque obsidian layer above or to any other culture I could think of. The variations in numbers of layers in a band (from three to five layers in Band 3, for instance) are due to the fact that the soil in one area steadily accumulated, while at the same time a spot nearby was being eroded. Over hundreds of years the otherwise thick layer of one period merged with a worn-away segment of another (this can be seen in Fig. 141, p. 360). A similar situation occurred on the beach ridges at Cape Krusenstern, where one beach was sometimes fused into another.

Beneath the earliest layer of the Norton-like deposits came a few inches to a foot or more of yellowish sandy loam, largely sterile (containing few artifacts or none), and under this was another sandwich-like zone containing from three to five charcoal-bearing layers. This we called Band 3, and we could see from the projection of the cut from one wall to another that this was the band that encompassed the Old Hearth layer I had dug down to earlier in the season. Its materials were far more Indian-like than were those immediately above, and in some ways it anticipated the layer with the opaque obsidian at the top of Band 2.

Obviously a great deal of time had been required for the accumulation of these many layers. Could there be more of this remarkable layer-cake stratigraphy below? Unfortunately, we were not to have the whole answer at the end of 1961. Nearly everywhere by then we had reached frost in or just below Band 3. In one exceptional area, however, the frost gave way more rapidly than elsewhere, and Paul Dayton took advantage of this to trowel the spot as much as possible until, just as we were about to leave, he found that beneath the Band 3–Old Hearth layer was still another layer of sterile loam, and, below that, at least three deeper layers, each containing charcoal, bits of red ocher, and an occasional flint chip. The season thus ended with a widening knowledge of cultures and the prospect that after we had dug more extensively at Onion Portage, we would have a new view of Eskimo penetration into the forest, and insight as well, perhaps, into how Eskimos had met with, or given way to, incursions of Indians.

The original problem of the microblade and cores that I had found in House 1 in 1941—and that had prompted my return to the site—had not yet been solved, however, for although several microblades had been found in the Old Hearth layer and in layers above, they were crude in comparison to those of House 1 or to Denbigh microblades. These other microblades, in fact, were not even definitely made from prepared cores—a first requirement for the striking of true, multiple-faceted microblades.

IT WAS NEARLY two years before I returned to Onion Portage, for the 1962 field season and part of 1963 were spent with my family on a sabbatical year in Denmark. There, at the National Museum in Copenhagen, working with specialists on sites of Greenland and other parts of the Arctic, I was continually reminded of the questions that might be answered in part, at least, at Onion Portage. In studying the collections of the Greenland specialist Count Eigil Knuth, for instance, I learned of a remarkable series of sites on high terraces in northernmost Greenland that Count Knuth demonstrated to me as having an older, crude, Denbigh-like phase (Independence I) and a later, Dorset-like period (Independence II).

This kind of information made me hasten to finish other work in order to prepare for a lengthy dig in a truly stratified Arctic site. My Danish colleagues agreed that Onion Portage held great promise. Until now we had been content when we found as many as three layers in real stratigraphy: at Cape Denbigh, and in Greenland— the latter with a stratified site at Disko Bay that was excavated by Helge Larsen and Jørgen Meldgaard. There, in clearly separate layers, Sarqaq culture (an eastern relative of late Denbigh) was at the bottom; Dorset, next; and Thule at the top. Other stratigraphy, representing an even longer time span, had been reported by R. S. MacNeish at Engigstciak on the Firth River of western Canada, but this seemed to lack the clear separation of layers that would make possible the isolation of artifacts into distinct and unmixed cultural phases.

Onion Portage gave promise of showing us in its acre-wide expanse just how the site must have been at each of its various periods of occupation. Ideally, an archeologist with the necessary time and funds would plan to dig the whole area of a site like this, level by level, scanning each layer across its entire breadth and removing from it the artifacts left by the people of its time before digging lower to the next, clearly separate level containing artifacts of an older generation or culture—and this was now my hope for Onion Portage.

After a delightful and instructive half-summer in 1963 excavating sites of Sarqaq culture with a Danish National Museum group in Greenland under the able direction of Hans Berg, I returned to Copenhagen to meet my son Jim, then sixteen, and say good-bye to the rest of my family who were going back to our home in Rhode Island. Jim and I then boarded a jet plane bound for Anchorage, Alaska. We reached Onion Portage and began work with a small crew of Eskimos on August 1, 1963.

The ground below our 1961 excavation had now thawed to a good depth, and we decided to start digging in the middle and largest of the three test pits. For two years the barely discerned and unexplored layers that lay beneath the Old Hearth band had excited our curiosity, and now, at last, we would see if they, too, held campsites or artifacts. In the winter following their excavation, the Old Hearth's material had been studied and analyzed at the Haffenreffer Museum, and the resemblances of end scrapers and bifaced blades to similar objects of Old Whaling culture on the coast had led me to believe that the two cultures roughly paralleled each other in time, although in many respects they differed. If contemporary with Old Whaling, the Old Hearth culture would be roughly 3,700 years old. At Cape Krusenstern we had found no clearly defined cultures preceding Old Whaling except the much earlier (5,000-year-old) and much different Denbigh Flint complex. There was nothing intermediate between the two cultures on the beach ridges.

What, then, would be the contents of Band 4? For it became almost immediately obvious to Jim and me that more layers, necessarily older because of their greater depth in the ground, did indeed lie below Band 3. Might we find, as on the beaches, that the earlier people at the site were Denbigh campers?

We exposed the old surfaces in six-foot squares, one at a time, finding a sterile layer of yellowish sandy loam separating the Old Hearth band from Band 4. Then in the top layer of Band 4 we began to uncover a fireplace (Fig. 136). As we did so, a thin sliver of red jasper stood out above all else, and I saw with an excited glance that it was a burin spall, one of those minute implements used by Denbigh people (Fig. 103). Next came raw flakes, and soon, a microblade—a true one this time, with three facets like those from Cape Denbigh (Fig. 102). In my mind's eye I pictured with amusement my old friends Nakarak and Sokpilak squatting along the edge of my cut here and nodding wisely at this new manifestation of their "little people."

Following rapidly came fragments of two small arrowpoints of a type sharp at both ends, ground at the edges of the stem, and finely serrated along both edges toward the tip (Fig. 137). These points, only an inch long, had extremely fine diagonal flake scars across both faces, and their curvature showed that they had been made from microblades. Other objects soon turned up, identical in every respect to artifacts and flakes of the Denbigh Flint complex, and together they announced, as if given voice, that Denbigh people,

136. Large stone hearth uncovered in Band 4 (Denbigh culture), Onion Portage, 1963.

137. Diagonally flaked arrowpoint made from a microblade, Denbigh Flint complex, Band 4, Onion Portage. Length, 1 in. (2.5 cm.).

formerly known to have lived at the forest edge where trees meet tundra or bare mountain slopes, had also camped, here at Onion Portage, deep within the woods. Soon other hearths turned up as we continued widening our cut in six-foot squares, and I noted with some puzzlement that they contained white bone meal like that found in fireplaces of Bands 3 and 2 above. This was an element not found in hearths on the coast. Later, when much more was learned of the site, I concluded that the making of bone meal was a custom that was shared by all the many generations of people at Onion Portage, even though in other respects their cultures often differed completely.

Even our Eskimo helpers were amazed at the depth of the stratigraphy, for the Denbigh levels lay some five feet deep. Almond Downey had come up from the coast with his family to join us, and John Custer and Wilson Tickett, Eskimo residents of Shungnak, completed our group. We all speculated on the length of time required for so many people, who made arrow and spearpoints in such different ways, to have succeeded each other at this single site at Onion Portage. Almond, almost as familiar as I with the range of Denbigh flaking, was particularly impressed with finding our old and early acquaintances from the coast so well established in this forested environment halfway up the Kobuk River. If the Denbigh people at Onion Portage were contemporary with those on the coast, these layers of former ground surfaces had been camped on at least four or five thousand years ago.

Pausing only briefly to speculate, we continued with our excavations, though at different rates from one block to the next. It soon became apparent that not only had thaw penetrated deep into the ground but the ice had disappeared entirely, and there was no frozen ground below. This was a pleasant surprise, for I had become reconciled to the bit-by-bit thawing. At the depth we had reached we could see that the ground bore only a frozen topping, no more than six feet at most. Once through this zone of frost, we could be free of the strictures imposed by scraping at ice and could excavate as rapidly as the findings in each layer allowed. This advantage was offset somewhat, though, by the fact that the lack of ice meant little or no preservation of perishable materials in the lower levels.

I decided to excavate the older layers myself. First plotting on mapping paper the areas to be examined, I staked out large blocks on the surface and set my companions to work removing sod and trowelling out the upper layers of these squares, each worker carefully recording the exact position of each artifact as it was uncovered along with all other pertinent data. I myself dug deeper each day into my twelve-by-twenty-foot trench.

Band 4, the Denbigh band, had from three to five cultural layers, each within an inch or less of the next over most of the cut. Beneath, there came another sterile layer. What, if any, culture would I find deeper than Denbigh; and was there no limit to the depth of the site? The trowelling seemed painfully slow as I dug ever deeper. Would there, perhaps, be spearheads of the Early Man types of the Great Plains? What chance was there that a notched point like those of Palisades II at Cape Krusenstern might show up to support my proposed dating of that site and give proof to my colleagues that the culture of Palisades II was older than Denbigh?

Under a broad layer of sterile, sandy loam, a fifth band at length revealed itself, lying as deep as seven feet in places below the top of my cut (Fig. 138). As I uncovered its three to five cultural layers, I was struck by the fact that none of these Band 5 levels contained accumulations of stones—that is, there were no large stones outlining a hearth (such as that shown in Fig. 136), nor were there fire-cracked pebbles such as Denbigh people had presumably used for cooking. What few stones there were lay among the flint chips at the edges of the fired areas, suggesting their use as hammers or anvils rather than as hearthstones.

The hearths themselves displayed a feature I had not seen in other fireplaces here or elsewhere: at the base of a thick deposit of charcoal and ash, often containing quantities of white bone meal, there lay frequently a bed of red ocher. The people of Band 5 apparently powdered and distributed a good portion of this substance over the ground before lighting their first fires. In view of the association of red ocher with religious practices, as in the

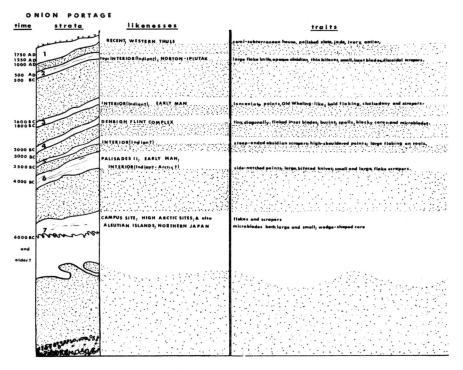

time	strata	likenesses	traits
1750 AD 1250 AD 1000 AD	1	RECENT, WESTERN THULE	semi-subterranean house, polished slate, jade, ivory, antler,
		top INTERIOR(Indian?), NORTON -IPIUTAK	large flake knife, opaque obsidian, thin bifaces, small, inset blades, discoidal scrapers.
500 AD 500 BC	2		
1600 BC 1800 BC	3	INTERIOR(Indian?), EARLY MAN	lanceolate points, Old Whaling-like, bold flaking, chalcedony and scrapers.
		DENBIGH FLINT COMPLEX	tiny, diagonally, flaked inset blades, burins, spalls, blocky cores, and microblades.
2000 BC 3000 BC	4	INTERIOR(Indian?)	steep-ended obsidian scrapers, high-shouldered points, large flaking on tools.
3500 BC 4000 BC	5 6	PALISADES II, EARLY MAN, INTERIOR(Indian? Arctic?)	side-notched points, large, bifaced knives, small and large, flake scrapers.
6000 BC	7	CAMPUS SITE, HIGH ARCTIC SITES, & also ALEUTIAN ISLANDS, NORTHERN JAPAN	flakes and scrapers microblades both large and small, wedge-shaped core
and older?			

138. The bands of culture found at Onion Portage.

burials of many North American Indians and other early people elsewhere in the world, I could not help but wonder if this red base might have had some mystical association with fire in the beliefs of its users.

As I dug more widely, the old ground surfaces of Band 5 slowly gave me an impression of the early hunters who had camped there. An immediate difference between them and their successors, the Denbigh people of Band 4, was that the Band 5 people used neither microblades nor other distinctly Denbigh-like implements, and to an uncommon extent they preferred obsidian as a material. They flaked their tools and weapons rather carefully, but without the deft touch and refinements of the Denbigh craftsmen. Besides large bifaced blades and many end scrapers, two edges of which were usually retouched, the Band 5 artifacts included an intriguing weapon point with a square base that widened toward the center and then drew with a changed angle of the two straight edges to a sharp tip (Fig. 139a). This was a form I had not previously encountered so far north in Alaska, but it proved to be a basic type of projectile point used by Band 5 people.

My trowel now led me deeper, through another relatively sterile section of sandy loam, to still more culture-bearing layers! These, at least twelve in all as viewed along the walls of my excavation, formed Band 6. Most of these layers proved to contain hearths, and at their greatest depth they were some ten feet below the ground surface, so that I was quite hidden from the view of those digging in other areas nearby. The depth I had now reached below such sheer walls caused me a moment or two of worry, in fact, for the sandy walls were by no means guaranteed stable, but then a new excitement drove all else from my mind. With a shout to my fellow workers, I picked up, from one of the upper layers of Band 6, a side-notched point, the first of many subsequently found (Fig. 139b). Here was proof, from ancient layers deep in stratigraphy, that notched points elsewhere so rare in the Arctic were indeed old, and this at once strongly fortified my belief that the notched points found at the Palisades site back beyond all the beach ridges were of equally great age (see Fig. 130). Had we, in the two sites, evidence of a group of people heretofore unknown?

As excavations continued, I could see that now a full comparison between the levels of Onion Portage and the beaches at Cape

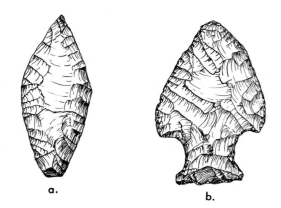

a.

b.

139. Points found in 1963:
a) square-based, high-shouldered weapon point from Band 5
b) side-notched point from Band 6. Length, 2¼ in. (5.6 cm.)

Krusenstern was possible. A culture found in "horizontal stratigraphy" at Cape Krusenstern could be linked in time and placement to the same culture in "vertical stratigraphy" at Onion Portage. For instance, digging from the present ground surface at Onion Portage down to the lower part of Band 2 with Norton artifacts was like walking back from the sea at Cape Krusenstern to Norton Beaches 36–44, 2,000–2,500 years old at both sites. The Band 3 levels at Onion Portage bore artifacts (especially end scrapers) like those of the Old Whaling culture on Beach 53 at Cape Krusenstern, dating around 3,700 years ago.

Farther back at the Cape, the 5,000-year-old Denbigh Beaches 78–104 had microblades and small tools like those in Denbigh Band 4 at Onion Portage. Band 5 had no counterpart on the beach ridges, but seemed to represent a period when Indians had lived there. This was the case, too, in the period represented by the top layer of Band 2, a time more recent than that of Norton people.

Finally, the numerous notched points we soon found in Band 6 gave us the feeling we had crossed all the beaches at Cape Krusenstern and climbed to the top of the Palisades, the more recent artifacts of which I had rather tenuously estimated as dating from barely post-glacial times, perhaps 8,000 years ago. The graphic depth in stratigraphy and consequent great age of these notched points at Onion Portage were the proofs I had hoped for in support of my views of antiquity for the Palisades II notched points, and I must admit feeling lively satisfaction.

OTHER OBJECTS collected from the wide and deep hearths of Band 6 were end scrapers, bifaced knives, and large and small projectile points, the last invariably provided with ground notches near their bases, like the point shown in Fig. 139b. While by no means all these objects were duplicated in the small Palisades II collection, a portion of them were nearly identical. The hearths, some containing quantities of red ocher, as in Band 5, also displayed bone meal, which I now regarded with certainty as a characteristic of the site. Whatever its dating might ultimately prove to be, Band 6 represented a period earlier than all the beach ridges at Cape Krusenstern and was presumably as old as the more recent deposits at the Palisades site.

In the lower layers of Band 6, I found two chopper tools

resembling in general form, if not in detail, those of Palisades I, the older of the two Palisades assemblages. The Onion Portage artifacts, however, had not deteriorated chemically, as they had at Cape Krusenstern, nor were they of the fine-grained materials that had been chosen at the coastal site.

By the end of our month at Onion Portage in 1963 I had pressed two shafts far deeper than the layers of Band 6 but had encountered no more chips. I did find, though, that under a slight depth of sterile loam beneath Band 6 was still another series of horizontal layers, each containing charcoal in quantity and an occasional streak of red ocher, showing that men had camped here at an even earlier time.

The lower part of this band, Band 7, intrigued me the most, for I could see that wide areas of charcoal and red ocher had been folded over and over, as in the solifluction lobes at Cape Denbigh (Fig. 105). Ranging from six inches to two feet in thickness, these folds at Onion Portage marked some phenomenon of weather extremes that had not affected any of the later deposits or those under, at least to a depth of six more feet. I wondered if this might have had to do with a period of climate that was mainly very cold, but interspersed with short periods of warmth, such as would have been the case just as the Wisconsin period of continental glaciation was ending. At any rate, we had indeed penetrated a long way into the past.

Below Band 7, which I felt would undoubtedly reveal flints when there was time for more thorough digging over a wider area, I continued my downward trowelling and found brownish, coarser sands, some displaying limited streaks of charcoal, but none closely similar to the hard-packed surfaces of the layers above.

Finally, at a depth of about seventeen feet, I came to a layer of river gravel, from a few inches to a foot deep, that seemed to mark a time when the river had cut across at the foot of these hills, probably in the path of the "portage" for which the site is named: a distance of two miles, in contrast to the meandering seven that the river now takes. On the gravel lay bits of wood and other organic matter such as one might expect to lodge along a river's edge.

THE RANGE of stratigraphy and the remarkable promise of Onion Portage were thus revealed at the end of that summer of

1963, and the site was never out of mind all winter as we studied the collections in detail at the Haffenreffer Museum.

If a truly Early Man site were to be found anywhere in the interior of Alaska, what more likely candidate could there be than this? Surely the same conditions that brought hundreds of subsequent generations to butcher meat and render bones of herd animals at Onion Portage would have attracted whoever had been in the region in very early times. Finding their oldest sites should tell much of what these people were like, when they were there, and perhaps even where they came from.

As soon as practicable in 1964, I went back to the Kobuk eager to learn what exciting new information the Onion Portage site might hold. My family joined me this time—Bets, Jim, Russ, and Ann—and as student assistants we had John Cook, Roger Hirschland, and Norton Grubb, rounded out by our good Eskimo helpers (Fig. 140). Doug Anderson was there to help early in the season before he flew to the Noatak River north of us to look

140. The 1964 crew at Onion Portage. Left to right: John Cook, Russell Giddings (front foreground), Norton Grubb, Roger Hirschland, Tommy Lee, Truman Cleveland, Shield Downey, and Jim, Bets, and Ann Giddings. The flat area on the right was the floor of a Denbigh camp. Small boxes hold artifacts.

for sites that might tie in with our stratigraphy, and later on Dr. Emil Haury of the University of Arizona joined us at Onion Portage to give us the benefit of his views and experience.

We chose the pleasant, airy, birch-covered ridge top as the place to set up our sleeping tents, and our view of the sharply turning Kobuk was superb. For a change in scene, we had only to look behind, through the trees, to the snow-capped mountains of the Brooks Range. Five and sometimes six Eskimo assistants, together with their families, brought the number of people in our village to more than forty, not to mention the dogs staked out close by.

The Eskimos chose to put their tents along the bank of the river, sheltered by poplars and spruce. Though this denied them our panorama, they could concentrate on the water, watching for signs of fish, protecting their nets from floating pieces of drift, and meeting the many visitors from neighboring villages who ply the river in boats with outboard motors during the summer season. We "hilltop people" maintained a large mess and recreation tent on the gravel near the site, and after dinner in the evenings our youthful members, equipped with guitars, met their Eskimo counterparts over hot chocolate and coffee around the ample roughhewn table.

Difficulties are many in resuming the excavation of a site as deep as this at Onion Portage. The carefully preserved, sheer wall faces of the previous summer are held intact through the winter's freeze, but with the coming of spring thaws the sandy silt layers tend to shift and slide, carrying artifacts and earth down to a great potpourri at the bottom. Before work can resume in the summer, the fallen materials must all be dug out of the pits, and the included artifacts must be abstracted by sifting, then labeled as "mixed," with no proof as to the level from which they originated. Often the bottoms of the pits are filled with water or buried snow, and this must be drained away before the arduous job of removing tons of sifted sand with shovel and wheelbarrow can begin. The prospect of new things to come, though, inspires us to get on with these chores, and when new revelations of artifacts begin to appear, we feel more than repaid.

The 1964 season, as in much of the United States, was unusually dry, and later on, swimming in the river was pleasant for those who did not mind the battalions of mosquitos hovering for attack on shore. The mosquitos were a constant plague. All of us, except John Cook, wore two layers of clothing as protection, no matter how uncomfortable, or how hot the day. John, who served as my chief field assistant that summer, constantly amazed us by working oblivious of these insects, clad only in a T-shirt and trousers. He had previously worked in the eastern Canadian Arctic, and we finally attributed his great unconcern to the fact that he had been immunized by Canadian insects and ours of the Kobuk River now found him untasty.

The dryness of the season made our task of clearing the previous season's excavations somewhat easier, and it was not long before more hearths and camping places of the site's divergent peoples began to appear. It seemed to us that all the residents of Onion Portage throughout the years had been there for the same reasons: to meet the herds of passing animals and procure for themselves the essential meat, fat, and, undoubtedly, skins for bedding, clothing, and tent covers. The bones of small animals and fish in the hearths of all periods testified to the fact that many Onion Portage visitors took advantage of the whole range of seasonal foods available there. Some bones smaller than those of caribou and some that appeared to differ from any of the animals now found at the site suggested that there were small variations in the kinds of game hunted in the earlier periods, and just possibly we shall find bones of extinct species after we have had time to make detailed analyses.

How this layer-cake stratigraphy formed over the years is an interesting speculation. In order to understand it better, we extended trenches to the edge of the riverbank, giving us an increased perspective. I saw that the nearly sterile layers of sandy loam in the deepest parts of the site were the result of a slow creep of soil down the slopes at periodic intervals. This probably occurred during regular spring thaws. In some years storms must have created small avalanches that quickly deposited a thick layer of mud and sand over the leavings of former campers—the sterile layers we now find. Not only would such deposits contain few artifacts, but campers would not inhabit the slopes until the weather again became dependable. The dark strata in our excavations, and the white ones of sand, on the other hand, seem to have formed over long periods lasting for dozens and hundreds of years and they represent the soils under the surface sods at different times.

In cross-cuts across the trenches that reached toward the river's edge, we found that the loam gradually pinched out and the bands tended to come together as they approached the river, then widened again near the water's edge through the inclusion of more white sand. The layers of the bands thus became thin and black, alternating with thick layers of coarse white sand obviously deposited by exceptionally high waters of the river (Fig. 141). The proportions between cultural periods near the river remained essentially the same as those farther back, the bottom of Band 6 throughout the site being nearly as far again below the middle of Band 4, the Denbigh band, as Band 4 was beneath the present surface.

WITH EACH DAY'S WORK we learned increasingly more about the many levels at Onion Portage, and slowly accumulated enough

141. A view of the stratigraphy at Onion Portage in 1964, looking from the hillside out toward the Kobuk River. Note the thick band of silt at the right. This must have been washed downhill during a very rainy period—a time just after Band 4's occupation by Denbigh people. Band numbers are at the right.

flint and sometimes bone and antler artifacts to make possible a sharp definition of cultures for each layer and period. Many of the layers, or periods of continuous layers, formed aspects of culture not yet dignified with names of their own. There was not time in 1964 to expose any layer fully enough to learn its complete story. In future digging, we hope to find a great deal more in the layer containing opaque obsidian in Band 2, just before the Western Thule to modern layers, so that we will see why this phase of culture so sharply contrasts with others in the site. It has no coastal counterpart, and may be evidence that the Onion Portagers of its day accepted no intruders from the coast.

The preceding Norton, Old Hearth, and Denbigh phases correspond in varying degrees to cultures on the coast, but then the deeper Band 5 must be treated as a new form of culture. Were its residents Indians who were eased out when a strong Denbigh people moved up the Kobuk from the sea? And Band 6: its great depth alone is proof of great age; perhaps further excavations will reveal indisputable connections between this band and the Palisades II site at Cape Krusenstern with its similarly notched points.

And what of Band 7? Just when we were becoming discouraged at finding no artifacts, and doubting that we might find a cultural bridge between these ancient levels and cultures of Asia, three live layers turned up deep in the site. Band 7 had given us nothing but trouble for a while. Because of its depth and the consequent sogginess from melting spring snow, we could not dig it much until midsummer. Also, the careful work we were doing in the upper bands prevented our getting down to the top of this dense band except in three small cuts. Finally, when we could, we gingerly began to dig our trowels into its clear-cut layers. The reason for our extreme care was that although no chips had turned up in previous tests, we had found charcoal in three or more of the upper layers—some of it so well preserved as to show the ring structure of the original spruce wood.

Below these upper layers of Band 7 and ranging much deeper in the ground was the curious folded layer or zone that contained in its fold both red ocher and charcoal. The material in the folded layer was claylike and full of rusty inclusions that seemed to have formed about bits of organic matter. This consistency made trowelling difficult in every way, for we could neither clean a surface easily nor cut through at an angle without quickly tiring our wrists.

All our work here was done as cautiously as if we expected momentarily to find diamonds, and we noted that our delicacy in trowelling was soon copied by Eskimos Truman Cleveland and Shield Downey working under Roger's supervision in the upper bands, for they barely moved their wrists as they wielded their trowels.

As we moved down in our separate pits to the bottom of Band 7, past high columns of unexcavated earth, for whole days finding nothing at all, we began to anticipate less and to wish we could concentrate our attention on the upper levels where artifacts and chips lent continuing interest and rewarded our efforts. The mere labor of hauling the heavy back dirt up and out of our deep pits, step by step, to a place where Jim could load it in a wheelbarrow and cart it away, became more and more tedious. However, we reminded ourselves how ancient the band must be, and hope of finding an artifact of great antiquity never left us.

JUST TWO WEEKS before the 1964 season ended, I was aroused one morning from my work in a very small pit by noise from the greater excavation where most of the crew labored. Something had been found in Band 7, came the excited report. Unlikely though it seemed, in view of our previous disappointments, I hastened over to check. Roger Hirschland held a chert artifact, while the others gathered to hear my opinion. It was without doubt a segment of a microblade core. At first I thought there must be some error, as we had found no trace of microblade technology in all of Band 6 and most of Band 5, yet something kept me from saying this. I examined the object again, checked the circumstances of its finding, and assured myself that it had indeed come from Band 7. The core fragment was evidently the cap from which microblades had been struck, but unlike cores with which I was familiar, this one had as one of its two broad faces a natural plane caused by a thin dike, or fault, of quartz in the original rock. As it was neither a broad-topped Denbigh-type core (Fig. 102), nor one of the narrow, wedge-shaped cores known from the Campus site or the Gobi Desert, the fragment was baffling.

For the next few hours, as the rest of us continued our fruitless digging, we all cast expectant glances toward Roger to see what more he could find. Soon he turned up small flakes in two upper layers of Band 7 and also in the folded layer of solifluction from which his core cap had come. Then later that same afternoon he found two more pieces, one apparently a large microblade and the other a wedge-shaped fragment. I saw at once that the latter had one flat face, and on examining the three pieces together, found that they were all parts of a single microblade core (Fig. 142), one segment of which—another thick microblade—was still missing.

John Cook suggested that this core resembled certain ones from the Anangula site of the Aleutian Islands that we had recently seen in the collections of the University of Alaska when we had stopped at Fairbanks en route to Onion Portage, and that it also resembled photographs of cores from the pre-pottery sites of Hokkaido, in northernmost Japan. The treatment of the striking plat-

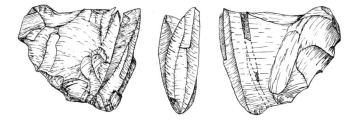

142. Three views of the microcore (as reconstructed) found in the deepest cultural level at Onion Portage in 1964. Height, 1¾ in. (4.6 cm.).

form of this piece was similar to that of the Aleutian, the Japanese, and the Campus site cores. The Japanese pieces are called Shirataki keeled scrapers, and were used by people 11,000 years ago. Later in the fall we learned that Doug Anderson had found a number of nearly identical cores farther north on high terraces along the Noatak River.

The Aleutian Island specimens aroused our particular speculation that day, however, for until recently it had been difficult to tie Bering Strait archeology directly to that of the Aleutians in any of the later periods, including that of the Denbigh Flint complex. Then tests made by William Laughlin, archeologist, Robert Black, geologist, and their associates deep in a stratified sandbank on Anangula Island showed curious burins unlike any known from northern Alaska because of a blow struck across the end rather than at steep angles or along lateral edges. These burins were associated with thick microblades of varying lengths and with cores ranging from conical to narrow and asymmetrical.

While our core was not as close to any of these as it was to the Japanese examples, the radiocarbon dates for the Anangula artifacts indicated an age of more than 8,000 years ago, and this in itself was stimulating for the possibilities suggested. According to Anangula's excavators, toward the end of the last glacial period the site was connected not only to the neighboring large island of Umnak but also, in all probability, to the whole combined continent of Asia and America near the edge of the "land bridge" that existed because of lower sea level. In those remote ages of a land bridge between continents, and with few barriers to travel, a somewhat uniform culture was conceivable for the whole area. This view might be strongly reinforced with the finding of a real kinship in flints between diverse Arctic sites at a very early period.

In later, postglacial times, when water covered the land bridge and the vast Bering and Chukchi seas separated the peoples of the Aleutians, Asia, and Alaska from one another, a lack of rapport in flint technology became readily understandable, for not only had contact between former neighbors become difficult, if not impossible, but their adaptations to divergent climates and habitats would eventually have erased whatever similarities they had once shared. So we trowelled a bit more urgently here at this spot that had been host to so many generations of hunters.

Our hope of quickly establishing some far-ranging connections in culture, and learning the meaning of this microblade technology in the lower bands of Onion Portage was short-lived, however. No new, definitive artifact came to light in our last few days at the site that summer. More microblades, it is true, did turn up in the lowest culture layer, and these were the thick, narrow ones that we now anticipated from the shape of the reconstructed core, but despite our eager trowelling nothing else that was different appeared.

At least we did now have evidence of two kinds from deep within the site. First, the core and microblades were proof that these layers had been trodden by man in some very ancient time; and, second, we had the geological evidence that man had been at Onion Portage long before the strange folding phenomenon of Band 7 took place—a hint that this band did, indeed, lie far back in the history of mankind in America. For further answers about early men at the site, we would have to return to Onion Portage another season.

Reluctantly we packed up the artifacts for shipment to Rhode Island, distributed a few excess cans of food equally among our Eskimo friends who then headed homeward, and waited for the float plane that would come to take the students away first. After they had left and we were alone, my family and I stood at dawn a day or so later waiting for our own plane to touch gently down on the calm water at the bend of the river. As we admired the sunrise, we also regarded speculatively the deep gashes we had made in the side of the hill and the sheer faces of our excavations. The deepest went down twenty feet below the present surface, into the gravel of the old riverbed, and we wondered what we would learn in seasons to come when every layer of every band had been dug out inch by inch.

What kind of people had made the microblade core and discarded it on the ground of Band 7? And what else might they have left for us to find in reconstructing their culture? Was it possible that even earlier people had been at the site whose leavings we would uncover when all the levels were taken down, perhaps to the original surface? And how would the objects from Onion Portage fit in with all the other known cultures throughout the Arctic and for thousands of miles to the east, south, and west?

We could only regret the short length of the digging season and look forward with pleasure to the study of the artifacts at the Haffenreffer Museum over the winter and then a joyous return to the Kobuk in 1965 for a further picking of its secrets and treasures.

EPILOGUE

THE UNTIMELY DEATH of Dr. Giddings in December 1964 was a great loss to American archeology. His unfinished work and questions have become the legacy of others. In the 1965 season Brown University, supported by a grant from the National Science Foundation, returned an archeological expedition to the Onion Portage site. Leader of this expedition was Dr. Giddings's longtime friend, Dr. Froelich Rainey, director of the University Museum, Philadelphia, assisted by Mr. Douglas D. Anderson of Brown University, Mrs. J. L. Giddings, curator of the Haffenreffer Museum, and Dr. Sten Florin, geologist of the University of Uppsala, Sweden.

Tons of earth were laboriously removed with shovels and trowels by expedition members as they enlarged and deepened the excavations of previous years. Foremost among the new findings was the uncovering of three Denbigh houses—the first definitely known to have been inhabited by Denbigh people—probably the oldest houses in the Arctic. Two were found in Band 4, the Denbigh band, and the other, still older, in the topmost level of Band 5. The Band 4 houses, though now of course fallen to ruins, had been built in a circular area excavated to a foot in depth. Around the perimeter, the Denbigh people had placed poles upright against the low wall, pulling the ends of the rods together at the top to form a dome, and covering the exterior with skins or bark, making a commodious house with a central fireplace. The house floors were richly scattered with typical Denbigh artifacts: small, finely executed arrowpoints, side blades, and burins. The still older house, some two and a half feet deeper, was rectangular in outline, with rounded corners, though otherwise similarly constructed. Probably a "first generation" of Denbigh people had lived here, for the implements found on the house floor, though of a Denbigh type, were more crudely made than those of their successors in the Denbigh band proper.

As excavations continued, it was seen that the deepest band, 7, of 1964 really was separable into two distinct bands, each with many layers. Thus Band 8 became the lowermost band, and it was from this section that the ancient, perhaps 8,000-year-old core was found the season before. In 1965, chips and microblades were retrieved from the earliest levels, and a number of thick pockets of charcoal from man-made hearths were found. Band 7 has so far given little, but other bands in 1965 continued to yield profuse quantities of things unwittingly left by the site's many inhabitants. Samples of charcoal from all levels are being tested by the radiocarbon method, obsidian artifacts will be treated and examined for age, and soil samples will be analyzed for their contents—the combined findings, together with the archeology, giving the most reliable proofs possible in dating the many cultures at Onion Portage.

Yet much more may be learned, for fully half the site's contents lie still buried beneath the soil. As this volume goes to press, Douglas Anderson for Brown University is making plans for another two years of digging at Onion Portage and along the Kobuk River, and very possibly these new seasons' finds will, as Dr. Giddings hoped, clearly tie together the Onion Portage, Cape Krusenstern, and other sites, both coastal and inland, both Eskimo and Indian, allowing the writing of many chapters of prehistory. Perhaps, too, unsuspected new things are yet to come from the remarkably stratified site that is Onion Portage.

EDITOR

BIBLIOGRAPHY

Chapter II • A SEARCH FOR OLD BEACHES

COLLINS, HENRY B.
 1932. "Prehistoric Eskimo Culture on St. Lawrence Island,"*Geographical Review*, Vol. 22, No. 1. New York.
 1937. *Archeology of St. Lawrence Island, Alaska.* See Ch. VIII.

ELLIOTT, HENRY W.
 1887. *Our Arctic Province, Alaska and the Seal Islands.* New York.

GIDDINGS, J. L.
 1957. "Round Houses in the Western Arctic." See Ch. X.
 1960. "The Archeology of Bering Strait," *Current Anthropology*, Vol. 1, No. 2. Chicago.
 1960. "First Traces of Man in the Arctic," *Natural History*, Vol. 69, No. 9. New York.
 1961. "Cultural Continuities of Eskimos," *American Antiquity*, Vol. 27, No. 2. Salt Lake City.
 1964. *The Archeology of Cape Denbigh.* See Ch. XII.
 1966. "Cross-Dating the Archeology of Northwestern Alaska," *Science*, Vol. 153, No. 3732. Washington.

HENRY, THOMAS R.
 1955. "Ice Age Man, the First American," *National Geographic*, Vol. 108, No. 6. Washington.

LARSEN, HELGE
 1951. "De Dansk-amerikanske Alaska-ekspeditioner 1949–50," *Geografisk Tidsskrift*, 51 Bind. Copenhagen.
 1961. "Archaeology in the Arctic, 1935–60," *American Antiquity*, Vol. 27, No. 1. Salt Lake City.

LARSEN, HELGE and FROELICH RAINEY
  1948. *Ipiutak and the Arctic Whale Hunting Culture.* See Ch. VI.

MOORE, G. W. and J. L. GIDDINGS
  1962. "Record of 5000 Years of Arctic Wind Direction Recorded by Alaskan Beach Ridges," *Geological Society of America Special Paper No. 68.* New York.

VON KOTZEBUE, OTTO
  1821. *A Voyage of Discovery into the South Sea and Beering's Straits for the Purpose of Exploring a North-east Passage, undertaken in the years 1815–1818, etc.* London.

Chapter III • THE OUTER BEACH AND THE CHANGING ESKIMOS

BEECHEY, FREDERICK WILLIAM
  1832. *Narrative of a Voyage to the Pacific and Beering's Strait to Cooperate with the Polar Expeditions: performed in His Majesty's Ship Blossom . . . in the years 1825, 1826, 1827, and 1828.* Philadelphia.

COOK, JAMES and JAMES KING
  1784. *A Voyage to the Pacific Ocean . . . to Determine the Position and Extent of the West Side of North America, etc.,* Vol. 3. London.

DU HALDE, J. B.
  1736. *The General History of China.* London.

ELLIOTT, HENRY W.
  1887. See Ch. II.

GIDDINGS, J. L.
  1952. "Driftwood and Problems of Arctic Sea Currents," *Proceedings of the American Philosophical Society,* Vol. 96, No. 2. Philadelphia.

GOLDER, F. A.
  1914. *Russian Expansion on the Pacific, 1641–1851: An Account of the Earliest and Later Expeditions Made by the Russians along the Pacific Coast of Asia and North America, etc.* Cleveland.

MAGUIRE, ROCHFORD
  1854. "Proceedings of Commander Maguire, H. M. Discovery Ship 'Plover,'" *Parliamentary Reports, 1854,* No. XLII. London.

PIM, BEDFORD
  1863. *The Gate of the Pacific.* London.

SAUER, MARTIN
  1802. *An Account of the Geographical and Astronomical Expedition to the Northern Part of Russia . . . Performed by Captain Billings in the years 1785–94.* London.

SEEMANN, BERTHOLD
  1853. *Narrative of the Voyage of H.M.S. Herald, during the years 1845–51,* Vol. 2. London.

VON KOTZEBUE, OTTO
  1821. See Ch. II.

ZAGOSKIN, L. A.
  1847. *Account of Pedestrian Journeys in the Russian Possessions in America.* St. Petersburg.

Chapter IV • THULE: ARCTIC ARCHEOLOGY BEGINS

BIRKET-SMITH, KAJ
  1929. *The Caribou Eskimos,* Report of the Fifth Thule Expedition 1921–24, Vol. 5. Copenhagen.
  1945. *Ethnographical Collections from the Northwest Passage,* Report of the Fifth Thule Expedition 1921–24, Vol. 6, No. 2. Copenhagen.
  1959. *The Eskimos.* London.

BOAS, FRANZ
  1964. *The Central Eskimo.* Lincoln, Nebraska.

CRANZ, DAVID
  1767. *The History of Greenland: Continuing a Description of the Country,* etc. London.

FREUCHEN, PETER
  1935. *Arctic Adventure.* New York.

GIDDINGS, J. L.
  1962. "Seven Discoveries of Bering Strait," *Proceedings of the American Philosophical Society,* Vol. 106, No. 2. Philadelphia.

MATHIASSEN, THERKEL
  1927. *Archaeology of the Central Eskimos,* Report of the Fifth Thule Expedition 1921–24, Vol. 4, Parts 1 and 2. Copenhagen.
  1928. *Material Culture of the Iglulik Eskimos,* Report of the Fifth Thule Expedition 1921–24, Vol. 6, No. 1. Copenhagen.
  1930. *Archaeological Collections from the Western Eskimos,* Report of the Fifth Thule Expedition 1921–24, Vol. 10, No. 1. Copenhagen.

RASMUSSEN, KNUD

1927. *Across Arctic America*. New York and London.

1930. *Intellectual Culture of the Caribou Eskimos*, Report of the Fifth Thule Expedition 1921–24, Vol. 7, Nos. 2 and 3. Copenhagen.

1931. *The Netsilik Eskimos*, Report of the Fifth Thule Expedition 1921–24, Vol. 8, Nos. 1 and 2. Copenhagen.

1932. *Intellectual Culture of the Copper Eskimos*, Report of the Fifth Thule Expedition 1921–24, Vol. 9. Copenhagen.

1942. *The Mackenzie Eskimos*, ed. H. Ostermann; Report of the Fifth Thule Expedition 1921–24, Vol. 10, No. 2. Copenhagen.

1952. *The Alaskan Eskimos*, ed. H. Ostermann; Report of the Fifth Thule Expedition 1921–24, Vol. 10, No. 3. Copenhagen.

RINK, HENRY

1887. *The Eskimo Tribes*, Meddelelser om Grønland, Vol. 2. Copenhagen and London.

STEENSBY, H. P.

1917. *An Anthropogeographical Study of the Origin of the Eskimo Culture*, Meddelelser om Grønland, Vol. 53. Copenhagen.

Chapter V • WESTERN THULE

COLLINS, HENRY B.

1937. "Cultural Migrations and Contacts in the Bering Sea Region," *American Anthropologist*, Vol. 39, No. 3, Part 1. Menasha.

1940. "Outline of Eskimo Prehistory," *Smithsonian Miscellaneous Collections*, Vol. 100. Washington.

1954. *Arctic Area*, Program of the History of America, Vol. 1, No. 2. Comision de Historia. Mexico.

1956. "The Tl Site at Native Point, Southampton Island, N. W. T.," *Anthropological Papers of the University of Alaska*, Vol. 4, No. 2. College.

FORD, JAMES A.

1959. *Eskimo Prehistory in the Vicinity of Point Barrow, Alaska*, Anthropological Papers of the American Museum of Natural History, Vol. 47, Part 1. New York.

HOLTVED, ERIK

1954. *Archaeological Investigations in the Thule District. III Nûgdlît, and Comer's Midden*, Meddelelser om Grønland, Vol. 146, No. 3. Copenhagen.

JENNESS, DIAMOND

1928. "Archaeological Investigation in Bering Strait," *Annual Report of the National Museum of Canada 1926*, Bulletin 50. Ottawa.

LARSEN, HELGE
 1961. "Archaeology in the Arctic, 1935–60," *American Antiquity*, Vol. 27, No. 1. Salt Lake City.

MASON, J. ALDEN
 1930. "Excavations of Eskimo Thule Culture Sites at Point Barrow, Alaska," *Proceedings of the 23rd International Congress of Americanists*. New York.

MATHIASSEN, THERKEL
 1927. See Ch. IV.
 1930. See Ch. IV.
 1958. *The Sermermiut Excavations 1955*, Meddelelser om Grønland, Vol. 161, No. 3. Copenhagen.

MELDGAARD, JØRGEN
 1960. "Origin and Evolution of Eskimo Cultures in the Eastern Arctic," *Canadian Geographic Journal*, Vol. 60, No. 2. Montreal.

NELSON, E. W.
 1899. See Ch. VI.

STEFANSSON, VILHJALMUR
 1914. "The Stefansson-Anderson Arctic Expedition of the American Museum: Preliminary Ethnological Report," *Anthropological Papers of the American Museum of Natural History*, Vol. 14, Part 1. New York.

TAYLOR, WILLIAM E., JR.
 1963. "Hypotheses on the Origin of Canadian Thule Culture," *American Antiquity*, Vol. 28, No. 4. Salt Lake City.

Chapter VI • THE ARTISTS AND MAGICIANS OF IPIUTAK

BAROVKA, GREGORY
 1928. *Scythian Art*. London.

CHARD, CHESTER S.
 1958. "An Outline of the Prehistory of Siberia; Part 1, the Pre-Metal Periods," *Southwestern Journal of Anthropology*, Vol. 14, No. 1. Albuquerque.
 1960. "Recent Archaeological Work in the Chukchi Peninsula," *Anthropological Papers of the University of Alaska*, Vol. 8, No. 2. College.
 1963. "The Old World Roots: Review and Speculations," *Anthropological Papers of the University of Alaska*, Vol. 10, No. 2. College.

GIDDINGS, J. L.
 1940. "The Application of Tree-Ring Dates to Arctic Sites," *Tree-Ring*

Bulletin, Vol. 7, No. 2. University of Arizona, Tucson.

1941. *Dendrochronology in Northern Alaska*, University of Arizona Bulletin, Vol. 12, No. 4. Tucson.

1962. "Development of Tree-Ring Dating as an Archeological Aid," in *Tree Growth*, ed. Theodore T. Kozlowski. New York.

JENNESS, DIAMOND
1957. *Dawn in Arctic Alaska*. Minneapolis.

JOCHELSON, WALDEMAR
1910–26. *The Yukaghir and Yukaghirized Tungus*, Memoirs of the American Museum of Natural History, Vol. 13, Part 2. New York.

LARSEN, HELGE
1954. "The Position of Ipiutak in Eskimo Culture," *American Antiquity*, Vol. 20, No. 1. Salt Lake City.

LARSEN, HELGE and FROELICH RAINEY
1948. See Ch. II.

LEVIN, M. G.
1963. *Ethnic Origins of the Peoples of Northeastern Asia*, Arctic Institute of North America, Anthropology of the North; Translations from Russian Sources No. 3, ed. Henry N. Michael. Toronto.

MICHAEL, HENRY N.
1958. *The Neolithic Age in Eastern Siberia*, Transactions of the American Philosophical Society, Vol. 48, Part 2. Philadelphia.

MURDOCH, JOHN
1892. *Ethnological Results of the Point Barrow Expedition*, Bureau of American Ethnology, 9th Annual Report. Washington.

NELSON, E. W.
1899. *The Eskimo about Bering Strait*, Bureau of American Ethnology, 18th Annual Report, Part 1. Washington.

OKLADNIKOV, A. P.
1959. *Ancient Population of Siberia and Its Cultures*, Russian Translation Series of the Peabody Museum of Archaeology and Ethnology, Harvard University, Vol. 1, No. 1. Cambridge.

RASMUSSEN, KNUD
1952. See Ch. IV.

STALLINGS, W. S.
1949. *Dating Prehistoric Ruins by Tree-Rings*, The Tree-Ring Society. University of Arizona, Tucson.

VAN STONE, JAMES W.
1962. *Point Hope: An Eskimo Village in Transition*, American Ethnological Society. Seattle.

Chapter VII • IPIUTAK BEACHES

BANDI, HANS-GEORG and JOHANNES MARINGER
1953. *Art of the Ice Age.* New York.

BANDI, HANS-GEORG and JØRGEN MELDGAARD
1952. *Archaeological Investigations on Clavering Ø, Northeast Green-land,* Meddelelser om Grønland, Vol. 126, No. 4. Copenhagen.

CRANZ, DAVID
1767. See Ch. IV.

GIDDINGS, J. L.
1960. See Ch. II.

GIDDINGS, J. L. and HANS-GEORG BANDI
1962. "Eskimo-archaologische Strandwalluntersuchungen auf Kap Krusenstern Nordwest-Alaska," *Germania,* Vol. 40, No. 1. Halb-band.

HEIZER, ROBERT F.
1947. "Petroglyphs from Southwestern Kodiak Island, Alaska," *Proceedings of the American Philosophical Society,* Vol. 91, No. 3. Philadelphia.
1952. "Incised Slate Figurines from Kodiak Island, Alaska," *American Antiquity,* Vol. 17, No. 3. Salt Lake City.

JOCHELSON, WALDEMAR
1910–26. See Ch. VI.

DE LAGUNA, FREDERICA
1947. *The Prehistory of Northern North America as Seen from the Yukon,* Memoirs of the Society for American Archaeology, No. 3; Supplement to *American Antiquity,* Vol. 12, No. 3, Part 2. Menasha.

LARSEN, HELGE and FROELICH, RAINEY
1948. See Ch. II.

Chapter VIII • WIDENING HORIZONS

COLLINS, HENRY B.
1930. "Prehistoric Eskimo Culture in Alaska," *Smithsonian Institution Explorations and Field-work, 1929.* Washington.
1935. "Archeology of the Bering Sea Region," *Annual Report of the Smithsonian Institution, 1933.* Washington.
1937. *Archeology of St. Lawrence Island, Alaska,* Smithsonian Miscellaneous Collections, Vol. 96, No. 1. Washington.

1951. "The Origin and Antiquity of the Eskimo," *Annual Report of the Smithsonian Institution, 1950.* Washington.

GEIST, OTTO WILLIAM and FROELICH G. RAINEY
1936. *Archaeological Excavations at Kukulik, St. Lawrence Island, Alaska,* Miscellaneous Publications of the University of Alaska, Vol. 2. Washington.

HOOPER, C. L.
1882. "The Cruise of the Corwin," *The Californian,* Vol. 5, Parts 1 and 2. San Francisco.

HRDLIČKA, ALEŠ
1930. "Anthropological Survey of Alaska," *46th Annual Report of the Bureau of American Ethnology.* Washington.

JENNESS, DIAMOND
1922. "The Life of the Copper Eskimos," *Report of the Canadian Arctic Expedition 1913–18,* Vol. 12. Ottawa.
1928. See Ch. V.
1929. "Little Diomede Island, Bering Strait," *Geographical Review,* Vol. 19, No. 1. New York.
1941. "Prehistoric Culture Waves from Asia to America," *Annual Report of the Smithsonian Institution, 1940.* Washington.
1946. "Material Culture of the Copper Eskimo," *Report of the Canadian Arctic Expedition 1913–18,* Vol. 16. Ottawa.

LEVIN, M. G.
1963. See Ch. VI.

MUIR, JOHN
1917. *The Cruise of the Corwin.* Boston and New York.

NELSON, E. W.
1899. See Ch. VI.

RUDENKO, S. I.
1961. *The Ancient Culture of the Bering Sea and the Eskimo Problem,* trans. Paul Tolstoy; Arctic Institute of North America, Anthropology of the North; Translations from Russian Sources No. 1. Toronto.

STEFANSSON, VILHJALMUR
1913. *My Life with the Eskimo.* New York.
1914. See Ch. V.

A few sources on the Dorset culture:

COLLINS, HENRY B.
1956. See Ch. V.
1958. "Present Status of the Dorset Problem," *Proceedings of the 32nd*

International Congress of Americanists, Copenhagen, 1956.
Copenhagen.

1962. "Bering Strait to Greenland," in 'Prehistoric Cultural Relations
Between the Arctic and Temperate Zones of North America,' ed.
J. M. Campbell; *Arctic Institute of North America Technical
Paper No. 11.* Montreal.

1963. "Paleo-Indian Artifacts in Alaska: An Example of Cultural Retardation in the Arctic," *Anthropological Papers of the University of Alaska,* Vol. 10, No. 2. College.

HARP, ELMER, JR.

1953. "New World Affinities of Cape Dorset Eskimo Culture," *Anthropological Papers of the University of Alaska,* Vol. 1, No. 2.
College.

1964. *The Cultural Affinities of the Newfoundland Dorset Eskimo,*
National Museum of Canada, Bulletin 200. Ottawa.

JENNESS, DIAMOND

1925. "A New Eskimo Culture in Hudson Bay," *Geographical Review,*
Vol. 15, No. 3. New York.

KNUTH, EIGIL

1952. See Ch. XII.
1954. See Ch. XII.
1958. See Ch. XII.

LARSEN, HELGE

1938. *Archaeological Investigations in Knud Rasmussen's Land,* Meddelelser om Grønland, Vol. 119, No. 8. Copenhagen.

LARSEN, HELGE and JØRGEN MELDGAARD

1958. *Paleo-Eskimo Cultures in Disko Bugt, West Greenland,* Meddelelser om Grønland, Vol. 161, No. 2. Copenhagen.

LAUGHLIN, WILLIAM S. and WILLIAM E. TAYLOR, JR.

1960. "A Cape Dorset Culture Site on the West Coast of Ungava Bay,"
*National Museum of Canada Bulletin No. 167, Anthropological
Series No. 48.* Ottawa.

MATHIASSEN, THERKEL

1958. See Ch. V.

MAXWELL, MOREAU S.

1962. "Pre-Dorset and Dorset Sites in the Vicinity of Lake Harbour,
Baffin Island, N. W. T.," *National Museum of Canada Bulletin
No. 180,* Contributions to Anthropology, 1960, Part 1. Ottawa.

MELDGAARD, JØRGEN

1952. "A Paleo-Eskimo Culture in West Greenland," *American Antiquity,* Vol. 17, No. 3. Salt Lake City.

1960. See Ch. V.

1962. "On the Formative Period of the Dorset Culture," in 'Prehistoric Cultural Relations Between the Arctic and Temperate Zones of North America,' ed. J. M. Campbell; *Arctic Institute of North America Technical Paper No. 11.* Montreal.

TAYLOR, WILLIAM E., JR.

1959. "Review and Assessment of the Dorset Problem," *Anthropologica,* Vol. 1, Nos. 1 and 2. Ottawa.

1962. "Pre-Dorset Occupations at Ivugivik in Northwestern Ungava," in 'Prehistoric Cultural Relations Between the Arctic and Temperate Zones of North America,' ed. J. M. Campbell; *Arctic Institute of North America Technical Paper No. 11.* Montreal.

1962. "Comments on the Nature and Origin of the Dorset Culture," in 'Problems of the Pleistocene and Arctic,' *Publications of McGill University Museums,* Vol. 2, No. 2. Montreal.

Chapter IX • NORTON BEACHES

GIDDINGS, J. L.
1961. See Ch. II.
1964. See Ch. XII.

LARSEN, HELGE and FROELICH RAINEY
1948. See Ch. II.

Chapter X • CHORIS

GIDDINGS, J. L.
1957. "Round Houses in the Western Arctic," *American Antiquity,* Vol. 23, No. 2. Salt Lake City.
1960. "First Traces of Man in the Arctic." See Ch. II.
1961. See Ch. II.

LARSEN, HELGE
1963. "The Trail Creek Caves on Seward Peninsula, Alaska," *Proceedings of the 34th International Congress of Americanists, Vienna, 1960.* London.

WORMINGTON, H. M.
1957. See Ch. XII.

Chapter XI • OLD WHALERS

GIDDINGS, J. L.
1961. See Ch. II.
1962. "Side-notched Points Near Bering Strait," in 'Prehistoric Cul-

tural Relations Between the Arctic and Temperate Zones of North America,' ed. J. M. Campbell; *Arctic Institute of North America Technical Paper No. 11*. Montreal.
1966. See Ch. II.

HEIZER, ROBERT F.
1943. "Aconite Poison Whaling in Asia and America, an Aleutian Transfer to the New World," *Bureau of American Ethnology Bulletin 133*. Washington.

MURDOCH, JOHN
1892. See Ch. VI.

RADIOCARBON
1966. Vol. 8, ed. Edward S. Deevey, Richard F. Flint, Irving Rouse. New Haven.

RAINEY, FROELICH G.
1947. "The Whale Hunters of Tigara," *Anthropological Papers of the American Museum of Natural History*, Vol. 41, Part 2. New York.

Chapter XII • DENBIGH

CAMPBELL, JOHN M.
1962. "Cultural Succession at Anaktuvuk Pass, Arctic Alaska," in 'Prehistoric Cultural Relations Between the Arctic and Temperate Zones of North America,' *Arctic Institute of North America Technical Paper No. 11*. Montreal.

COLLINS, HENRY B.
See Ch. VIII (Dorset).

GIDDINGS, J. L.
1951. "The Denbigh Flint Complex," *American Antiquity*, Vol. 16, No. 3. Salt Lake City.
1956. "The Burin Spall Artifact," *Arctic*, Vol. 9, No. 4. Ottawa.
1964. *The Archeology of Cape Denbigh*. Providence.
1966. See Ch. II.

HARP, ELMER, JR.
1958. "Prehistory in the Dismal Lake Area, N. W. T.," *Arctic*, Vol. 11. No. 4. Montreal.
See also Ch. VIII (Dorset).

HOPKINS, DAVID M. and J. L. GIDDINGS
1953. "Geological Background of the Iyatayet Archeological Site, Cape Denbigh, Alaska," *Smithsonian Miscellaneous Collections*, Vol. 121, No. 11. Washington.

IRVING, WILLIAM
    1951. "Archaeology in the Brooks Range of Alaska," *American Antiquity*, Vol. 17, No. 1. Salt Lake City.

KNUTH, EIGIL
    1952. "An Outline of the Archaeology of Peary Land," *Arctic*, Vol. 5, No. 1. Ottawa.
    1954. "The Paleo-Eskimo Culture of Northeast Greenland Elucidated by Three New Sites," *American Antiquity*, Vol. 19, No. 4. Salt Lake City.
    1958. "Archaeology of the Farthest North," *Proceedings of the 32nd International Congress of Americanists, Copenhagen, 1956.* Copenhagen.

LARSEN, HELGE
    1938. See Ch. VIII (Dorset).

LARSEN, HELGE and JØRGEN MELDGAARD
    1958. See Ch. VIII (Dorset).

MACNEISH, RICHARD S.
    1956. "The Engigstciak Site on the Yukon Arctic Coast," *Anthropological Papers of the University of Alaska*, Vol. 4, No. 2. College.
    1959. "Men Out of Asia; As Seen from the Northwest Yukon," *Anthropological Papers of the University of Alaska*, Vol. 7, No. 2. College.
    1962. "Recent Finds in the Yukon Territory of Canada," in 'Prehistoric Cultural Relations Between the Arctic and Temperate Zones of North America,' ed. J. M. Campbell; *Arctic Institute of North America Technical Paper No. 11.* Montreal.

MARINGER, JOHN
    1950. "Contributions to the Prehistory of Mongolia," Publication 34, *The Sino-Swedish Expedition.* Stockholm.

MATHIASSEN, THERKEL
    1958. See Ch. V.

MAXWELL, MOREAU S.
    1962. See Ch. VIII (Dorset).

MELDGAARD, JØRGEN
    1952. See Ch. VIII (Dorset).

NELSON, N. C.
    1937. "Notes on Cultural Relations Between Asia and America," *American Antiquity*, Vol. 2, No. 4. Menasha.

OAKLEY, KENNETH P.
    1959. *Man the Tool-Maker.* Chicago.

RAINEY, FROELICH G.
  1939. "Archaeology in Central Alaska," *Anthropological Papers of the American Museum of Natural History*, Vol. 36, Part 4. New York.

SKARLAND, IVAR and J. L. GIDDINGS
  1948. "Flint Stations in Central Alaska," *American Antiquity*, Vol. 14, No. 2. Menasha.

SOLECKI, RALPH S.
  1951. "Notes on Two Archaeological Discoveries in Alaska, 1950," *American Antiquity*, Vol. 17, No. 1. Salt Lake City.
  1951. "Archaeology and Ecology of the Arctic Slope," *Annual Report of the Smithsonian Institution*, 1950. Washington.

TAYLOR, WILLIAM E., JR.
  1962. See Ch. VIII (Dorset).

WORMINGTON, H. M.
  1957. *Ancient Man in North America*, Denver Museum of Natural History Popular Series No. 4. Denver.
  1963. "The Paleo-Indian and Meso-Indian Stages of Alberta, Canada," *Anthropological Papers of the University of Alaska*, Vol. 10, No. 2. College.

Chapter XIII • THE INTERIOR—INDIAN OR ESKIMO

GIDDINGS, J. L.
  1954. "Tree-Ring Dating in the American Arctic," *Tree-Ring Bulletin*, Vol. 20, Nos. 3 and 4. Tucson.
  1954. "Early Man in the Arctic," *Scientific American*, Vol. 190, No. 6. New York.
  1956. "A Flint Site in Northernmost Manitoba," *American Antiquity*, Vol. 121, No. 3. Salt Lake City.

Chapter XIV • ARCTIC WOODLANDERS

GIDDINGS, J. L.
  1941. See Ch. VI.
  1944. "Dated Eskimo Ruins of an Inland Zone," *American Antiquity*, Vol. 10, No. 2. Menasha.
  1948. "Chronology of the Kobuk-Kotzebue Sites," *Tree-Ring Bulletin*, Vol. 14, No. 4. Tucson.
  1952. *The Arctic Woodland Culture of the Kobuk River*. Museum Monographs, University Museum. Philadelphia.

1956. *Forest Eskimos*, University Museum Bulletin, Vol. 20, No. 2. *Anthropological Papers of the University of Alaska*, Vol. 6, No.

1961. *Kobuk River People*, Studies of Northern Peoples, No. 1. College, Alaska.

Chapter XV • BEFORE BEACH RIDGES

CAMPBELL, JOHN M.
1959. "The Kayuk Complex of Arctic Alaska," *American Antiquity*, Vol. 25, No. 1. Salt Lake City.

1961. "The Tuktu Complex of Anaktuvuk Pass," *Anthropological Papers of the University of Alaska*, Vol. 9, No. 2. College.

1961. "The Kogruk Complex of Anaktuvuk Pass, Alaska," *Anthropologica*, Vol. 3, No. 1. Ottawa.

1962. See Ch. VIII (Dorset).

1963. See Ch. VIII (Dorset).

GIDDINGS, J. L.
1960. "First Traces of Man in the Arctic." See Ch. II.

1961. See Ch. II.

1962. See Ch. XI.

1966. See Ch. XVI.

HAAG, WILLIAM G.
1962. "The Bering Strait Land Bridge," *Scientific American*, Vol. 206, No. 1. New York.

HOPKINS, DAVID M.
1959. "Cenozoic History of the Bering Land Bridge," *Science*, Vol. 129, No. 3362. Washington.

IRVING, WILLIAM
1951. See Ch. XII.

1957. "An Archaeological Survey of the Susitna Valley," *Anthropological Papers of the University of Alaska*, Vol. 6, No. 1. College.

MacNEISH, RICHARD S.
1954. "The Pointed Mountain Site near Fort Liard, Northwest Territories, Canada," *American Antiquity*, Vol. 19, No. 3. Salt Lake City.

1962. See Ch. XII.

RAINEY, FROELICH G.
1939. See Ch. XII.

SKARLAND, IVAR and CHARLES J. KEIM
1958. "Archaeological Discoveries on the Denali Highway, Alaska,"

Anthropological Papers of the University of Alaska, Vol. 6, No. 2. College.

SOLECKI, RALPH S.
1951. See Ch. XII.

WORMINGTON, H. M.
1957. See Ch. XII.

Chapter XVI • ONION PORTAGE

BLACK, ROBERT F. and WILLIAM S. LAUGHLIN
1964. "Anangula: A Geologic Interpretation of the Oldest Archeologic Site in the Aleutians," *Science,* Vol. 143, No. 3612. Washington.

GIDDINGS, J. L.
1956. See Ch. XIV.
1961. See Ch. XIV.
1962. "Onion Portage and Other Flint Sites of the Kobuk River," *Arctic Anthropology,* Vol. 1, No. 1. Madison, Wisc.
1965. "A Long Record of Eskimos and Indians at the Forest Edge," in *Context and Meaning in Cultural Anthropology,* ed. Melford E. Spiro. New York and London.
1966. See Ch. II.

KNUTH, EIGIL
See Ch. XII listings.

LARSEN, HELGE and JØRGEN MELDGAARD
1958. See Ch. VIII (Dorset).

LAUGHLIN, WILLIAM S.
1963. "Eskimos and Aleuts: Their Origins and Evolution," *Science,* Vol. 142, No. 3593. Washington.

LEECHMAN, DOUGLAS
1954. "The Vanta Kutchin," *National Museum of Canada Bulletin No. 130, Anthropological Series No. 33.* Ottawa.

MACNEISH, RICHARD S.
1956. See Ch. XII.

STUCKENRATH, ROBERT and DOUGLAS D. ANDERSON
—. "Radiocarbon Dates from the American Arctic" (in press), *American Antiquity.* Salt Lake City.

GLOSSARY

abrader An implement, generally of sandstone, used to shape, smooth, or polish an object.

adz A cutting or planing tool with the blade's cutting edge in a line horizontal to the handle.

artifact Any object or part of an object that was made or altered by primitive man.

babiche Narrow strips of deer or moose rawhide used for such things as lines and webbing.

back dirt The earth removed from an archeological excavation as digging progresses.

baleen Commonly known as whalebone; a horny substance from the upper jaw of certain whales who use it to strain out plankton and other minute foods from sea water. It is light, flexible, tough, and fibrous.

barb A projection on the head of a weapon (spear, arrow, etc.) that anchors the head in place after it enters the flesh of an animal. *See* Fig. 77a.

basalt A fine-grained, igneous rock, dark gray or black.

beluga Commonly called the white whale, this is a mammal of the dolphin-porpoise family that reaches a length of 10 to 18 feet.

bifaced A term describing an artifact that has been worked both front and back.

bitumen Mineral pitch or asphalt.

bladder dart A long shaft with a loose barbed point used in hunting sea mammals. A line is fastened between point and shaft and an inflated seal bladder is additionally attached to the shaft. When the point becomes embedded in an animal, the shaft falls away, and both shaft and bladder act as drags. *See* Fig. 17a.

blade and core   A term referring to the technique of producing, from a specially prepared stone core or nodule, narrow, parallel-sided flakes to be fashioned into tools or weapons. A bone punch, placed against the flat, prepared surface of the core, is struck with a hammer stone, causing the desired flakes to fall off.

blowout   A valley or depression blown out by the wind in areas of shifting sand or light soil.

bodkin   A pointed bone or ivory tool, eyed or not, used to sew or pierce skins. *See* Fig. 24c.

boiling stones   Fist-sized stones that are heated in a fire and then dropped into wood, bark, or skin vessels containing food. The heat from the stones cooks the food.

bola   A missile made of two or more lines weighted at the ends with pieces of stone, bone, ivory, or antler. Flung through the air, the bola entangles the legs or wings of animals or birds, facilitating capture. A bola weight is shown in Fig. 17c.

bow brace   A shaped piece of bone or antler that is pegged or lashed to the inner face of a bow to stiffen or strengthen it.

brow band   A curved piece of ivory, often decorated, that is tied across the forehead to enhance the wearer's appearance on ceremonial occasions.

burin   A chisel-like tool with a narrow, heavy blade—used to cut or groove hard organic substances such as bone, antler, and ivory.

chalcedony   A variety of quartz with a waxy luster.

chert   A fine-grained rock similar to flint.

chips   The small waste pieces that result when a stone is flaked into an implement.

Chukchi   The most easterly inhabitants of Siberia.

Circassian tobacco   A type of tobacco grown in and traded from the North Caucasus region of Circassia.

composite house   A structure consisting of several rooms or houses joined together.

condyle   A prominence on a bone: a joint.

conglomerate   A rock that includes other miscellaneous rocks or fragments, all cemented together into one whole; also called puddingstone.

dart   As used here, a barbed harpoon.

dendrochronology   A method of determining dates from the examination and comparison of the growth rings of trees.

discoidal scraper   A disc-shaped scraping tool.

dowitcher   A long, slender-billed bird resembling a snipe or sandpiper.

drill bow   A small bow used for turning a drill. The string of the bow is wrapped once around the drill's shaft, and a sawing motion of the bow causes its string to revolve the shaft, the sharp point of which bores a hole in an object.

dune   A wind-formed hill or ridge of sand or loess.

end blade   A blade attached to the end of any tool or weapon to serve as a cutting edge.

Eocene   Earliest geologic epoch in the Tertiary period extending from seventy million to forty-five million years ago.

facet   One of several or many small, flat or nearly flat surfaces of an artifact.

feather setter   A tool used in affixing feathers to arrow shafts.

fiber temper   The mixing of a fibrous material, such as grass, with clay in making pottery. This "tempering" of the clay makes the pots more durable.

flake   Any piece of stone removed purposefully from a larger stone.

flakeknife   A flake sharp enough to be used as a knife just as struck from the core (*see* blade and core); or it may be further sharpened or refined by additional chipping.

flaker   An implement of bone or other material used to chip off flakes from a stone.

flint   A very hard, smooth stone, highly desirable for fashioning into tools and weapons because of the extremely sharp edges obtained by flaking or chipping.

flint knapper   One who breaks and shapes flint and flintlike stone.

flints   A term popularly used to denote all chipped and flaked stone artifacts made by men of the Stone Age.

fluted point   A bifaced weapon point with one or both faces thinned at the center from the base toward the tip. The thinning permits insertion into a shaft that has been split to receive it. *See* Figs. 99 and 133b, c.

foreshaft   The part of a harpoon assemblage that holds the head.

fossil animal   An animal of a past geological era whose bones or other parts have been preserved in the earth.

fossil beach   An antiquated beach or shore, no longer at the water's edge.

glyph A carved figure or character, either incised or in relief; a carved pictograph.

graver A small, pointed stone tool used to engrave bone, antler, or ivory.

grindstone Abrasive stone, usually sandstone, used to shape or sharpen tools or weapons.

groover A stone tool used to cut longitudinal grooves in bone, antler, or ivory, often to facilitate splitting.

ground squirrel A burrowing member of the squirrel family. The Arctic species is yellowish-brown sprinkled with gray; it grows to twelve inches with a five-inch tail.

guillemot A bird of the northern hemisphere, member of the awk family, but with a narrower bill. It is an expert swimmer and diver.

harpoon A shafted weapon with detachable head used for hunting sea mammals. A line fastened at one end to the head is secured at the other by the hunter. When the head of the weapon enters the flesh of an animal, a tug on the line rotates (toggles) the head enough so that it cannot be pulled out.

head The part of a weapon that may either itself pierce an animal or hold a point which is the piercer.

house mound A visible protuberance in the land, like a small hill, indicating an abandoned and collapsed house.

Ice Age The glacial epoch; see Pleistocene.

ideograph A symbol or character painted, written, or inscribed that represents an idea or concept.

igneous rock Rock produced by a solidification of molten material within the earth.

jade A very hard stone, usually green. Though harder to work than most rock, it was used in toolmaking and can be given a high polish.

jasper An impure variety of quartz found in various opaque colors. It can be highly polished.

jet A black, coal-like mineral that takes a high polish.

kayak A one-man, covered-deck boat formed by stretching skins or canvas over a wooden frame. In rare instances, a kayak can carry two men.

kazigi Clubhouse and ceremonial center where men gather for recreational and religious purposes.

labret An item of personal adornment worn through a perforation in the lower lip.

lemur A small animal, related to the monkey, with a pointed snout, large eyes, long tail, and handlike paws.

lichen   A small, mosslike plant that grows extensively in the north. One variety, called "reindeer moss," is the primary food of caribou and reindeer.

mandible   The lower jawbone.

mattock   A heavy, hoe-like tool of stone or bone used for digging.

Mesolithic   The cultural period between the Paleolithic and Neolithic periods; that is, from about 10,000 B.C. to 8000 B.C., when farming and pottery-making began in the Near East. The culture reached other places later.

microblade   A small blade, less than one and a half inches in length, produced by the blade-and-core technique.

microcore   The nodule or core used in the production of microblades.

midden   A refuse heap.

Middle Stone Age   Same as Mesolithic.

mold   The earthen impression of a wooden post or artifact that remains after the wood has rotted away.

mound   An artificial hill or elevation of earth.

muck bank   A thawed or partially thawed, fine-grained deposit with high organic content.

murre   Like the guillemot, a member of the awk family of swimming, diving birds of the north. Also called a razor-billed awk.

muskeg   A sphagnum or peat bog, especially one with grassy tussocks.

Neolithic   The cultural period following the Mesolithic. It began about 8000 B.C. in the Near East and later elsewhere. Neolithic men ground and polished their stone and bone tools, made pottery, domesticated animals, and cultivated grain.

obsidian   Volcanic glass.

Paleo-Indians   The people who inhabited the New World during and just after the last glacial advance. They lived by hunting large animals, now extinct, such as the mammoth, with finely made stone weapons.

Paleolithic   The "Old Stone Age." This was the period when man had his beginnings and gradually learned to improve his techniques of chipping stone tools. The period ended about 10,000 B.C. when the Mesolithic period began.

patinated   Possessing a surface appearance changed or mellowed by long use or exposure to the elements.

pay dirt   Soil profitable to excavate because of its valuable minerals; colloquially: a bonanza.

pit house   A house built over an excavated pit. Often called a "semi-subterranean house."

placer gold field   A glacial or alluvial deposit containing gold that may be extracted by washing.

plane table   An instrument for plotting lines in surveying.

Pleistocene   The glacial epoch, extending from 1½ million years ago until about 10,000 years ago. Also called the Ice Age.

polyhedral core   The many-faceted core remaining after the removal of a quantity of blades.

potsherd   A piece or fragment of broken pottery.

pressure flaking   The process of removing chips or flakes from a piece of stone by pressure rather than by a direct, hard blow.

pressure retouch   Sharpening, edging, or re-edging a tool or weapon by pressure flaking.

prong   One of several sharp forward projections on a weapon shaft, any or all of which may penetrate the prey (generally birds or fish). *See* Fig. 65d.

ptarmigan   A northern game bird of the grouse family. In summer it is gray or brown, and in winter turns white. Like other grouse, it has completely feathered feet.

puffin   A bird of the awk family with short neck and deep, thick bill. It nests on rocky ledges or crevices near the sea.

radiocarbon dating   A method of determining the age of an organic archeological specimen by measuring the degree of disintegration of its carbon-14 atoms.

sandstone   A sedimentary rock containing sand and other minerals, used mainly for grinding or polishing.

schist   A metamorphic, crystalline rock that splits rather easily along parallel lines.

sealing dart   A seal-hunting weapon with a barbed head permanently affixed to a four- or five-foot shaft.

sedge   A grasslike plant that grows in tufts.

shaft stem   The part of a weapon head that fits into or is fastened to the shaft. *See* Fig. 11.

shaman   A priest or conjurer, loosely a medicine man, who uses inherited or acquired powers to intercede between man and the spirits. Shamans may cure or cause illness or death, influence weather and game, and make prophecies.

shrew   A tiny, chiefly nocturnal mammal, sometimes as little as two inches long, with velvety fur and pointed nose.

side blade   A blade attached to the side of a tool or weapon to serve as a cutting edge. *See* Figs. 7 and 109.

silicified slate   Slate that is extra hard because of its silica content.

silt   A river deposit of mud or other sediments.

sinew   A tendon; specifically, one used as a cord, thread, or the like.

sinew twister   An implement used to twist and tighten sinew that has been put on the back of a bow for reinforcement.

slate   A fine-grained rock that separates along parallel lines, the surfaces along the break being fairly smooth.

sledge shoe   A strip of bone, antler, or wood pegged onto the bottom of the wooden runner of a sledge. The "shoes" receive most of the wear and are easily replaced when worn out.

soapstone   A soft stone named for its soapy feel. When freshly mined, it is rather easily carved, and it hardens after exposure to air.

socket piece   The part of a weapon assemblage that is lashed to the main shaft and hollowed out (socketed) either to hold the head directly or to hold the foreshaft which, in turn, holds the head of the weapon.

sphagnum   Peat moss.

stratigraphy   Natural, often differing, deposits that have accumulated in one place over a period of time and now lie layered under the earth's surface, the oldest deposits being deepest. "Horizontal" stratigraphy, as here used, refers to a series of beaches, not buried, but similarly deposited in time, the oldest now being farthest from the sea.

swale   Low-lying ground, often marshy.

tarsier   A large-eyed, small animal with strong hind legs for jumping and adhesive foot disks that enable it to spend its life in trees. Like the lemur, it is a member of the primate group.

tern   A gull-like bird with a forked tail, also called a sea swallow.

theodolite   A surveying instrument for measuring angles.

toggle   A piece so constructed that once it is inserted through an opening it cannot easily be removed, as a button or weapon head. *See* harpoon.

tree-ring dating   *See* dendrochronology.

tundra   A treeless, moss- and lichen-covered plain of the northern Arctic.

umiak   A large, open boat holding eight or ten people. Its wooden frame is skin covered, and it is used for transportation and whaling.

INDEX

A Note about the Author

J. LOUIS GIDDINGS was born in Caldwell, Texas, in 1909. He graduated from the University of Alaska in 1932, earned his master's degree from the University of Arizona in 1941, and his doctorate at the University of Pennsylvania in 1951. He became interested in Bering Strait research while an undergraduate at the University of Alaska, and spent many summers excavating archeological sites at Cape Denbigh, the Seward Peninsula, and Kotzebue Sound in western Alaska, frequently with the help of research grants from the National Science Foundation. He was also the pioneer of Arctic dendrochronology, or tree-ring dating. His studies led him to challenge the popular scientific concept of ancient mass migrations from Siberia through Arctic North America. He believed that there was, rather, a "circumpolar drift" of peoples, ideas, and techniques all the way from central Siberia to Greenland.

Dr. Giddings was Professor of Anthropology at Brown University and director of its Haffenreffer Museum from 1956 until his untimely death, following an automobile accident, on December 9, 1964. His wife, the former Ruth Warner, who with their three children often accompanied him on his expeditions to the Far North, is now curator of the Haffenreffer Museum in Bristol, Rhode Island.

A Note on the Type

THE text of this book was set in a typeface called Primer, designed by Rudolph Ruzicka for the Mergenthaler Linotype Company and first made available in 1949. Primer, a modified modern face based on Century broadface, has the virtue of great legibility and was designed especially for today's methods of composition and printing.

Primer is Ruzicka's third typeface. In 1940 he designed Fairfield, and in 1947 Fairfield Medium, both for the Mergenthaler Linotype Company.

Ruzicka was born in Bohemia in 1883 and came to the United States at the age of eleven. He attended public schools in Chicago and later the Chicago Art Institute. During his long career he has been a wood engraver, etcher, cartographer, and book designer. For many years he was associated with Daniel Berkeley Updike and produced the annual keepsakes for The Merrymount Press from 1911 until 1941.

Ruzicka has been honored by many distinguished organizations, and in 1936 he was awarded the gold medal of the American Institute of Graphic Arts. From his home in New Hampshire, Ruzicka continues to be active in the graphic arts.

The book was composed and bound by The Haddon Craftsmen, Inc., Scranton, Penn., and printed by Halliday Lithograph Corporation, West Hanover, Mass. Typography and binding design by Anita Karl.

DATE DUE

MR 5- '68	MY 29 '74		
AP 12 '68	AG 11 '74		
AP 26 '68	OCT 4 '75		
FE 22 '69	OCT 0 1 2000		
MR 5 - '69	AUG 2 3 2010		
DE 1 - '69			
AP 23 '70			
MY 13 '70			
AUG 31 1970			
MY 7 - '71			
MY 17 '71			
MY 23 '71			
JA 27 '72			
FE 10 '72			
OC 16 '72			
FE 20 '73			
MR 7 '73			
MR 6 '74			PRINTED IN U.S.